REMEMBERING JULIUS NYERERE IN TANZANIA

History, Memory, Legacy

Edited by Marie-Aude Fouéré

MKUKI NA NYOTA
DAR-ES-SALAAM

PUBLISHED BY
Mkuki na Nyota Publishers Ltd
P. O. Box 4246
Dar es Salaam, Tanzania
www.mkukinanyota.com

In association with
French Institute for Research in Africa (IFRA)
P.O.Box 52979 - 00100,
Nairobi, Kenya.
www.ifra-nairobi.net
©French Institute for Research in Africa (IFRA), 2015

ISBN: 978-9987-753-26-0

All rights reserved. No part of this publication may be reproduced, stored in a retrieval system or transmitted in any form or by any means, electronic, mechanical, photocopying, recording, or otherwise, without the prior written permission of Mkuki na Nyota Publishers Ltd.

Visit www.mkukinanyota.com to read more about and to purchase any of Mkuki na Nyota books. You will also find featured authors, interviews and news about other publisher/author events. Sign up for our e-newsletters for updates on new releases and other announcements.

Contents

Acknowledgements vii
Authors ix
Acronyms xiii

PART 1: 'CAPTURING' JULIUS NYERERE

Chapter 1
"Julius Nyerere": The Man, the Word, and the Order of Discourse
Marie-Aude Fouéré 3

Chapter 2
Julius Nyerere, Ujamaa and Political Morality in Contemporary Tanzania
Marie-Aude Fouéré 33

PART 2: ENTERING AND SECURING THE POLITICAL SPACE

Chapter 3
Julius Kambarage Nyerere: His Formative Years
Thomas Molony 65

Chapter 4

Julius Nyerere, the Arusha Declaration, and the Deep Roots of a Contemporary Political Metaphor

Emma Hunter 73

PART 3: IN SEARCH OF A TUTELARY FIGURE

Chapter 5

Nyerere's Ghost: Political Filiation, Paternal Discipline, and the Construction of Legitimacy in Multiparty Tanzania

Kristin D. Phillips 97

Chapter 6

Different 'Uses of Nyerere' in the Constitutional Review Debates: A Touchstone for Legitimacy in Tanzania

Aikande C. Kwayu. 127

PART 4: JULIUS NYERERE & HIS CRITICS

Chapter 7

Julius Rex: Nyerere through the Eyes of His Critics, 1953-2013

James R. Brennan 143

Chapter 8

Julius Nyerere in Zanzibar: The Revolution, the Union and the Enemy of the Nation

Marie-Aude Fouéré. 171

PART 5: POLITICS & POETRY

Chapter 9

Tanzanian Newspaper Poetry: Political Commentary in Verse

Kelly Askew 213

Chapter 10

The Poetry of an Orphaned Nation: Newspaper Poetry and the Death of Nyerere

Mary Ann Mhina 251

PART 6: POST-MWALIMU EDUCATION?

Chapter 11

The University of Dar es Salaam: A Post-Nyerere Institution of Higher Education? Legacies, Continuities and Changes in an Institutional Space (1961-2012)

Olivier Provini 277

Chapter 12

Ward Secondary Schools, Elite Narratives and Nyerere's Legacy

Sonia Languille 303

Acknowledgements

This volume has its origin in my encounter with the figure of Julius Kambarage Nyerere as it was narrated in the Tanzanian media in the early 2000s. This triggered a quest for understanding the appropriation of, or detachment from, Mwalimu in contemporary Tanzania that took several years and followed different paths. Along the way, I soon discovered that my interest was shared with many other scholars in Tanzania and abroad, most of them senior academics while I was still a budding researcher. The present book embodies this collective endeavour to give insight into the collective memories and narratives that make Nyerere the *primus inter pares* – to be lionized, or to be debunked – in Tanzania. I would like to thank all the contributors for embracing the idea of this edited volume when I approached them and for their patience throughout the long process until its actual publication. Each contribution casts a different light on the theme discussed, but resonates with all the others contributions, thus resulting in both a tuned and complementary collection.

This collection is definitely not a biography of Julius Nyerere, even less another tribute or hagiography of Tanganyika's then Tanzania's first president. It does not aim either at evaluating the politics of Nyerere's time – assessing one more time Ujamaa's successes and shortcomings – or digging into the relation between Nyerere's personality, political thought and political action. Rather, this book is about how Nyerere is remembered by Tanzanians from all levels of society, in what ways, on which occasions, and for what purposes. It is about what Julius Nyerere stands for today, as well as about his legacy, in relation to collective representations and practices of what the Tanzanian nation was, is and should be. The few contributions that slightly depart from this overall frame of analysis about contemporary political imagination provide essential historical elements for the readers to understand the issues at stake.

I wish to express my sincere thanks to Walter Bgoya for his enthusiastic and enduring support since the beginning of this project, and to his son Mkuki Bgoya. The introduction to the volume gained from the watchful eye of Joost Fontein, Hervé Maupeu, Sandrine Perrot and Justin Willis. James Brennan has always showed supportive of my work, not only prompting discussions but also providing rich scholarly insights. William Bissell and Martin Walsh are thanked for setting the bar high when commenting upon some early writings. Other friends and colleagues shared their views at different steps of this work. This volume owes them all a great debt as they definitely enriched my understanding and enabled me to supervise it. I would like to thank in particular Hélène Charton, Dominique Connan, Jean Copans, Christine Deslaurier, Eloi Ficquet, Ahmed Gurnah, Muhammad Juma, Kjell Havnevik, Emma Hunter, Jérôme Lafargue, Amos Mhina, Thomas Molony, Haroub Othman, Jean-Claude Penrad, Ahmed Rajab, Alain Ricard, Mohamed Saleh, Etienne Smith, and Iain Walker.

Contributors are indebted to the Tanzanian Commission for Science and Technology (COSTECH), the National Archives and the Zanzibar Government for enabling them to conduct research in Tanzania. The Mwalimu Nyerere Foundation (MNF), through its Executive Director Joseph Butiku, always remains a thoughtful interlocutor. In the preparation of the manuscript, I am most grateful to the patient and efficient team of Mkuki na Nyota. The introduction tremendously benefitted from the work of Suzan Nolan and Leila Whittemore, language editors at BlueSky International. Lastly, this edited volume would not have been possible without the continuous backing of the French Institute for Research in Africa (IFRA) in Nairobi, Kenya.

Authors

Kelly Askew is Director of the African Studies Center and Associate Professor of Anthropology and Afroamerican/African Studies at the University of Michigan. Her works include *Performing the Nation: Swahili Music and Cultural Politics in Tanzania* (University of Chicago Press, 2002); *African Postsocialisms* (co-editor, Edinburgh University Press, 2006); *The Anthropology of Media* (co-editor, Blackwell, 2002); and two documentary films: *Poetry in Motion: 100 Years of Zanzibar's Nadi Ikhwan Safaa* (70 min., 2012); *The Chairman and the Lions* (46 min., 2012).

James Brennan researches the histories of twentieth-century Tanzania and Kenya, examining themes of urban history, decolonization, media history, and the Indian Ocean World. He is author of the book *Taifa: Making Nation and Race in Urban Tanzania* (Ohio University Press, 2012), as well as numerous journal articles and book chapters.

Marie-Aude Fouéré is a Lecturer in Anthropology at the *Ecole des hautes études en sciences sociales* (EHESS) in Paris and was the Deputy Director of the French Institute for Research in Africa (IFRA) in Nairobi (2011-2014). Her first book was on joking relationship in Tanzania (L'Harmattan, 2008). Her current research interests cover collective memories, belonging and the use of archives in contemporary Tanzania, focusing on the figure of Julius Nyerere and the Revolution of 1964 in Zanzibar

Emma Hunter has been a Lecturer in History and Fellow of Gonville and Caius College, Cambridge, since 2008. Her first book, *Languages of Democracy in Tanzanian Decolonization: Global Discourses and Local Politics*, is forthcoming with Cambridge University Press. She is currently working on a new project, funded by the British Academy, called 'Concepts of Democracy in mid-twentieth-century Africa'.

Aikande Kwayu holds a PhD in Politics and International Relations from the University of Nottingham and is a research affiliate of the University of Oxford. Her doctoral work analyzed the relationship between the UK government and faith group. She currently works as a research and development consultant at BUMACO Ltd. Tanzania. She is also a column contributor of the Continent Observer and runs a blog.

Sonia Languille holds a PhD in Development Studies from the School of Oriental and African Studies (SOAS). Her research interests cover the political economy of education in Africa, the textbook industry, and social mobilisation around school provision and aid management. She has an extensive professional experience as a development practitioner in education planning and financing, public finance management and decentralisation.

Mary Ann Mhina originally became interested in representations of Nyerere in media and literature as an undergraduate student studying Swahili and Social Anthropology at the School of Oriental and African Studies (SOAS) around the time of his death. Her interest in Tanzania continued as a post-graduate student Goldsmiths College London. She is now an independent writer, anthropologist and facilitator working on women's rights, equality and literature in East and Southern Africa.

Thomas Molony is Lecturer in African Studies at the University of Edinburgh. He is author of *Nyerere: The early years* (Oxford: James Currey, 2014), the most detailed account to date of Nyerere's formative years as a student and his early political life leading up to his presidency of Tanzania.

Kristin D. Phillips is a Lecturer in Anthropology and African Studies at Emory University who has studied citizenship, development, and social change in Singida Region in Tanzania since 2004. She is finishing a book manuscript, titled *Subsistence Citizenship: Hunger, Development, and the Politics of Poverty in Tanzania*.

She has published and presented on numerous themes related to Tanzanian development, including education, participatory development, postcolonial policymaking, electoral politics, and food, farming and hunger.

Olivier Provini is a PhD student in political science (*Université de Pau et des Pays de l'Adour*, France) and a former research fellow at the French Institute for Research in Africa (IFRA) between 2011 and 2013. He works on transfers of higher education reforms in four public universities in East Africa: Dar es Salaam (Tanzania), Makerere (Uganda), Nairobi (Kenya) and Burundi (Burundi).

Acronyms

CA	Constituent Assembly
CCM	Chama Cha Mapinduzi (Party of the Revolution)
CHADEMA	Chama Cha Demokrasia na Maendeleo (Party for Democracy and Progress)
CRC	Constitutional Review Commission
CUF	Civic United Front
DP	Democratic Party
GoT	Government of Tanzania
MP	Member of Parliament
MNF	Mwalimu Nyerere Foundation
NEC	National Elections Commission
NCCR	Mageuzi National Convention for Construction and Reform - Changes
TAA	Tanganyika African Association
TANESCO	Tanzania Supply Electric Company
TANU	Tanganyika African National Union
TAWA	Tanganyika African Welfare Association
TAZARA	Tanzania-Zambia Railway Authority
TBC	Tanzania Broadcasting Corporation
TPDF	Tanzania's People Defence Force
UDSM	University of Dar es Salaam
UKAWA	Umoja wa Katiba ya Wananchi (Coalition for a People's Constitution)
URT	United Republic of Tanzania

PART 1:

'Capturing' Julius Nyerere

Chapter 1

"Julius Nyerere": the Man, the Word, and the Order of Discourse

Marie-Aude Fouéré

> "When I use a word," Humpty Dumpty said in a rather scornful tone, "it means just what I choose it to mean – neither more nor less."
> "The question is," said Alice, "whether you can make words mean different things."
> "The question is," said Humpy Dumpty, "which is to be master, that's all."
> *Through the Looking Glass,* Lewis Caroll

> "489. Ask yourself: On what occasion, for what purpose, do we say this? What kinds of action accompany these words? (Think of greeting.) In what kinds of setting will they be used; and what for?"
> *Philosophical Investigations,* Ludwig Wittgenstein

"His Eternity" Nyerere? A risk of déjà vu

The political 'afterwards' in the late postcolony

Anthony Kirk-Greene once worried that any new publication about African heads of state might risk déjà vu (Kirk-Greene, 1991). During the 1980s, an influential literature reflected upon leadership, personal rule and national trajectories in Africa. It adopted a comparative and typological approach that discussed scholarly studies in political history published from the mid-1960s to the late 1970s (Jackson and Rosberg, 1982; Cartwright, 1983). Did the first generation of postcolonial political leaders belong to the category of prince, autocrat, prophets or tyrant? Or should one view "His Eternity," "His Eccentricity," or "His Exemplarity" (Kirk-Greene, 1991) as modern versions of Janus, both prince and autocrat or philosopher and tyrant, like Jomo Kenyatta in Kenya or Sékou Touré in Guinea? Biographies of the most renowned leaders – usually the founding fathers of the fledgling sub-Saharan African nation-states – added to these debates about personal power and styles of leadership, the better to interrogate the foundations of legitimacy in early African postcolonial regimes. This profound interest – fascination, even – in the thoughts and conduct of rulers has not diminished, in Africa or elsewhere.

Yet in the mid-2010s, an era one might call the "After-life" or "Afterwards"[1] of most of those African statesmen who had stepped down from power and/or passed away, we contend that the imperative question concerns the memories and legacies of their personalities and leadership, and how these weigh on the present of African societies. The question is timely: independence jubilee celebrations across the continent have prompted African countries, their diasporas, their former colonial powers and international academics to take stock of post-independence successes and failures. Most such assessments, however, have tended to gloss over the relationships built between states and citizens, and have ignored both postcolonial national narratives and the figures who embodied nation, power and authority (Charton and Fouéré, 2013). The legacies and memories of the anti-colonialism leaders and the national Fathers still play out in contemporary modes of government, shaping representations and senses of national belonging; they demand reassessment. The present volume will address one compelling and, we will argue, exemplary case.

Debating the meanings of 'Nyerere'

The interrogations we propose here aim to decentre the perspectives on leadership that dominated political science in the 1980s – in particular, those that identified ideal leadership models or adopted the "national synonymity" viewpoint in which leader equals nation and vice versa (Chabal, 1984: 108; Kirk-Greene, 1991: 167).[2] Gavin

---

[1] Unlike Southall and Mercer (2006) in their discussion of the political "Afterwards" (not in the metaphysical but historical sense of the term), this volume does not address the actual role former heads of state continued to play in politics after they retired from office (see also, for Tanzania, Hodd, 1998; Legum and Mmari, 1995; Mbelle, Mjema and Kilindo, 2002; McDonald and Sahle, 2002). We focus here on the traces they left on leadership and political imagination after their presence faded or they passed away.

[2] This shift gained its footing in the mid-1980s in political science and political anthropology, though from different perspectives, in an effort to capture key aspects of the politics of contemporary African societies "from below" (Bayart, 1981, 1993 [1989]), "from within", "on the ground" or, to quote yet another metaphor, by "fixing the camera at eye level and engage with politics as it is played out in everyday life" (Chabal, 2009: xi).

Kitching has argued, for instance, that Nyerere "entirely determined" the general thrust of Tanzanian post-independence policy (Kitching, 1982: 117).[3] Yet many early works of political science fell into the trap of personalizing the nation,[4] thus missing the complex interplay between social actors through which state and citizens are produced, and therefore through which state-formation occurs – a conflicting and largely involuntary historical process entwined with disorder, confrontations and compromises, rather than a simple building of state institutions (Berman and Lonsdale, 1992; see also, in the case of Tanzania, Geiger, 1998; Maddox and Giblin, 2005).

Departing from these past perspectives on leadership, the decentred approach adopted here emphasizes how individuals and groups use the past – and within this past, the figure of one statesman in particular, Julius Kambarage Nyerere, the first President of Tanganyika and first President of Tanzania – to reflect upon their present and act upon it. Rather than scrutinizing Nyerere the statesman and his political philosophy, this volume asks how the state and Tanzanians, from all levels of society, appropriate the figure of Nyerere today, reworking it and harnessing it to different representations of power and authority. We will consider how 'Nyerere' becomes a political language and metaphor for debating and shaping the present, and how collective memories and legacies can transform current political and social practices – both through ingrained modes of thought and doing and through strategic transactions.[5] We will, in short, take 'Nyerere' as a point of departure for the discursive dimension of contemporary Tanzanian politics.

Therefore, this book is not about Julius Nyerere; it is about what Julius Nyerere means and stands for in Tanzania today. It does not answer the question of who Julius Nyerere was in his private life and as a public figure, or what he genuinely thought and did. Rather, it addresses what institutions and people say that Julius Nyerere was, and of what they think of the impact of his thoughts and deeds for the present. The people

---

3 Our approach does not refute the idea that statesmen indeed have some bearing on the historical trajectory of their country, as aptly shown by John Lonsdale's intellectual biography of Jomo Kenyatta (2002: 34).

4 The recent political science literature on ruling regimes and power configurations has made tremendous progress in analysing governing practices by giving insight into the complex interplay between political structures, elite alliances and state institutions. See for instance Stacher on 'autocratic continuity' in North Africa and the Middle East (2012), or Bueno des Mesquita et al. (2003) on leaders' 'political survival'.

5 The use of the past not only owes to tactics and strategies intentionally deployed by actors, but are also the product of enduring and incorporated traces – or "sedimentation" (Bayart and Bertrand, 2006) – which shape political and historical consciousness today.

considered are not just those who were closely associated with Nyerere, retelling their personal memories of interactions with Nyerere. They are Tanzanians in general, of all generations and social conditions, who excavate their memories of Nyerere (and/or what they have heard of him) to revisit his salience and significance in contemporary Tanzania. In the words of Cohen and Comaroff (1976), this book is about the everyday "management of meaning" in Tanzanian society – here, the meaning of 'Nyerere' – in situations where people debate their present and seek to shape it.

From Mwalimu-in-Power to Mwalimu-in-Memoriam

Tanzaphilia and Nyererephilia

Like most founding fathers of the early postcolonial African states, Julius K. Nyerere appears in scores of works of history, politics and memoirs;[6] these have explored his style of leadership, his political thought, intentions and actions, in great detail. To Crandford Pratt, "[Nyerere] has always been a leader with strong convictions about his people's needs. Nyerere has been, above all, a teacher, a *mwalimu*. He is a teacher of a special sort (…). He is a *mwalimu*-in-power – a moral teacher who is a political leader with a great deal of authority and power" (Pratt 1976: 256). This laudatory depiction of Nyerere from 1976 seems to have weighed heavily on subsequent scholarly works about Nyerere in the 1980s.[7] In 1982, Robert H. Jackson and Carl G. Rosberg asserted that:

Julius K. Nyerere, the socialist president of Tanzania, provides one of the best contemporary illustrations of the importance of mean and ideas as factors in historical change, of history not as "destiny and necessity" but as "chance and contingency". He is an example of a ruler who recognizes that considerable structural impediments and constrains stand in the way of planned, socialist-inspired change in Africa, but who believes that appropriate action can be taken to rationally deal with these obstacles. Nyerere offers the students of African rulers and regimes an example of a leader whose personal ideals will have made a significant difference not only to personal relations of power in the state,

---

6 I do not present an exhaustive summary of the existing literature on Nyerere, which is both vast and dispersed. Instead, I critically engage the corpus of texts I find the most relevant for my argument. For a detailed overview of this literature and its discussion, see Bjerk (2010).

7 For an earlier lookalike depiction of Nyerere as the guiding teacher of Tanzania's people, see also Hyden (1967) who states that "[t]he leader of the Revolution in Tanzania is the humble teacher, who is not teaching his pupils – the Tanzanian people – for the sake of teaching, but for the sake of making their education relevant to their life" (p. 34).

but also to social relations in the wider society (Jackson and Rosberg, 1982: 219). These two authors portray Nyerere as a "Prophet" and the "best example of the moral agent in political history" in Black Africa (Ibid: 220).[8] This depiction of Nyerere has become commonplace in most academic writings, either those centered on Nyerere or addressing African leadership generally,[9] a point underscored by Coulson (1982) and Kirk-Greene (1991).[10] This has made it difficult to move away from the figure of Nyerere in exploring Tanzania's politics. These early assessments reflect the largely uncritical reception of Nyerere and the Tanzanian experiment among Westerners in the 1960s-70s – what Ali Mazrui (1967) ironically characterized as "Tanzaphilia" and "the mystique of Nyerere" (Ibid: 165, 168).[11]

A primus inter pares among a 'few good men'

Academics have long analyzed two major aspects of Nyerere's time in power, sometimes separately and sometimes together: his political philosophy and political action. Many works on Nyerere's political philosophy, officially referred to as Ujamaa or African socialism – sometimes even "Nyererism" – address Nyerere's conception of political power and the nation as a coherent body of ideas and principles drawn from various intellectual influences.[12] Certain analyses stress, on the one hand, the traditional values of work, mutual cooperation and solidarity, as well as the reciprocal generosity and egalitarianism of northwestern Tanzania.[13] But scholars have also highlighted his

---

8 In the authors' vocabulary, a Prophet is one who can "foretell a new and better world and (…) inspire and guide others towards its attainment. (…) [He] is a political agent, but he is also a moral agent – a political-religious man" (Ibid: 182).

9 For instance, in their discussion of the figure of the Big Man in Africa, Chabal and Daloz (1999) mention in passing that "exceptional leaders", "like Nyerere or Museveni" who had "a relatively modest personal need for the status of Big Man", genuinely aimed "to transcend the short-term view in favour of longer-term development" though, they assert, the forms of political legitimacy in use during their time in power limited their capacity to transform the political system (p. 162).

10 To Coulson, this literature often leaves the reader "with an impression of Nyerere as a far-seeing superman" (Coulson, 1982: 5). As Kirk-Greene reminds us, the "national synonymity" syndrome applied to Nyerere as well as to other African heads of the state: "Tanzania was Nyerere and Nyerere stood for Tanzania and African Socialism" (Kirk-Greene, 1991: 168).

11 On "Nyererephilia", see also Bennett (1968), Leys (1968), Samoff (1989), Constantin (1988), and more recently, Hunter (2004), Fouéré (2009, 2014), and Becker (2013).

12 Similar approaches have been adopted to account for the thoughts of leftist African 'intellectual politicians' like Sékou Touré, Patrice Lumumba or Kwame Nkrumah (see for instance Williams, 1984)

13 Nyerere was born in the village of Butiama, in a region populated by people designated by the ethnic name of Zanaki, and situated 50 km from Musoma town on the shore of Lake Victoria in northwestern Tanzania. Nyerere describes his youth, saying: "I grew up in a

exposure to classical liberalism, British socialism, anti-colonialism and pan-Africanism during his studies in Edinburgh.[14] The relative importance assigned to these influences varies.[15] Some scholars have elected to trace shifts from Nyerere's earlier writings and speeches to his later declarations, with a view to revealing the "dynamic development of Nyerere's thinking" (Havnevik, 2010: 41).[16] Others have preferred to highlight discontinuities, self-contradictions, or even what they see as inconsistency in Nyerere's intellectual stance, and how it translated – or failed to translate – into practices.

When it comes to political action, past scholarship has often presented Nyerere as the sole driving force behind the anti-colonial struggle and the first years of independence, and above all, behind the Tanzanian experiment, from the Arusha Declaration in 1967 – the blueprint for African socialism – to his retirement from presidency in 1985. More recent historiography has questioned this view of Nyerere as the only architect of Tanzanian nationhood. By interrogating Tanzanian nationalist ideology and official historical narratives, such works have re-situated Nyerere in the various milieus that made his rise to power possible (Said, 1998).[17] Other writers – skeptical of the biographical approach focused on exceptional figures, the "few good men" (Denoon and Kuper, 1970) – have reassessed the role of various collective actors and movements in the anti-colonial struggle.

Susan Geiger, for example, has questioned the gendering of this model in her work on women activists in TANU and their relation to Nyerere (Geiger, 1996).[18] However, the conception of Nyerere as the *primus*

---

perfectly democratic and egalitarian society" (in Stöger-Eising, 2000: 119). This contrasts with a different depiction of Zanaki society by Nyerere himself in Smith (2011 [1973]: 34-44).

14 See in particular Listowel (1965), Mohiddin (1968), Hatch (1976), Assensoh (1998), Stöger-Eising (2000), and Mwakikagile (2010: 78-109).

15 In contrast to this tradition-vs.-modernity binary, some have argued the relative futility of untangling the Western and indigenous elements of Nyerere's thought (Eckert, 2001: 323) – the supposed "Africanness of his ideas" (Meyns, 2000: 158).

16 Nyerere has produced numerous writings, gathered in several volumes, which Michael Twaddle calls both "a skilful constructed ideological monument to the Tanzanian future" (1968: 669).

17 Mohamed Said (1998), for instance, notes that the circle of educated Muslim townsmen of Dar es Salaam (led by the Sykes family, founders of the first nationalist organisation in the country, the Tanganyika African Association (TAA)), helped Nyerere reach the summit of power. They did so once they realised he was "a highly educated person with admirable debating skills" (Ibid: 111) who could be made president of the association, and of the political party that would emerge in 1954, the Tanganyika Africa National Union (TANU) (Ibid: 111).

18 Geiger shows that women activists in the 1950s "did not 'learn nationalism' (so to speak) from Nyerere or when they joined TANU. Rather, they brought to TANU and to their public, political party activism an (sic) ethos of nationalism already present as trans-ethnic, trans-

inter pares of the "few good men" who changed the country's destiny has remained entrenched among many scholars, and unmistakably remains at the heart of the Tanzanian nationalist and statist metanarrative.

Building Utopian Tanzania

Lastly, many commentators over the years have portrayed Nyerere as a utopian, aiming to realize an ideal state in Tanzania.[19] In the late 1960s Ahmed Mohiddin characterized Nyerere's stance as "unrestrained idealism" (1968: 137); one year after the Arusha Declaration was adopted,[20] he drew attention to the sweeping vision in Nyerere's own description of his objectives, the precepts that would underpin Ujamaa. By deploying "Herculean efforts to create a better world" (Hartmann, 1988: 165) – one detribalized, deracialized and unified under a shared sense of nationhood – Ujamaa represented a political ideology that cast economic and social issues in a "familiar popular idiom" (Ferguson, 2006: 76).[21] The historian Emma Hunter (2008) has shown that, as it permeated Tanzanian society, the Ujamaa political lexicon transformed into a popular language, one utilized by common citizens to think and debate about social, political, and economic morality and state/citizens relations, thus connecting local issues to the broader national framework of socialist-appropriate behaviours and attitudes.[22]

Forty years later, James Scott, analyzing the failures of high-modernist schemes of social engineering around the world, associated Nyerere with the "hubris" of the utopian planners and intellectual advocates, while conceding the sincerity of their desire to improve the human condition (Scott 1998: 342).

---

tribal social and cultural identity" (Geiger, 1996: 468–469). They thus helped shape and spread a nationalist consciousness throughout the country "for which TANU was the vehicle" (Ibid: 478) – and, one may add, for which Nyerere was the talented spokesperson before he became its inventive composer through the language of Ujamaa.

19 Nyerere, however, rather saw himself a "realistic idealist" (Nyerere, 1967).

20 See also John Lonsdale who, in an article published shortly after the Arusha Declaration, recounts that the Lutheran pastor Reverend Mushendwa "compared the Arusha Declaration with the Sermon on the Mount" (1968: 344) to underline the Utopian character of Ujamaa and its religious and moral overtones.

21 See Nyerere's own writings (1966, 1968, 1973).

22 See also Martin (1988) who characterizes Ujamaa as a "dynamic utopia" based upon coercive measures and "cohesive political" languages. Yet, James Ferguson argues that, in Tanzania as well as in Zambia, for instance, "state moralizing (…) was intensely interested, self-serving, and very often fraudulent" (Ibid.).

Because Nyerere has often been cast as both an intellectual *sui generis* and a man imbued with a deep sense of morality, later academic works rarely attribute the failures of Ujamaa to his actions.[23] Since the 1990s, the prevailing interpretation has blamed external circumstances – the international economic situation, his fellow politicians and the administration, the reluctance of Tanzanian farmers to embrace new work practices and their evasive manoeuvres to avoid state "capture" (Hyden, 1980). Discussions of village collectivization – probably the most controversial of Nyerere's policies, due to its coercive nature – exemplify his exoneration from this "*idée fixe*" (Meyns, 2000: 163): as Leander Schneider has argued, direct responsibility for coercive action has gone to anonymous "'officials,' as well as 'policies' and 'campaigns' without authors or initiators." As a result, Nyerere emerges from these narratives as a "tragically failing hero", whose good intentions were subverted in implementation (Schneider 2004: 346). Such defenses of the genuine intentions of Tanzania's "philosopher-king", "kingmaker", "teacher-president" or "philosopher president" (as his most apologetic commentators variously described him), and the idea that he could or should not be held accountable for "unsavoury" abuses or failures (Saul 2002: 20), underpin most accounts of Mwalimu-in-power.

It is perhaps less surprising, then, that most postmortem scholarly and historically-minded works on Nyerere now available in Tanzania consist of romantic retrospectives of Mwalimu and pay tribute to the Father of the Nation – sometimes under the guise of critical scholarship, sometimes in a hybrid scholar-cum-admirer mode. Rather than unsettling the reigning interpretations of the Mwalimu-in-power era, they renew them in the present.

Discussing Nyerere's role within the CCM party (Chama Cha Mapinduzi, the Party of the Revolution) and on the international scene after he voluntarily stepped down from the presidency in 1985 (Nyerere, notably, took a strong part in mediations in Burundi and Rwanda), Roger Southall stresses his singularity, egalitarianism and his "down-to-earth" mien (Southall, 2006: 233). Echoing the earlier exonerations and "tragic" views noted above, Chambi Chachage and Annar Cassam (2010) assert a project both celebrating the man and reassessing the shortcomings

---

23 It is impossible to quote all the publications on the successes and failure of Ujamaa, which are numerous (see, notably Civille and Duggan, 1976; Coulson, 1982; Boesen et al, 1986; McHenry, 1994; Rugumamu, 1997; Scott, 1997; Ibhawoh and Dibua, 2003). Samoff's position that "the clash of sharply conflicting positions – Tanzania's economic strategy has been a great failure vs. Tanzania has in fact done no worse than most other African states and a good deal better than some – is no more definitively resolved here than it is elsewhere" (1989: 178) provides a concise assessment of the dead-ends of these discussions.

of his policies (see e.g. Manji, 2010: x). In lieu of critical scholarship, most of these publications gather personal memoirs and anecdotal contributions – often drawn from recycled secondary literature rather than recent first-hand materials.[24] This gives them "something of the air of a matey ramble down Memory Lane", as Justin Willis ironically phrases it (1996: 465).

Looking Through Nyerere

Capturing 'Nyerere'

This background sets a high bar for the present volume, which aims to move away from scholarly former conceptions and look afresh at Nyerere, or rather through Nyerere. The contributions gathered here come from a young generation of scholars in varied disciplines (history, anthropology, political science) who have not been closely associated with Nyerere as colleagues, friends, family members, or observers of the Tanzanian experiment during his political tenure. This distance from the man Nyerere, we suggest, makes it possible for them to avoid the trap of romanticizing both Nyerere and Ujamaa, and instead critically engage the existing literature, drawing upon materials recently collected through extensive fieldwork and archival research. Nor do their interrogations replay the now "obsolete debates" (Bjerk, 2010: 276) at the heart of years of scholarly literature on the Tanzanian experiment. Therefore, rather than assessing once again the failure and successes of Ujamaa or exploring the origins of Nyerere's political philosophy, they focus on the production of a usable past for a contemporary (re)imagination of nationhood (Anderson, 2006). Beyond a variety of approaches and themes, they share key common interests: in the power of words and narratives – delimiting, in a positive or negative way, the moral standards for the exercise of power and the contours of national sentiment; in the interplay between state-orchestrated memorializing and counter-hegemonic political repertoires, through remembering and forgetting; in the weight of a failed teleology of modernization when reimagining the state-citizen relationship today. In this sense, they shift away from the dominant scholarly interest in the colonial

---

24 Various non-scholarly volumes that pay tribute to Nyerere have been published over the last 10 years, among them Othman (2007), the Russian Academy (2005), and Kaduma (2010). Several volumes of Nyerere's speeches that had not yet been transcribed have recently been released by the Mwalimu Nyerere Foundation – an organisation created by Julius Nyerere in 1996 with the aim to preserve and transmit his memory and legacy – and some of his most famous writings have been reprinted, thus adding to the sum of new publications associated with Tanzania's former President.

legacy, and instead explore the imprint of the early postcolonial years on contemporary African politics and political culture, in words and in practices.

Chapter 2 by Marie-Aude Fouéré gives a panorama of Nyerere's iconic presence in the Tanzanian public space since his death in 1999. It complements this introduction with empirical and historical information about the various contexts and actors engaged in appropriating and mobilizing Nyerere. After the decline in his popularity from the mid-1970s to the mid-1980s, Tanzania's *Baba wa Taifa* (Father of the Nation) has reappeared on the public scene as an acclaimed symbol of humility, integrity and incorruptibility. The state and the media have propagated a laudatory official memory of Nyerere for the purposes of nation-building and the ruling party's political hegemony. As in other nations, the effigy of the head of state appears everywhere, in the public as well as in the domestic space (Mbembe, 1992). Political parties and politicians also lionize Nyerere when they try to gain or reassert political legitimacy by claiming to walk in Nyerere's footsteps and represent his moral legacy (see also Fouéré, 2006, 2009; Phillips, 2010), a theme elaborated by Kristin Phillips in Chapter 5. And among common citizens, popular discussions about post-liberalization hardships, religious, ethnic and political cleavages, and the absence of patriotism among political leaders also recur to a positive image of Nyerere – though criticism is not absent (Becker, 2013). Thus, Nyerere may appear associated with the "good old days" when the government provided free health care, subsidized food, and social security; and citizens' mobilisation and popular discontent against the neoliberal order may invoke Nyerere to ground dissent upon a narrative of the moral standards he supposedly set, understandable by all (Kelsall, 2003; Monson, 2006, 2013; Kamat, 2008; Chachage, 2010).

This shows that among ordinary citizens – and despite variations between the sociological groups considered – Nyerere has increasingly offered a terrain for holding the state and political leaders accountable and reminding them of their responsibilities, on the ground of the ethical norms Nyerere promoted during his lifetime. These actors will invoke Nyerere in moments of what Ferguson calls "abjection" (Ferguson, 1999), affecting different levels of Tanzanian society – the perceived failure to deliver on the liberation struggles' pledges of modernization, enrichment, and social justice. Yet the fact that Nyerere is invoked at all levels of society and in so many contexts – indeed, as a benchmark against which Tanzanians measure political leadership – argues a complicit dialogue or other transactions between the state and citizenry, rather than a simple, top-down exercise of state power. This definitely sheds light on what others have coined "collaborative nationalism" to depict the dynamics of a nationhood mutually constructed by the state and its citizens (Edmondson, 2007: 17-18).

Securing the political space

In Chapter 4, Emma Hunter asks: "[W]hy it is that memories of Nyerere serve so effectively as a site at which to reflect on wider questions of Tanzania's past, present and future?" The question appears all the more pertinent given that the Arusha Declaration and the socialist Tanzania experiment have increasingly appeared in retrospective as a failed economic model. Hunter's contribution re-examines the political and discursive context of the Arusha Declaration. The author ascribes the contemporary power of Nyerere's memory to the role that the Arusha Declaration played in re-founding the Tanzanian nationalist project, and in securing Nyerere's position – fragile in the first years after independence – both in the country and within TANU. In her view, the moment when Julius Nyerere firmly committed Tanzania to a path of Ujamaa (socialism) and Kujitegemea (self-reliance) constitutes the foundation of modern memories of him, since it was then that he established himself as the champion of morality who would fight corruption and speak up for the poor against the rich. This narrative of Nyerere as a "Titan" (Mazrui, 2002) became conventional wisdom because the state and the party efficiently deployed it throughout the socialist era. This deeply anchored the association between Nyerere and the nation in the collective imagination, in spite of later attacks against him in the mid-1980s.

In this connection, Thomas Molony (Chapter 3) provides key biographical landmarks to understand the ambiguities of a Nyerere who was a modest man opposed to personality cult, and still used his power to strategically build his own national representation. Molony's chapter provides an overview of the formative years of Nyerere, from his childhood through his times in Great Britain to his early political engagement in Tanzania[25] – the latter epoch marking the emergence of Nyerere's own voice, notably through the words of his best biographer during his lifetime, the *Time* correspondent William Edgett Smith (2011 [1973]).

---

25 For a fresh, detailed insight into the first thirty years of the life of Nyerere before he formally entered politics, see Molony (2014).

The nation-building language of Nyerere and his party were much more than top-down rhetoric; they became durable artefacts of vernacular political discourse. By the 1960s-70s, Ujamaa had already come into use among ordinary Tanzanians as a tool for attacking corrupt officials (Hunter, 2008), demonstrating the continuity in Tanzanian political languages. These may vary over time with reworkings of historical symbols, but they remain harnessed to the past (Crozon, 1996, 1998). However, these political languages may become emptied of their former content, as demonstrated by the anthropologist Kelly Askew (2006) in her compelling analysis of the songs of lamentation composed after Nyerere's death. Although the vocabulary of peace, unity, solidarity, and the elimination of tribalism and religious divisiveness – an array of terms used in the Tanzanian state ideology – appears in song after song, the term 'Ujamaa' rarely occurs, with little mention of the socialist orientation and economic policies of the Tanzanian experiment, as if to avoid recalling the dark side of the socialist times. The present volume will return to the significance of such vernacular reworkings below.

A tutelary figure

Chapter 5 and 6 explore in greater detail the strategic use of Nyerere on the Tanzanian political stage. Analyzing the 2005 and 2010 presidential and parliamentary elections, and touching upon the run up to the 2015 elections, Kristin Phillips (Chapter 5) shows how political parties and politicians tried to convince the electorate of the legitimacy and efficacy of their leadership through the symbolic manipulation of Nyerere's name, memory, and legacy. This invocation takes place within a broader political rhetoric of eldership and youth, fathers and sons, and illicit eating and legitimate consumption (see notably Bayart, 1993; Schatzberg, 2001), a dynamic perfectly illustrated by the political cartoons included in the chapter. Symbolic filial descent from Nyerere – both personal and party-based – therefore becomes central to the construction of political legitimacy in Tanzania. Such a discourse denies political change, rhetorically asserting a false continuity between past and present governance. The author also casts light on how citizens draw on the figure of Nyerere – sometimes with irony and sarcasm – in order to leverage their electoral power to influence government agendas, performance and conduct. Nyerere becomes a touchstone of good governance, co-opting elite discourses of filial descent to morally discipline the government with projections of paternal displeasure. Interestingly, the controversy over which political party had the right to claim the legacy of Nyerere, a central feature of party jockeying in 2005, seemed to have lost its salience in the 2010 campaign.

Aikande Kwayu's contribution to this volume (Chapter 6) deeply resonates with that of Phillips. In surveying current debates at the Constitutional Assembly, the author shows how Nyerere's words and ideas are invoked not only for moral authority but to justify debate over the country's destiny, and most notably the structure of the Union government. Kwayu identifies three different models for the Union proposed through recourse to Nyerere, either to ground their promoters' views or to delegitimize other factions: those of the CCM leadership, of the Chairman of the Commission Joseph Warioba and his adherents, and of the opposition group Umoja wa Katiba ya Wananchi (UKAWA, the Coalition for a People's Constitution). Each proposes a different view of Nyerere's advocacy and intentions over time, and each recurs to the notion of symbolic filial descent from Nyerere – the content of this legacy provoking more debate than its present-day relevance. Kwayu also makes it clear that the manipulation of Nyerere, figured as the founding father of the nation, tends to delimit the thinkable and the unthinkable in Tanzania's politics – the death of Tanzania as a nation-state. Shortly before the demise of Tanzania's Ujamaa, Jackson and Rosberg noted that "the real test for the Tanzanian experiment will occur after Nyerere exits from the political stage that he has dominated for so long" (1984: 440). One might add that today's debates test the very concept of Tanzania as a nation.

Vilifying Nyerere?

The public use of Nyerere to debate nationhood – and the scholarly literature that has tended overwhelmingly to eulogize Nyerere's time in power – should not obscure his political critics. In his contribution to this volume, James Brennan (Chapter 7) presents three distinct groups of detractors, all sharing a sharp frustration with how Nyerere used his image – humble intellectual and paragon of morality – as a political weapon to control political debate and silence opposition. These groups include the disillusioned paternalist Anglo-American elites who had followed Nyerere's ascent to power; Western anti-socialist writers who witnessed the Tanzanian experiment and its failure (e.g. Naipaul, 1979; Daniels, 1988); and, since the country's return to multiparty elections in the early 1990s, Tanzanian political opponents who experienced Nyerere's autocratic power (e.g., Muhsin, 2002; Mwijage, 1994). The author shows that the production of political criticism against Nyerere calls for a sociological characterization of actors and requires historical contextualization: the coercive nature of village collectivization was a watershed, turning enthusiasts into fierce critics. Yet, these "counter-mythologies" have little impact on everyday discussions because they take the form of confidential writings, such as foreign newspapers articles or prison letters, which are shared only among Tanzania's educated elite. Lionizing Nyerere remains the rule.

This echoes Marie-Aude Fouéré's chapter (Chapter 8), describing popular Nyerere-bashing in contemporary Zanzibar as a tool for the production of counter-hegemonic narratives of nationhood. Retracing how anti-Nyerere sentiment entails rewriting the history of the 1964 Revolution in Zanzibar and the Union with the former Tanganyika, she shows how present-day anti-Nyerere criticism owes something to the spread of publications by his fierce political opponents – most of them belonging to Brennan's third group. Critics used various channels to disseminate their views throughout Zanzibar society, eventually shaping popular historical consciousness and informing political mobilization. As a consequence, ordinary citizens can also produce critical accounts of Nyerere (see also Becker, 2013; Kamat, 2008). Most of these critical voices, however, do not come from Tanzania's academics (for exceptions, see notably Shivji, 1974; Othman in Yahya-Othman, 2014). Brennan aptly reminds us that for years, protest or disagreement within the Tanzanian national borders had to be muffled or uttered off the record; in the case of scholars, it required "the panoplies of deeply abstracted theory," e.g. debates on socialism at the University of Dar es Salaam.

Poetry as political performance

Two chapters on the genre of newspaper poetry, focused on non professional praise poems about Nyerere, enrich our understanding of channels of production and transmission of ordinary political debates about the nation. They remind us of the deep imprint of Swahili oral and print culture on Tanzanian national culture. In Chapter 9, the anthropologist Kelly Askew contrasts non-elite poems about Tanzania's first president with poems published decades earlier, during colonial times, about Kaiser Wilhelm II and King George V. Mary Ann Mhina (Chapter 10) reviews the specific form of Swahili popular poetry published in the ruling party newspaper, *Uhuru*, during the mourning period of Nyerere in 1999. Both chapters give complementary insight into this genre of poetry as a "repository of popular political debate," in Askew's words. The genre bears witness to the engagement of Tanzanian citizens with politics, in the broad sense of the term, reflecting at once a particular *zeitgeist* and individual creativity. A comparative historical perspective captures variations in popular perceptions of a leader and their ties to distinct political moments. Praise poetry about Nyerere consequently follows the ups and downs of citizen investment in the national project. During Nyerere's early tenure, especially after the Arusha Declaration, newspaper poetry not only resonated with the modernization faith and the left-leaning development promises of the new postcolonial regime, but also reflected the cultural "revolution" of the fledgling nation, aimed at making arts and culture a vehicle for nation-building. In a period where art was seen as serving and representing society, popular poetry too performed versions of patriotism (see notably Askew, 2002, 2005; Edmondson, 2007; Ivaska, 2011).

With the demise of socialism and the decline in Nyerere's popularity since the end of the 1970s, poems increasingly articulated discontent and critique – often conveyed, however, by way of metaphor and innuendo. And in the post-Nyerere period, patriotic poets have flourished again and newly re-assert Nyerere's central position in the political imagination, as Mhina demonstrates. This rekindled investment is two-sided, however. It can be used as a means to foster the legitimacy of CCM in a fiercely competitive multi-party system, and it may replay the symbolic filiation between the previous and current political leaders, in ways similar to those described by Phillips and Kwayu in their chapters. Yet the panegyric ode to Nyerere can also serve as sharp critique of the new big-bellied elite of bureaucrats and politicians, as against the idealized national leader whose "conspicuous lack of a belly was perhaps as symbolically potent as his rejection of material luxury" (Ferguson, 2006: 76, quoted in Kristin Phillips' chapter). While the social impact of the printed word in verse or in prose goes beyond the scope of their analysis, Askew and Mhina remind us of an important paradox: one cannot postulate an autonomous popular domain of thought and action outside state narratives and practices, but the state's efforts at citizen control remain partial and imperfect – liable, in fact, to turn against the state and those associated with it.

Post-Mwalimu education

The last two chapters of this collection explore Nyerere's legacy in the field of education, a field bearing his lasting imprint. Theoretically, these essays differ slightly from the other contributions: they do not simply excavate memory narratives of Nyerere that inform debates on politics and belonging, but rather demonstrate how Nyerere's words and Ujamaa policies play out in current institutional and bureaucratic practices. Olivier Provini (Chapter 11) argues that the University of Dar es Salaam occupies a space set between transition (through the implementation of a new neoliberal agenda) and continuity (maintaining representations and practices related to a socialist approach), notably in the state's financial engagement with the university budget. Nyerere's shadow still lingers over the implementation of reforms as well as in teacher and student visions of education. The author details how the policy of cost-sharing among governments, parents and students gave rise to demonstrations invoking the tutelary protection of Mwalimu. Students asserted that the government should follow Mwalimu Nyerere's example by prioritizing education for all eligible students, not simply the well-off. Student-government negotiations finally resulted in budgetary reforms which did not, however, fully embrace the neoliberal model originally intended. This outcome signals the uniqueness of Tanzania's higher education system – what we could call a "post-socialist" system, characterized by both ruptures and continuities with Tanzania's past.

In her study of the ward secondary schools policy introduced in 2006 (Chapter 12), Sonia Languille skillfully argues that public policy-making in the field relies on narratives of legitimation and justification, which in turn draw upon Nyerere's educational philosophy as a discursive resource. Asserting that the 2006 policy blatantly contradicts Nyerere's actual concept of education's purpose – that is, to prepare children for their roles within the community – she identifies a rigid "performative" adherence to a Nyerere orthodoxy among policy-makers. However, such invocations of Nyerere rarely address the contradictions between Ujamaa egalitarian rhetoric and the reality of an elite produced and reproduced under the present system. But Languille highlights one significant legacy from the socialist past in the dominant narrative of youth-centred legitimacy, mobilized to justify the ward secondary schools policy. This narrative brings back the ambivalent socialist view of Tanzanian youth – at once servants of the nation and threatening raw minds and bodies, prone to idleness, crime and transgression (Burton, 2005, 2006; Burgess, 2005; Brennan, 2006, 2010; Ivaska, 2011), especially in the city (Brennan, Burton and Lawi, 2007).

'Nyerere' as a Political Struggle

Floating 'Nyerere'

The foregoing should establish the variety of uses and attributes configured by "Julius Nyerere" in contemporary Tanzania: sometimes hero and sometimes villain, king-philosopher or cynical dictator. In all instances, 'Nyerere' becomes a political metaphor for debating and acting upon the present. More precisely, 'Nyerere' attains it meaning by virtue of having something done with it. 'Nyerere' can be brandished in a street demonstration for better education or freedom of speech – thus becoming a referent of liberty, justice and equality. It can be harnessed to nostalgia for social services in the 1960s-1970s as against neoliberal reforms, in street-corner discussions between friends, colleagues and acquaintances – thus becoming synonymous with social equity, national welfare and solidarity. Or it can be dropped on the stage during a political rally to promise a walk in Nyerere's footsteps if elected – as a rallying point for political commitment, incorruptibility, and integrity. In the language of semiotics and philosophy, 'Nyerere' is a floating signifier: it has no fixed or definite signified attached, but rather ambiguous, flexible, and variable signifieds, assigned according to the occasions and settings of its use. As Ernesto Laclau and Chantal Mouffe remind us, it is impossible to fix "ultimate meanings" to floating signifiers (Laclau and Mouffe, 2001: 111). In other words, 'Nyerere' means different things to different people – it has a plurality of signifieds, always contextual in character.

Although 'Nyerere' appears as a floating signifier due to its polysemy, indeterminacy and indexical character, we contend that it is not "empty" – it does not float in a space of freedom in which one could assign any type of meaning to it. If its meanings are highly variable, as we contend above, they are not free from any determinacy: 'Nyerere' remains embedded in a system of existing signifiers and signifieds historically constructed throughout his life and since his death and disseminated through Tanzanian society. 'Nyerere' is not blank and unfilled, because Julius Nyerere possesses a historicity. Social and cultural conditions also constrain and limit how a given society negotiates and contests its past. In Arjun Appadurai's words, "the past is (not) a limitless and plastic symbolic resource," subject to contemporary interests and warped by contemporary ideologies, since culturally variable norms "regulate the debatability of the past" (1981: 201). The thinkable and the unthinkable, the debatable and the un-debatable remain largely framed by history and culture. If 'Nyerere' is discursively constituted in the present and by the present, the present uses of 'Nyerere' also depend upon the past.

The present volume depends upon disconnecting the entity and the word, to borrow Foucault's formulation (1966) – divorcing the signifier "Nyerere" from the historical referent Julius Nyerere – while acknowledging that the existence of that referent constrains public debate about the signifier's meanings. This indeed explains two core issues at stake. First, it accounts for the fact that most debates about what Nyerere stands for today – whether deliberate or the product of less articulated practices – translate into specifying what 'Nyerere' means. This prompts endless interpretations and arguments, be they banal and mundane or learned and erudite, rooted in living experience of the past or grounded in second-hand oral or written accounts. People make continuous efforts to arrest the flow of meanings and construct fixed signification – in our case, striving to make of 'Nyerere' a "privileged discursive point of partial fixation" or a "nodal point" (Laclau and Mouffe, 2001: 112).[26] Second, highlighting the indexical or contextual nature of words shows us that assigning meanings is a political struggle; debates over the possible meanings of 'Nyerere' construct ideas, ideals, conceptions and representations of what the society should be, and prompt actions that may transform society.[27] Any signifier is always, therefore, a performing signifier (Austin, 1962). People manipulate words, struggle over their definitions, contest the legitimacy of given actors to use them and to attribute other meanings to them – not simply for the sake of it, but to accomplish certain ends, in contingent contexts where power is at play.

---

26 We contend that biographies of Nyerere, transcripts of his speeches and publications of his writings, and essays at analysing his political thought constitute efforts by some gatekeepers to arrest the ordinary continuous flow of meanings of Nyerere and sustain a certain image – or what they see as a certain 'truth' harnessed to 'objective facts' in order to fight 'distortions' – of the man and the politician, though the written word, like the spoken words, also generates debates and may trigger contest.

27 See also Chambi Cachage who, in his contribution "Mwalimu in our popular imagination", shows that when the name 'Nyerere' is uttered in the public space, it generates "public debates on issues of importance to society" (2010: 3). Yet, that the name 'Nyerere' may prompt debates has to do with its nature of floating signifier, not to any ability of collective debating which Julius Nyerere would have passed on to Tanzanians.

Post-socialist nationhood

This leads us to several observations. First, scholars who attempt to map the various meanings attributed to 'Nyerere' in Tanzania face an endless task. Perceptions, memories and descriptions of Julius Nyerere vary greatly in time and place – from his lifetime to the present, and from one social environment to another. A merely inventorial perspective on this variety is rapidly exhausted; we propose, instead, to cast light on efforts to produce "partially fixed" meanings and how these operate in a given social situation. We cannot escape historicizing and contextualizing the uses of 'Nyerere', and all contributors to this volume have brilliantly taken up the challenge.

This collection calls for a reappraisal of contemporary politics – one which, instead of continuously looking back onto the colonial legacy, explores continuities and discontinuities with the early postcolonial period. Following Crawford Young, it suggests that the colonial referent has lost its pertinence in current governance and shows that Tanzania no longer situates itself in the "post-colonial moment", having shed "routines, practices and mentalities" inherited from the colonial state (2004: 23-24; see also Burton and Jennings, 2007). Since the demise of the socialist order, Tanzania has entered the "post-socialist" moment (Askew, 2006; Askew and Pitcher, 2006) with continuities as well as ruptures with the socialist paradigm. Ongoing debates around Nyerere clearly indicate that a new historical moment is taking shape, characterized by efforts at reimagining the Tanzanian nation.

Second, we propose revisiting the liberally-applied scholarly concept of "collective memory." This is often conceived as a set of representations of the past, shared by a given social group – a village community, people who went through the same experience, a generation who have lived specific historical events, a nation. However, since the initial reflections of Ernst Renan (1996 [1882]) and Maurice Halbwachs (1980 [1950]), this conception of memory has come into question.[28] In the case of the nation-state, memory narratives have a powerful presence among various constituents of society, because they reflect the power of the state to control their terms, contours and modes of transmission, notably through institutions such as museums, school curricula, the media,

---

28 From different perspectives, both authors show how remembering and forgetting are social processes in the service of conceptions and needs of the present through which the 'content' of memory is constantly reshaped. Efforts to physically inscribe mental representations in space or in repetitive social practices like rituals and commemorations clearly point to the malleability of collective memories which societies – or certain segments within society – may try to control.

etc. (Roberts, 2000: 521). As Moses Finley has aptly argued (1965: 297), memory is "the transmittal to many people of the memory of one man or a few men" for given purposes. Memory is therefore about mediation, oralisation, textualization, and acts of communication more generally: when Tanzanians "remember" Nyerere, they re-narrate and re-define him. The struggle over the meanings of Nyerere will not recede – and the floating yet historically and culturally constrained nature of Nyerere as a signifier will not vanish – as long as the political imagination that underpins conceptions of the Tanzanian nation and Tanzania-ness has its anchor in the figure of the first president.

One should also stress that local memories rather than grand national narratives may affect the esteem that citizens accord Nyerere. In her work on women's mobilisation in the late 1950s, Susan Geiger noted a "moral claim on Nyerere and the party", with echoes in today's generation of politically involved women; this should not be dismissed as simple nostalgia (2005: 286) or as the product of state and party hegemony. It also derives from vivid memory of Nyerere, their *mwanangu* (son) – a nickname given to him before he became the father of the nation – who publicly recognized their role in the independence struggle on several occasions. Ordinary citizens, therefore, can locate the origins of their memory narratives of Nyerere in their own shared experience, and such narratives may intertwine – or not – with the more strategic uses of his figure by politicians and the state.

Last, why is it that in Tanzania Nyerere remains such a paramount figure at various levels of society, while many other African Fathers of the Nation have been challenged or debunked – such as Léopold Ségar Senghor in Senegal or Sékou Touré in Guinea (see Charton and Fouéré, 2013)? Other countries such as Kenya have created a pantheon of national heroes, fostering a sense of plural and multipolar nation building. But in Tanzania, when the official historiography has foregrounded other personae, they are located in the pre-colonial past and seen as Nyerere's forebears (Sunseri, 2000; Roberts, 2000). Personalities who had a tremendous political role during the Nyerere era and are reclaimed today, such as former Prime Minister Rashid Kawawa, cannot overshadow Nyerere in the state narrative. We contend that the socialist national narrative and its embodiment in Nyerere have had powerful effects on political consciousness and the national ethos. Tanzania under Nyerere managed to create deep-rooted repertoires of subjectivity with which Tanzanians still identify in part, and which they draw upon to express their conception of the polity. To borrow a still-pertinent usage from Max Weber, we might say that the early postcolonial era has led to "types of men" (*Menschentum*) who share a specific ethos of respectability, honour, and dignity (Weber, 1964).[29] As in many African countries, economic liberalisation changed the state-society relationship and brought about demoralization and disillusion; but in Tanzania, this new context violently collided with the postcolonial repertory that had undergirded political subjectivities.

This may explain the rekindled investment in the figure of Nyerere and how it has translated into political discussions and discourses at all levels of society, whether in the media, on political podiums or in street-corner talks. This reminds us that, as above, popular narratives do not necessarily take shape in opposition to the dominant state narrative, but arise within the same repertoire of representations (Roberts, 2000: 522). However, shifts are occurring in the Tanzanian nationalist ethos, and new figures and repertoires of success have emerged from prevailing conditions of social, political and economic transformation (see, e.g. Weiss, 2009). Only the passing of generations, therefore, will tell us whether the relevance of Nyerere – the values and ideals he represents in the nation's present – will remain intact. In a speech in Accra on 6th March 1997 marking the 40th anniversary of Ghanaian independence, Nyerere challenged new generations of Africans, saying: "My generation led Africa to political freedom. The current generation of leaders and peoples of Africa must pick up the flickering torch of African freedom, refuel it with their enthusiasm and determination, and carry it forward" (Nyerere, 2000: 31).[30] Today, the question is less whether these new generations are ready to take up this challenge, but whether they see it as a challenge at all.

---

29 Nyerere himself clearly expressed how national ethics supply the foundation of national identity: "What was needed (Nyerere said) was a national ethic that enabled the government to say, 'That we cannot tolerate, that is un-Tanganyikan.' Without such an ethic, said Nyerere, 'no constitution, however, framed, could insure that the people would not become victims of tyranny'" (Smith, 2011 [1973]: 84).

30 In this speech, Nyerere makes reference to his own words at the Tanganyika Legislative Assembly on 22nd October 1959, when he expressed his hope that the torch of freedom "would shine beyond our border, giving hope where there was despair, love where there was fate, and dignity where there was before only humiliation".

References

ANDERSON, Benedict. *Imagined Communities: Reflections on the Origin and Spread of Nationalism*. London: Verso, 2006.

APPADURAI, Arjun. "The Past as a Scarce Resource." *Man* 16, no. 2 (1981): 201–209.

ASKEW, Kelly M. "Sung and Unsung: Musical Reflections on Tanzanian Postsocialism." *Africa* 76, no. 1 (2006): 15–43.

ASKEW, Kelly M. "Jacks-of-all-Arts or Ustadhi? The Poetics of Cultural Production in Tanzania." In *In Search of a Nation. Histories of Authority & Dissidence in Tanzania*, ed. Gregory H. Maddox and James L. Giblin, 304–327. Oxford: James Currey Ltd, 2005.

ASKEW, Kelly M. *Performing the Nation: Swahili Music and Cultural Politics in Tanzania*. Chicago: University of Chicago Press, 2002.

ASSENSOH, A. H. *African Political Leadership. Jomo Kenyatta, Kwame Nkrumah and Julius K. Nyerere*. Malabar, Fl.: Krieger Publishing Company, 1998.

AUSTIN, John L. *How to Do Things with Words: The William James Lectures delivered at Harvard University in 1955*, ed. J.O. Urmson and Marina Sbisà. Oxford: Clarendon Press, 1962.

BAYART, Jean-François. *The State in Africa: The Politics of the Belly*. Heinemann: London, 1993. Originally published in Jean-François Bayart, trans. *L'Etat en Afrique. La politique du ventre* (Paris: Fayard, 1989).

BAYART, Jean-François. "La politique par le bas en Afrique noire: question de méthode [Politics from Below in Black Africa: A Methological Issue]." *Politique africaine* 1 (1981): 53–82.

BAYART, Jean-François, and Romain BERTRAND. "What Colonial Legacy Are We Talking About?" Originally published in Jean-François Bayart and Romain Bertrand, trans., "De quel 'legs colonial' parle-t-on?" *Esprit* (Dec., 2006): 134–161).

BECKER, Felicitas. "Remembering Nyerere: Political Rhetoric and Dissent in Contemporary Tanzania." *African Affairs* 112, no. 447 (2013): 1–24.

BENNETT, George. "Tanzania and Tanzaphilia: A Review Article." *African Affairs* 67, no. 268 (Jul., 1968): 248–252.

BERMAN, Bruce, and John LONSDALE. *Unhappy Valley. Conflict in Kenya and Africa*. Portsmouth: James Currey, 1992.

BJERK, Paul. "Sovereignty and Socialism in Tanzania: The Historiography of an African State." *History in Africa* 37 (2010): 275–319.

BOESEN, Jannik, Kjell J. HAVNEVIK, Juhani KOPONEN and Rie ODGAARD. *Tanzania. Crisis and Struggle for Survival.* Uppsala: Scandinavian Institute of African Studies, 1986.

BRENNAN, James. "Blood Enemies: Exploitation and Urban Citizenship in the Nationalist Political Thought of Tanzania, 1958–75." *Journal of African History* 47 (2006): 389–413.

BRENNAN, James R. "Youth, the TANU Youth League and Managed Vigilantism in Dar es Salaam, 1925-1973." In *Generations Pasts. Youth in East African History*, ed. Andrew Burton and Hélène Charton-Bigot, 196–220. Ohio University Press: Athens Ohio, 2010.

BRENNAN, James R., Andrew BURTON and Yusuf LAWI. *Dar es Salaam: Histories from an Emerging African Metropolis.* Dar es Salaam: Mkuki na Nyota, 2007.

BUENO DES MESQUITA, Bruce, Alastair Smith, Randolph R. Siverson, and James D. Morrow. *The Logic of Political Survival.* Cambridge, MA: MIT Press, 2003.

BURGESS, Thomas G. "Introduction to Youth and Citizenship in East Africa." *Africa Today* 51, no. 3 (Spring 2005), 'Youth and Citizenship in East Africa': vii–xxiv.

BURTON, Andrew. *African Underclass.Urbanisation, Crime and Colonial Order in Dar es Salaam.* Nairobi: The British Institute in Eastern Africa, 2005.

BURTON, Andrew. "Raw youth, school-leavers and the emergence of structural unemployment in late-colonial urban Tanganyika." *Journal of African History* 47 (2006): 363–387.

BURTON, Andrew, and Michael JENNINGS. "The Emperor's New Clothes? Continuities in Governance in Late Colonial and Early Colonial Postcolonial East Africa." *International Journal of East African Histories* 40, no. 1 (2007): 1–26.

CARROLL, Lewis. *Through the Looking Glass and What Alice Found There.* London and Sydney: Pan Books, 1977 (1st ed. 1871).

CARTWRIGHT, John. *Political Leadership in Africa.* London, New York: Croom Helm, St. Martin's Press, 1983.

CHABAL, Patrick. *Africa: The Politics of Suffering and Smiling.* London: Zed Books, 2009.

CHABAL, Patrick, and Jean-Pascal DALOZ. *Africa Works. Disorder as Political Instrument.* Oxford, Bloomington: James Currey, Indiana Press, 1999.

CIVILLE, John R., and William R DUGGAN. *Tanzania and Nyerere. A Study of Ujamaa and Nationhood.* Maryknoll: Orbis Books, 1976.

CHACHAGE, Chambi. "Mwalimu in Our Popular Imagination: the Relevance of Nyerere Today." In *Africa's Liberation: the Legacy of Nyerere*, ed. Chambi Chachage and Annar Cassam, 4–6. Cape Town: Pambazuka Press, 2010.

CHACHAGE, Chambi, and Annar CASSAM. *Africa's Liberation. The Legacy of Nyerere*. Kampala: Fountain Publishers; Cape Town, Dakar, Nairobi, Oxford: Pambazuka Press, 2010.

CHARTON, Hélène, and Marie-Aude FOUÉRÉ. "Présentation." Special issue 'Héros nationaux et pères de la nation en Afrique [National Heroes and Fathers of the Nation in Africa],' *Vingtième Siècle* 118 (Apr.-Jun., 2013): 3–14.

COHEN, Anthony P., and John L. COMAROFF. "The Management of Meaning: On the Phenomenology of Political Transactions." In *Transactions and Meaning: Directions in the Anthropology of Exchange and Symbolic Behavior*, ed. Bruce Kapferer, 87–107. Philadelphia: Institute for the Study of Human Issues, 1976.

CONSTANTIN, François. "Les images de la Tanzanie en France, mythes et parti pris [The Images of Tanzania in France, Myths and Biais]." In *Arusha (Tanzanie), vingt ans après*, ed. François Constantin & Denis-Constant Martin, 1–13. Pau: Université de Pau et des Pays de l'Adour, 1988.

CONSTANTIN, François. "L'héritage de Nyerere: débuts d'inventaire [Nyerere's Legacy: An Early Inventory]." *Canadian Journal of African Studies* 23, no. 3 (1989), 454–457.

COULSON, Andrew. *Tanzania: a Political Economy*. Oxford: Oxford University Press, 1982.

CROZON, Ariel. "Dire pour séduire: Langages et politique en Tanzanie [Speaking to Seduce: Languages and politics in Tanzania]." In *Nouveaux langages du politique en Afrique orientale*, ed. Denis-Constant Martin, 115–185. Paris: Karthala, 1998.

CROZON, Ariel. "Maneno wa siasa, les mots du politique en Tanzanie [Maneno wa siasa: The Words of Politics in Tanzania]." *Politique Africaine* 64 (1996): 18–30.

ECKERT, Andrea. "An African Statesman: A Portrait of Julius Nyerere as Politician, 1950s to 1980s." In *Afrikanische Beziehungen, Netzwerke und Räume / African Networks, Exchange and Spatial Dynamics / Dynamiques spatiales, réseaux et échanges africains*, ed. Laurence Marfaing and Brigitte Reinwald, 309–325. Münster: LIT, 2001.

EDMONDSON, Laura. *Performance and Politics in Tanzania. The Nation on Stage*. Bloomington and Indianapolis: Indiana University Press, 2007.

FERGUSON, James. *Global Shadows: Africa in the Neoliberal World Order*. Durham, N.C.: Duke University Press, 2006.

FERGUSON, James. *Expectations of Modernity: Myths and Meanings of Urban Life on the Zambian Copperbelt*. Berkeley, Calif.: University of California Press, 1999.

FINLEY, Moses I. "Myth, Memory, and History." *History and Theory* 4, no. 3 (1965); 281–302.

FOUCAULT, Michel. *The Order of Things: An Archaeology of the Human Sciences*. New York, Pantheon Book, 1970. Originally published in Michel Foucault, trans. *Les Mots et les choses: Une archéologie des sciences humaines* (Paris: Gallimard, 1966).

FOUÉRÉ, Marie-Aude. "Julius Nyerere, Ujamaa and Political Morality in Contemporary Tanzania." *African Studies Review* 57, no. 1 (2014): 1–24.

FOUÉRÉ, Marie-Aude. "Tanzanie: la nation à l'épreuve du postsocialisme [Tanzania: The Nation Put to the Test of Postsocialism]." *Politique Africaine* 121 (2011): 69–85.

FOUÉRÉ, Marie-Aude. "J. K. Nyerere entre mythe et histoire: analyse de la production d'une culture nationale en Tanzanie post-socialiste [J. K. Nyerere Between Myth and History: An Analysis of the Production of a National Culture in Post-socialist Tanzania]." *Les Cahiers d'Afrique de l'Est* 4 (2009): 197–224.

GEIGER, Susan. *TANU Women: Gender and Culture in the Making of Tanganyikan Nationalism, 1955-1965*. Portsmouth NH: Heinemann, 1997.

GEIGER, Susan. "Tanganyikan Nationalism as 'Women's Work': Life Histories, Collective Biographies and Changing Historiography." *Journal of African History* 37 (1996): 465–478.

GEIGER, Susan. "Engendering & Gendering African Nationalism. Rethinking the case of Tanganyika (Tanzania)." In *In Search of a Nation: Histories of Authority and Dissidence in Tanzania*, ed. Gregory Maddox and James Giblin, 278–289. Oxford: James Currey, 2005.

HALBWACHS, Maurice. *The Collective Memory*. New York: Harper & Row Colophon Books, 1980. Originally published in Maurice Halbwachs, *La mémoire collective* (Paris: Presses Universitaires de France, 1950).

HARTMANN, Jeanette. "President Nyerere and the State." In *Tanzania after Nyerere*, ed. Micheal Hood. London: Pinter Publishers, 1988.

HATCH, John. *Two African Statesmen: Kaunda of Zambia and Nyerere of Tanzania*. London: Secker and Warburg, 1976.

HAVNEVIK, Kjell. "A Historical Framework for Analyzing Current Tanzanian Transitions: The Post-independence Model, Nyerere's Ideas and Some African Studies Review Interpretations." In *Tanzania in Transition: From Nyerere to Mkapa*, edited by Kjell HAVNEVIK and Aida C. ISINIKA, 19–55. Dar es Salaam: Mkuki na Nyota, 2010.

HODD, Michael. *Tanzania after Nyerere*, London, New York: Pinter Publishers, 1988.

HUNTER, Emma. "British Tanzaphilia, 1961–1972." Unpublished MA thesis, University of Cambridge, 2004.

HUNTER, Emma. "Revisiting Ujamaa: Political Legitimacy and the Construction of Community in Post-Colonial Tanzania." *Journal of Eastern African Studies* 2, no. 3 (2008): 471–485.

HYDEN, Goran. "Mao and Mwalimu: The Soldier and the Teacher as Revolutionary." *Transition* 34 (Dec. 1967-Jan.1968): 24–30.

HYDEN, Goran. *Beyond Ujamaa in Tanzania: Underdevelopment and an Uncaptured Peasantry*. London: Heinemann, 1980.

IBHAWOH, Bonny, and Jeremiah I. DIBUA. "Deconstructing Ujamaa : The Legacy of Julius Nyerere in the Quest for Social and Economic Development in Africa." *African Journal of Political Science* 8 no. 1 (2003): 59–83.

IVASKA, Andrew. *Cultured States: Youth, Gender, and Modern Style in 1960s Dar es Salaam*. Durham: Duke University Press, 2011.

JACKSON, Robert H., and Carl G. ROSBERG. "Personal Rule: Theory and Practice in Africa." *Comparative Politics* 16, no. 4 (Jul., 1984): 421–442.

JACKSON, Robert H., and Carl G. ROSBERG. *Personal Rule in Black Africa. Prince, Autocrat, Prophet, Tyrant*. Berkeley, CA: University of California Press, 1982.

KADUMA, Ibrahim. *Maadili ya Taifa na Hatma ya Tanzania: Enzi kwa Mwalimu Julius K. Nyerere*. Dar es Salaam: Knowledge Printers and Publishers, 2010.

KAMAT, Vinay. "This is not Our Culture! Discourse of Nostalgia and Narratives of Health Concerns in Post-Socialist Tanzania." *Africa* 78, no. 3 (2008): 359–383.

KELSALL, Tim. "Governance, Democracy and Recent Political Struggles in Mainland Tanzania." *Commonwealth and Comparative Politics* 41, no. 3 (2003): 55–82.

KIRK-GREENE, Anthony H. "His Eternity, His Eccentricity, or His Exemplarity? A Further Contribution to the Study of HE the African Head of State." *African Affairs* 90, no. 359 (Apr., 1991): 163–87.

KITCHING, Gavin. *Development and Underdevelopment in Historical Perspective: Populism, Nationalism, and Industrialization*. London: Methuen, 1982.

LACLAU, Ernesto and Chantal MOUFFE. *Hegemony and Socialist Strategy. Towards a Radical Democratic Politics*. London and Brooklyn: Verso, 2001 (1st ed. 1985)

LEYS, Colin. "Inter Alia-or Tanzaphilia and All That." *Transition* 34 (Dec., 1967-Jan., 1968): 51–53.

LEGUM, Colin, and Geoffrey MMARI. *Mwalimu: The Influence of Nyerere*. London: James Currey, 1995.

LISTOWEL, Judith. *The Making of Tanganyika*. London: Chatto and Windus, 1965.

LONSDALE, John. "Jomo Kenyatta, God & the Modern World." In *African Modernities. Entangled Meanings in Current Debate*, ed. Jan-Georg Deutsch, Peter Probst and Heike Schmidt, 31–66. Portsmouth: Heinemann, Oxford: James Currey, 2002.

LONSDALE, John. "The Tanzanian Experiment." African Affairs 67, no. 269 (Oct.,1968): 330–344.

MADDOX, Gregory, and James GIBLIN. *In Search of a Nation: Histories of Authority and Dissidence in Tanzania*. Oxford: James Currey, 2005.

MANJI, Firoze. "Preface. How We Wish You Were Here: A Tribute to Mwalimu Nyerere." In *Africa's Liberation. The Legacy of Nyerere*, ed. Chambi Chachage and Annar Cassam, ix–xi. Kampala: Fountain Publishers; Cape Town, Dakar, Nairobi, Oxford: Pambazuka Press, 2010.

MARTIN, Denis-Constant. *Tanzanie: L'invention d'une culture politique*. Paris: Presses de la Fondation nationale des sciences politiques/ Karthala, 1988.

MAZRUI, Ali A. *"The Titan" of Tanzania: Julius K. Nyerere's Legacy*. Binghamton, Ind.: Institute of Global Cultural Studies, 2002.

MAZRUI, Ali A. "Tanzaphilia." *Transition* 31 (1967): 20–26.

McDONALD, David A., and Eunice Njeri SAHLE. *The Legacies of Julius Nyerere: Influences on Development Discourse and Practice in Africa*. Trenton, New Jersey: Africa World Press, 2002.

McHENRY, Dean E. *Limited Choices: The Political Struggle for Socialism in Tanzania*. London: Lynne Riener, 1994.

MBELLE, Ammon, Godwin D. MJEMA and Ali A. L. KILINDO. *The Nyerere Legacy and Economic Policy Making in Tanzania*. Dar es Salaam: Dar es Salaam University Press, 2002.

MBEMBE, Achille. "Provisional Notes on the Postcolony." *Africa*: 62, no. 1, (1992): 3–37.

MEYNS, Peter. "The Quest for Freedom. Reflections on Julius Nyerere's Political Thinking and Practice." In *Tanzania Revisited: Political Stability, Aid Dependency and Development Constraints*, ed. Ulf Engel, Gero Erdmann and Andreas Mehler, 151–166. Hamburg: Institut für Afrika-Kunde, 2000.

MOHIDDIN, Ahmed. "Ujamaa: A Commentary on President Nyerere's Vision of Tanzanian Society." *African Affairs* 67 no. 2 (1968): 130–43.

MOLONY, Thomas. *Nyerere: The early years*. Oxford: James Currey, 2014.

MONSON, Jamie. "Defending the People's Railway in the Era of Liberalization." *Africa* 76, no. 1 (2006): 113–130.

MONSON, Jamie. "Remembering Work on the TAZARA Railway in Africa and China, 1965–2011: When New Men Grow Old." *African Studies Review* 56, no. 1 (2013): 45–64.

MWAKIKAGILE, Godfrey. *Nyerere and Africa: End of an Era*. Pretoria. Dar es Salaam: New Africa Press, 2010 (5th amended edition).

MUHSIN, Ali. *Conflicts and Harmony in Zanzibar, Memoirs*. Dubai: self-published, 2002.

MWIJAGE, Ludovick S. *The Dark Side of Nyerere's Legacy*. London: Adelphi Press, 1996 (1994).

NYERERE, Julius K. *Africa Today and Tomorrow*. Dar es Salaam: Mwalimu Nyerere Foundation, 2000 (2nd ed.).

NYEREREe, Julius K. *Freedom and Socialism/ Uhuru na Ujamaa. A Selection from Writings and Speeches 1965-67*. Dar es Salaam: Oxford University Press, 1968.

NYERERE, Julius K. *Freedom and Development/ Uhuru na Maendeleo. A Selection from Writings and Speeches 1968-1973*. Dar es Salaam: Oxford University Press, 1973.

NYERERE, Julius K. *Freedom and Unity/ Uhuru na Umoja. A Selection from Writings and Speeches 1952-65*. Dar es Salaam: Oxford University Press, 1966.

OTHMAN, Haroub. *Sites of Memory. Julius Nyerere and the Liberation Struggle of Southern Africa*. Dar es Salaam: ZIFF, 2007.

PHILLIPS, Kristin D. "Pater Rules Best: Political Kinship and Party Politics in Tanzania's Presidential Elections." *PoLAR: Political and Legal Anthropology Review* 33, no. 1 (2010): 109–132.

PITCHER, Anne, and Kelly M. ASKEW. "African Socialisms and Postsocialisms." *Africa* 76 (2006): 1–14.

PRATT, Cranford. "Julius Nyerere: Reflections on the Legacy of his Socialism." *Canadian Journal of African Studies* 33, no. 1 (1999): 137–152.

PRATT, Cranford. *The Critical Phase in Tanzania, 1945-67. Nyerere and the Emergence of a Socialist Strategy*. Cambridge, NewYork: Cambridge University Press, 1976.

ROBERTS, Richard. "History and Memory: The Power of Statist Narratives." *The International Journal of African Historical Studies* 33, n° 3 (2000): 513–522.

RUGUMAMU, Severine R. *Lethal Aid: The Illusion of Socialism and Self-Reliance in Tanzania*. Trenton NJ: Africa World Press, 1997.

Russian Academy of Sciences Institute for African Studies. *Julius Nyerere. Humanist, Politician, Thinker*. Dar es Salaam: Mkuki na Nyota, 2005.

SAID, Mohamed. *The Life and Times of Abdulwahid Sykes: The Untold Story of the Muslim Struggle against British Colonialism in Tanganyika*. London: Minerva Press, 1998.

SAMOFF, Joel. Review of *Tanzania after Nyerere*, by Michael Hood. *The International Journal of African Historical Studies* 22, no. 1 (1989): 177–180.

SAUL, John. "Julius Nyerere and the Theory and Practice of (Un) Democratic Socialism in Africa." In *The Legacies of Julius Nyerere: Influence on Development Discourse and Practice in Africa*, ed. David A. McDonald and Eunice Njeri Sahle, 15-26. Trenton, New Jersey: Africa World Press, 2002

SCHATZBERG, Michael. *Political Legitimacy in Middle Africa: Father, Family, Food*. Bloomington: Indiana University Press, 2002.

SCHNEIDER, Leander. "Freedom and Unfreedom in Rural Development: Julius Nyerere, Ujamaa Vijijini, and Villagization." *Canadian Journal of African Studies* 38 (2004): 344–392.

SCOTT, James C. *Seeing Like a State: Wow Certain Schemes to Improve the Human Condition Have Failed*. New Haven: Yale University Press, 1998.

SHIVJI, Issa G. *The Silent Class Struggle*. Dar es Salaam: Tanzania Publishing House, 1974.

SMITH, William Edgett. *Nyerere of Tanzania. The First Decade 1961-1971*. Harare: African Publishing Group, 2011 (first published 1972 by Random House Inc. New York with the title *We Must Run While They Walk*; and published 1973 by Victor Golancz Ltd, London).

SOUTHALL, Roger, and Henning MELBER. *Legacies of Power: Leadership Change and Former Presidents in African Politics*. Uppsala: Nordiska Afrikainstitutet, 2006.

SOUTHALL, Roger. "Troubled Visionary: Nyerere as a Former President." In *Legacies of Power: Leadership Change and Former Presidents in African Politics*, edited by Roger Southall and Henning Melber, 233–55. Uppsala: Nordiska Afrikainstitutet, 2006.

STÖGER-EISING, Viktoria. "'Ujamaa' Revisited: Indigenous and European Influences in Nyerere's Social and Political Thought." *Africa* 70, no. 1 (2000): 118–43.

TWADDLE, Michael. "The Words of Nyerere." Review of *Freedom and Unity/Uhuru na Umoja: A Selection from Writings and Speeches 1952-65*, by Julius K. Nyerere. *The Journal of African History* 9, no. 4 (1968): 668–669.

YAHYA-OTHMAN, Saida. *Yes, In My Lifetime. Selected Works of Haroub Othman*. Dar es Salaam, Dakar: Mkuki na Nyota, CODESRIA, 2014.

YOUNG, Crawford. "The End of the Post-Colonial State in Africa? Reflections on Changing African Political Dynamics." *African Affairs* 103, no. 410 (Jan., 2004): 23–49.

WILLIAMS, Michael W. "Nkrumahism as an Ideological Embodiment of Leftist Thought Within the African World." *Journal of Black Studies* 15, no. 1 (Sept., 1984): 117–134.

WILLIS, Justin. Review of *Mwalimu: The Influence of Nyerere*, by Colin Legum and Geoffrey Mmari. *African Affairs* 95, no. 380 (Jul., 1996): 465–466.

WITTGENSTEIN, Ludwig. *Philosophical Investigations*. Wiltey-Blackwell: Blackwell Publishing Ltd, 2009.

Chapter 2

Julius Nyerere, Ujamaa and Political Morality in Contemporary Tanzania

Marie-Aude Fouéré

After two decades of popular and academic expectations since the transition from the Ujamaa national development path to a free-market economy and a multiparty political system, Tanzania has witnessed the return in the public sphere of a reconfigured version of Ujamaa as a set of moral principles.[1] In popular discourses, in the political arena, and in the media, this revisited philosophy is being used as a moral code in debates about social, political, and economic morality in a postsocialist situation characterized by increasing concerns about economic inequality, threats to national cohesion, and the high visibility of corruption in the political sphere. This new version of a national ethos, which constitutes a nebulous set of broad and flexible moral concepts from which individual and collective actors can draw to pursue different agendas and connect to other political repertoires of morality, has gained coherence through its embodiment in the figure of the tireless promoter of the 1960s-1970s version of Ujamaa, the first president of Tanzania, Julius Kambarage Nyerere.

Indeed, after Nyerere's death on the 14th October 1999, the relative eviction of "Mwalimu" (the teacher) from the political landscape in the mid-1980s – when he became associated with the economic failure of Ujamaa – was suddenly reversed. The *Baba wa Taifa* (father of the nation) reappeared on the scene and was brandished as a symbol of humility, integrity, and incorruptibility in the face of today's corrupt economic and political elite.

---

* This text was first published in the *African Studies Review* vol. 75, no. 1 (2014), pp. 1–24. It is reprinted with permission.
1 Officially, the United Republic of Tanzania (1998) still follows the policy of Ujamaa. The 1977 Constitution of Tanzania states that the building of the nation is to be accomplished through the pursuit of the policies of socialism and self-reliance.

The state and the media have been instrumental in propagating a laudatory official memory of Nyerere for the purpose of nation-building and the maintenance of the political hegemony of the ruling party. Claiming to walk in Nyerere's footsteps has also become a common stand among politicians of both the ruling party and the opposition as they strive to build their personal legitimacy and attract votes. In a similar vein, popular discussions about present-day hardships, religious, ethnic, and political cleavages, and the absence of patriotism among political leaders tend to resort to a revisited positive image of Nyerere. Yet the prominent presence of the iconic figure of Nyerere in the public space does not mean that there is no critical perspective, if not alternative historical memories of Nyerere. Notably, negative figurations of Nyerere are promoted by opposition parties in the margins or in regions that resent being relegated to the periphery, with Zanzibar occupying first place.

Any analysis of either the laudatory or critical narratives of Nyerere needs to go beyond an assessment of their accuracy with regard to historical reality – that is, their veracity with regard to the facts of the past – to explore how such narratives are productive in the present in conceptualizing the political space and acting upon it through a dialogue between the past and the present. The persisting traces of Nyerere and Ujamaa in the postsocialist context, and their appropriation as instruments for constructing a claim to a collective moral and political project, are therefore, to borrow a phrase from Ricoeur (2004 [2000]), the product of "a narrative configuration": a rereading, refiguring, and reinterpreting of the past, entailing both remembering and forgetting.[2] The figure of Nyerere as a discursive *lieu de mémoire* ("place of memory"; see Nora, 1989, 1997) is consequently revisited in the face of present socioeconomic and political conditions, especially the disillusionment, disenchantment, and "demoralization" of the political space (Ferguson, 2006) that now have largely replaced optimistic expectations about the promises of neoliberal modernity. In this sense contemporary narratives of Nyerere constitute a "politicised historical memory" (Werbner, 1998); they do not necessarily translate into actual political practices or economic measures enforced by the state, but rather constitute a shared

---

2 This article acknowledges the shift from history to memory that has characterized recent approaches in historiography, anthropology, and political science on topics concerning the discursive construction of identities (including national identity or nationhood) and the past. Works that inaugurated such a shift include Halbwachs (1980 [1950]) and White (1973). On nationhood, narration, and memory, see Renan (1996[1882]); Anderson (1983); Hobsbawm (1990).

political language employed in collective debates and controversies about politics, morality, and national consciousness – a language intended, in short, to shape contemporary imaginaries of the nation (Anderson, 1983; Hobsbawm, 1990). This article, therefore, explores how and why a shared historical memory of Nyerere in association with a reconfigured Ujamaa political language is being built and used by official and nonofficial actors to define, mediate, and construct Tanzanian conceptions of morality, belonging, and citizenship in the polis today. It also provides insight into the relation between the production and uses of alternative narratives – not eulogistic, but on the contrary, strongly pejorative – about Nyerere, and related alternative narratives of the nation in contemporary Tanzania.

The Past Ups and Downs of Nyerere and Ujamaa

In scholarly circles as well as among common people, in Tanzania as well as abroad, the figure of Julius Nyerere, the first president of newly independent Tanganyika in 1961 and the United Republic of Tanzania in 1964, is undeniably linked to what was referred to as the "Tanzanian experiment" and conflated with the ideas and values of Ujamaa. Ujamaa ("familyhood" in Swahili), the "basis of African socialism" (Nyerere, 1967) which Nyerere and the single-party of TANU (Tanganyika African National Union) instituted as a government policy at the Arusha Declaration in 1967, consisted of a societal project that combined nation-building policies with a social and economic development strategy. Based on the idea that development could be achieved only in a condition of full autonomy (Kujitegemea, "self-reliance"), rather than by relying upon foreign aid or investment, Ujamaa as a political thought articulated modernist socialist principles and a set of values and ways of living considered traditional and typically African.[3] Promoting a "moral economy" (Green, 1995) based upon justice and equality for all, it was built upon concrete government policies such as the communitization of the work force, the collectivization of the means of production, the nationalization of private businesses and housing, and the provision of public services – notably in health care and education (Cliffe & Saul, 1972; Coulson, 1982). The implementation of this development strategy relied upon the installation of a powerful state controlled by the bureaucracy and a single party. A Leadership Code was adopted as a moral framework and as a set of concrete prescriptions to control the

---

3 On the romanticizing of the past and tradition in Ujamaa, see Stöger-Eising (2000), Martin (1988).

activities of political leaders (ministers, MPs, TANU officials, and civil servants). Because Nyerere was, at the time of the socialist experiment, Tanzania's most prominent political figure – but also because he was "one of the most reflective and articulate African socialist leaders" (Mohiddin, 1968: 130), had developed his political thought in several influential essays, and was a gifted public speaker and outspoken advocate of Ujamaa principles – not only was Ujamaa equated with Nyerere and vice versa (as expressed by the term "nyerereism"; see Lwaitama, 2002), but the development policies implemented by the government of Tanzania were also conflated with his powerful presence in the political life of the country.

Indeed, at the time of the Tanzanian experiment Ujamaa was more than strictly a development strategy: it provided a new political lexicon that the state used to articulate its national narrative.[4] Referring to Nyerere's oft-cited definition that "the foundation, and the objective, of African socialism is the extended family" (Nyerere, 1967) as a point of departure, many academic works have analyzed Ujamaa's key concepts, showing how official conceptions of national belonging were expressed, as in other parts of Africa, through the discursive fields of family and community (e.g., *wananchi*, literally the "children of the country," for "citizens"; *ndugu*, "extended family members," for "comrades") (see, e.g., Schatzberg, 2001). But far from fostering only inclusion as a nation-building strategy, the socialist rhetoric also drew upon metaphors of exploitation and blood-sucking (*unyonyaji*) to define and exclude "enemies of the nation" (Brennan, 2006), among them *mabeberu* (imperialists), *mabepari* (capitalists), and *kupe* (parasites). As it permeated the whole society, the Ujamaa official political lexicon was also transformed into a popular language used widely by common citizens to reflect upon the new political landscape. Emma Hunter (2008), for example, through her close reading of the local press in the Kilimanjaro area in the months after the Arusha Declaration, shows that the vocabulary related to Ujamaa and Kujitegemea was appropriated by common citizens to think, argue, and debate about social, political, and economic morality, thus connecting local issues to the broader national framework of socialist-appropriate behaviors and attitudes. The popular appropriation of the state's official language was possible because the set of ideas, values, and principles developed in the context of Ujamaa was

---

4 As several academic works have shown, state nationalism had no monopoly on the production of nationalist thought and actions in Tanzania. Other nationalist narratives not only existed alongside Ujamaa, but also engaged in dialogues with it. See Brennan (2006); Geiger (1997); Maddox and Giblin (2005).

broad enough to allow a large range of concerns to fit in it, and flexible enough to resonate with strictly local or panethnic idioms of morality. But through this process of popular appropriation of the official language crafted by TANU cadres, government authorities, and academics, shifts in content and meaning occurred, and new categories emerged. As James Brennan (2006) underlines, a specific urban vocabulary developed to speak about a growing economic differentiation that the state tended to ignore, and consequently, that Ujamaa categories were unable to grasp: the personages of *kabwela* and *naizi* embodied, respectively, the ordinary poor yet cunning town dweller and the recently emerged wealthy "middle-class" as two products of an urban world whose existence and specific living conditions, in the rural-oriented state ideology and policies, were not fully acknowledged, much less taken into account.

The retreat from socialism, which was in sight since the end of the 1970s when the economic shortcomings and failures of Ujamaa became manifest, took place in the 1980s with the adoption of a National Economic Survival Programme (1981-82) and successive structural adjustment plans (1982-86). At that time the Ujamaa lexicon was abandoned in favor of a vocabulary related to change and modern capitalism: *mageuzi* (trade liberalization), *kwenda na wakati* (going with the times), *utandawazi* (globalization), or *utajirisho* (increased wealth) (see Askew, 2006; Crozon, 1996). If the opposition took the lead in introducing this new political language, the state and politicians of the CCM ruling party (Chama Cha Mapinduzi, Party of the Revolution) adopted it, too. Meanwhile, the Ujamaa-bashing of this decade was prejudicial to the iconic image of the wise Mwalimu that had been propagated abroad in enthusiastic developmental intellectual spheres and diffused in the country by Tanzanian authorities, notably through the media.[5] It showed in full light the existence of fault lines in what had long been presented as a popular consensus on African socialism, and consequently on the head of the state who embodied it.[6] From the end of the 1970s, comical or pejorative nicknames started to be associated with Nyerere in popular discussions; examples include

---

5 With the Newspaper Ordinance Bill of 1968, the President of Tanzania could ban any material from the press that was considered subversive. Konde (1984: 56) quotes Nyerere declaring that the Standard newspaper published by the Tan- ganyika Standard Ltd. parastatal "will be a socialist paper. It will support the socialist ideology of Tanzania as defined in the Arusha Declaration, Part One and Two."

6 Mazrui's neologism "tanzaphilia" (1967) is an ironic expression of the way most Western intellectuals in the 1960s-1970s uncritically supported Ujamaa and an idealized Nyerere. For a detailed overview of the academic reception of Nyerere's political thought, see Havnevik (2010).

Sungura (the rabbit), which targeted his cunning and trickiness; *Mussa* (Moses), which pointed ironically to his pretence of guiding and saving the Tanzanian people; *Haambiliki* (the stubborn, literally, "the one who cannot be advised"), which hinted at his refusal to heed advice about the need for economic and political reforms; and *Mchongameno* ("the one who sharpens teeth"), which highlighted his cruelty. At the same time, Ujamaa and Kujitegemea were lampooned as Unyama (bestiality) or Utamaa (lust/ambition) and *kujimegea* (to serve oneself first).

Although he voluntarily stepped down from the presidency in 1985, Nyerere continued to be a political force and a dominating figure on the national political scene. He remained the leader of CCM until 1990, for example, and influenced debates about political pluralism and the union between Tanzania Mainland and Zanzibar. He was also an important figure on the African political scene, being strongly involved in the mediation process in Burundi and Rwanda (Southall, 2006). But as he remained largely on the sidelines of the political turmoil of the 1990s, Nyerere slowly came to epitomize the figure of the wise old man concerned about national and international peace and aspiring mostly to rest, read, and write literary and philosophical works and meditate at home in Butiama-Mwitongo (Gakunzi & Obe Obe, 1995), his natal village in northwestern Tanzania. After the decrease in his popularity from the mid-1970s to the mid-1980s, his commitment to furthering international peace-building and his manifest search in retirement for the wisdom and peace of age worked to maintain and ensure his elevated status at home and abroad. A rehabilitation process of Nyerere as a moral political figure therefore took place during his "Afterwards" or "After-Life" (Kirk-Greene, 1991: 183; Southall & Melber, 2006) period as former president, which also corresponded to the time when the newly introduced neoliberal reforms started to reveal their fault lines: growing economic differentiation, a fragile national cohesion, an increased competition for power and wealth, and an overall "demoralization" of the public space (Ferguson, 2006) in a country marked by more than two decades of intense socialist "moralization."[7] Nyerere's public funerals in October 1999, following his death from leukaemia in a London hospital, were characterized by the media as "perhaps the greatest outpouring of grief ever witnessed in sub-Saharan Africa" (Southall, 2006: 253) as his coffin was borne through the streets of Dar es Salaam, bearing witness to the renewed popular emotional investment in Nyerere at the end of

---

7 On alarming assessments about national cohesion and identity cleavages in Tanzania, see notably the discussion in Jennings and Mercer (2011).

the 1990s and the existence of a shared feeling of belonging among the Tanzanian citizenry (Maddox & Giblin, 2005).

Since his death, a posthumous historical memory of Nyerere is being built and tends to take the shape of myth-building and personality cult – what we may call "Nyerere-philia."[8] Indeed, as in other national contexts, the posthumous creation of Nyerere as a historical figure has entailed a simplifying of the intricacies of history and politics. The personality, life, and actions of Nyerere are reduced to striking images, familiar terms, and moral examples that are used as a reservoir of positive moral principles, metaphors, and beliefs – what may also be called a "moral toolbox" or "moral matrix" – from which individual and collective actors can draw for their particular agendas.[9] It is partly this selective and reconfigured image of Nyerere, especially as it is conflated with similarly adapted and reshaped Ujamaa tenets, that is articulated and debated in contemporary representations of the nation as an entity united by a shared set of values and political and cultural attributes (Anderson, 1983). This article, far from asserting that today's "making" or "invention" of Nyerere is an imposition of the hegemonic state upon popular imaginaries of the nation, seeks to demonstrate that it is the product of an ongoing dialogue between citizens and the state in which the use of a shared political language reflects an effort to remoralize the public space in the post-liberalization context.[10]

---

8 Recent books contributing to this Nyerere-philia include Legum and Mmari (1995); Chachage and Cassam (2010). For a recent depiction of Nyerere-philia and political criticism against Nyerere, see also Becker (2013).

9 In Schatzberg's work (2001), the concept of "moral matrix" designates a set of metaphors upon which actors draw in order to think and speak about power and state-citizen relations.

10 The term "invention" is used with reference to Mudimbe's (1988) use of the word to highlight how the reiteration of Nyerere's attributes entails interpretations and reconstruction processes through which the contemporary figure of Nyerere is being composed.

The Contemporary State-Built Imagery of Nyerere

As in other national contexts, keeping alive Nyerere's memory by a saturation of the public space with his images and words definitely serves state nationalism (Anderson, 1983; Hobsbawm, 1990). The Tanzanian state is a major player in the current production of an official public memory of Nyerere as a "Titan" (Mazrui, 2002). Various government measures and rhetorical strategies of memorialization have been implemented in the 2000s to create "places of memory" (Nora, 1989, 1997) of Nyerere in the form of tangible sites, images, performances, and narratives. Nyerere is increasingly referred to as *Baba wa Taifa,* a term that was less commonly in use during his life (Schatzberg, 2001) though not absent in the public space (Smith, 2011: 14). Every year on 14th October the country celebrates Nyerere Day, the public holiday marking the anniversary of his death, with official ceremonies of commemoration organized in the major cities during which local or national politicians deliver speeches that pay tribute to Nyerere. In Butiama-Mwitongo, Nyerere's birthplace and resting place, a special mass brings together Nyerere's family members, government or administrative officials, and common citizens, followed by a clergy-led procession to the Nyerere mausoleum on the family property. There, in the presence of Maria Nyerere, Nyerere's widow, as well as other family members and government officials, the clergymen conduct a prayer service at Nyerere's grave. The nearby Mwalimu Nyerere Museum, officially opened on 2nd July 1999, as the custodian of Nyerere's heritage, presents the leader's personal and political biography, displays various portraits (sculptures, photos, printed fabric, paintings), and exhibits official presents that were bestowed upon him in Tanzania and abroad as well as personal objects such as his radio, his shoes, and his favorite tea set. Comments jotted down on the visitors' book by officials and other visitors express respect and deference for Nyerere, thus reflecting the museum's raison d'être of honoring Nyerere and revering the Tanzanian nation at the same time: "The contribution of Mwalimu to this nation is incommensurable, it's big and he really gave himself to the nation" (2 September 2009); "I've been very much touched by the patriotism of our father of the nation so much so that I wish he would still be alive" (18 September 18, 2010); "He worked a lot for this nation and his people for the benefit of the nation (28 July 2011).[11] Displaying a narrative of nation-building in which Nyerere is the central figure, the museum acts

---

11 Author's fieldwork in Butiama, 2010, 2011, 2012.

as a mnemonic device that plays a crucial role in bringing Nyerere into the present and shaping contemporary feelings of Tanzania-ness.

Elsewhere, written texts, iconography, and statuary are also used to saturate the public space with the *Baba wa Taifa*. Short biographies of Nyerere have been produced in Swahili, directed to both children and adults.[12] Statues of Nyerere are being erected in major political sites of the country; in the capital city of Dodoma, for example, an impressive Stalin-like statue stands in front of the Parliament. Streets, squares, and official buildings have been renamed in his honor, such as Julius Kambarage Nyerere International Airport. Public offices as well as private businesses are required to hang a photograph of Nyerere next to that of the current president. The expenses incurred by the project of memory making, though mainly included in the national budget, are also assumed by foreign countries. In 2009, for example, the Sino-Tanzania Friendship Association, in collaboration with the Dar es Salaam City Council, announced that it would build, at an estimated cost of U.S.$1.5 million, a statue of Nyerere and a memorial hall at Mnazi Mmoja grounds in Dar es Salaam, an open space in the heart of the city used for official political occasions where Nyerere used to welcome foreign politicians on their official state visits.[13] Although financially and institutionally independent from the state, the Mwalimu Nyerere Foundation, an organization created by Nyerere in 1996 that aims to preserve Nyerere's memory and pass down his legacy to future generations, also contributes to the visibility of his image: it has published several collections of his writings and speeches and is currently working on collecting and transcribing original manuscripts of speeches that have not been published. It is also planning a television series broadcasting interviews with members of his family, close friends, and fellow politicians and is preparing a video documentary of his life with the contribution of U.S. scholars.

The media – sometimes acting as simple sounding boards of political concerns, but more often as instruments of the state in a country where the control of the media remains strong – is another major channel of diffusion of an idealized image of Nyerere and the propagation of his official memory in the public space.[14]

---

12 Books for children include TEMA Publishers (2002); Maillu (2010). Books for adults include Mwakilasa (2010); Thomas (2009); Nikata (n.d.).

13 "Mwalimu Nyerere Statue Set to Be Erected in Dar City", *The Guardian*, 23 February 2009.

14 Since the passing of the Newspaper Act of 1976, directors of the main newspapers have been appointed by the President of Tanzania; their activities are supervised by a subcommittee

The press has been particularly active, for example, in celebrating the anniversary of Nyerere's death. Since the early 2000s, the headlines of most newspapers remind readers that October 14 is Nyerere Day, and the main national publications print extensive supplements.[15] Every October Nyerere's voice can be heard on the radio and television channels of the government (such as Tanzania Broadcasting Corporation, TBC) or media groups close to the regime (ITV, Radio One, or Radio Uhuru). In the morning of the 14th October 2010, three songs of lamentation by famous Tanzanian singers and music bands (Remmy Ongala, Tanzanian One Theatre, and African Star Band) were transmitted in a continuous loop on TBC television praising Nyerere's qualities and mourning his death. The same channel showed a recent documentary on his life and legacy, 'Mwalimu: The Legacy of Julius Kambarage Nyerere' (2009), which presents Nyerere in a positive light. Images from the archives of major political events of the 1960s-1970s and clips of his speeches, most of them now well known among Tanzanians, were shown on ITV. Academics and renowned journalists discussed the legacy of Nyerere on programs such as Star TV's *Tuongee Jamii,* which broadcast "Kumbukumbu ya Mwalimu Nyerere" (Memories of Nyerere). On TBC radio the "Wosia wa Baba" (The father's speeches), an assemblage of short recorded speeches of Nyerere, are broadcast all year long, several times a day, at peek audience hours. Nyerere's media visibility is particularly high during the run-ups to national elections, which are held every five years during the month of October, the same month as Nyerere Day. Most speeches broadcast during the time of elections emphasize the importance of national unity, the qualities expected of political leaders, the importance of political incorruptibility, and the need to respect the Union and the Constitution.

Most of the articles published on Nyerere Day focus more on the man than on history and politics. Many articles feature short hagiographic biographies. The titles are evocative: "Nyerere: A Human Star That Twinkles since Childhood"; "Nyerere: A Glimmer of Hope That Left Us in Darkness"; "Mwalimu Was a Universal Gift to the World".[16]

---

linked to the leading party. The press, often accused of calumny or of jeopardizing social peace and national unity, is regularly suspended or banned (see Sturmer, 1998).

15 Government newspapers include the *Daily News* and *Habari Leo* of the parastatal Tanzania Standard Newspapers and newspapers of media groups close to the regime, most notably The Guardian (owned by Reginald Mengi's IPP Media), *The Sunday Observer, Nipashe, and Taifa Letu.*

16 *Nipashe*, 13 October 2004; *Majira*, 14 October 2004; *Daily News*, 14 October 2011 respectively.

Selected excerpts of speeches given by heads of state who attended his national funerals are reprinted, emphasizing Nyerere's magnificence: he was a "hero", a "great man", an "example to follow". Articles praise his personal qualities of simplicity, absence of ostentation, honesty, and generosity and describe the food he liked (*ugali*), the way he dressed, the simplicity of his houses in Dar es Salaam and Butiama, and his slim body (Schatzberg, 2001: 170) – all examples of his "rejection of material luxury" (Ferguson, 2006: 76).[17] Readers are reminded that "Mwalimu," was not just a nickname: Nyerere had indeed been a teacher, but he deliberately chose this title to highlight his modesty and ability to explain things in a simple and clear manner (Smith, 2011: 25). Similarly, the moral values he promoted during his lifetime – freedom, justice, unity, and equality – are presented as a transposition of Nyerere's personal qualities into the social, political, and economic realm.

According to Memel-Fotê (1991), the production of idealized images of "fathers of the nation" in Africa typically follows a three-step process consisting of predestination, initiation, and symbolical rebirth. In the case of Nyerere, too, the laudatory details of his life are often presented implicitly within this larger symbolic framework. His childhood and youth are explored in order to highlight premonitory signs of his future career: the even temper that would serve him well when confronted with the stresses and responsibilities of politics; his hard-working attitude that would later become socialist discipline; the generosity that augured his future commitment to equality and justice. His education is presented as an initiation rite he successfully overcame to enter the age of wisdom, and his decision to leave the classroom and join the liberation movement is interpreted as a turning point in his life, a kind of symbolical "rebirth". Recurring analogies with the figure of Moses and Jesus conflate political power with the sacred, producing a shift from knowledge to imaginaries, history to myth, and the secular to the sacred: all of these translations fostering, finally, the contemporary "invention" of Nyerere.

In this context, the canonization of Nyerere that was launched in January 2006 by the Church of Tanzania (see Fouéré, 2008b; Mesaki & Malipula, 2011) is particularly significant. Cardinal Polycarp Pengo, who had celebrated the national mass for Nyerere's death at St. Joseph Church in Dar es Salaam on October 20, 1999, announced in 2006 that

---

17 Ugali is a thick porridge made of maize flour. Nkrumah's khaki suits, communist- inspired "Chou-En-Lai" vests, and safari costumes all shared the common features of simplicity and absence of ostentation. In Dar es Salaam, Nyerere lived with his family in a modest house in the area of Masaki.

Nyerere had been declared a "Servant of God" – the first step toward sainthood – by the Vatican. He claimed that the Church's selection of Nyerere for canonization was based on two criteria: the life he had lived "as a Christian" and the influence of his faith on his entire career.[18] The initiative of the Church is puzzling, given that the separation of religion and politics was considered an important basis for national unity and religious tolerance in post-independence Tanzania.[19] In 1965 Nyerere himself stated in *The Nationalist* newspaper, the publication of TANU, that "[h]istory has shown how disastrous it is to mix politics and religion... That is why it is imperative that religion must be isolated from the political life of our country" (quoted in Westerlund, 1980: 57). The cause for canonization reinforces the current process of extracting Nyerere from the secular realm and elevating him to the sacred: a disconnection which, if it were finally to take place, would definitely erase the historical, political, and intellectual context of the 1950s-80s that gave birth to the man and the values he defended, producing instead an utterly decontextualized moral figure.

Also striking is the way in which most references to Ujamaa and Nyerere are built on a "national silence on socialism" (Askew, 2006: 32) as a development strategy. As Kelly Askew (2006) points out in her analysis of the songs of lamentation composed after Nyerere's death, peace, unity, solidarity, and the elimination of tribalism and religious divisiveness are referred to in song after song, but the term "Ujamaa" rarely appears and little mention is made of the socialist orientation and economic policies of the Tanzanian experiment (see also Ibhawoh & Dibua, 2003; Schneider, 2004). Thus a set of abstract moral principles is disconnected from the specific historical context in Tanzania and reconnected to global repertoires of religion and human rights. At the national level, the disjunction between political morality and African socialism makes it possible for the political elite to capitalize on the past to build political legitimacy, renew national consciousness, and strive to impose the state's hegemony on common citizens. The imaginary continuity thus drawn between socialism and postsocialism allows for the promotion of a national ethos, and the fostering of citizens' adherence to an imagined national community sharing basic moral tenets.

---

18 "Tanzania's First President to Become a Saint?", *Young African*, 26 September 2006.

19 John Hatch, Nyerere's biographer, attests that Nyerere "always practised his religion and participated in its observances" (1976: 78). Nyerere is also said, in this text, to have told his friend Cardinal Laurian Rugambwa that without a daily mass, it would have been impossible for him to do his work.

Such a disjunction also reassures international donors that socialism, as a political and economic system, will never come back to Tanzania (Fouéré, 2011).

Nyerere and Ujamaa Through the Lens of Party Competition

Politicians of the CCM ruling party, and most notably President Jakaya Kikwete, have taken the lead in capitalizing on the *Baba wa Taifa* myth (Schatzberg, 2001). During the run-up to the 2005 presidential elections, Kikwete, then the CCM presidential candidate, did not even wait for the official launch of the electoral campaign to publicize and promote his candidacy by means of a May meeting with Maria Nyerere in Butiama. Even though the actual content of their discussion was not released, the present of a Bible that Kikwete received from Nyerere's widow was abundantly recounted and analyzed in the media – both the implicit anointing of Kikwete as Nyerere's descendant and also the specific suggestion that Kikwete, a Muslim, stood for both the underlying principles of Nyerere's Christianity and also the values of religious tolerance. The meeting with Maria Nyerere also had a special significance for a man who, in 1995, had been overlooked as a presidential candidate by Nyerere, who instead had supported Benjamin Mkapa. As Kristin Phillips (2010: 120) asserts in her analysis of political rallies and idioms in the 2005 campaign, this episode showed that Kikwete derived his authority to govern "through a myth of maturity and of lineal descent from the national father – Nyerere."

But in the competition for power, controversies between political parties over who can claim to be the legitimate heir of the moral legacy of Nyerere are heated. In the mid-1990s opposition parties appropriated the rhetoric of economic liberalization and free competition to attract people disillusioned by socialism and the ruling party. Yet shifts occurred in the mid-2000s when the opposition started to advocate for social equality and economic justice with manifest references to the political principles that Nyerere had stood for. The controversy that emerged toward the end of the third multiparty election campaign (October-December 2005) between CCM and the CHADEMA opposition party (Chama cha Demokrasia na Maendeleo, or Party of Democracy and Development) over the public use of the name and memory of Nyerere is a good example of the return of the figure of Nyerere to the political arena.[20] During campaign rallies, the presidential aspirant on the ticket of CHADEMA, Freeman Mbowe, did not only insist on his close friendship with the former president, but he also repeated many times that CCM "had died with Nyerere." According to this claim, what remained was a party of politicians whose only goal was "to exploit the wealth of their country to get rich while the rest of the population was stuck in abject poverty".[21]

Such an assertion – whether true or false – might have been designed as just another strategy for political legitimacy comparable to that of many other presidential candidates, except that it irritated CCM members intensely and became a matter for public debate. The then chief CCM campaign strategist and chief political advisor to President Benjamin Mkapa, Kingunge Ngombale-Mwiru, declared that, like many ex-CCM politicians in Tanzania, Mbowe had indeed known Nyerere but had never been a close acquaintance.[22] Ngombale-Miwru went on to say that the opposition candidates, Mbowe included, were using Nyerere's name as a means of endearing themselves to the electorate, "although their calibre and integrity [were] nowhere near Mwalimu's" and that Kikwete, the CCM candidate, had "never used Mwalimu Nyerere's name to earn cheap publicity".[23] The CHADEMA spokesman, Mwisiga Baregu, replied in turn that Nyerere was neither a personal property nor the property of any political party,[24] and President Mkapa (of the CCM) asserted that "no one can claim to respect Nyerere more than Chama Cha Mapinduzi".[25] Undeniably, this party competition over Nyerere's legacy was a proxy for the struggle for votes and, more broadly, for political legitimacy.

---

20 This overview of the use of Nyerere in the 2005 elections is notably based on Fouéré (2005; see also 2009).

21 "CCM hapo ilikufa na Nyerere–Mbowe" (Today's CCM died with Nyerere), *Taifa Letu*, 5 September 2005.

22 "Kingunge awajia juu ya akina Mbowe" (Kingunge comes back to Mbowe and Cie), *Majira*, 2 December 2005.

23 "Don't Misuse Mwalimu's Name, Opposition Warned", *The Guardian*, 2 December 2005.

24 "CCM yaonywa Mwalimu Nyerere si mali ya mtu" (CCM warns that Mwalimu Nyerere is not a personal property), *Majira*, 5 December 2005.

25 "Mkapa awashambulia wapinzani" (Mkapa attacks opposition), *Mtanzania*, 21 October 2005.

During the last general elections of October 2010, the figure of Nyerere was used again by politicians for a similar purpose. CHADEMA's presidential candidate, Willbrod Slaa, repeatedly associated his accusations of corruption within the CCM with invocation of Nyerere's memory. He promised that, when in power, he would "consider the position of Julius Nyerere, that is to say to ensure that public services in health and education are provided at the expenses of the state" and "follow in Nyerere's footsteps of a meaningful leadership so as to bring the country to a better place".[26] On October 26, 2010, the newspaper *Tanzania Daima* printed a picture of CHADEMA's supporters waving a banner bearing the words "Kutoka Nyerere hadi Slaa" (From Nyerere to Slaa) – representing an effort to replace Kikwete with Slaa in the symbolic filial descent from Nyerere (see Philips, 2010). Interestingly, the controversy over which party had the right to claim the legacy of Nyerere, which had become central in the 2005 campaign, seemed to have lost its salience in 2010. Nevertheless, the 2010 campaign reinforced the degree to which Nyerere, over the past five years, had become an icon of morality against which politicians are judged. Especially since the end of 2007, when successive scandals of grand corruption, or *ufisadi*, made front page news and resulted in the resignation of Prime Minister Edward Lowassa (Fouéré, 2008a), opposition parties have resorted massively to the rhetoric of political and economic morality. This war of words did not end with the 2010 elections, as CHADEMA has remained strongly vocal, organizing post-electoral rallies to denounce electoral manipulation and rampant corruption, blaming the state for the use of violence after CHADEMA's supporters were killed by the police in Arusha and Mbeya in January 2011, publicizing corruption scandals while pointing the finger at corrupt CCM leaders, and finally reaffirming its commitment to walk in Nyerere's footstep by paying tribute at his gravesite in May 2011. On this occasion CCM reacted to CHADEMA's pilgrimage to Butiama, complaining that CHADEMA politicians were hypocritically going to "cry on Nyerere's grave" while they were a party of "capitalists" and reminding the country of Nyerere's words, uttered when he stepped down in 1985, that "without a solid CCM, the country will become unstable" (*"bila CCM imara nchi itayumba"*).[27]

---

[26] "Slaa anamtumia Nyerere kummaliza Kikwete" (Slaa uses Nyerere to get over with Kikwete), *Raia Mwema*, 6-12 October 2010.

[27] "Mukama: Chadema mabepari waliokubuhu" (Mukama: Chadema as experienced capitalists), *Jambo Leo*, 16 May 2011.

Once again, however, there is an obvious silence on Ujamaa (Askew, 2006) and the socialist experiment in these attempts to built individual or party legitimacy by claiming Nyerere's legacy. On the rare occasions when Ujamaa is mentioned, it is widely dismissed as an old-fashioned ideology in the new liberal global economy. The need to revise the Constitution and erase references to Ujamaa and Kujitegemea are frequently asserted not only by politicians but also in the academic sphere. The disjunction between Ujamaa as a development path and Ujamaa as a moral reservoir embodied in the figure of Nyerere has thus been reaffirmed in the political competition, which now both reflects and directs how Nyerere and the time of Ujamaa are remembered among common citizens.

Popular Re-imaginations of Nyerere and Ujamaa

The language of Ujamaa is still a shared popular lexicon in everyday interactions in Tanzania. Nostalgic narratives about education and health care reforms are commonly heard among the generations that grew up under socialism and compare former imaginaries and concrete measures of social justice and equity with today's harsh conditions. As Vinay Kamat (2008) argues in his work on popular perceptions of change in the health system in Tanzania, in situations in which nostalgia for socialist times arises, Nyerere is associated with the "good old days" when the government provided free health care, subsidized food, and social security. The socialist ethos built in the 1960s and 1970s, rooted in expectations of change for the better and a shared imaginary of Tanzanian-ness, still permeates how the past is remembered in the present. However, the older generations with personal memories of socialism are gradually disappearing, leaving new generations with no first-hand experiences of Nyerere's Tanzania. Those who are negatively affected by neoliberal reforms tend to long for a past that has been remembered by others and reconstructed as a golden age, while those who benefit economically from the opportunities opened up by the market economy tend to be dismissive of the legacy of Ujamaa and of those who regret it or call for its return. Especially in regions where neoliberal measures have brought the greatest opportunities of increased wealth, forging new models and figures of success, Tanzania's socialist past has virtually sunk into oblivion.

Nevertheless, it is interesting to observe the ways in which the critique that accompanies social struggles since the post-liberalization period has continued to appropriate the formerly shared language of

Ujamaa to mobilize citizens and articulate popular discontent. The case of the Tanzania Zambia Railway (TAZARA), built with the financial and technical help of Communist China at the beginning of the 1970s in order to link the port of Dar es Salaam to the heart of the Zambian Copperbelt, is a good example of the re-appropriation of Ujamaa and early post-independence expectations of modernity as a repertoire of morality (see Bailey, 1976; Monson, 2006, 2013). When, in 1994, the management of Tazara planned to privatize the railway, Tazara's workers and the leaders of villages situated along the rail- way sent letters of protest to the Tazara directors and the national authorities invoking the "language of exhortation that had been used by the socialist state" (Monson, 2006: 113–14). In 2002 songs of praise to Julius Nyerere were sung by workers of Tanzania Electric Supply Company (TANESCO) who opposed the privatization of the national enterprise and its sale to a South African firm (see Kelsall, 2003). Since the end of 2007, successive scandals of corruption have also triggered imaginaries of political and economic morality related to the socialist period.[28] Considering that the free-market economy has facilitated the development of practices of straddling, by which the national elite occupy both the political arena and the economic sphere, strong calls to re-establish the Leadership Code (abolished in 2001 at the Zanzibar Declaration) have emerged in civil society and received strong visibility in the media. Once again, the criteria of political and economic morality upon which such appeals are based are drawn from the idealized figure of Nyerere and the return to leadership principles, if not concrete measures, associated with the Ujamaa period.

In other words, Ujamaa and Nyerere are contemporary popular "tool-boxes" used to give intelligibility to the present and to produce alternative representations of good leadership and good governance in a demoralized political space. It shows that one cannot simply attribute the re-appropriation of the Nyererist rhetoric in social struggles to the existence of a deep-seated socialist ethos or *habitus* as a set of incorporated "durable, transposable dispositions" (Bourdieu, 1977: 72) built by a hegemonic state. Indeed, a number of scholars shown that, even in Nyerere's own time, popular adherence to socialism was variable and malleable (Jennings & Mercer, 2011), and citizens remained partly "uncaptured" by the state (Hyden, 1980). Ujamaa and Nyerere should consequently be conceptualized not so much within the theoretical

---

[28] On the "EPA" and "Richmond" scandals that rocked the country in 2007, see, e.g., Fouéré (2008a).

framework of *habitus* than as a political language shared at all levels of Tanzanian society, providing notions, ideas, images, and metaphors of power to speak and act in the present. Such language is selected, rearranged, and invested with different meanings to construct a claim to moral and public morality, and it can be combined with other moral reservoirs such as the language of religion or the international language of democracy and good governance (Fouéré, 2011).

It is noticeable that, from 2004 to 2010, a shift slowly occurred in the use of the moral toolbox represented by the figure of Nyerere: although laudatory comments about Nyerere are still very much present in the media, they have increasingly given way to the figuration of the first president as a standard of morality in the political arena. During the last 2010 general elections, Nyerere Day was again the occasion to revere Nyerere and to wonder which presidential candidate he would have supported if he were still alive. On 14th October the headline of *The Citizen*, a critical newspaper publishing the opinions of political analysts and renowned intellectuals, suggested "Why Nyerere wouldn't have okayed many candidates" and presented "Mwalimu's probable stance in the elections" on the following page.

Contesting Mwalimu, Contesting the Nation

The prominent presence of the idealized figure of Nyerere in the public space does not mean that there is no alternative perspective.[29] For instance, in the mid-2000s, the leader of the populist opposition Democratic Party (DP), Christopher Mtikila, suggested that the failures of Ujamaa were deliberately organized by Nyerere and that Nyerere had been possessed by the devil. In the weeks that followed the death of Nyerere, Mtikila was accused of disseminating recorded tapes vilifying and insulting the deceased, calling him a "devil," and referring irreverently to him as a "corpse." An unpublished essay from 2006 by Mtikila, entitled "The Information of the Democratic Party on the Sins of Julius Kambarage Nyerere" ("Taarifa ya Democratic Party juu ya madhambi ya Julius Kambarage Nyerere"), accuses Nyerere of having stolen citizens' money and stirring religious divisiveness.

Mtikila has been the only politician who has tried to dismantle the iconic imagery of Nyerere in such a radical way, although other publications exist that purport to reveal the dark, hidden facets of Tanzania's former president. In *The Life and Times of Abdulwahid*

---

29 For critical perspectives among ordinary citizens, in Mtwara region notably, see Becker (2013).

Sykes (1998), Mohamed Said retells the history of the building of the nationalist movement before independence, highlighting the decisive role of numerous urban political activists who eventually were erased from the official history. He not only challenges the official historical narrative that presents Nyerere as the sole nationalist leader, but he also reintroduces the religious factor in the nationalist movement, showing how the national educated elite committed to the fight for independence were, for the most part, Muslims (among them, the Sykes family). The book is now well known among the educated Muslim elite who are determined to reveal the Christian bias of CCM and the government, and selected excerpts have been printed in the mainland Muslim newspaper *An-Nuur*. In a historical account entitled *The Dark Side of Nyerere* (1994), Ludovick Mwijage tells the story of his years of persecution and imprisonment, which he attributes to Nyerere's despotic rule. Aiming to unveil the murky facets of the Nyerere regime, depicted as a reign of arbitrary rule and personal power, the book points to the fate of many political companions turned opponents who were imprisoned or forced to exile, such as the second most prominent figure of the early post-independence government, Oscar Kambona, or the most active female figure in the political mobilization of women in the pre-independence movement, Bibi Titi Mohamed (see Geiger, 1997). Written in an accusatory tone or from the point of view of victimization, these books uncover painful life histories and troubling historical episodes in which the actual role of Nyerere is revisited, and the official idealized image of Nyerere is contested.

Such autobiographical works and narratives of revisionist history reflect practices of "negative commemoration" (Posel, 2008: 122) that are evident in other works produced on the African continent since the demise of single-party systems in the mid-1990s.[30] Similar writings propagating a pejorative view of Nyerere in particular have been produced in Zanzibar. Drawing upon the collective memories of the Revolution of 1964 and the presidency of Abeid Amani Karume, the first postrevolutionary president of Zanzibar (1964-75), members of populations targeted by the revolutionary regime and mostly in exile in Europe and on the Arabic Peninsula (opponents of the then-Zanzibar Nationalist Party and people of foreign origin, the more vocal among them being people of Arab origin), have published biographies

---

30 Such practices are common in all former single-party regimes in the world. On postcommunist Europe see, e.g., Berry (1995); Smith (1996).

and histories challenging the official image of Nyerere.[31] A nationalist-oriented newspaper called *Dira* was particularly active in articulating and diffusing this narrative more widely (Fouéré, 2012). The feuilleton article published in several issues in 2002 by the editor-in-chief, Ali Mohamed Nabwa, entitled "Nyerere si Malaika" (Nyerere is not an angel), contained personal memories of the author plus re-readings of the words and actions of Nyerere. The article depicts Nyerere as a condescending, disloyal, and self-interested man who resorted to backroom deals, intrigues, and machinations to acquire and retain power, maneuvered to get rid of popular politicians who got in his way, and stabbed even faithful companions in the back. It also reveals the role purportedly played by Nyerere, in great secrecy, in the revolution that overthrew the post-independent constitutional monarchy of Zanzibar during the night of the 11-12th January 1964 (see Lofchie, 1965; Clayton, 1981), and in bringing about the union between Tanganyika and Zanzibar three months later. Nyerere, according to this article, is said to have abetted these two events on the basis of Zanzibar's history as the centre of the slave trade in East Africa. He also, according to the article, considered Zanzibar as a place where cosmopolitan Arab and Islamic Swahili culture flourished over the centuries, creating collective attitudes of distinction from the African continent and discrimination against black Africans. Similarly, a recent book titled *Kwaheri Uhuru, Kwaheri Ukoloni!* (Goodbye Independence, Goodbye Colonialism!) (Ghassany, 2010) asserts, based on personal testimonies of people who were involved in or witnessed the 1964 Revolution, that Nyerere, along with his right-hand man at the time, Oscar Kambona, masterminded the coup d'état that overthrew the government.[32] Concerning the Union of April 1964 between Tanganyika and Zanzibar, it claims that under pressure from the United States, which feared that Zanzibar might become the "Cuba of Africa" (Wilson, 1989), Nyerere worked to undermine the Marxist influence of the Umma Party and its popular leader, Abdulrahman Mohamed Babu, and impose a black African regime. The *Dira* article even asserts that the Union was not just meant to control the political destiny of Zanzibar, but also had the underlying objective of destroying the economy and the culture of a place that, not so long before, as the author reminds the reader, Nyerere had wanted to

---

31 See Fairooz (1995); Muhsin (2002); Al-Barwani (2003).

32 The veracity and reliability of the personal testimonies presented in Harith Ghassany's book (2010) is questioned by foreign scholars and strongly debated by members of the Zanzibari educated (personal communications, 25-26 May 2011).

"tow out into the middle of the Indian Ocean".[33] Thus both the article and the book portray Nyerere as an *adui wa taifa* ("enemy of the nation," with "nation" referring to Zanzibar) who dismissed the central role of Islam in the Swahili coastal culture and did his utmost to limit the diffusion of Islam and control its thriving social and political influence on the mainland (Fouéré, 2014).

Dira was banned by the government of Zanzibar only one year after it was launched. The aim of the newspaper had clearly been the construction of a historical narrative that would compete with the national official history and ideology and, in doing so, destabilize the political elite who, to this day, have based their political legitimacy on their lineal descent, both imaginary and real, from the revolutionaries. Articulating a historical memory of Nyerere that challenges the compelling imagery in circulation today served this purpose well and underpinned the production of alternative conceptions of identity and sovereignty in Zanzibar based on hybridity, creolization, interconnectedness, and transnationalism throughout the Indian Ocean. In the politically and economically peripheral society of Zanzibar, Nyerere is thus the centre of a national narrative of resentment. Perhaps ironically, however, the legacy of Nyerere, whether it is used positively or negatively, is the basis of a shared political language employed in the present to articulate conceptions of morality, belonging, and citizenship.

Conclusion

Unlike many African countries whose so-called fathers of the nation have been challenged or debunked – like Léopold Ségar Senghor in Senegal (Havard, 2009), Moussa Traoré in Mali (De Jorio, 2003), or Sékou Touré in Guinea (McGovern, 2004), to cite but a few – Tanzania still holds Julius Nyerere, the first president of the country, in high esteem. Along with very few other national figures – most notably, Nelson Mandela – he belongs in the popular imagination to the category of "exceptional leaders" who genuinely aimed "to move the political system beyond its present rationality" and continued to pursue a constructive role in their retirement (Southall & Melber, 2006). The widely shared memory of Nyerere in Tanzania, therefore, as well as his association with the Tanzanian national project, is based in Nyerere's personality and leadership: his vision for the nation and fostering of economic development, his well-articulated principles of Ujamaa, and

---

33 The sentence pronounced by Nyerere, "If I could tow that island out into the middle of the Indian Ocean, I'll do it," is reported in Smith (2011: 90) and has been quoted repeatedly by most nationalist informants since then.

the constructive roles he played both nationally and internationally in his retirement. However, memory-making does not belong to the past only, but also to the present. The contemporary narrative of Nyerere in Tanzania is also due undeniably to the present socioeconomic woes, growing inequality, concerns about religious and national fragmentation, the high visibility of corruption, and the overall context of disillusionment after two decades in which the promises of neoliberal modernity have not materialized.

The official memory propagated and reproduced by the state and employed as a device to maintain national cohesion, revive political legitimacy, and control popular protest is univocally eulogistic. Places of memory in the form of tangible sites, images, and performances saturate the public space with the figure of Nyerere. Political parties and politicians participate in the dissemination of this homogeneous narrative of Nyerere as they try to gain or reassert political legitimacy by claiming to walk in Nyerere's footsteps and represent his moral legacy. The coincidence of the commemoration of Nyerere's death and election campaigns in the month of October helps explain why both the ruling party and the opposition capitalize on the memory of Nyerere. The significant electoral success of the CHADEMA opposition party during the last general election of 2010, while not translating into a change of power, can be attributed partly to the capacity of its presidential candidate, Willbrod Slaa, to shift the notion of filial descent from the incumbent President, Jakaya Kikwete, to himself. Among common citizens, the popular memories of Nyerere and of the development path of Ujamaa are more diverse and malleable. Nostalgia for the old regime varies along generational and socioeconomic lines, as the generations who experienced socialist times slowly disappear and the new liberal order makes its way in society, forging new models and figures of success. This may explain why a depersonalized Nyerere and a revisited Ujamaa have become the basis for a common political language for thinking, arguing, and debating questions of social, political, and economic morality. A striking feature of the varied memories of Nyerere that circulate in Tanzanian society today is that they converge in a vision of Nyerere as a benchmark against which political leadership is being measured, producing imaginaries of morality rooted in standards associated with the past. In a country marked by an abandoned moral contract between the state and citizens, Nyerere and Ujamaa are employed as a language and repertoire of ideas, values, images, and metaphors to define, mediate, and construct conceptions of morality today and the meaning of Tanzanian-ness.

At the same time, the trend of negative commemoration of Nyerere that has gathered momentum since the democratization and liberalization of the public space points to the existence of alternative memories of Nyerere. Based upon autobiographic narratives and the rewriting of history that draw from personal and community remembrances of the past, they attempt to unveil the dark side of Nyerere's regime and of the man, highlighting the fact that the making of a national icon is built upon the forgetting of ambiguous, if not reprehensible, political actions. If such memorial narratives challenge nation-building by producing alternative conceptions of nationhood, notably within the framework of the contested Union between Tanzania Mainland and Zanzibar, they nevertheless show that, whether used positively or negatively, Nyerere constitutes a shared political language employed to articulate morality, belonging, and citizenship in the present. The symbolic association between Nyerere and the nation is a striking feature of the national imagination at all levels of Tanzanian society.

References

AMINZADE, Ron. "From Race to Citizenship: The Indigenization Debate in Post-Socialist Tanzania." *Comparative Studies in International Development* 38, no. 1 (2003): 43–63.

ANDERSON, Benedict. *Imagined Communities: Reflections on the Origin and Spread of Nationalism.* London: Verso, 1983.

ASKEW, Kelly. "Sung and Unsung: Musical Reflections on Tanzanian Postsocialisms." *Africa* 76, no. 1 (2006): 15–43.

BAILEY, Martin. *Freedom Railway: China and the Tanzania–Zambia Link.* London: Collings, 1976.

al-Barwani, Sauda A., et al. *Unser Leben vor der Revolution und danach—Maisha yetu kabla ya Mapinduzi na baadaye. Autobiographische Dokumentartexte sansibarischer Zeitzeugen.* Köln: Köppe Verlag, 2003.

BECKER, Felicitas. "Remembering Nyerere: Political Rhetoric and Dissent in Contemporary Tanzania." *African Affairs* 112, no. 447 (2013): 238–61.

BERRY, E. E. *Postcommunism and the Body Politics.* New York: New York University Press, 1995.

BOURDIEU, Pierre. *Outline of a Theory of Practice.* Cambridge, U.K.: Cambridge University Press, 1977.

BRENNAN, James R. "Blood Enemies: Exploitation and Urban Citizenship in the Nationalist Political Thought of Tanzania, 1958–1975." *Journal of African History* 47, no. 3 (2006): 389–413.

CAMPBELL, John. "Nationalism, Ethnicity And Religion: Fundamental Conflicts and the Politics of Identity in Tanzania." *Nations and Nationalism* 5, no. 1 (1999): 105–25.

CHACHAGE, Chambi, and Annar CASSAM. *Africa's Liberation: The Legacy of Nyerere*. Kampala: Fountain Publishers, 2010.

CLAYTON, Anthony. *The Zanzibar Revolution and Its Aftermath*. London: C. Hurst & Company, 1981.

CLIFFE, Lionel, and John SAUL. *Socialism in Tanzania: An Interdisciplinary Reader*. Nairobi: East African Publishing House, 1972.

COULSON, Andrew. *Tanzania: A Political Economy*. Oxford: Clarendon Press, 1982.

CROZON, Ariel. "Maneno wa siasa, les mots du politique en Tanzanie [Maneno wa siasa, the Words of Politics in Tanzania]." *Politique africaine* 64 (1996): 18–30.

DE JORIO, Rosa. "Narratives of the Nation and Democracy in Mali: A View from Modibo Keita's Memorial." *Cahiers d'études africaines* 172 (2003): 827–55.

FAIROOZ, Amani T. *Ukweli ni huu—Kuusuta uwongo*. Dubai: self-published, 1995.

FERGUSON, James. *Global Shadows: Africa in the Neoliberal World Order*. Durham, N.C.: Duke University Press, 2006.

FOUÉRÉ, Marie-Aude. "Recasting Julius Nyerere in Zanzibar: The Revolution, the Union, and the Enemy of the Nation." *Journal of Eastern African Studies* 8, no. 3 (2014): 478–496.

FOUÉRÉ, Marie-Aude. "Reinterpreting Revolutionary Zanzibar in the Media Today: The Case of *Dira* Newspaper." *Journal of Eastern African Studies* 6, no. 4 (2012): 672–98.

FOUÉRÉ, Marie-Aude. "L'imaginaire national à l'épreuve du post-socialisme [Tanzania: The Nation Put to the Test of Postsocialism]." *Politique africaine* 121 (2011): 69–85.

FOUÉRÉ, Marie-Aude. "J. K. Nyerere entre mythe et histoire: Analyse de la production d'une culture nationale en Tanzanie post-socialiste [J. K. Nyerere Between Myth and History: An Analysis of the Production of a National Culture in Post-socialist Tanzania[." *Les Cahiers d'Afrique de l'Est* 4 (2009): 197–224.

FOUÉRÉ, Marie-Aude. "A Democratic Purge? Financial Scandals and Political Turmoil in Tanzania." *Mambo! La lettre d'information de l'IFRA* 7, no. 4 (2008a): 1–4.

FOUÉRÉ, Marie-Aude. "La fabrique d'un saint en Tanzanie postsocialiste: Essai d'analyse sur l'Eglise, l'Etat et le premier président Julius Nyerere [Making a Saint in Post-socialist Tanzania: An Tentative Analysis of the Church, The State and First President Julius Nyerere]." *Les Cahiers d'Afrique de l'Est* 39 (2008b): 101–51.

FOUÉRÉ, Marie-Aude. "The Legacy of J. K. Nyerere and the Tanzanian Elections of Oct.-Dec. 2005." In *Annuaire de l'Afrique Orientale 2005*, Hélène Charton & Claire Médard. Nairobi: IFRA, Paris: L'Harmattan, 2006.

GAKUNZI, David, and Ad' OBE OBE. *Rencontre avec Julius K. Nyerere* [Meeting with Julius K. Nyerere]. Paris: Descartes & Cie, 1995.

GEIGER, Susan. *TANU Women: Gender and Culture in the Making of Tanganyika Nationalism, 1955–1965*. Portsmouth, N.H.: Heinemann, 1997.

GHASSANY, Harith. *Kwaheri uhuru, kwaheri ukoloni! Zanzibar na Mapinduzi Afrabia* [Goodbye Independence, Goodbye Colonialism! Zanzibar and the Revolution of Afrabia]. Tring, Herts: Anno Domini, 2010.

GREEN, Reginal H. "Vision of Human-Centred Development: A Study in Moral Economy." In *Mwalimu, the Influence of Nyerere*, ed. Colin Legum and Geoffrey Mmari, 80–107. London: James Currey, 1995.

HALBWACHS, Maurice. *The Collective Memory*. New York: Harper & Row Colophon Books, 1980. Originally published in Maurice Halbwachs, *La mémoire collective* (Paris: Presses Universitaires de France, 1950).

HATCH, John Charles. *Two African Statesmen: Kaunda of Zambia and Nyerere of Tanzania*. Chicago: Regnery, 1976.

HAVARD, Jean-François. "Tuer les Pères des indépendances: Comparaison de deux générations politiques post-indépendances au Sénégal et en Côte d'Ivoire [Killing the Fathers of Independence: A Comparison Between Two Post-Independence Political Generations in Senegal and Côte d'Ivoire]." *Revue internationale de politique comparée* 16, no. 2 (2009): 315–31.

HAVNEVIK, Kjell. "A Historical Framework for Analyzing Current Tanzanian Transitions: The Post-independence Model, Nyerere's Ideas and Some Interpretations." In *Tanzania in Transition: From*

Nyerere to Mkapa, ed. Kjell Havnevik and Aida C. Isinika, 19–55. Dar es Salaam: Mkuki na Nyota, 2010.

HOBSBAWM, Eric. *Nations and Nationalism since 1780: Programme, Myth, Reality.* Cambridge, U.K.: Cambridge University Press, 1990.

HUNTER, Emma. "Revisiting Ujamaa: Political Legitimacy and the Construction of Community in Post-colonial Tanzania." *Journal of Eastern African Studies* 2, no. 3 (2008): 471–85.

HYDEN, Goran. *Beyond Ujamaa in Tanzania: Underdevelopment and an Uncaptured Peasantry.* London: Heinemann, 1980.

IBHAWOH, Bonny, and Jeremiah I. DIBUA. "Deconstructing Ujamaa: The Legacy of Julius Nyerere in the Quest for Social and Economic Development in Africa." *African Journal of Political Science* 8, no. 1 (2003): 59–83.

JENNINGS, Michael, and Claire MERCER. "Réhabiliter les nationalismes: convivialité et conscience nationale en Tanzanie post-coloniale [Rehabilitating Nationalisms: Conviviality and National Consciousness in Post-colonial Tanzania]." *Politique africaine* 121 (2011): 87–106.

KAISER, Paul J. "Structural Adjustment and the Fragile Nation: The Demise of Social Unity in Tanzania." *The Journal of Modern African Studies* 34, no. 2 (1996): 227–37.

KAMAT, Vinay. "'This Is Not Our Culture!' Discourse of Nostalgia and Narratives of Health Concerns in Post-Socialist Tanzania." *Africa* 78, no. 3 (2008): 359–83.

KELSALL, Tim. "Shop Windows and Smoke-Filled Rooms: Governance and the Re-Politicization of Tanzania." *Journal of Modern African Studies* 40, no. 4 (2002): 579–619.

KELSALL, Tim. "Governance, Democracy and Recent Political Struggles in Mainland Tanzania." *Commonwealth and Comparative Politics* 41, no. 2 (2003): 55–82.

KIRK-GREENE, A. H. 1991. "His Eternity, His Eccentricity, or His Exemplarity? A Further Contribution to the Study of HE the African Head of State." *African Affairs* 90, no. 359 (1991): 163–87.

KONDE, Hadji S. *Press Freedom in Tanzania.* Lederbogen, Utz.: Eastern Africa Publications, 1984.

LEGUM, Colin, and Geoffrey MMARI. *Mwalimu: The Influence of Nyerere.* London: James Currey, 1995.

LEVILAL, Lekoko P. Ole. *Mwalimu: The Legacy of Julius Kambarage Nyerere.* Atlanta, Ga.: Savannah Films Production, 2009.

LOFCHIE, Michael F. *Zanzibar: Background to Revolution*. Princeton, N.J.: Princeton University Press, 1965.
LWAITAMA, Azaveli F. "Nyerereism in the 21st Century in East And Central Africa: A Theoretical Appraisal of Pan-Africanist Sensibilities under Globalization." Paper presented to the Third International AmFiTan Development Ethics Conference, University of Helsinki, August 12-15, 2002.
MADDOX, Gregory, and James GIBLIN. *In Search of a Nation: Histories of Authority and Dissidence in Tanzania*. Oxford: James Currey, 2005.
MAILLU, David G. *Julius Nyerere: Father of Ujamaa*. Nairobi: Longhorn Publishers, 2010 (2005).
MARTIN, Denis-Constant. *Tanzanie: L'invention d'une culture politique*. Paris: Presses de la Fondation nationale des sciences politiques/ Karthala, 1988.
MAZRUI, Ali. "Tanzaphilia." *Transition* 31 (1967): 20–6.
MAZRUI, Ali. *"The Titan" of Tanzania: Julius K. Nyerere's Legacy*. Binghamton, Ind.: Institute of Global Cultural Studies, 2002.
McGOVERN, Michael. "Unmasking the State: Developing Modern Political Subjectivities in 20th Century Guinea." Ph.D. diss., Emory University, 2004.
MEMEL-FOTÊ, Harris. "Des ancêtres fondateurs aux Pères de la nation; Introduction à une anthropologie de la démocratie." *Cahiers d'études africaines* 31, no. 3 (1991): 263–85.
MESAKI, Simeon, and Mrisho MALIPULA. "Julius Nyerere's Influence and Legacy: From a Proponent of Familyhood to a Candidate for Sainthood." *International Journal of Sociology and Anthropology* 3, no. 3 (2011): 93–100.
MOHIDDIN, Ahmed. "Ujamaa: A Commentary on President Nyerere's Vision of Tanzanian Society." *African Affairs* 67, no. 2 (1968):130–43.
MONSON, Jamie. "Defending the People's Railway in the Era of Liberalization." *Africa* 76, no. 1 (2006): 113–30.
MONSON, Jamie. "Remembering Work on the TAZARA Railway in Africa and China, 1965–2011: When New Men Grow Old." *African Studies Review* 56, no. 1 (2013): 45–64.
MTIKILA, Christopher. "Taarifa ya Democratic Party juu ya madhambi ya Julius Kambarage Nyerere." 2006.
MUDIMBE, Valentin Y. *The Invention of Africa*. Bloomington: Indiana University Press, 1988.
MUHSIN, Ali. *Conflicts and Harmony in Zanzibar, Memoirs*. Dubai: self-published, 2002.

MWAKILASA, Michael T. *Tanzania. Tutakukumbuka Milele Baba wa Taifa*. Dar es Salaam: Sisikazi Economic Empowerment Centre, 2010 (2000).

MWIJAGE, Ludovick S. *The Dark Side of Nyerere's Legacy*. London: Adelphi Press, 1996 (1994).

NIKATA, Camillius A. n.d. *Mwalimu Julius K. Nyerere*. Songea: Tanganyika Mission Press.

NORA, Pierre. *Les lieux de mémoire* [Places of Memory]. Paris: Gallimard, 1997 [1984–87].

NORA, Pierre. "Between Memory and History: Les lieux de mémoire." *Representations* 26 (1989): 7–24.

NYERERE, Julius K. *Freedom and Unity, Uhuru na Umoja: A Selection from Writings and Speeches 1952–1965*. London: Oxford University Press, 1967.

NYERERE, Julius K. *Freedom and Development, Uhuru na Maendeleo: A Selection from Writings and Speeches 1968–1973*. London: Oxford University Press, 1973.

PHILLIPS, Kristin. "Pater Rules Best: Political Kinship and Party Politics in Tanzania's Presidential Elections." *PoLAR: Political and Legal Anthropology Review* 33, no. 1 (2010): 109–32.

POSEL, Deborah. "History as Confession: The Case of South Africa's Truth and Reconciliation Commission." *Public Culture* 20, no.1 (2008): 119–41.

RENAN, Ernest. "What is a Nation?" In *Becoming National: A Reader*, ed. Geoff Eley and Ronald Grigor Suny, 41–55. New York and Oxford: Oxford University Press, 1996. Originally published in Ernest Renan, trans. "Qu'est-ce qu'une nation?" (Lecture at Sorbonne, 11 March 1882).

RICOEUR, Paul. *Memory, History, Forgetting*. Chicago: University of Chicago Press, 2004. Originally published in Paul Ricoeur *La mémoire, l'histoire, l'oubli* (Paris: Seuil, 2000).

SAID, Mohamed. *The Life and Times of Abdulwahid Sykes: The Untold Story of the Muslim Struggle against British Colonialism in Tanganyika*. London: Minerva Press, 1998.

SCHATZBERG, Michael. *Political Legitimacy in Middle Africa: Father, Family, Food*. Bloomington: Indiana University Press, 2001.

SCHNEIDER, Leander. "Freedom and Unfreedom in Rural Development: Julius Nyerere, Ujamaa Vijijini, and Villagization." *Canadian Journal of African Studies* 38, no. 2 (2004): 344–392.

SMITH, Kathleen E. *Remembering Stalin's Victims: Popular Memory and the End of the USSR*. Ithaca, N.Y.: Cornell University Press, 1996.

SMITH, William E. *Nyerere of Tanzania*. London: Victor Gollanez, 1973.

SOUTHALL, Roger. "Troubled Visionary: Nyerere as a Former President." In *Legacies of Power: Leadership Change and Former Presidents in African Politics*, ed. Roger Southall and Henning Melber, 233–55. Uppsala: Nordiska Afrikainstitutet, 2006.

SOUTHALL, Roger, and Henning MELBER. *Legacies of Power: Leadership Change and Former Presidents in African Politics*. Uppsala: Nordiska Afrikainstitutet, 2996.

STÖGER-EISING, Viktoria. "'Ujamaa' Revisited: Indigenous and European Influences in Nyerere's Social and Political Thought." *Africa* 70, no. 1 (2000): 118–43.

STURMER, Martin. *The Media History of Tanzania*. Mtwara: Ndanda Mission Press, 1998.

TEMA Publishers. *Mashujaa Wetu 1: Mwalimu Julius Kambarage Nyerere*. Dar es Salaam: TEMA Publishers, 2002.

THOMAS, Jacob N. *Historia fupi ya Mwalimu J.K. Nyerere, Rais wa Kwanza wa Tanzania*. Dar es Salaam: Livanga Publishers, 2009.

WERBNER, Richard. "Beyond Oblivion: Confronting Memory Crisis." In *Memory and the Postcolony: African Anthropology and the Critique of Power*, ed. R. Werbner, 1–17. New York: Zed Books, 1998.

WESTERLUND, David. *Ujamaa na Dini: A Study of Some Aspects of Society and Religion in Tanzania, 1961–1977*. Stockholm: Borgströms Tryckeri, 1980.

WHITE, Hayden V. *Metahistory: The Historical Imagination in Nineteenth-Century Europe*. Baltimore: John Hopkins University Press, 1973.

WILSON, Amrit. *US Foreign Policy and Revolution: The Creation of Tanzania*. London: Pluto Press, 1989.

PART 2:

Entering and Securing the Political Space

Chapter 3

Julius Kambarage Nyerere: His Formative Years

Thomas Molony

Kambarage Nyerere, as Julius Nyerere was called before he was baptised into the Catholic Church, was born on 13th April 1922 in the village of Butiama, near the east coast of Lake Victoria. In that area of north-west Tanzania the European presence was negligible, and from infancy he was used to doing small jobs around the *shamba* (smallholding) and tending to the animals. Nyerere later recalled how he grew up like all the other boys "in a surrounding of basic rural equality. There were no special privileges because of the office of my father".[1] His father was Chief Nyerere Burito (1860-1942) of the Zanaki tribe. Nyerere's mother, Mugaya, was the fifth wife of 22. She married while he was forty-seven and she fifteen, and had Kambarage as the second of the four sons and four daughters she bore to him, of whom six survived.[2] Nyerere's father seems to have had the greatest influence on him, as he himself said: "To the extent that I have some humanity, I took it from my father" (Smith, 1973: 41). Burito was slow and careful before acting and always insisted on giving his people their rights. One commentator, writing much later, attributes the Zanaki culture as the foundation on which Nyerere's moral and political sensibilities were built, long before the later influences of his formal education (Stöger-Eising, 2000). Kambarage's formal education began in 1934 when he attended the Native Administration School at Mwisenge, Musoma. He was apparently bored by the lack of learning and challenges at school, but came top in the territorial examination of 1936, and the following year advanced to Tabora Government School. Nyerere said that 'Tabora Boys', as it

---

* This text was first published as "Nyerere: The formative years" in 2009 in *Julius Kambarage Nyerere: Life, Times, Legacy*, 32–35. London: FIRST. It is reprinted with permission. References have been added to this version.

1 Stöger-Eising interview with Nyerere, Butiama, 9th December 1995 (Stöger-Eising, 2000: 123–4).

2 I have revised Mugaya's position from 'fourth wife of 23', and Burito's age from 61 (Molony, 2014: 34–5).

was often called, was "as close to Eton as it could have been in Africa – fagging, sportsmanship, fair play, all that. If you went through it for six years, and succeeded, that was really something".³ While at the school Nyerere decided to become a Catholic and took catechism at The White Fathers mission. He completed his secondary studies in 1942. Nyerere then obtained a bursary to Makerere College in Uganda the following year to undertake a Teacher Training Course. He was baptised in the Nyegina mission chapel outside Musoma on 23rd December 1943, one of the first Zanaki to become a Roman Catholic. In his second year he co-founded the Tanganyika African Welfare Association (TAWA), which was quickly dropped in favour of reinvigorating the campus chapter of the Tanganyika African Association (TAA).

The Makerere branch of the TAA provided Nyerere with his first experience of direct political organisation at exactly the same time as the first stirrings of a national concept of politics in Tanganyika. Nyerere left Makerere in 1945 with a Teachers' Diploma. He spent the summer in Zanaki district building a house for his widowed mother, and received an offer to return to Tabora Government School to teach. He remained in Tabora, but chose St Mary's, a new Catholic secondary school in the town. In Tabora he became secretary of the local TAA branch and used the organisation to mobilise opinion in the district against Britain's manipulation of elections. While teaching in Tabora, in 1946 Nyerere wrote: "The educated man is not important in himself, his importance lies in what he can do for the community of which he is a member".⁴ This is probably the first time that his philosophy of education for self-reliance was actually shared for publication.

Nyerere applied to the University of Edinburgh in 1948. According to one of Nyerere's childhood friends, however, his continuing interest in politics almost prevented him from the next move in his career as a student (Smith, 1973: 48). So the account goes, a local British official wrote to the Governor in the belief that he should be prevented from studying overseas because he was 'politically minded and might be dangerous when he returned' (Ibid.). In October 1949 Nyerere was accepted for entry at the University of Edinburgh's Faculty of Arts to study for a Master of Arts degree. Nyerere's choice of degree subject was simple, as he put it at the time in a letter from Edinburgh: "if I can be

---

3 Nyerere, quoted in Smith (1973: 45).

4 Nyerere to the editors of *Makerere* magazine, November 1946, (headed with 'Makerere 1, n°1 (1946): 35'); CLX-A-16/1, Shepperson Collection, Special Collections, Edinburgh University Main Library, Edinburgh. (Hereafter 'Shepp.Coln.'.) Also Hatch (1976: 24–5).

useful to my country after my studies here, I will be more useful if I take an arts rather than a science degree".[5] Writing to the Colonial Office, David Carmichael, the Colonial Office Welfare Officer in Edinburgh, described Nyerere's performance while at the university as "well above average",[6] while the report from the Secretary of State for the Colonies to the Government of Tanganyika was that he was "in every way a satisfactory student".[7] At university, a picture of Nyerere emerges as more than just a political person, but also a leader who was deeply philosophical, something that he could develop thanks to the flexibility to explore beyond his formal studies that the course options he chose allowed for: "I found that I had ample time to read many other things outside my degree ... I evolved the whole of my political philosophy while I was there".[8] A close friend of Nyerere while in Scotland, the Church of Scotland missionary Reverend Kenneth Mackenzie, felt that this period in Edinburgh "had a very direct and powerful influence upon his development as a politician. He was slowly building up his life-view, his basic orientation about things like the nature of government... [and] the rights of the individual".[9] Although dealing with many contemporary issues of African politics during his time in Edinburgh, there is no evidence that Nyerere ever had any meetings with those Africans who were to become prominent politicians around the same time as him, among them Hastings Banda, who would become the first president of Malawi. Nyerere never became much of a platform politician on the university campus itself. He was certainly politically aware though, and maintained regular correspondence with the few other Tanganyikans in Britain, informing and discussing with them the situation back home. Apparently, speaking on behalf of the Tanganyikan students, in 1951 Nyerere asked the authorities for the opportunity for a number of his fellow countryfolk to meet the African chiefs from home coming to the Festival of Britain, then taking place in London, and which would last until the coronation of Queen Elizabeth the following year.[10] Nyerere got in touch with David Makwaia, his Makerere friend who he had fallen out with in 1947 over Britain's manipulation of the local elections,

---

5 Nyerere to Mitford-Barberton, 22nd April 1949, CO981/34/11007/16556/32, Colonial Office files, National Archives, Kew, London. (Hereafter 'NACO'.)
6 NACO981/16556/68.
7 NACO981/16556/104.
8 Nyerere to Shepperson, Letter, 5th May 1960, CLX-A-16-17/8/1, Shepp.Coln..
9 MacKenzie in 'Portraits of Our Time', 'No.2: Julius Nyerere', a BBC broadcast on 12th July 1964. Transcript of broadcast, p.1. Facsimile in author's possession.
10 Nyerere to Crook, Letter, 17th July 1951, NACO981/34/11007/16556/94.

and who he was later to call "our Hamlet" because, in Nyerere's view, Makwaia could never make up his mind whether to join the nationalists (Smith, 1973: 53). David Makwaia had studied philosophy and politics at Lincoln College, Oxford, during which time he and Nyerere may have resolved their differences. Their improving relationship in Britain during July 1951 appears to have been of considerable importance to the future of Tanganyika, for shortly after Nyerere had left Edinburgh for home, Makwaia facilitated his friend's political rise by winning him British support as well as by securing the allegiance of Sukuma chiefs to TANU. At independence Nyerere repaid his friend by abolishing the role of chiefs, and temporarily banished Makwaia to a remote region.

Those who knew Nyerere in Edinburgh recall him as "quiet and unassuming", "not the usual type", and "a very decent fellow" (Lowe, 2000: 135). There is nothing to suggest, as Herbert Neve (1976: 33) assumes, that as a student at Edinburgh Nyerere suffered problems of self-esteem. Outside formal tuition he also spent time with university staff, and this sympathetic student-staff relationship may have had some part in moulding his multi-racial outlook. Among the staff with whom Nyerere spent much time with was Kenneth Little, the distinguished social anthropologist with whom he discussed the roots of colonial rule at a meeting of the Cosmopolitan Club run by colonial students, and the historian Don Nichol who was a convert and Catholic intellectual. There is scant detail on Nyerere's involvement in Catholicism while studying for his Master's degree, however, although we know that in Edinburgh he used to find peace by sitting on his own in church, and that he apparently contemplated ordination while in Britain. But Nyerere already knew that his vocation lay elsewhere: "There was no moment when it all clicked into place. It wasn't a sudden inspiration; I didn't suddenly see the light. At Edinburgh, I was certain I was coming back [to Tanganyika] to get myself involved in full-time politics. I had made up my mind that my life would be political".[11]

Nyerere graduated with an Ordinary Degree of Master of Arts in July 1952 and was "anxious to get back to work as soon as possible".[12] Before returning home, however, he sought to make the most of the available opportunities to further his knowledge. He had initially applied to remain in Britain to take a diploma in Education after his degree course but was refused because, along with insufficient funds and the fact that he already held a Teacher's Diploma from Makerere, his employers at The

---

11 Nyerere; cited in Smith (1973: 50). Also Listowel (1965: 208).
12 NACO981/34/11007/16556/130.

White Fathers Mission required him to return to teaching duties. Instead he was granted a shorter British Council visitorship to study educational institutions in England and, foregoing a trip to the Continent, Nyerere's stay was lengthened so that he could see the schools operational during term time. From mid-July 1952 until at least the end of September he was based at 1 Hans Crescent in London's Kensington from where he took short visits as part of the visitorship to Oxford and Cumberland. In contrast to the efforts of the Colonial Office in facilitating Nyerere's time in Britain – from allowing him to extend his stay for further training, to putting pressure on the Tanganyika government when his dependents' allowance payments were late – the Union Castle Shipping Company with whom he was due to return home with were far less accommodating. He was booked to sail on 3rd October 1952, with the SS Kenya Castle, but issues of race (that bore a striking similarity to race problems in East Africa that he wrote about while at Edinburgh) got in the way. While the Union Castle Shipping Company would not refuse outright to accept 'coloured' people on their boats if they could accommodate them all together, "for odd individuals, unless they have accommodation available, such as a berth in a 2 or 4 berth cabin, where they have already sat coloured persons, they will not accept".[13] Again the Colonial Office stepped in on Nyerere's behalf and asked the company for an official declaration of their policy as regards 'coloured' students, to which they replied that they were "not prepared either to have a half empty cabin or to double up white and coloured individuals".[14] Lt.Col. Crook, the Colonial Office's Liaison Officer for East African students, offered another African student in order to obviate the difficulty but received a flat refusal and a categorical statement that "because Nyerere was coloured, his booking had been cancelled".[15] The matter was finally settled when Crook gained authority from the Government of Tanganyika to use air travel instead, and on 7th October 1952 Nyerere took a flight from London to Nairobi and on to Dar es Salaam, where he arrived on 9th October.

Back in Tanganyika, Nyerere took up a post to teach history at St Francis' College in Pugu, just outside Dar es Salaam. We know little of his communication with friends in Edinburgh when he was back home, although it was a busy time that would have made much written correspondence difficult. Within three months Nyerere was

---

13 NACO981/16556/Minute Paper entry 141.
14 NACO981/16556/142.
15 Ibid.

elected president of the Tanganyika African Association, and when independence was attained in 1961 he insisted that only his friends the Wilsons, who had acted as a surrogate family for him during his stay in Edinburgh, would be invited to stay in his official residence during the celebrations (Neath, 1985: 15). Mrs Wilson was also invited to the Republic celebrations in 1962, and then went on to work in his private office and in State House. Nyerere returned to Edinburgh in 1959 and again in 1962 to receive the Honorary Degree of Doctor of Law from the University. The following year he was a candidate for the post of Rector of the University, and had "given an undertaking to be in Edinburgh whenever he is required".[16] He was defeated by James Robertson Justice, a popular Anglo-Scottish film actor.

Nyerere's final trip to his alma mater was in 1997 when he taught and conducted seminars at the Centre of African Studies and delivered the Lothian European Lecture, 'Africa: The Third Liberation', in which he appealed for African countries to be allowed to develop their own forms of democracy (Nyerere, 1997). On 14th December 1999, exactly two months after his death in London, the university held a Celebration and Thanksgiving for the Life of Mwalimu Julius Nyerere.

References

HATCH, John. *Two African Statesmen: Kaunda of Zambia and Nyerere of Tanzania*. London: Secker and Warburg, 1976.

LISTOWEL, Judith. *The Making of Tanganyika*. London: Chatto and Windus, 1965.

LOWE, Martin, "Dr Julius K Nyerere: Distinguished Graduate and Honorary Graduate of the University of Edinburgh." In *Nyerere: Student, Teacher, Humanist, Statesman*, ed. Thomas Molony and Kenneth King, 135–138. Edinburgh: Centre of African Studies, University of Edinburgh, 2000.

MOLONY, Thomas. *Nyerere: The early years*. Oxford: James Currey, 2014.

NEATH, Ronald. "Who was to stay where?" In *The Nyerere Years: Some Personal Impressions by Friends*, ed. Britain-Tanzania Society, 15. London: Britain-Tanzania Society, 1985.

NEVE, Herbert. "The Political Life of Julius K. Nyerere in Religious Perspective." *Africa Today* 23, no. 4 (1976): 29–45.

---

16 'Vote Nyerere', 1963 Rectorial Election campaign pamphlet, CLXA-16-17/8/1, Shepp.Coln..

NYERERE, Julius. "Africa: The Third Liberation." Occasional Paper 70, Centre of African Studies, University of Edinburgh, Edinburgh, 1997.
SMITH, William. *Nyerere of Tanzania*. London: Victor Gollancz, 1973.
STÖGER-EISING, Viktoria. "'Ujamaa' Revisited: Indigenous and European Influences in Nyerere's Social and Political Thought." *Africa* 70, no. 1 (2000): 118–43.

Chapter 4

Julius Nyerere, the Arusha Declaration, and the Deep Roots of a Contemporary Political Metaphor

Emma Hunter

In the autumn of 2009, Tanzanians prepared to mark the tenth anniversary of the death of their first President, Julius Kambarage Nyerere, who had died in London in October 1999. Yet at the same time as Tanzanians were commemorating their former President, they were also invoking his memory as a guide to the future. In Dar es Salaam, Tanzanians who had been children when Nyerere died but who were now young adults spoke to me about their plans to organise events to mark Nyerere Day on 14th October, and to seek inspiration from Nyerere's life and thought to develop new political visions for the future. In Tanzania's lively Swahili-language press, Nyerere's memory was often mobilized, functioning as a powerful political metaphor.

As Marie-Aude Fouéré and others have shown, allusions both to the historical figure of Nyerere and to his era have come to serve as a shorthand in political discourse, contributing to creating a common language of political debate which, while not all-inclusive, nevertheless offers the potential for those who accept its parameters to discuss Tanzania's present and imagine its future (Fouéré, 2011: 69–70). Writing shortly after the 2010 elections, Fouéré demonstrated the ways in which the ruling Chama Cha Mapinduzi party (CCM) had constructed a series of *lieux de mémoire* which put Nyerere at the centre of public discourse and enabled Tanzanians to use Nyerere's name as a metaphor for a distinctive political morality (Fouéré, 2014 and in this volume). In a similar vein, Felicitas Becker has contrasted the official discourse produced by the ruling CCM party in which Nyerere is held up as a symbol of the peace and unity which only CCM can provide with a counter-discourse from below, characterizing him as "failed despot" or "advantage-seeker" (Becker, 2013: 248).

---

*I am grateful to COSTECH for granting research permits in 2005-2006 and 2009-2010 which enabled me to carry out the research on which this chapter is based.

Yet within the terms of what Becker describes as the 'official' discourse, she too identifies ways in which Nyerere's name has been mobilised as a means of criticising official greed and corruption and speaking up in defence of the poor, concluding that this demonstrates a more open political society than conventional models of political analysis have allowed us to see.

But this still leaves open the question of why it is that memories of Nyerere serve so effectively as a site at which to reflect on wider questions of Tanzania's past, present and future. In this chapter, I argue that to understand the power of Nyerere's memory as a metaphor in contemporary political discourse, we need to return to the 1960s and specifically to the turning point constituted by the Arusha Declaration of February 1967 – the moment when Julius Nyerere firmly committed Tanzania to a path of Ujamaa na Kujitegemea, translated at the time and since as 'socialism and self-reliance'. It is this moment which, I argue, constitutes the foundational point of modern memories of Nyerere. Moral critiques of excessive wealth and corruption were a commonplace of the Swahili-language press in late colonial and early independent Tanzania. Nyerere did not create this context, but he did have to operate within it. The Arusha Declaration constituted a radical attempt by Nyerere to establish himself as the champion of this moral critique. Nyerere's language of Ujamaa was, in turn, adopted by Tanzanians and used to critique immoral behaviour in ways which served to link Nyerere with this moral undertaking. This served as the basis of a distinctive cultural memory (Rigney, 2005), created in part through the circulation of texts and other media, both in the present and in the past.

To make this argument, I start by setting out in more detail the way in which memories of Nyerere have recently been employed as a political metaphor, then move on to make the argument that the Arusha Declaration was a response not only to a growing political crisis but also to the inability of the new TANU (Tanganyika African National Union) government to put a stop to moral critiques of growing inequalities of wealth and rising corruption which had been heard since the late colonial period.

A Powerful Political Metaphor

During the 2010 elections, the trend for political speeches and newspaper articles to make explicit reference to Julius Nyerere was even more apparent, at least on a cursory glance, than it had been during the 2005 elections. Moreover, in making reference to Nyerere, politicians and columnists seemed to be making reference not simply to an individual, but to a political ideology embodied in that individual. The nature of that political ideology was in some ways lacking in specificity, but a general body of content can be identified: opposition to corruption, a concern with the relationship between rich and poor, and an attachment to peace and national harmony.

Different aspects of this nexus were employed by different political parties. The CCM ruling party emphasised Nyerere's commitment to peace and national harmony, and as the October elections approached, supporters of CCM in the press employed references to Nyerere as a way of suggesting that CCM alone could guarantee that Tanzania would remain united. A particularly evocative example of this trope was offered in the pages of the CCM-supporting *Daily News* on 13th October 2010, the day before the tenth anniversary of Nyerere's death. To survive in a difficult world, the *Daily News* argued, Tanzania needed to maintain the Union between mainland Tanzania and Zanzibar. Referring to Nyerere's famous speech about the Union, it went on: "Mwalimu speaks so loudly about it and equates the cancer of division to cannibalism. 'Once you have eaten meat of another human being you will always go on to do so,' he says".[1]

In contrast, the CCM's major rival on the mainland, CHADEMA (Chama Cha Demokrasia na Maendeleo, the Party for Democracy and Progress), sought to reject CCM's claim that they were the sole party who could govern Tanzania. CHADEMA argued that their legitimacy came in part from their claim to embody Nyerere's legacy. Strikingly, Nyerere's name appeared five times in the CHADEMA manifesto. In particular, CHADEMA emphasised that their mission to root out corruption from Tanzanian politics was a continuation of Nyerere's approach to politics.[2]

But Nyerere's memory also served as a means of framing debate and legitimizing criticism of the ruling party beyond partisan politics. This was possible because of Nyerere's emphasis that his CCM party should remain true to high ethical standards, and his criticisms of those politicians who failed to do so. Towards the end of his life, he said "CCM is not my mother", a statement which newspaper columnists and correspondents have drawn on to argue that it is possible to conceive of Tanzania without CCM. In the weekly newspaper *Raia Mwema*, frequently extremely critical of CCM, a columnist writing under the

---

1 J. Lawi, "To honour Mwalimu: coming polls demand integrity", *Daily News*, 13 October 2010.
2 CHADEMA, *Ilani ya Uchaguzi Mkuu wa Rais, Wabunge na Madiwani, Oktoba 31 2010*, August 2010.

alias 'Msomaji Raia' argued that if CCM was not Nyerere's mother, and thus could not make the unconditional claims of respect and loyalty associated with parenthood over Nyerere, nor could it do so over Tanzanians. Rather, he wrote, "the relationship between Tanzanians and CCM lies in its policies, its beliefs and its actions". If this contract broke down, then the relationship between CCM and Tanzanians would cease.[3]

In a similar vein, others argued that since Nyerere's death CCM itself had changed. On 20th October 2010 James Irenge, an elderly man who said that he had been Nyerere's teacher, was interviewed in another weekly newspaper called *Mwanahalisi* which, like *Raia Mwema*, was often fiercely critical of the government and was subject to regular government bans and suspensions of publication as a result.[4] The teacher complained that while Nyerere had listened to the old, CCM leaders of today did not. CCM had been the party of farmers and workers, now it was the party of the rich. In a telling phrase, reminiscent of critiques of economic and political liberalization elsewhere in Africa, he linked the death of Nyerere with a rise in individualism and a concomitant decline in moral standards, saying that since his death, the country had become "one in which each person does what he likes".

One of the chief ways in which moral standards are deemed to have declined is in the sense that corruption is increasing, particularly high-level corruption, called *ufisadi* in Swahili. As it launched its campaign for the 2010 elections, the CHADEMA manifesto turned to this issue on the second page of its introduction. Under the heading "What is corruption?" the manifesto cited a speech which Nyerere had made in 1960 in which he emphasised the danger that corruption posed to the welfare of the people.[5] Nyerere's words were recalled from their 1960 context to provide a clear example for today. Elsewhere, his actions rather than his words were called to mind, as in an article in *Raia Mwema* which stressed that Nyerere "did not wait for the decision of the courts" before distancing himself from corrupt officials.[6]

Allusions to Nyerere's life and work seem to have come to serve as a shorthand for a better, more idealistic and more moral time. Even as his

---

3 Msomaji Raia, "CCM haikumzaa Nyerere, haiwezi kuwazaa Watanzania", *Raia Mwema*, 20 October 2010.

4 G. Marato, "Mwalimu wa Nyerere ataka CCM iadhibiwe", *Mwanahalisi*, 20 October 2010.

5 CHADEMA, *Ilani ya Uchaguzi Mkuu wa Rais, Wabunge na Madiwani, Oktoba 31 2010*, Agust 2010, p. 6.

6 "Mbivu na mbichi kuwa Jumapili", *Raia Mwema*, 27 October 2010.

memory is used by competing political parties for competing political ends, appeals to his memory constitute a shared language which helps make political disagreement possible. This use of Nyerere's words extends far beyond the domain of high politics, and can be found in a range of settings, from the driver of a bus from Dar es Salaam to Arusha evoking Nyerere's words in a debate on mineral extraction (Chachage, 2010: 4), to elderly villagers on the outskirts of Dar es Salaam comparing the heavily subsidized healthcare of the Ujamaa years with the privatized health services of today (Kamat, 2008: 360) or villagers living alongside the Tazara railway seeking to defend its services in the face of economic liberalization policies (Monson, 2006: 121–122).

However this particular use of Nyerere's memory as a shared moral language runs counter to alternative narratives. In the first place, it runs counter to a narrative in which the economic choices most closely associated with Nyerere are understood to have failed. As Anne Pitcher and Kelly Askew have suggested, the agents and institutions of neo-liberalism have worked to de-legitimise socialism and give the impression that Tanzania's socialist past was a disastrous dead end, best forgotten so that the country can make a new start (Pitcher and Askew, 2006). At the same time, it runs counter to a narrative which links Nyerere's African socialism with the violence and authoritarianism of villagization (Becker, 2013; Scott, 1998). Among scholars beyond Tanzania, it is this narrative of failure that remains the more powerful (Schneider, 2004). Why is it then that memories of Nyerere can serve as such a powerful metaphor today? It might seem it is Nyerere's association with Tanzania's independence struggle and his status as 'Baba wa Taifa' or 'Father of the Nation' (Schatzberg, 2001: 12; Fouéré, 2014 and in this volume) that allow him to stand above the policy failings of his time in office. But the Nyerere recalled in contemporary discourse is not specifically the Nyerere of the struggle for independence. Rather, I shall argue, it is the Nyerere of the Arusha Declaration.

Nyerere and the Early Years of Tanzania's Independence

Tanzania's post-colonial trajectory stands out from that of other states in the post-colonial world, both in Africa and beyond. Tanzania was able to avoid the coups which toppled many post-colonial leaders in the mid-1960s and 1970s. Instead, the nationalist party which had led Tanzania to independence sought, particularly through the Arusha Declaration of 1967, to re-legitimize itself as a party whose claim to authority derived not only from its role in bringing independence but also from its promise to create a more just society. But in the early 1960s, it was by no means clear that TANU, and Nyerere, would succeed in staying in power. So to put the Arusha Declaration in context, we must first return to the difficult first few years which followed independence in December 1961. We will first set out some of the political and economic challenges which Nyerere, and the TANU government which he led, faced in the years immediately after independence, and then look in more detail at the wider intellectual context and the political languages which circulated and which provide crucial context for this reading of the Arusha Declaration.

Political and economic challenges

A snapshot of the challenges which Tanzania's new government faced is provided by a report written in late 1965 by the British diplomat Malcolm MacDonald, following a meeting with Nyerere. The message he had taken away from their meeting was that Nyerere was deeply concerned about the slow pace of economic development. Macdonald reported that: "[h]e emphasised again and again that Tanzania's major problem is that of economic development. So far multitudes of ordinary people in the country have gained little or nothing from Independence... If the common people do not see good results in their own daily lives before the next General Election a few years hence, then the present Government will be overthrown, with unhappy results. Therefore his first priority is the achievement of such development – and he spends a lot of time reading, thinking, planning and trying to act about it".

These challenges were not, of course, unique to Tanzania. Recent work by historians of early post-colonial Africa has stressed the ways in which post-colonial states struggled to live up to the expectations which nationalist mobilisation had encouraged in their citizens. Writing about the Luapula province of Zambia, Macola has argued that a "fundamentally acquisitive notion of independence" developed in the period before independence, engendering an expectation of "immediate and tangible rewards" which could not be delivered (Macola, 2006: 45-46; see also Ferguson, 1999). In Tanzania too, expectations of what independence would mean went far beyond what any government could offer. In 1965, the journal *Africa* published a letter which the anthropologist Robert F. Gray had received from his informant Gideon Mbee who lived in the district of Mbugwe. In his letter, Mbee recalled the enthusiasm of independence, writing that "when the day arrived all doubts were thrown aside and there was only rejoicing". Indeed, "everyone believed in Freedom; there was no one, young or old, who had not had it explained to him" (Mbee, 1965: 199). The trouble, Mbee continued, was that "the elders and the youths interpret self-rule in different ways". For the elders, self-rule should mean a return to old ways, without taxes or laws controlling such matters as the hunting of game. This, for Mbee, was a fundamental misunderstanding, and, he went on, "[w]e young men tried to explain the meaning of Freedom under modern conditions, but the elders would not listen to us" (Mbee, 1965: 199).

Young and old in Mbugwe disagreed about the types of knowledge which should be used to protect crops, that of the rainmaker or that of the new agricultural expert. But even among those who agreed about the broad developmental aims of the post-colonial state, for whom independence should mean the provision of the schools and hospitals which the colonial state had failed to provide and which TANU had promised, there were arguments over speed and priorities. TANU could never quite succeed in silencing these arguments. Michael Jennings has described the process whereby the government's failure to meet the costs involved in staffing and sustaining new schools and dispensaries built by enthusiastic citizens responding to calls for 'self-help' led to a reassertion of governmental control and attempts to redirect efforts firmly into the directions desired by the government, at the expense of meaningful popular participation (Jennings, 2003: 185). Yet while the authoritarian edge of the nationalist government was increasingly apparent over the course of the 1960s, it was never quite able to silence dissent.

Reading the Swahili-language press and the archival record from the mid-1960s, it is very clear that many of the developmental criticisms which were destabilising leaders across Africa were present too in Tanzania. Andrew Ivaska has described the way in which the newspaper *Ngurumo* served as a space which, while not constituting an organised force opposing the nationalist government, was nevertheless a space in which the priorities and choices of the government could be critiqued; and indeed, a steady stream of letters to *Ngurumo* in the mid-1960s raised questions of the speed with which development policies were being implemented (Ivaska, 2011: 30).

Some of these letters were from areas of the country which felt they were neglected, such as the residents of Kilwa who in 1965 lamented the fact that travel around the south of the country in the rainy season continued to be difficult, and called on the government to make the improvement of roads in the region a priority in the next five year development plan.⁷ Others focused on specific areas, and education was a particular bone of contention. TANU had repeatedly attacked the colonial government's record on providing school places, and particularly on providing secondary school places, much to the colonial government's frustration as it felt that TANU was ignoring the progress which the colonial state was making. Yet at the same time as it was criticising the colonial government publicly, behind the scenes TANU's leadership was increasingly aware that difficult choices would have to be made after independence. On 10th November 1958 Nyerere wrote to Solomon Eliufoo to ask him to start thinking seriously about what TANU's programme should be once responsible government was achieved, and to consult with "your friends, the Missionaries, and get their opinion".⁸ The choice, Nyerere suggested, was between a goal of maintaining current numbers of children at primary school, around 40%, but enabling all to continue to Standard Eight, or allowing a larger percentage to reach Standard Six. Alongside this letter was a memo from the Director of Education to Nyerere spelling out the costs of offering eight years of education to all, and the secondary school costs which would ensue from a major expansion of primary education – figures of £6 million for the annual running cost of the secondary schools, £5 million to train the staff and capital costs of £20-40 million were listed.⁹

Choices would have to be made, and in the end despite TANU's criticism of the colonial government's failure to provide secondary schools, the emphasis was placed on primary education. The result was growing dissatisfaction with the ongoing lack of places in secondary school, and with the fate of those who failed to gain a place. One correspondent, P. R. Banzi of Morogoro, wrote to the newspaper *Ngurumo* complaining that despite its various development plans, the government seemed to have no plans for those youth who would not continue into the ninth grade – were they simply to be left to work "selling peanuts on the street?"¹⁰ He called on the government to provide some form of training, for otherwise Tanzania would soon be faced with all sorts of criminality caused by this youth, and the government would only have itself to blame.

---

7   Letter from Mshamu Mkuli, 'Barabara ya Kilwa', *Ngurumo*, 1 January 1965, p. 2.
8   Letter from Julius Nyerere to Solomon Eliufoo, 10 November 1958, CCM Acc 1/NPP/003, no f.
9   Memo from Director of Education to Nyerere, 7 January 1958, CCM Acc/1/NPP/OO3, f. 3. On Tanzania's post-colonial education policy, see Resnick (1968).
10 Letter from P.R. Banzi, 'Wanafunzi Darasa la 8', *Ngurumo*, 26 February 1965, p. 2.

If economic development posed a challenge, at the same time, the political pressures on Nyerere's government were mounting. In February 1966, shortly after the military coup which overthrew Nigeria's civilian government, information reached the Australian High Commission in Dar es Salaam that Julius Nyerere had met senior officers of the Tanzanian police and military (TPDF) and talked to them about his fears that Tanzania would also face a military coup. In the High Commission's report, sent to Whitehall, it was recorded that: "According to our information Nyerere said that the coup was due basically to resentment at corruption in government; that it contained lessons for Tanzania; and that if the army and police were thinking of doing the same in Tanzania he hoped that they would do it without bloodshed".[11] 1966 would turn out to be the year in which many founding fathers across Africa were deposed by their people, most famously the Ghanaian leader Kwame Nkrumah who had made history as the first nationalist in Sub-Saharan Africa to win independence during the wind of change.[12] Because we know that Nyerere survived the challenges of the mid-1960s, it can be easy to overlook the insecurity of the period. It is, however, worth returning to one specific aspect of that time – the fear expressed by Nyerere in his meeting with senior security officials that the processes which had led to coups elsewhere were also at work in Tanzania. As we shall see, there was some evidence to justify such a fear.

The report from the Australian High Commission did not come as a surprise to officials in London, who had long been concerned that Nyerere's position was fragile. In January 1964, revolution in Zanzibar had been followed swiftly by a series of army mutinies in Tanganyika, Kenya and Uganda. The army mutiny in Dar es Salaam shook Nyerere on two counts. First, it suggested that he was not entirely in control at home, and second, he was forced to rely on Britain, the former colonial power, for support.[13] In discussion later, Bishop Trevor Huddleston maintained that this had been a profound experience for Nyerere. Huddleston described the "humiliation the President had suffered in having to call in foreign troops to put down a mutiny in his own army", which he maintained had 'produced an element of bitterness in

---

11 Australian High Commissioner to Department of External Affairs, Canberra, 'Tanzania: Role of the Army and Police', 15 February 1966, TNA/PRO/DO/213/103, f. 65a.

12 The stresses and strains of 1966 are effectively captured in Paul Nugent's *Africa since Independence* (2004: Ch. 5).

13 British Embassy, Washington to Commonwealth Relations Office, 17 November 1964, TNA/DO 185/8.

President Nyerere".[14] To understand the sense of humiliation provoked by the army mutiny, we must remember that the shame of dependence had been at the heart of TANU's arguments for self-government and independence. And in the context of the mid-1960s, relying on Britain also posed a distinct challenge to Tanganyika's attempts to avoid taking sides in the increasingly hot Cold War.

At the same time, Zanzibar's revolution had brought the Cold War to East Africa in dramatic fashion, prompting panic in Western capitals at the sight of Chinese and East German advisers arriving on the island. Incorporating Zanzibar into the new state of Tanzania in April 1964 was in part an attempt to stop the situation escalating, and Zanzibar becoming a new Cuba (Speller, 2007). But it was an uneasy Union, compared by the *Economist* to a python which had swallowed its prey, but failed fully to digest it.[15] If the Union with Zanzibar seemed to serve as evidence that Tanzania was being pulled to the East, Tanzania was also caught on the boundary between white-dominated southern Africa and independent Africa to the north. Nyerere's decision to welcome freedom-fighters from the Portuguese colonies and South Africa to Tanzania had provoked the wrath of Portugal's ruler Salazar.

The result of these pressures was that when, in November 1964, the Foreign Minister Oscar Kambona claimed to have detected a 'Western Plot', Nyerere reacted angrily.[16] The alleged plot turned out to have been a fake, based on forged documents, but Nyerere's frustration with the challenges he faced was evident when he sought to explain his response and calm emotions at a meeting attended by 20,000 people in Dar es Salaam. In the speech he touched on the difficulties posed by Cold War politics and his relations with China, saying that when Tanzania needed weapons, he asked the Chinese to provide them, and to come to Tanzania to show the Tanzanians how to use them. "We sent for seven Chinese to come to help us; and this too has become a problem! Towards a mere seven Chinese, people have reacted as if they were 70,000 Chinese! And those seven Chinese are to stay for only six months! There was such a big row about this that I had to call a press conference and lash out like a mad man. I am tired of being questioned about the Chinese".[17]

---

14 'Visit of Bishop Huddleston', April 1966, DO 214/30, f. 113.

15 Editorial, 'The Perils of Nyerere', *The Economist*, 13 June 1964, p. 1217.

16 High Commissioner, Dar es Salaam to Secretary of State for Commonwealth Relations, 'Alleged Western Plot', DO 185/8, 1 February 1965.

17 'Translation of speech given by Mwalimu Julius K. Nyerere, Kijangwani Playing Fields, Dar es Salaam, Sunday 15 November', DO 185/8.

He described threats issued by Salazar against Tanzania, and threats made by Malawi's leader, Hastings Banda, to expel Tanzanians from the country. It was in this context, he argued, that they had reacted as they did to the alleged Western plot. "My brothers, we are not Gods. We are human beings. We have been threatened too much in the past. What should we have done?"[18]

Both the army mutiny and the 'Western plot' incident revealed the continued strains in relations between Nyerere and Oscar Kambona, and outside observers were certain that if Nyerere were unseated, Kambona and his allies would be responsible.[19] They also demonstrated the challenges involved in pursuing a non-aligned course. These internal and external political pressures had economic consequences too, as breaking diplomatic relations with Western capitals risked interrupting the supply of development aid, essential to meet the demands of post-colonial citizens.

Freedom and justice

Independence brought new challenges in terms of heightened expectations of improved living standards and the challenges of navigating a world divided by the Cold War, but there were also continuities from the late colonial period, particularly in terms of discourses around corruption, inequality of wealth and morality. In the public sphere of the 1940s and 1950s, complaints about growing inequality of wealth had been a common theme, as letter writers and African editors worried aloud about the impact of growing individualism on social relations (Hunter, 2014). Expectations of independence were not only material. James Brennan has shown the importance of the concept of *unyonyaji* or exploitation in urban nationalist thought, and the idea encouraged by nationalist politicians that freedom would also mean freedom from exploitation (Brennan, 2006: 394–500). This concern about inequality was not restricted to urban areas: similar concerns were heard in the rural areas and in places far from Dar es Salaam.

Nationalist politicians had promised that independence would address these concerns, yet not only had they not disappeared, they were exacerbated by growing expectations that finite resources would now be distributed more fairly. The complaints heard in the Swahili press

---

[18] 'Translation of speech given by Mwalimu Julius K. Nyerere, Kijangwani Playing Fields, Dar es Salaam, Sunday 15 November', DO 185/8.

[19] Telegram from British Embassy in Washington to Foreign Office, 'Western Plot', 24 November 1964, DO 185/8.

about the continued lack of social services were thus not only about the limited resources available, but also about how resources were allocated. Central to the question of how many school places were available was the question of who was selected for those places that were available. A letter published in *Ngurumo* in January 1967 asked why education was proving more of a problem in Tanzania than in neighbouring Zanzibar, Kenya or Uganda.[20] Not only was the number of secondary schools not increasing sufficiently, students seemed to be selected for those schools which did exist on dubious grounds, and many good students were missing out on places.

The suggestion of corruption at work reflected wider currents, and was part of a broader critique of local officialdom. Sometimes this focused on allegations of corruption, at other times on the wealth of officials and their attitude to that wealth. The former civil servant and original member of the African Association Zibe Kidasi attacked the benefit of 'Africanisation' when it seemed to mean that officials who had once rented a room for 50 Shs. now rented it for 250 Shs., or officials who had once "drunk two bottles now ordered the entire case".[21] He called on them instead to put their money in the bank where it could be used for the benefit of the country and its citizens.

Criticism of the behaviour of local officials was countered with appeals to the people to respect their leaders. But criticism of profligate officials spoke to larger themes and was not so easily shut down. One answer was to turn the focus onto non-Africans, both Europeans and Asians (Brennan, 2012). But by the mid-1960s, this strategy seemed to be becoming less successful. An editorial in *Ngurumo* in January 1965 targeted the so-called 'Mabeberu Waafrika', or African Capitalists. The editor reminded readers that where it had once been assumed that those who engaged in exploitation [*unyonyaji*] were non-Africans, it was becoming increasingly apparent that Africans could be equally guilty of exploiting their fellow citizens.[22] Class consciousness and concern about inequality of wealth was a growing theme in the Swahili press.[23]

---

20 Letter from Mohamed Alli Seffu, D.M. Kilimira and William Mtambo, 'Matatizo ya Shule', *Ngurumo*, 10 January 1967, p. 2.

21 Letter from Zibe Kidasi, 'Waafrika wenye vyeo', *Ngurumo*, 15 March 1965, p. 2. On Zibe Kidasi see Iliffe (1979: 408). Competition for urban housing and its growing cost was a constant theme in the Swahili press of the period, on which see Brennan (2006).

22 Editorial, 'Mabeberu Waafrika', *Ngurumo*, 11 January 1965, p. 2.

23 See Brennan (2006: 408–413) on the use of class rhetoric as a means by which the poor constructed a claim to urban citizenship.

The language of Ujamaa, present in the public sphere already in the late colonial period but circulating more widely after independence, offered another way in which moral questions could be discussed. While in some contexts Ujamaa functioned as a direct translation of the English word 'socialism', particularly in left-leaning publications such as the TANU party newspaper *Uhuru*, it also functioned as a word with which to reflect on positive social relations more broadly, following from the way in which it was employed by Julius Nyerere in his 1962 pamphlet, *Ujamaa* (Hunter, 2008). However the term was amorphous, and not as explicitly tied to a clear vision of the future as it would later become.

The period immediately after independence was therefore not simply one in which the developmental expectations placed on independence and promised by TANU as independence approached were seen not to be being met, but also one in which the moral dilemmas which TANU had promised to resolve, and particularly the perceived crisis of relations between rich and poor, seemed to be persisting. It is in this context that we should interpret the Arusha Declaration as a rhetorical move.

The Arusha Declaration

In this reading of Tanzania's early post-colonial period, the Arusha Declaration of 1967 played a foundational role in setting Tanzania on a new course.[24] Where other post-colonial leaders were overthrown in coups or pushed aside by rivals, Nyerere was able to create a new narrative which put himself at the centre of a struggle against illegitimate accumulation and corruption in politics, redefining politics as a moral struggle. We might therefore see the process of creating a cultural memory of Nyerere as a leader who fought corruption and spoke up for the poor against the rich and against inequality of wealth beginning not with the foundation of TANU in 1954 or even with independence in 1961, but rather with the political events of 1967. Thus while, as we shall see, on one level the Arusha Declaration was a political manoeuvre, which shored up support and eliminated rivals, it also served to recapture and re-moralize public space, re-enchanting nationalist discourse in a narrative that put Nyerere firmly at the centre as author of the new aims of TANU. We start by briefly discussing the Arusha Declaration as a political move, and then consider how it served to capture the public sphere.

---

24 The following two sections draw on arguments developed in Emma Hunter (2015).

A political move

The Arusha Declaration, published on 5th February 1967 after consultation with TANU's National Executive Committee (NEC) but based on ideas formulated by Nyerere, marked a bold shift. It announced that where TANU had once been open to all who wished to fight for Tanzania's self-government and independence, it would henceforth be a party only for those committed to building a society based on the principles of Ujamaa. Immediately afterwards a series of nationalisations were announced, along with 'Education for Self-Reliance', a new educational system which aimed to educate all in a way fitting to Ujamaa rather than focusing attention on an academic few, and a plan for rural resettlement and villagisation. A Leadership Code made clear that those who held political office must be fully committed to TANU's objectives, and must give up any private or business interests which contradicted those objectives and placed them in the class of 'exploiters' (Coulson, 1982: 177-179).

Once understood primarily as a development strategy and assessed for its successes and failure in bringing economic development (Coulson, 1982: 176; McHenry, 1994: 2-3; Scott, 1998: 234; Rugumamu, 1997), the Arusha Declaration was also, as Andrew Coulson pointed out, a political triumph. Coulson wrote that "[e]verywhere Nyerere was the hero, and the villains were the politicians and civil servants who had been growing fat at the expense of the masses" (Coulson, 1982: 183). Reflecting on the demonstrations held in support of the Declaration, Coulson wrote that such scenes had not been seen "since independence itself" (Coulson, 1979: 3).

The Arusha Declaration constituted a decisive attempt to recapture the initiative and tackle directly the criticisms of local officials deemed to behave unjustly or corruptly, while also confronting critics within the party – men such as the veteran nationalist and leading minister Oscar Kambona who would soon leave Tanzania and go into exile. It was an attempt to put earlier criticisms in the past, and begin again from a new basis. This aspect was quickly understood by outside observers. Reflecting on the events of the preceding months in August 1967, the American Embassy in Dar es Salaam remarked on the speed with which Kambona had been marginalised from the political scene. Crucially, they saw the Arusha Declaration as a reassertion of control by Nyerere, arguing that "[w]hichever way things go in Tanzania, it is certain that Nyerere will be making the decisions." The report went on to detail speeches in support of the Arusha Declaration given by both the Vice President, Abeid Karume, and the Prime Minister, Rashid Kawawa, in sharp contrast to the response to some of Nyerere's previous interventions which had quickly been undermined by close colleagues.[25]

Within Tanzania, government officials stressed that the Arusha Declaration laid the foundations for TANU to continue to lead the country. The Area Commissioner of Musoma, O.S. Madawa said in a public meeting that "TANU has not died and nor is there any expectation of death: it will continue to lead this country forever in order that it reaches its goal of self-reliance." He told his audience that the task ahead for TANU was now even greater than that of bringing independence, and that "[t]he Arusha Declaration is the best foundation" to fulfil the promises of progress which TANU's constitution had always made.[26]

In the letters' pages of the Swahili press, the Arusha Declaration was understood as an answer to the sorts of problems which had led to the fall of Nkrumah's government in Ghana, and links were sometimes explicitly made to circumstances in Nkrumah's Ghana. A letter which appeared in *Ngurumo* lamented the great wealth which many politicians had acquired and asked: "where have they acquired this wealth if not from injustice?" In Ghana, he wrote, one of Nkrumah's ministers had "bought a gold bed", and this bed had now been seized by the new government and would be sold. There were lessons here, he argued, for Tanzania, writing that "[i]f we have discovered this sickness, and we seem to have done so in announcing the Arusha Declaration and the policy of *ujamaa*, should we not also seek out this remedy? There is only one remedy – this property should be seized and the money which is received should be put into the Government purse."[27]

The Arusha Declaration provided a new language for attacking corrupt officials. Thus on 21st October 1967 an article entitled 'Against *Ujamaa*' reported that C.R. Chipanda, working in the office of the Ministry of Lands in Mtwara, had appeared in court for the offence of having failed to pay his servant enough and for not having paid for insurance for him. While the defendant claimed that the servant was a relative, the judge asserted that "exploitation has many faces", and that this was an example of misusing the principle of African brotherhood [*undugu*].[28]

---

25 When Nyerere gave the speech discussed above which sought to put a stop to the 'Western Plot' allegations, Kambona continued giving speeches in which he emphasised the threat posed by Western powers. High Commissioner, Dar es Salaam to Secretary of State for Commonwealth Relations, 'Alleged Western Plot', DO 185/8, 1 February 1965, p. 8.

26 'Tanu haijafa na haitakufa milele', *Ngurumo*, 5 August 1967, p. 3.

27 Letter from John Rungimba, 'Heko Chogga', *Ngurumo*, 3 November 1967, p. 2.

28 'Kinyume cha Ujamaa', *Ngurumo*, 21 October 1967, p. 2.

Recapturing the public sphere

But beyond the role of the Arusha Declaration in re-legitimising TANU through re-establishing its claim to authority, no longer simply as the party which brought freedom from colonialism but as the party which would combat corruption and ensure justice for all, I particularly wish to emphasise two further aspects of the Arusha Declaration. First, the *moral* content of the Arusha Declaration and second, the way that it was presented as Nyerere's personal intervention as President of TANU.

One way in which this moral aspect was manifested was in the way that processes which had long been criticised were now re-described as a 'sin' (*dhambi*), this shift being directly attributed to the Arusha Declaration. This argument was made in an editorial in *Ngurumo* on 7th February 1967. "In a socialist country [*nchi ya ujamaa*], capitalism and feudalism are sinful. To be masters and slaves is sinful. And also laziness, indolence, idleness and gossiping are sinful and there is no country which follows socialism which tolerates such things".[29] A language of sin was picked up in other letters. A letter published in *Ngurumo* in April 1967 from P.G. Mattaka of Morogoro entitled 'Unyonyaji' or 'Exploitation' opened with the statement that: "As a result of the Arusha Declaration, the word *unyonyaji* is sinful".[30]

Crucially, as suggested in the American Embassy's report, the struggle launched at Arusha was specifically attributed to Nyerere. As we have seen, Ujamaa language already had wide currency in the Tanzanian public sphere and was used in ways which Nyerere could not control (Ivaska, 2011; Brennan, 2006; Hunter, 2008), but it is nevertheless important to note that the Arusha Declaration was presented as his personal initiative. His initial speech to the Party Congress was presented to the public as his call to TANU to push forward in new directions in 1967. As the headline in the TANU party newspaper *Uhuru* stated in 1967: "Nyerere says: this year TANU should achieve Ujamaa".[31] When the Arusha Declaration was announced to the nation at large, it was again framed as Nyerere's initiative. *Uhuru* reported that "Mwalimu Julius Nyerere wants leaders of TANU, Government, other national agencies and all citizens to help the Ruling Party to fulfil through its

---

29 Editorial, 'Ujamaa', *Ngurumo*, 7 February 1967, p. 2.

30 Letter from P.J. Mattaka, 'Unyonyaji', *Ngurumo*, 3 June 1967, p. 2. Nyerere himself was very comfortable with a language of sin. The American diplomat James William Spain recalled a meeting with Nyerere when he asked: 'Mr. Ambassador, can you remember from your school days what is the 'ultimate sin'? (1998: 166).

31 'Nyerere Asema: Mwaka 1967 TANU itekeleze Ujamaa', *Uhuru*, 24 January 1967, p. 1.

actions a policy of socialism and self-reliance [*ujamaa na kujitegemea*]. He has said that Tanzania cannot accept ticks continuing to suck the blood of their fellows".[32]

As a political move, the Arusha Declaration constituted an attempt to regain TANU's moral high ground and to re-establish it as the rightful party of governance. In this context, the specific ideological import of 'African socialism' is in some ways less important than the moral message which it sent out, and the way in which Nyerere's name was indelibly linked to this moral message. When we look at the way in which contemporary political discourse employs Nyerere's name or his era as a shorthand for a more moral time, it is the process of discursive construction and the political narrative established in 1967 which is being recalled.

Creating Cultural Memory

In the Arusha Declaration of 1967, Julius Nyerere both drew on and reformulated an existing set of discourses about political morality and offered up a new language of Ujamaa with which to critique immoral behaviour (Hunter, 2008). But of course this is not enough in itself to explain the renewed power of this association in contemporary Tanzania. After all, Nyerere's particular brand of African Socialism, for which he used the Swahili term Ujamaa has increasingly come to be remembered either in terms of a failed economic model or as a time characterised by the authoritarian rule symbolised by forced villagisation (Becker, 2013). Moreover, many of those who today employ Nyerere's name as a political metaphor were not yet born at the time of the Arusha Declaration and have no personal memory of his time in office which, after all, ended nearly three decades ago. To understand the continued power of this association, we therefore need to reflect further on the process by which memories are created.

A great deal of recent work has focused on the ways in which collective memory can serve as a counterpoint to official narratives, setting up a distinction between 'memory' and 'history' (Rigney, 2005: 13). In our case, this might suggest a contrast between an official memory of Nyerere constructed by the ruling party and a counter-narrative based in the experience of economic suffering and forced villagisation. As we have seen, the situation is not as straightforward as this model might suggest. But if, drawing on the concept of 'cultural memory' as developed by Jan Assmann and Aleida Assmann, we instead understand

---

[32] 'Mwalimu alitangazia Taifa juu ya 'Azimio la Arusha', *Uhuru*, 6 February 1967, p. 1.

memories of the past as "the product of mediation, textualization and acts of communication" (Rigney, 2005: 14), we can better understand the continued power of an alternative narrative.

The origins of the connection between Julius Nyerere and a particular sort of political morality began in the 1960s. As we have seen, the Arusha Declaration was a foundational moment in rhetorically linking Nyerere to a new kind of political morality, and this link was reinforced by the official Tanzanian press and the wider media in the years after 1967. In turn, this official discourse was picked up and developed by those writing in Tanzania's public sphere, for example in letters sent to the Swahili-language press in the period immediately after the Arusha Declaration (Hunter, 2008).

The same interplay between official discourses and their use in the wider public sphere is apparent in the contemporary construction of memory. The clips of Nyerere's speeches which filled Tanzanian television screens in the summer of 2010 and the references to Nyerere's words and actions in office invoked in newspapers, political speeches and in everyday discourse in buses and bars both served to recall lived memories of the late 1960s and 1970s, passed on through oral as well as written channels, and to allow a younger generation to experience the past vicariously. It is this combination of oral narrative, texts and images which provide the building blocks with which Tanzanians construct a powerful shared memory for today.

Conclusion

The starting point for this chapter was a question. Why is Nyerere remembered for having presided over a more moral era, an era when politicians cared about social justice and battled corruption? After all, we know that this period was one when many of the policies which sought to address questions of social and economic justice, particularly those flowing from the Arusha Declaration of February 1967, served ultimately to disappoint. My argument has been that to understand the way in which Nyerere's association with a more moral time overrides alternative discourses of economic failure and authoritarianism requires both that we situate the Arusha Declaration with a set of discourses about morality in politics and that we think carefully about the active production of cultural memory.

Now often associated by scholars with the inauguration of a set of policies which would lead towards the increasing authoritarianism of the 1970s, characterised by economic crises and food shortages, viewed in the context of the time the Arusha Declaration was a deliberate move to forget the political challenges of the mid-1960s and re-establish TANU on a new basis. It was a political move, but one based on a moral argument and which sought to respond to a perceived moral problem. It had the pragmatic aim for Nyerere and for TANU of allowing TANU to regain the initiative and avoid suffering the fate which other nationalist parties had encountered across Africa in the mid-1960s. These nationalist parties, like TANU, were facing the disappointments of populations who had high 'expectations of independence', and struggling to deliver the development goals they had promised. It was also, crucially, a move by Julius Nyerere to reassert his personal authority over his fellow leaders, as well as his party and the country.

Through the Arusha Declaration Nyerere presented himself as an individual separate from the Party, and stood above it, advocating a moral project of fighting corruption and defending the poor against the rich. The language of Ujamaa, with Nyerere now at its centre, was quickly adopted in popular discourse, both during Nyerere's lifetime and since his death. It is this construction, recreated and re-imagined in the years which followed through texts and visual media, which contemporary Tanzanian writers are calling upon when they conjure up Nyerere's memory as ideological shorthand, and which provides the foundation of modern memory.

References

ANDERSON, Benedict. *Imagined Communities: Reflections on the Origin and Spread of Nationalism*. London: Verso, 2006.

BRENNAN, James. *Taifa: Making Nation and Race in Urban Tanzania*. Athens, OH: Ohio University Press, 2012.

BRENNAN, James. "Blood Enemies: Exploitation and Urban Citizenship in the Nationalist Political Thought of Tanzania, 1958–75." *Journal of African History* 47 (2006): 389–413.

CHACHAGE, Chambi. "Mwalimu in Our Popular Imagination: the Relevance of Nyerere Today." In *Africa's Liberation: the Legacy of Nyerere*, ed. Chambi Chachage and Annar Cassam, 4–6. Cape Town: Pambazuka Press, 2010.

CONFINO, Alon. "Collective Memory and Cultural History: Problems of Method." *American Historical Review* 102 (1997): 1386–1403.

COULSON, Andrew. *Tanzania: a Political Economy*. Oxford: Oxford University Press, 1982.

COULSON, Andrew. *African Socialism in Practice: the Tanzanian experience*. Nottingham: Spokesman Books, 1979.

DE JORIO, Rosa "Narratives of the Nation and Democracy in Mali: A View from Modibo Keita's Memorial." *Cahiers d'études africaines* 43 (2003): 827–855.

FERGUSON, James. *Expectations of Modernity: Myths and Meanings of Urban Life on the Zambian Copperbelt*. Berkeley, Calif.: University of California Press, 1999.

FOUÉRÉ, Marie Aude. "Julius Nyerere, Ujamaa and Political Morality in Contemporary Tanzania." *African Studies Review* 57, n°1 (2014): 1–24.

FOUÉRÉ, Marie-Aude. "Tanzanie: la nation à l'épreuve du postsocialisme [Tanzania: The Nation Put to the Test of Postsocialism]." *Politique africaine* 121 (2011): 69–85.

GEIGER, Susan. *TANU Women: Gender and Culture in the Making of Tanganyikan Nationalism. 1955-1965*. Portsmouth NH: Heinemann, 1997.

HOBSBAWM, Eric. *Nations and Nationalism since 1780: Programme, Myth, Reality*. Cambridge: Cambridge University Press, 1992.

HUNTER, Emma. *Political Thought and The Public Sphere in Tanzania : Freedom, Democracy and Citizenship in the Era of Decolonization*. New York: Cambridge University Press, 2015

HUNTER, Emma. "A History of *Maendeleo*: the Concept of 'Development' in Tanganyika's Late Colonial Public Sphere." In *Developing Africa: Concepts and Practices in Twentieth Century Colonialism*, ed. Joseph Hodge, Martina Kopf and Gerald Hoedl. Manchester: Manchester University Press, 2014.

HUNTER, Emma. "Revisiting Ujamaa: Political Legitimacy and the Construction of Community in Post-Colonial Tanzania." *Journal of Eastern African Studies* 2, no. 3 (2008): 471–485.

ILIFFE, John. *A Modern History of Tanganyika*. Cambridge: Cambridge University Press, 1979.

IVASKA, Andrew. *Cultured States: Youth, Gender, and Modern Style in 1960s Dar es Salaam*. Durham: Duke University Press, 2011.

JENNINGS, Michael. "We Must Run While Others Walk: Popular Participation and Development Crisis in Tanzania, 1961-69." *Journal of Modern African Studies* 41 (2003): 163–187.

KAMAT, Vinay. "This is not Our Culture! Discourse of Nostalgia and Narratives of Health Concerns in Post-Socialist Tanzania." *Africa* 78, no. 3 (2008): 359–383.

LENTZ, Carola. 2013, "The 2010 Independence Jubilees: the Politics and Aesthetics of National Commemoration in Africa." *Nations and Nationalism* 19, no. 2 (2013): 217–237.

LENTZ, Carola. "Ghana@50: Celebrating the Nation – Debating the Nation." University of Mainz Working Papers Nr. 120 (2010), www.ifeas.uni-mainz.de/workingpapers/AP120.pdf, accessed 9 February 2014.

MACOLA, Giacomo. "It Means as if We Are Excluded from the Good Freedom': Thwarted Expectations of Independence in the Luapula Province of Zambia, 1964-6." *Journal of African History* 47 (2006): 43–56.

MAZRUI, Ali. "Tanzaphilia." *Transition* 31 (1967): 20–26.

MBEE, Gideon. "Letter from Mbugwe, Tanganyika." *Africa* 35 (1965): 198–208.

McHENRY, Dean E. *Limited Choices: The Political Struggle for Socialism in Tanzania*. London: Lynne Riener, 1994.

MONSON, Jamie. "Defending the People's Railway in the Era of Liberalization: Tazara in Southern Tanzania." *Africa* 76, no. 1 (2006): 113–130.

NUGENT, Paul. *Africa since Independence: a Comparative History*. Basingstoke: Palgrave Macmillan, 2004.

OLICK, Jeffrey K., and Joyce ROBBINS. "Social Memory Studies: From "Collective Memory" to the Historical Sociology of Mnemonic Practices." *Annual Review of Sociology* 24 (1998): 105–140.

PITCHER, Anne, and Kelly M. ASKEW. "African Socialisms and Postsocialisms." *Africa* 76 (2006): 1–14.

RESNICK, Idrian N. *Tanzania: Revolution by Education*. Arusha: Longmans, 1968.

RUGUMAMU, Severine R. *Lethal Aid: The Illusion of Socialism and Self-Reliance in Tanzania*. Trenton NJ: Africa World Press, 1997.

SCHATZBERG, Michael. *Political Legitimacy in Middle Africa: Father, Family, Food*. Bloomington: Indiana University Press, 2002.

SCHNEIDER, Leander. "Freedom and Unfreedom in Rural Development: Julius Nyerere, Ujamaa Vijijini, and Villagization." *Canadian Journal of African Studies* 38 (2004): 344–392.

SCOTT, James C. *Seeing Like a State: Wow Certain Schemes to Improve the Human Condition Have Failed*. New Haven: Yale University Press, 1998.

SPAIN, James W. *In Those Days: a Diplomat Remembers*. London: Kent State University Press, 1998.

SPELLER, Ian. "An African Cuba? Britain and the Zanzibar Revolution." *Journal of Imperial and Commonwealth History* 35 (2007): 283–302.

PART 3:

In Search of a Tutelary Figure

Chapter 5

Nyerere's Ghost: Political Filiation, Paternal Discipline, and the Construction of Legitimacy in Multiparty Tanzania

Kristin D. Phillips

Figure 1: Cartoon by Nathan Mpangala, *Majira* (14 October 2004). Cartoon re-printed with permission.

Introduction

During his life, and especially since his death in 1999, Julius Kambarage Nyerere has served for many mainland Tanzanians as an icon of legitimacy – moral, political, and economic. In his depiction of an urban Tanzanian landscape, artist and political cartoonist Nathan Mpangala (*Majira*, 14 October 2004; Figure 1) captured Tanzanians' propensity to invoke and pay tribute to this legitimacy in their everyday endeavors by naming everything after Nyerere.[1] In the cartoon, a man drinking at a streetside table says to his companion: "I want to open a bar. I'll call it 'Nyerere'. What do you think?" All around them are city street signs that mark "Nyerere Road," "Nyerere Internet Café," "Nyerere Pub," "Nyerere Airport," "Nyerere Book Shop," and "Nyerere Spare Parts." It is predictable then that – as Tanzania's political parties compete in five-year general election cycles to convince the electorate of the legitimacy and efficacy of their leadership – Nyerere's legacy should feature so centrally in political discourse. And it is perhaps equally unsurprising that Nyerere's memory should be wielded so frequently during election campaigns as a weapon of political shaming by citizens leveraging their electoral power to influence government agendas, performance, and conduct.

This chapter explores how both of these projects – party jockeying and popular political critique – involve the symbolic manipulation of Nyerere's name, memory, and legacy within a broader political rhetoric in Tanzania that turns on shifting, and sometimes contradictory, conceptions of eldership and youth, fathers and sons, and illicit eating and legitimate consumption. It demonstrates that central to the construction of political legitimacy in Tanzania is filiation to Nyerere – both personal and party – and it shows how Nyerere's name and political views are employed in electoral politics to a variety of diverging ends. At the same time popular critiques of political candidates increasingly use Nyerere – Tanzania's one authorized critic (see Brennan, 2014

---

* Portions of this chapter have appeared in *PoLAR: Political and Legal Anthropology Review* (Phillips, 2010). They are reprinted with permission. This chapter and prior iterations of it have benefited tremendously from the comments and insights of Marie-Aude Fouéré. Aikande Kwayu offered important insights on recent rhetorical developments. James Hoesterey provided fresh eyes on the manuscript at critical junctures. I would also like to thank Amy Stambach, Sharon Hutchinson, Angelique Haugerud, Deborah McDowell, Brandi Hughes, Cynthia Hoehler-Fatton, and colleagues at Michigan State University and the Carter G. Woodson Institute of African-American and African Studies at the University of Virginia for their comments on earlier iterations and presentations of this material. Any errors of fact or interpretation are my own.

1 This cartoon was also re-printed and discussed in Fouéré (2011: 70).

and this volume) – as a touchstone for good governance, co-opting elite discourses of filiation to morally discipline the government with projections of paternal displeasure.

The data for this chapter emerged from nineteen months of ethnographic research in Tanzania between 2004 and 2006, and shorter visits in 2007 and each year from 2010 to 2014. The initial period of research took place in Singida Region – a very poor region situated in the center of the country – during a charged political environment created by severe food and water scarcity and a presidential election year.[3] As I participated in everyday village life, conducted interviews with rural and urban people, attended political rallies in both town and village, and accumulated an array of English- and Swahili-language newspapers,[2] two themes quickly jumped out: the structural advantage of the ruling party, CCM (*Chama Cha Mapinduzi*, or Party of the Revolution); and the rich symbolism of politics in Tanzania that centered on idioms of kinship and food (Bayart, 1993; Phillips, 2009; Schatzberg, 2001). My challenge in examining the "arts of politics" became, as Angelique Haugerud has urged, to "recognize the power of images and aesthetics, but not to divorce images from (contested versions of) history, or to treat the culture of politics as a domain autonomous from material political-economic processes" (1993: 52).

Toward this end I explore the lived landscape of political parties in Tanzania in three electoral periods (2005, 2010, and mounting anticipation of the 2015 elections) by building on Eric Wolf's analysis of structural power. For Wolf, "relations that command the economy and polity and those that shape ideation interact to render the world understandable and manageable" (1999: 5–6), even when it is experienced as unjust. I flesh out the particular forms and figurations of paternalism in the political landscape of mainland Tanzanian and the way it pivots on particular (and always partial) constructions of Julius Nyerere. I focus on this political narrative in order to, following Wolf, "identify the instrumental, organizational, or ideological means that maintain

---

2 I conducted over 140 interviews in 80 homesteads with rural WaSingida between 2004 and 2007. Interviews included oral history and life history components, and surveys of household economic and village development issues. I attended campaign rallies; took part in development meetings; conducted interviews and archival research; and participated in everyday life from my residence in a single room of one rural village's government office. Data presented on the 2010 and run-up to the 2015 elections emerge from interviews conducted during follow-up visits to Dar, Singida, and Dodoma, media reports, email communications and phone interviews. I also draw extensively on political cartoons and news reports from Swahili- and English-language newspapers to illustrate popular national discourses about politics.

custom or underwrite the search for coherence. There may be no inner drive at the core of a culture, but assuredly there are people who drive it on, as well as others who are driven. Wherever possible we should try to identify the social agents who install and defend institutions and who organize coherence, for whom and against whom" (1999: 67).

By moving back and forth between local ethnography from fieldwork in Singida Region and data on broader public perceptions of national politics in media and historical sources, I combine levels of analysis to show how the ruling elite, the political opposition, the media, and the voting populace deploy filiation to Nyerere to explain and manipulate contemporary political and economic relationships in accordance with historical and cultural narratives.

Constructing the Nyerere Line: Filiation in Tanzanian Political Rhetoric

The peaceful transition to independence and the uniting of many ethnic groups under one national flag and one African language are, in the eyes of Tanzanians, Nyerere's greatest achievements (Askew, 2006; Becker, 2013; Lofchie, 2014; Mwakikagile, 2006). With several of Tanzania's neighbors torn apart by revolutions, violence or dictatorship, Tanzanians regularly applaud Julius Nyerere (popularly known as the "Father of the Nation" or *Baba wa Taifa*) for Tanzania's relative peace. Nyerere, unlike many of his post-independence presidential contemporaries in Africa, is also praised by Tanzanians for his "thinness" (Schatzberg, 2001: 170) – his prudent lack of personal feasting on what Bayart (1993) has termed, "the national cake." As James Ferguson has noted, "…given his avowed refusal to eat his fellow man, Nyerere's conspicuous lack of a belly was perhaps as symbolically potent as his rejection of material luxury" (2006: 76). Public accolades of Nyerere today by many Tanzanians construct an idealized – even sanctified – image of Nyerere at the same time as they project a glossy national self-portrait of Tanzania as a nation-family bound together by peace, cooperation, and family ties.

A number of scholars have noted the way in which the "cultural intimacy" (Herzfeld, 1997) of domestic images is deployed to extract loyalty from citizens and consolidate state power (Askew, 2002; Herzfeld, 1997; Lakoff, 2002). People of Singida Region in central Tanzania, for example, have long conceptualized Nyerere as a patriarch who promised protection and peace.

In 1967, anthropologist Marguerite Jellicoe noted how – since independence – Nyerere had taken the place of the Sun as the key symbol of unity and paternalism in rural Singida:

> Nowadays, the Sun as a symbol of unity is becoming overlaid by other and more human symbols (...). The most meaningful symbol is now a national one, the Presidency as manifested in the person of Nyerere (...) described in local songs as the herdsman of Tanzania who takes care of all his people as the homestead head takes care of the cattle which united the past, present and future (...). The symbol of Nyerere's delegated authority is his walking stick; this however, has in Singida been transformed into the herding stick carried by every homestead head – a symbol of protection as well as of rule (Jellicoe, 1978: 30).

In Singida in 2005 Nyerere remained a symbol of protection and domestic peace. As one widow narrated, "[t]he Father of the Nation came to strengthen the life of peace and cooperation together. He brought peace for all the tribes to live together without discrimination. Anywhere you go in the Republic of Tanzania you will not have a problem."[3]

Such domestic images have played a significant role in Tanzanian party politics. Nyerere's socialist vision, Ujamaa, centered on an idea of the "African Family" (Nyerere, 1968) and served to legitimate the vast CCM apparatus. After his retirement from politics, CCM increasingly referred to Nyerere as "the Father of the Nation." This, Schatzberg (2001) argues, was the means through which the CCM party machine secured its own legitimacy. For if Nyerere was father of the nation-family, then CCM could pronounce itself the father of the government.

Given Jakaya Mrisho Kikwete's relative youth in 2005 as the ruling party presidential candidate (he was 54 at the time), CCM devoted much political and symbolic work in that election to convince Tanzanians of the naturalness of the choice. In the process, Nyerere was resurrected time and time again during the electoral campaign to weigh in on candidates from his grave. Prior to receiving the CCM nomination for president, for example, Kikwete traveled to Nyerere's home of Butiama in northwestern Tanzania. Mama Maria (Nyerere's widow) bestowed upon the Muslim Kikwete the gift of a Bible. The gift served, in the first place, to publicize CCM's preference for Kikwete's candidacy; secondly, it posthumously conferred upon him the blessing of Nyerere (who in 1995 had overlooked him for candidacy); and thirdly, accepting a

---
3 Interview, Rural Singida, 7 February 2005.

Bible showed him to be a moderate Muslim in a nation where people are increasingly concerned about the emergence of religious tensions (Fouéré, 2009; Heilman & Kaiser, 2002).[4]

Nyerere then reappeared at the meeting of the CCM national congress in Dodoma where 1,500 representatives voted for Kikwete to be the CCM candidate: "a hush fell over the delegates, followed by gasps and waves of astonished laugher, when there emerged on-stage a slight man with graying hair, carrying a walking stick – a well-turned out look-alike of the popular leader who died in 1999" (Mnganya & Johnson, 2005). And before the 2005 elections Nyerere's voice could be heard each night in villages across Tanzania in radio broadcasts of the *Wosia wa Baba*, a series of carefully selected recorded speeches in which Nyerere reminds Tanzanians of the qualities needed for strong leadership. That Nyerere lives and leads on was so convincing in fact that, according to a *Majira* article, several Maasai elders arrived at the 2005 polls wanting to vote for Nyerere.[5] Although few Tanzanians are this far removed from national political currents, this news report testifies to many Tanzanians' sense that Nyerere, even postmortem, remains a powerful figure on the national political stage. Indeed, few political debates proceed without at least passing reference to the Father of the Nation's real or projected position on an issue, a topic to which I return later in the chapter.

But establishing political filiation to Nyerere is less about these explicit and rather obvious attempts to invoke Nyerere's memory for contemporary political gain, and more about establishing a sense of historical continuity for Tanzanians in a time of rapid political, economic, and social change, global political insecurities, and unprecedented possibilities to fall through the economic cracks. In such a context politicians from the ruling party seek to establish that they (and not others) represent three aspects of Nyerere's legacy: political seniority; paternal providership, and insistence on a happy, peaceful, and unified family even at the cost of silencing dissent. In the following pages I describe events from the 2005, 2010, and run-up to the 2015 presidential election campaigns and describe these three aspects of Nyerere's legacy. I then turn the analytical gaze from the ruling elite to explore how the political opposition, voting public and popular press have appropriated this particular crystallization of the myth of Nyerere-

---

4 In 2000 and again in 2005 the lead opposition party was the Civic United Front (CUF), a party perceived by many Tanzanians to have a Muslim base and religious agenda.

5 Kiliani, Faustine. "Wamasai: Nyerere hajafa tunamtaka achaguliwe rais" [Maasai: Nyerere has not died, we want him to be elected president], *Majira*, 15 December 2005.

as father, as protector, as provider – to stir public debate and discipline government actors.

Nyerere's Legacy: Seniority, Providership, and the Happy Nation-Family

In September 2005, the people of Singida welcomed ruling party presidential candidate Jakaya Kikwete to the soccer stadium in Singida Town. A tattered CCM flag whipped atop a tall tree pole; the day was windy and hot. By three in the afternoon, people of Singida streamed into the stadium. It was a river of yellow and green, with people sporting CCM baseball hats, scarves, *khangas*, and t-shirts that party touts had been doling out for weeks (see Figure 2). Kikwete's eyes were literally everywhere – his face peering out from the chests of jeering adolescents, from the foreheads of party officials, from the backsides of the dancing women. Kikwete posters lining the stadium were emblazoned with the CCM seal – its golden hammer and axe glinting in the unrelenting dry season sun.

Figure 2: CCM supporters sport campaign swag. Photo by author, 2005.

Kikwete was late. The Master of Ceremonies explained that supporters on his route from Manyoni district had prevented him from passing – that in the hopes of receiving a few words from the soon-to-be president, they had laid down in the road to block his passage. In the meantime, in Singida stadium, a band from Dar es Salaam played music and people danced, in time to CCM and Nyerere praise songs, *Bongo Flava* (Tanzanian hip hop), and *Mawindi*, the local Nyaturu dance.

As the sun drew near the horizon, word reached the stadium that Kikwete's caravan of sports-utility vehicles was drawing near. The MC worked the crowd into a cheering frenzy, "When he arrives, wave your hats and scarves. He who does not wave them and wears the hat of CCM, take it from him, for it is CCM who has clothed him." Reminding them of the gifts distributed freely for the rally, he suggested to voters that CCM was already fulfilling its fatherly duties to clothe its children. Senge, a 26-year-old young man from urban Singida recalled the scene:

> "People felt bad to have their presents taken, so they did as he requested, and said, "Karibu, Mheshimiwa!" (Welcome, your Honorable!), waving their hats and scarves". Kikwete arrived with so many people and presents to give out. He didn't talk many policies, like his opponents. He just made a lot of promises – to build roads, and hospitals, to bring water, and secondary schools. He didn't explain why these things are so late in coming or where the money for our minerals has gone. He spoke only good words, and people were happy. And then he talked about the opposition. He said, "The candidates come with a hunger and they are not suitable for your votes. A person with hunger, if you give him your vote, he won't implement a thing. He will just go to feed his family. And a youth of thirteen years old, would you give him a wife to take care of?" And people agreed you can't trust a thirteen-year-old with a wife and children. "And CUF [the main opposition party in Singida in 2005] is only thirteen years old since it was born, so you can't give it your vote because it's still too young. The vote must go to our father Nyerere's party, the father of our nation...."

Kikwete was not the first presidential candidate to come to Singida that election season. But he put on by far the best show. In contrast, his greatest rival for the region in 2005, the Civic United Front's (CUF) Professor Ibrahim Lipumba had stirred the crowd with his sharp critique of CCM rule. He fired up his audience with the substance of his speech – challenging the people of Singida to confront the political and economic disparities exacerbated by their current leadership – but put on neither paternal airs nor costly bells and whistles. Kikwete was welcomed into the town's largest venue – the soccer stadium – and from seated up on high was entertained by CCM performance troupes bused in from Dar es Salaam. Lipumba was welcomed onto an empty lot across from the stadium, where his audience waited soberly beneath trees, listening to the diatribe of a local CUF leader for hours before Lipumba's arrival. CCM parliamentary candidates and ward councilor candidates, dressed in *kitenge* shirts (tailored cotton print shirts of the style worn by wealthy government officials) of the CCM colors of gold and green, already looked official. They arrived in the long caravan of sports-utility vehicles with Kikwete, where they had the honor of being introduced and sanctioned by "the future president of Tanzania." Meanwhile their local CUF opponents emerged from the ranks of the audience beneath the trees to be introduced in the *mitumba* (second-hand clothes) that were their everyday wear.

For many voters in Singida, the sharp contrast between these two brief campaign visits supported a dominant discourse of electoral politics – one that asserts that the Tanzanian government is "father" to its citizen-children, and that only CCM possesses the qualities, resources, and descent from Nyerere to be that father. Ruling party candidates at campaign rallies argue that opposition parties are still "too young." Speakers draw on gendered and generational stereotypes to cast opposition parties as teenage troublemakers: out-of-work, hungry, discontented, and bearing all the strength of youth, but using it toward violent, self-serving, or exploitative ends. Extravagant spending on ruling party campaign events makes clear that it is only CCM who can provide for its nation-family. And minimal substantive engagement in political issues by CCM candidates suggests to voters that their guardianship will remain peaceable and they will safeguard the nation's unity. I will now discuss each of these aspects in turn.

The symbolic gerontocracy

A number of scholars have pointed out the need to consider 'age' as an analytic category (Abeles & Collard, 1985; Cole & Durham, 2006). "Age and generational symbolism," Cole and Durham argue, have long "been used to naturalize situations of conquest and rule" (2006: 7). Tanzania is no exception. Age and generation serve as complex and contested terrains upon which relations of hierarchy, dependency, and power are organized and challenged (Stroeken, 2005). On the one hand, eldership (*uzee*) remains a powerful cultural concept that organizes people, practices, and relationships. In Singida, for example, greeting, seating, and the distribution of labor are commonly organized around local conceptions of eldership and youth. But the technocracy of the colonial and postcolonial Tanzanian state has come to privilege education over eldership (Feierman, 1990). And hierarchies of formal education and the escalating mobility of youth have increasingly unsettled the organization of the political structure around primogeniture and notions of elderliness as godliness (Wagner, 1940). Leadership is now seen to require literacy, a mastery of technology, fluency in Swahili, physical stamina, and innovation: all powers associated with youth. It is the very old now, in addition to the very young, who have come to be characterized by "vulnerability" (the now-favored term in international development parlance) to famine, malnutrition, and a lack of access to health care and other social services (Cliggett, 2005). Young and dynamic MPs like Zitto Kabwe (of the opposition) and January Makamba (CCM) have ridden the wave of these challenges to the old guard, even calling in the current 2014 Constitutional Review Process for an amendment to the Constitution regarding the mandated age of the president – proposing 35 years of age instead of 40 (Mjema, 2014).[6]

Yet despite the declining status of old age in society and the ambiguous associations of youth as physically strong, literate, and technologically savvy on the one hand, and "hungry" and self-serving on the other, the symbolic power of age metaphors in East Africa remains strong. Consider two contrasting images that illuminate the paradox of age in Tanzanian political rhetoric and its strategic and sometimes contradictory deployment. On the one hand, a *Majira* cartoon by Nathan Mpangala, commenting on Kikwete's electoral victory, showed Kikwete as a large bull, leading the other presidential candidates who appear as small calves on wobbly legs. Kikwete is saying: "I am indeed their father, these others are only little calves" (*Majira*, 19 January 2006).

Yet paradoxically, while most Tanzanians acknowledged Kikwete's paternity and his rightful claim to the presidency as CCM's chosen one, they also referred to Kikwete (54 years old at the time and quite famously handsome) in 2005 as a "youth" (*kijana*). He is not yet seen to be *mzee*, an elder whose age and experience mandates a certain kind of respect. CCM even campaigned on Kikwete's youth with the slogan, "New Zeal, New Vigour, New Pace" (*Ari mpya, Nguvu mpya, Kasi mpya*).

A *Guardian* political cartoon by Haji Abeid shows Kikwete (in the lead) and former Prime Minister Edward Lowassa leading a race ahead

---

6 I am grateful to Aikande Kwayu for pointing this out to me. See Kibiriti, Rafael. "Zitto, Makamba Wautaka Urais", IPPMedia, 29 February 2012, http://www.ippmedia.com/frontend/?l=38953; Mjema, Daniel. "Wapendekeza umri mgombea urais upunguzwe", *Mwananchi*, 24 February 2014, http://www.mwananchi.co.tz/Katiba/
Wapendekeza-umri-mgombea-urais-upunguzwe/-/1625946/2219448/-/gecefyz/-/index.html.

of an overweight and bald Member of Parliament, who struggles to keep running (*Guardian*, 20 March 2006). The cartoon contrasts Kikwete's youth and energy with the old guard of CCM (whom Tanzanians call the *vigogo*, or "dead wood"), who are seen to have slowed the party for years. Age, this analysis suggests, remains a legitimizing narrative of Tanzanian political power in which a symbolic gerontocracy (not biological seniority) maps itself onto the technocracy and its youthful leadership in locally legitimate terms.

Though Kikwete was both older and more established as heir to the Nyerere line in 2010, campaign billboards from those elections still featured calculated constructions of Kikwete as the paternal head of household.

Figure 3 shows a photo of a campaign advertisement on a road sign which reads "Love for the Children: Vote CCM, Vote Kikwete". In the photograph, Kikwete gazes down with paternal affection on a Tanzanian youth, his "fatherliness" implying a commitment of guardianship for Tanzanians in the uncertain promise of the future. In Figure 4, a second road sign reads: "Friend of all the generations: Vote CCM, Vote Kikwete". This image, along with a third one that shows him seated next to his own mother and reads "Love of/for Mama: Vote CCM, Vote Kikwete," shows him as a loyal and loving son, showing deference and care for his elders and squarely positioning him as pater, protector, and progenitor to the next generation of Tanzanians and loyal son and heir apparent to Nyerere and the CCM legacy.

Figures 3 & 4: Photographs by Peter Bofin, 2010. Reprinted with permission.

Popular acceptance of Kikwete's seniority in 2005 above his opponents in other parties was closely linked to the widespread understanding, particularly in rural contexts, that the CCM party was senior to the government. Especially in rural contexts, the government has been largely dependent on the CCM party – which is seen to have "fathered" and "raised" the government. This became increasingly clear during my fieldwork. Between 2004 and 2006 I paid rent for my room in a village office in rural Singida. Like my neighbors – the village livestock expert and two primary teachers – I rented two small rooms and was asked by the chairman of the village to pay 1,000 shillings (approximately one dollar) per month to the village government. One day, a woman whom I knew very little appeared at my door, introduced herself as "my chairman," and demanded my rent. The request – from a woman whom I had not seen in months and whom I suspected was at the moment a patron of a nearby beer party, confused me. I told her I had made arrangements with the chairman and asked that she wait until I had spoken with him. When I tracked him down, the chairman concurred that this woman was indeed the party chairwoman for the local CCM branch, who had been temporarily on leave following childbirth. "But I will talk to her about your rent, and I will ask that she support our agreement." Still confused, I asked, "But the village office, does it belong to the party, or the government?" "It was built by the party during single-party rule," the chairman answered, "so it belongs to the party, but they let the government use it." "But what happens if another party would win the election? Shouldn't the office belong to the village, no matter whom they elect?" I persisted. "We have not yet faced that situation," said the chairman simply.

In subsequent interviews I asked my interlocutors in the village the same questions. Like others, Mzee Victorini, a party leader of his ten-household cell, responded,

> The government has no office here in the village, so we [the party] have welcomed them. But the office remains in the hands of the party. So the livestock expert who has his room there pays into the party pockets, as you will too. In the past, the leadership was *mzima* ["unified"]; there was only the party. Later, they decided it should be two: a party and a government. CCM is the elder of the government. It raised [*kulea*, as in, "to raise and educate a child"] the government and the nation. The party has raised the government to follow all the laws of the party.[7]

The party, he argued, fathered the state. This logic eventually resulted in the eviction of the village government from the village office. In 2010, the

---

7 Interview, Rural Singida, 7 June 2005.

CHADEMA opposition party (Chama cha Demokrasia na Maendeleo, Party for Democracy and Progress) won the parliamentary election in this constituency and several members of the village government were CHADEMA members and supporters. CCM subsequently reclaimed the office building (built by all villagers during one-party rule) and left the village government office-less. The government thereafter sought space to meet in the primary school building whenever a meeting was called.[8]

CCM inhabits not only the buildings of the government as its own, but also its structures and resources. In 2012 I interviewed Tundu Lissu – the Chief Opposition Whip in Parliament and MP for Singida East (CHADEMA) – about the campaign battle he waged and subsequently won in rural Singida in 2010. Lissu, a community organizer turned human rights lawyer, complained bitterly about the difficulty of extracting state institutions from the thickly woven web of party institutions, practices, and resources.

> Whatever CCM has in terms of buildings, all of them were built prior to 1992. They were built through forced contributions… prior to 1992. There was a provision in the national budget that 3 percent of the budget be allocated to CCM. It was in the budget! So CCM was not a political party as political parties go… CCM was part of the state! It was a *state* party! So therefore the Village Executive Director was also the Village CCM Secretary. The *Katibu Tarafa* was also the divisional executive secretary of CCM. The District Commissioner was also the district party secretary. This marriage of the state and party made it impossible to distinguish where the party ended and the government started. You know? And all the state offices were obtained through this state party, using primarily the state machinery to get resources for itself. You know? And we have not been able to outgrow that legacy of the state party.[9]

Lines drawn between the government and party were blurry indeed: I was often called to "village meetings" that turned out to be party elections or rallies. Without a viable opposition in the village, party and government became interchangeable. The "youth committee" and the "women's committee" were both in fact CCM committees. Likewise the government was entirely dependent on the party's ten-household cell

---

8 The village government proceeded to extract sponsorship to build a new village office from a wealthy government employee based in Arusha who intended to build a guesthouse within village borders. The office was mostly finished as of my most recent visit in 2014.
9 Interview, Dodoma Town, 28 June 2012.

structure (or *balozi*) for communication, the collection of development contributions, and general maintenance of the public order. MP Lissu went on to note,

> There are things which are very strange. You will be surprised, if you get arrested and are taken to court, these magistrates who should know better they will ask you… hey what's your name? Who is your ten-cell leader? The ten-cell leader is a CCM structure. But it's permeated into all levels of state![10]

It is then not surprising that a report on civic and voter education made note of low levels of civic knowledge amongst eligible voters. "It was discovered that some secondary schools students who are eligible voters [and who in rural areas are among the most highly educated] cannot distinguish between the government and the ruling party. Most of them thought that CCM is the government".[11] This conflation of party and government, that positions CCM as not only senior to the other parties, but as senior to the independent Tanzanian state leaves many Tanzanians with a categorical sense that they are beholden to CCM, the father-party of the party-father, Nyerere.

Paternal providership

In the political rhetoric of contemporary CCM politicians, the socialist period of Nyerere's rule is remembered as a period of political and economic paternalism, in which a big benevolent government "babied" its infant nation. Despite radical shifts in Tanzanian economic policy since that period, CCM has taken pains in recent elections to perpetuate the notion that it is the only party who can provide for the national family and to remind voters that opposition parties stand on very shaky ground when it comes to their financial resources. These efforts intensified in the face of the growing threat of opposition parties who have shaken public faith in CCM's ability to manage the household budget – that is, to contain government corruption. Though it looks ask if CCM may be changing its campaign tactics for the 2015 elections (I will return to this below), economic disparities between CCM and opposition parties have often been highlighted to emphasize that only CCM can provide for its political 'children'.

Material symbols like billboards and lavish spending on campaign rallies are particularly powerful cues in the context of Singida Region, a

---
10 Interview, Dodoma Town, 28 June 2012.
11 Berege, Simon. "Education on polls benefits tiny minority", *The Citizen*, 30 July 2005.

largely semi-arid region. In Singida, 28 percent of the population lives below the food poverty line and 55 percent lives below the basic needs poverty line, the highest regional percentage in all of Tanzania (National Bureau of Statistics, 2002). In such a food and resource insecure context, the symbolic and physical representation of party wealth as demonstrated in Kikwete's 2005 visit to Singida acquires particular force in decisions about whom to offer political allegiance. Lavish spending suggests not only a readiness and willingness to provide for constituents, but also the disinterestedness of independent wealth – a motivation for serving in public office that transcends the desire of the political elite to, in the Tanzanian idiom, fill one's own belly.

CCM candidates, as we saw from Kikwete's visit to Singida, use their money not only to put on a good show, but also for *takrima,* the gift economy of elections in Tanzania. Those who defend the practice argue that *takrima* is a form of hospitality intended to extend thanks to those who help with election campaigns, though most agree that its practice is abused when extended to offering gifts to voters, which has often been the case. In 2005, voters jokingly referred to campaign season as "harvesting season" – the season of exchanging votes for gifts of money, beer, meals, and party apparel referred to colloquially as "food," "soda," "sugar" or "tea." Gifts of t-shirts, hats, *khangas,* and scarves circulated widely. Though the 2010 elections saw *takrima* outlawed by a 2006 law, the practice of handing out payment or gifts for attendance at political rallies was, according to many people, more rampant than ever. One urban CCM supporter noted critically of her own party, "That law, it just existed on paper. I've never seen so much corruption like this year.... It was ridiculous. So much money. They paid people to come to rallies and gave out t-shirts, *khangas,* and lots and lots of money. People were saying it was a "fiesta-like" campaign."[12]

Unfortunately, very little *takrima* actually reaches the hands of the people who need it most. At the 2005 Singida rally, the concentration of green and gold (people who were given CCM's *khangas* and t-shirts) lay at the heart of the stadium, where officials, party cadres and active members sit, with thousands of people sitting on the outlying bleachers in the browns and greys of their worn secondhand clothes. They were left bearing witness to CCM's eminence, not enjoying it. Despite the fact that election "harvests" are unequally distributed and not all partake, *takrima* and CCM's public displays of wealth are powerful cues in a

---

12 Phone Interview, 5 December 2010.

context where the primary political platform is poverty reduction and a primary means of economic security is patronage.

It is important to note that CCM's financial and resource advantage over other parties is not, in itself, the reason for its overwhelming dominance in Tanzanian politics. As Abner Cohen has noted of the ideology produced by the political elite in Sierra Leone,

> ...the power mystique is a subtle, particularistic ideology developed by a privileged elite to validate and perpetuate their domination and thereby to support their own material interests. The cult consists of various techniques of mystification...to persuade the masses that it is only natural for this power elite to rule and that this is in the best interests of the society as a whole (1981: 5).

Cohen's observation rings true in Tanzania: CCM's material strength is most significant for its support of a social and political narrative that naturalizes CCM rule through its common-sense assertion that only a father can best look after his own child and that only CCM is materially positioned to provide for its political children.

And yet in the run-up to the 2015 presidential elections, both opposition and ruling parties appear to be scrambling to re-situate themselves on this political landscape. Political scientist Aikande Kwayu, in her provocative blog, notes the new "image strategy" of both CCM and the opposition. CCM, perhaps in response to charges of rampant corruption and aid profiteering and in light of quickly growing disparities in wealth and resources, appears to have shifted its rhetoric to make new claims to being a party of the people.[13] Photos of country tours by top party officials, she notes, portray them "taking the central rail train, building with people, farming with people using hoes,... eating *ugali* on plastic plates and on benches with *wananchi*".[14] UKAWA, the alliance of opposition parties that emerged in the 2014 constitutional review process (*Umoja wa Katiba ya Wananchi*, the Coalition for People's Constitution), she notes, has meanwhile begun flamboyantly executing a "Big Man" performance, complete with helicopters and traffic-disrupting convoys of expensive sports utility vehicles waving party flags. So, in an ironic twist, while UKAWA chases CCM's legacy of paternal providership by showcasing material and financial strength,

---

[13] For one such critique, see Ulimwengu, Jenerali. "A Broke Country with an Expensive Govt; Guess Who Pays the Price", *The East African*, 7 June 2014.

[14] See www.aikandekwayu.com, 19 May 2014.

CCM is now anxious to minimize social and economic distinctions between government and citizen, rather than emphasizing them.

Governing the happy family: The anti-politics of CCM

The marked difference in rhetorical strategies used by CCM's Jakaya Kikwete and CUF's Ibrahim Lipumba in their 2005 visits to Singida is illustrative of contemporary multi-party politics, particularly in the context of rural Tanzania. In his 2005 Singida speech, Kikwete spoke *maneno mazuri tu* ("only good words"), according to Senge, and "made lots of promises." CCM supporters I spoke with also noted Kikwete's "good words" that, to them, indicated a commitment to peace and security and symbolized continuity in years to come. Critics however emphasized the emptiness of Kikwete's words and famous smile, his avoidance of assuming any CCM responsibility for what many rural Tanzanians perceive as stalled development.

In 2005 Lipumba and his fellow CUF candidates satisfied those Singida residents thirsty for a more substantive message. A 2005 parliamentary candidate for CUF in Singida Town questioned, for example, why – if it were true that CCM has improved the economy – all the prices have gone up, but incomes have stayed the same. In an interview he observed, "we can't rely on takrima. Our words are that which pulls people to us. For us, our words are the money that will attract people to us."[15]

In 2010, people remarked on CHADEMA presidential candidate Willbrod Slaa's willingness to engage rural Tanzanians in substantive conversation about Tanzania's development.[16] One woman noted,

> Slaa made people think. He was *doing* civic education. He talked about poverty and housing, asking, "how can we claim that we live in the global village, with people in such pathetic housing? Where is humanity?" He talked about the level of education, about the ward schools that have no teachers. CCM put everything more positively: "See how many schools we have built? See how we have improved enrollment?"[17]

In general, CCM candidates avoid engaging in substantive issues at campaign rallies. Even as its candidates made promise after promise in 2010, CCM barred all its candidates from participating in televised campaign debates, rationalizing this move by stating that the party

---

15 Interview, Singida Town, 21 September 2005.

16 Before the 2010 elections, CHADEMA's popularity skyrocketed, particularly in urban areas and among younger segments of the population. Presidential Candidate Slaa won 27.1 percent of the popular vote and CHADEMA won 48 seats in the National Assembly.

17 Phone interview, 17 November 2010.

knows best how to present its policies to the public through campaign rallies. An editorial in the *Citizen* reacted: "We need to know this so that we can be sure that what they are promising is tenable. Telling voters how they are planning to implement the promises would give their promises weight. Otherwise their pledges will continue to be political statements meant to woo voters".[18] This refusal to engage in substantive debate with political opponents and the reliance on a one-way flow of propaganda to voters evokes doubt about the extent to which popular interests are and can be represented in national politics.

In rural areas the opposition's more direct approach to the politics of development has mixed effects. CCM candidates and supporters frequently charge opposition candidates with having *maneno mengi* ("too many words"), the sure sign of a trouble-maker in a land where people say that "the lip is an ankle-bell": it makes only meaningless noise. Accusations against opposition party members and leaders of "making trouble" (*kufanya fujo*) and being "argumentative" (*wabishi*) contribute to a climate of fear that has tended to cloud multi-party elections in Tanzania. Such accusations exacerbate existing fears that political dissent will incite violence, civil unrest, or worse, the "African tribalism" that Tanzanians pride themselves on avoiding.

Nyerere's own ambiguity toward multi-party politics is often invoked to delegitimize opposition politics as un-Tanzanian or even un-African.[19] A 2013 editorial in the *Guardian on Sunday* by Dr. Dalaly Peter Kafumu, a Member of Parliament for CCM from Igunga District, cited Nyerere's aversion to multi-partyism as a way of dismissing opposition parties' aspirations and claims to leadership. He noted:

> Mwalimu did not believe in multipartyism as he knew this will bring a negative dissection of the Tanzanian society (…). Yes, Mwalimu was right; building multiparty democracy in a poor country or a fragile toddler economy is synonymous to nurturing division and hate between the opposition and the ruling parties; between different communities with different cultural origins such as tribes and clans who in most cases create political parties

---

18 Mwakisyala, J. "Tanzanians tired of promises", *East African Business Week*, 13 September 2010.

19 With the collapse of the Soviet Union and increasing use of Western donor money to promote multipartyism, political reform movements were spreading across Africa. Still in his chairmanship of CCM, Nyerere himself began a strong campaign for multipartyism inside CCM. The government convened a group to examine popular opinion about the matter. In the Nyalali Commission's historic referendum, only 21 percent of people surveyed supported a multi-party system, with 78 percent in favor of the current single-party approach. Yet the commission's recommendations, noting the country's "best interests," supported the re-introduction of multipartyism. On May 7, 1992 Parliament approved a bill to make Tanzania a multi-party state.

to secure their interests. The fulfillment of Mwalimu Nyerere's vision on the danger of multiparty democracy in Africa and Tanzania is today unveiling before our eyes when democracy becomes a source of conflict among the people of nations in Africa.[20]

Like Kafumu, other CCM candidates make explicit and repeated connections between opposition politics and political violence (Makulilo, 2014; TEMCO, 2011). Government officials (of CCM persuasions) plead with their compatriots to keep the peace during elections, to not descend into the electoral and tribal violence that marks its East African neighbors. Despite Nyerere's leadership in the transition to a multi-party system in Tanzania, CCM supporters in rural Tanzania often invoke Nyerere's name to warn villagers about the threat to peace and security inherent in opposition politics.

At one village meeting I attended in rural Singida in 2005, a local CCM leader warned, "the opposition comes bringing its little threats. That's why Nyerere said these opposition parties, they have problems. They divide us by religion and tribe. Isn't this true?" That year, the aforementioned speeches by Nyerere played each night on Tanzanian government-sponsored radio, reaching millions of Tanzanians, repeated time and again Nyerere's entreaties to Tanzanians to refrain from violent conflict during the elections. Such incessant calls for peace (from Nyerere's grave, no less) functioned to constantly suggest to rural Tanzanians what the alternative to CCM rule would be: bloodshed.

Nyerere for the Opposition?

Efforts by the ruling party to establish its candidates as the true and deserving heirs to Nyerere's political line have never gone uncontested by the voting populace and opposition parties. Some Tanzanians pierce the hero image of Nyerere by articulating critiques of the suffering they underwent during the forced re-location of Nyerere's villagization policies, planned economy, and repression of political dissent. In response to Nyerere's possible canonization by the Catholic Church (Mesaki & Malipula, 2011), one editorial voiced, "Nyerere… A hero? No way…. Disagree with Nyerere at your own peril. You will find yourself in jail/detention. Many Tanzanians are still alive to attest to this".[21]

---

20 Kafumu, Dalaly Peter. "Mwalimu Nyerere: His Pain, Our Gain", *Guardian on Sunday*, 27 October 2013. http://www.ippmedia.com/frontend/?l=60871 (accessed 13 February 2014).
21 Kinsolyo, John. "Nyerere shouldn't be declared a saint", *The Guardian*, 3 February 2006.

Other critics highlight the co-optation of Nyerere's popularity for political ends that Nyerere would never have pursued. As one Internet blogger complained:

> JK [Kikwete] went to Butiama and was given a Bible by Mama Maria. This, we are told, is a symbol that he has been agreed upon by Mwalimu, so all of we Tanzanians should agree. This is just another political tool that we the citizens have given CCM to rule our lives. (....) now, this is what we get, that every time there are problems in this country like now with electricity, medicine, they announce anything about Mwalimu and just like that, we citizens quiet down.[22]

And as my neighbor in rural Singida (the only vocal supporter of the opposition in the village in 2005) complained to me in 2006: "We! I hate the *wosia wa baba* [the Nyerere speeches replayed on the radio] – it makes me sick! Every day that stupid song. His messages are good, but he's dead! Why are we listening to the politics of someone who's been dead for years? Let's talk about the politics of today!" In 2014, when I went to greet my old neighbor on a visit back to the village, he continued this rant without prompt from me, as if we had never been interrupted:

> What I hate most is all of this talk about Nyerere, saying but Nyerere said this, Nyerere said that. Don't you have any thoughts of your own? [Huna fikra zako?] Maybe around Nyerere Day, there could be one week when we could talk about Nyerere's opinions. But people never stop. It's like a prayer: every day, morning and evening.

Yet opposition parties, like the ruling party, also aim to cement their own legitimacy through re-constructing their lineage to the Nyerere line. A December 2005 *Majira* article reported that "CCM is warned that Mwalimu Nyerere is not their personal property"[23]. In 2005 the Tanzania Labor Party (TLP) disputed CCM's monopoly on Nyerere and featured their own "ghost" appearance of him during a campaign rally in Arusha:

> ...The late 'Mwalimu Julius Nyerere' who professed to have 'come from the dead' in order to 'put things straight' and 'apologize to Tanzanians,' appeared in Arusha and addressed a rally.... 'Nyerere' regretted that he had made a grave mistake during the

---

22 Field Marshall ES. Posting 8 October 2006, www.jamboforums.com (accessed 23 February 2008).

23 "CCM yaonywa Mwalimu Nyerere si mali ya mtu" [CCM is warned: Teacher Nyerere is not private property], *Majira*, 5 December 2005. Also discussed in Fouéré (2008, 2014 and in this volume).

first Multiparty Elections in 1995 by assisting the ruling party in its path to victory, adding that 'he had come back' to warn the local people here not to repeat the same mistake.[24]

In 2010, a campaign video for CHADEMA presidential candidate, Willbrod Slaa, showed a bright green CCM campaign shirt with Nyerere's face. The slogan, however, reads "I'm supporting Slaa".[25] And a 2013 CHADEMA Ohio campaign video replayed audio excerpts of a speech made by President Julius Nyerere in Dodoma in 1995. Overlaid on the faces of contemporary Tanzanians – young and old – one hears the voice of the deceased Nyerere echoing: "Tanzanians want change; if they fail to find it inside CCM, they will search for it outside of CCM. Tanzanians want change… Tanzanians want change… If they don't find it…inside CCM, they will look for it outside CCM. If they don't find it… inside CCM, they will look for it outside CCM".[26] This spectral echoing of Nyerere's voice suggesting Tanzanians might look beyond the ruling party for leadership makes it so: new political horizons have emerged.

In 2012, the Arusha by-election campaigns prompted a public debate over the use of Nyerere's name in contemporary politics. Referring to himself as Nyerere's son, CHADEMA's Member of Parliament for Musoma, Vincent Nyerere, said that "he had chosen to ditch CCM and his advice to Arumeru residents was (that) they should do the same" (Nkwame, 2012). In response to this, former President Benjamin William Mkapa charged Vincent Nyerere with fabricating his filial connection to Julius Nyerere, asserting that "I have worked with Mwalimu throughout his lifetime and buried him at Butiama in 1999. I have never heard of a son named Vincent Nyerere". The *Daily News* reported that "Mkapa has warned impostors using the names of national leaders for cheap popularity saying the late Father of the Nation, Mwalimu Julius Nyerere, had no son known as Vincent" and that "Mr. Mkapa said it was a serious offence for a person to impost a son, relative or acquaintance of the founding president for the sake of elections".[27] Ten days later,

---

24 "Weird Events Dominate Arusha as Election Fever Catches On", *The Guardian*, 6 August 2005.
25 Strong, Diane. "YouTube Video: Chagua Dr. Slaa2: The Hand that Giveth.mp4", http://www.youtube.com/watch?v=tIviJ1wzYI4. Uploaded 26 September 2010.
26 CHADEMA Ohio is a branch of the CHADEMA political party that represents Tanzanian CHADEMA members living in the state of Ohio in the United States. Chadema Diaspora. "Tangazo la Chadema; WaTanzania Wanataka Mabadiliko, Mwalimu Nyerere". http://www.jamiiforums.com/jukwaa-la-siasa/544934-tangazo-la-chadema%3B-watanzania-wanataka-mabadiliko-mwalimu-nyerere.html. Accessed 12 January 2014. English translation of Swahili speech done by author.
27 Marc Nkwame, "Mkapa Urges Arumeru Voters to Shun Imposters", *Tanzania Daily News*, 13 March 2012.

the Tanzanian *Business Times* triumphantly reported that Mkapa had apologized to Vincent Nyerere after being reminded that Mkapa himself had offered condolences to Vincent in 2000 following the death of his father Kiboko Nyerere (brother to Julius Nyerere). Though CHADEMA was vindicated through demonstrating publicly that Vincent Nyerere was indeed a blood relative – a "son" even – of Nyerere, both Mkapa's denunciation of Vincent and his apology succeeded in highlighting that descent was through a brother, not through the Father of the Nation himself.[28] A *Guardian* editorial called the whole debate "cheap politics", asking "How does the connection with Nyerere's family help the people of Arumeru East constituency whose main problems include land and poverty?… There's no justification to use Nyerere's name or family to win an election or using those personal issues as the main agenda".[29]

Increasingly, both the voting public and opposition parties use Nyerere – Tanzania's one authorized critic (see Brennan, 2014, and this volume) – as a mouthpiece for critiquing the government. If political rhetoric in 2005 centered primarily on filiation and the construction of legitimate party rule through descent from the Father of the Nation, it has since 2010 shifted to using the memory of Nyerere to shame today's political leaders for their political motives, conduct, and lack of success at fulfilling promises. In a context where open political critique is increasingly tolerated but direct attacks on the government are purported to violate a national ethos of solidarity (Phillips, 2011), projecting Nyerere's displeasure with contemporary leadership is a culturally and politically safe mode of expressing dissatisfaction. Thus, Nyerere is regularly invoked as a political touchstone – a gauge used to measure and comment upon the quality of today's political leadership.

This is most clearly expressed in a Nyerere Day[30] political cartoon by Abdul in which a contemporary government official in the post-Nyerere years is trying on a giant shoe belonging to Mwalimu (*Nipashe*, 14 October 2013). The government official is saddled with suitcases of money and drink, and is bewildered to find himself unable to fill Nyerere's shoes. Meanwhile, a bedraggled emaciated villager looks on in dismay in front of his makeshift house.

---

28 Karl Lyimo, "Playing the Devil's Advocate: Tanzania 'retired' state leaders abusing their positions." *Business Times*, 23 March 2012.

29 "Election campaigns should be about policies, not chaos and mudslinging." *Guardian on Sunday*, 25 March 2012. http://www.ippmedia.com/frontend/index.php?l=39843 (accessed 13 February 2014).

30 Tanzanians celebrate Nyerere Day each 14th October, the date of President Nyerere's death in 1999.

Figure 5: Cartoon by Gado. *The East African.* 18 October 2009. Cartoon re-printed with permission.

Paternal and educational discipline with Nyerere's signature walking stick are themes of other recent cartoons. One 2013 cartoon had Nyerere using his stick to push a personified "Government" off the ticking bomb on which he was sitting.[31] Another cartoon by Kenyan cartoonist Gado featured in a 2010 campaign video for CHADEMA (Figure 5). The caption reads: "If Mwalimu were alive today…" and depicts Nyerere in the process of spanking with his stick a long line of offenders, including Mkapa, Kikwete, Lowassa, a member of parliament, and a Roman Catholic dignitary. He is saying: "This place is a mess…and who told you I want to be made a saint?!"

In another Nyerere Day cartoon by King Kinya in the *Citizen* (14 October 2013), Nyerere snarls down from his obligatory perch on a framed photograph in a government office at an official caricatured as a pig dressed in a suit. The pig is seated at a table feasting on a plate of stacks of money with a fork, saying "yum, yum, yum!" but warily looking over his shoulder at the outraged Nyerere. A tiny devil pig (also in a suit) is egging him on by whispering in his ear "Don't worry. It's just a picture." No wonder another Nyerere Day cartoon self-published on Facebook by Muhidini Msamba Msamba depicted a hand-drawn

---

31 Msamba, www.facebook.com/muhidinimsamba.msamba (accessed 13 February 2014).

portrait of Nyerere with a caption on it: "The Man Whose Thoughts We Love to Forget!"[32]

In one final cartoon example that employs Nyerere for political critique, the artist FeDë depicts both the sense of jarring historical disjuncture and unsuccessful elite attempts to mask it. In the cartoon, "the period of Nyerere" is drawn as Nyerere the national father feeding a bottle to the suckling Tanzanian citizenry.

This era represents a sharp contrast to both the period of colonialism before it – depicted as a white farmer merrily drinking a bottle as he is pulled in a wagon by "TZ" personified as a child in chains who is also hoeing the earth – and the contemporary moment – depicted as a fat "Leader" urinating on the child Tanzania who is kneeling in a puddle of urine as the "Leader" spouts socialist rhetoric: "…let's continue to join together so that we uphold peace, love, and unity…"). Though the relationship between government and citizenry shows sharp fissures between these three eras, consistencies in political discourse elide discontinuities in governance from socialism to today.

Conclusion

What all of these cartoons suggest is that efforts to create a sense of historical continuity between the neoliberal present and the Nyerere-led past are not entirely – or even mostly – successful. What is significant however across the data from the 2005, 2010, and run-up to the 2015 elections is the fact that the specter of Nyerere structures political rhetoric in important ways. Nyerere becomes a political prism through which time is collapsed and messages distorted. It is this very polysemy of Nyerere symbolism that allows his memory to be used to both sustain the status quo as well as – potentially – to incite radical historical change.

Antonio Gramsci noted that where there is only one political party, the functions of that party "are no longer directly political, but… technical ones of propaganda and public order, and moral and cultural influence" (Gramsci, 1971: 149). The multi-party system in Tanzania is one that centers primarily on the elite of a single dominant party who have taken great pains to produce a rhetoric and practice of paternalism that provides narrative coherence to the political dominance and the socioeconomic disparities that govern Tanzanian lives. The memory of Mwalimu Nyerere serves as a key symbol in this rhetoric that organizes and serves as a referent for its propositions – namely that CCM and its candidates descend directly from Nyerere, that CCM is the only party

---

32 Msamba, www.facebook.com/muhidinimsamba.msamba (accessed 13 February 2014).

mature enough and materially positioned to support its family, and that any outsider trying to assume the role of father will only bring domestic discord to this already happy, unified family. Elites deploy these propositions to assert the common sense that it is naturally a father who can best look after his own child, to confirm rural Tanzanians' sense of themselves as citizens of a socialist gerontocracy, and to produce a sense of historical continuity in a time of volatile transformation.

This contemporary political idiom of paternity organizes and legitimates the political structure in four main ways. First, through its assertions of direct descent from the Nyerere line, CCM proclaims itself the sole heir and executor of Nyerere's political estate, which was secured through his legitimacy as "one who did not fill his own belly." This association complicates and contradicts a reality in which Tanzanians perceive their current leaders to be eating national resources (Phillips, 2009).

Second, CCM candidates draw on shifting, and sometimes contradictory, conceptions of eldership and youth to legitimize their political power. They alternately highlight, on the one hand, their candidates' youthfulness in a political environment that values the skills and attributes of the young, and on the other hand their eldership as candidates of the "father" party in a cultural context in which age carries symbolic weight as an indicator of status, prestige, and authority. In doing so, they map a symbolic gerontocracy and sense of tradition onto a technocracy and its youthful leaders in locally legitimate terms.

Third, CCM continues to rhetorically frame Tanzania as a national family, presided over by CCM, a political "father" who provides "gifts" to his political children. It must be noted that benevolent individuals giving away small commodities like t-shirts and phones during election years from their stores of private or party wealth is a far stretch from Nyerere's benevolent state committed to ensuring egalitarian access to rights or entitlements like education and healthcare. Yet few take serious note of this elision and *takrima* often successfully elicits a certain type of filial deference by citizens with respect to their leaders in both the electoral and local political realms.

Finally, it is the familial rhetoric of fatherhood (age superiority) – and not brotherhood (age equality) – that confers legitimacy on the drastic redistribution of power, national resources, and the burden of labor for national development that has occurred over the course of the last twenty years.

For as Bourdieu notes, in the *State Nobility*,

> There is no barrier more insurmountable than time, and all social bodies use it to maintain *an order of succession* (…) in other words, to maintain the distances that must be kept (…) because they are constitutive of the social order – those that separate tenants and claimants, fathers and sons, owners and heirs, masters and disciples, predecessors and successors, so many social ranks that are very often distinguished by nothing but time (1996: 333).

A narrative of fatherhood produces a discursive distance between Tanzanians and their ruling party that seeks to, and to some extent succeeds in, legitimating the disparities and stratification that mark the post-colonial, post-socialist, and neoliberal present in Tanzania. Through reframing governance and disparity in terms of the hierarchy of home, rather than of nation, political elites subject the distribution of political and economic power to regulation by "cultural" norms rather than political action. They thereby seek to neutralize political debate, rendering issues of political access and resource distribution insoluble by electoral processes.

Through attempting to re-politicize the symbolic terms in which governance and disparity have been framed in Tanzania, my intention is not to delegitimize CCM as a party worthy of power, nor to deny CCM's historical connection to Nyerere and role in post-independence nation-building, nor to glorify 'the opposition' and its potential to transform Tanzanian politics. For the ruling party's political practices today are (and have already been) easily co-opted into opposition politics; in fact most opposition parties are hard-pressed to conduct their political transactions outside the precedents that have been set. But I would like to conclude this essay on a more (cautiously) optimistic note, with the astute words of an opposition supporter from rural Singida: Godfredi, an undereducated man with seven children. Godfredi affirmed the predominance of this paternal narrative even as he contested its logic:

> Many Tanzanians still think of CCM as their father. They say that if you leave your father, whom will you be connected to? And me, I don't agree with this. Today's CCM is not like the father who raised you. CCM saved the Tanzanian from colonialism and from being ruled. But after saving Tanzania, CCM brought a new colonialism, one that I call colonialism of the thought. That means it rules the thoughts of people. We see that

there is no legitimate ruler but CCM. Yet we may choose a member of parliament or a ward councilor and he will look after his own profit more than that of his fellow Tanzanians[33].

To overemphasize the agency of the elite in defining the symbolic terms of politics in Tanzania would be a mistake. For, as Scott reminds us, "a hegemonic ideology must, by definition, represent an idealization, which therefore inevitably creates the contradictions that permit it to be criticized in its own terms" (1985: 317).

Godfredi went on to critique CCM in its own idiom: "Even if you go with the holy words (the Bible), they say that if you marry, you will leave your father and mother to be joined with your wife and you will become one. You will keep helping your parents if you get the good life. You will direct your own family and help your parents because they are your parents." Within this same paternal narrative lie cultural logics that not only affirm a political monopoly, but that also support a politics of autonomy, national dialogue and accountability. What is clear is that if Tanzanians want change, they will either find it inside CCM, or they will search for it outside CCM. And so long as his memory, words, and legacy continue to bring weight to bear on the debates of the day, Nyerere's specter looms.

References

ABÉLÈS, Marc, and Chantal COLLARD. *Age, pouvoir et société en Afrique Noire* [Age, Power, and Society in Black Africa]. Montréal, Paris: Presses de l'Université de Montréal, Karthala, 1985.

ASKEW, Kelly M. *Performing the Nation: Swahili Music and Cultural Politics in Tanzania*. Chicago: University of Chicago Press, 2002.

ASKEW, Kelly M. "Sung and Unsung: Musical Reflections on Tanzanian Postsocialism." *Africa* 76, no. 1 (2006): 15–43.

BAYART, Jean-François. *The State in Africa: The Politics of the Belly*. Heinemann: London, 1993. Originally published in Jean-François Bayard, trans. *L'Etat en Afrique. La politique du ventre* (Paris: Fayard, 1989).

BECKER, Felicitas. "Remembering Nyerere: Political Rhetoric and Dissent in Contemporary Tanzania." *African Affairs* 112, no. 447 (2013): 1–24.

BOURDIEU, Pierre. *State Nobility: Elite Schools in the Field of Power*. Cambridge: Polity Press, 1996. Originally published in Pierre

---

33 Interview, Rural Singida, 15 September 2005.

Bourdieu, trans. *La noblesse d'Etat. Grandes écoles et esprit de corps* (Paris: Editions de Minuit, 1989).

BRENNAN, James. "Julius Rex: Nyerere through the eyes of his critics, 1953-2013." *Journal of Eastern African Studies* 8, no. 3 (2014): 459–477.

CLIGGETT, Lisa. *Grains from Grass: Aging, Gender, and Famine in Rural Africa.* Ithaca: Cornell University Press, 2005.

COLE, Jennifer, and Deborah DURHAM. *Generations and Globalization: Youth, Age, and Family in the New World Economy.* Bloomington: University of Indiana Press, 2006.

FEIERMAN, Steven. *Peasant Intellectuals: Anthropology and History in Tanzania.* Madison: University of Wisconsin Press, 1990.

FERGUSON, James. *Global Shadows: Africa in the Neoliberal World Order.* Durham: Duke University Press, 2006.

FOUÉRÉ, Marie-Aude. "Julius Nyerere, Ujamaa and Political Morality in Contemporary Tanzania." *African Studies Review* 57, no. 1 (2014): 1–24.

FOUÉRÉ, Marie-Aude. "Tanzanie: la nation à l'épreuve du postsocialisme [Tanzania: The Nation Put to the Test of Postsocialism]." *Politique africaine* 121 (2011): 69–85.

FOUÉRÉ, Marie-Aude. "J. K. Nyerere entre mythe et histoire: Analyse de la production d'une culture nationale en Tanzanie post-socialiste [J. K. Nyerere Between Myth and History: An Analysis of the Production of a National Culture in Post-socialist Tanzania]." *Les Cahiers d'Afrique de l'Est* 4 (2009): 197–224.

FOUÉRÉ, Marie-Aude. "La fabrique d'un saint en Tanzanie post-socialiste: Essai d'analyse sur l'Eglise, l'Etat et le premier président Julius Nyerere [Making a Saint in Post-socialist Tanzania: An Tentative Analysis of the Church, The State and First President Julius Nyerere]." *Les Cahiers d'Afrique de l'Est* 39 (Dec., 2008): 47–97.

GRAMSCI, Antonio. *Selections from the Prison Notebooks.* New York: International Publishers, 1971.

HALL, Stuart. "The Problem of Ideology. Marxism without Guarantees." *Journal of Communication Inquiry* 10 (1986): 28–44.

HAUGERUD, Angelique. *The Culture of Politics in Modern Kenya.* Cambridge: Cambridge University Press, 1993.

HERZFELD, Michael. *Cultural Intimacy: Social Poetics in the Nation-State.* New York: Routledge, 1997.

HEILMAN, Bruce, and Paul KAISER. "Religion, Identity, and Politics in Tanzania". *Third World Quarterly* 23, no. 4 (Aug., 2002), pp. 691–709.

JELLICOE, Marguerite. *The Long Path: A Case Study of Social Change in Wahi, Singida District, Tanzania*. Nairobi: East African Publishing Company, 1978.

KELSALL, Tim. "Notes on Recent Elections: The Presidential and Parliamentary Elections in Tanzania, October and December 2005." *Electoral Studies* 26, no. 2 (2007): 525–529.

LAKOFF, George. *Moral Politics: How Liberals and Conservatives Think*. Chicago: University of Chicago Press, 2002.

LOFCHIE, Michael. *The Political Economy of Tanzania: Decline and Recovery*. Philadelphia: University of Pennsylvania Press, 2014.

MAKULILO, Alexander Boniface. "Why the CCM Is Still in Power in Tanzania? A Reply." 24 June 2014. Available at http://ssrn.com/abstract=2458778.Mnganya, Priscilla, and Phyllis Johnson. "We Must Run While Others Walk." *Southern African News Features* 05, no. 46 (May, 2005).

MWAKIKAGILE, Godfrey. *Tanzania Mwalimu under Nyerere. Reflections on an African Statesman*. Pretoria, Dar es Salaam: New Africa Press, 2006 (2nd edition).

National Bureau of Statistics. *Tanzania Demographic and Health Survey*, Dar es Salaam, National Bureau of Statistics, 2002.

NYERERE, Julius. *Ujamaa: Essays on Socialism*. London: Oxford University Press, 1968.

PHILLIPS, Kristin D. "Educational Policymaking in the Tanzanian Postcolony: Authenticity, Accountability and the Politics of Culture." *Critical Studies in Education* 52, no. 3 (2011): 235–250.

PHILLIPS, Kristin D. "Pater Rules Best: Political Kinship and Party Politics in Tanzania's Presidential Elections." *PoLAR: Political & Legal Anthropology Review* 33, no. 2 (2010): 109–132.

PHILLIPS, Kristin D. "Hunger, Healing, and Citizenship in Rural Tanzania." *African Studies Review* 52, no. 1 (2009): 23–45.

SCHATZBERG, Michael. *Political Legitimacy in Middle Africa: Father, Family, Food*. Bloomington: Indiana University Press, 2001.

SCOTT, James. *Domination and the Arts of Resistance: Hidden Transcripts*, New Haven, Yale University Press, 1990.

SCOTT, James. *Weapons of the Weak: Everyday Forms of Peasant Resistance*, New Haven, Yale University Press, 1985.

STROEKEN, Koen. "Immunizing Strategies: Hip-Hop and Critique in Tanzania." *Africa* 75, no. 4 (2005): 488–509.

TEMCO. *The Report of the 2010 General Elections in Tanzania*. Dar es Salaam: University of Dar es Salaam, 2011.

WAGNER, Gunter. "The Political Organization of the Bantu of Kavirondo." In *African Political Systems*, ed. Meyer Fortes and Edward E. Evans-Pritchard: 56–82. Oxford: Oxford University Press, 1940.

WOLF, Eric. *Envisioning Power: Ideologies of Dominance and Crisis.* Berkeley: University of California Press, 1999.

Chapter 6

Different 'Uses of Nyerere' in the Constitutional Review Debates: A Touchstone For Legitimacy in Tanzania

Aikande Kwayu

"There are many good and honest people who believe that those ideas, which in this country are associated with my name are now dead and should be properly buried. You will not be surprised to hear that I disagree! Great ideas do not die so easily; they continue nagging and every human society in history ignores them at its own peril..." (Julius Nyerere)

Tanzania is currently reviewing its Constitution promulgated in 1977. This constitution-making process is carried out under the Constitutional Review Act of 2011. The Act provisions include the establishment of the national Constitutional Review Commission (CRC)[1] for the purpose of coordinating and collecting public opinions. It has thus provided a mechanism through which Tanzanian citizens could widely and freely participate in expressing and transmitting their views and preferences on matters relating to the nation's 1977 Constitution through public fora organized throughout the country in 2012-2013. The Commission also consulted various groups in the society including civil society organisations, academic communities, and faith-based communities. These opinions were at the basis of the first draft of the Constitution, which was submitted to the public in June 2013. Councils were created at the district level – with members elected from the level of villages and streets to the ward level – in order to discuss and comment upon the draft Constitution. This led to the drafting of a second Constitution document, which the Commission presented to the President of Tanzania, Jakaya Mrisho Kikwete, in December 2013. This second

---

1 The CRC was formed on 6th April 2012, with retired judge Joseph Warioba as its Chairman.

draft was taken to the Constituent Assembly (CA)[2] on 18th March 2014. Thus, there have been three major platforms of debate about the new Constitution: the public, the councils, and the Constituent Assembly.

In all of these debates, the name of Mwalimu Julius Kambarage Nyerere has come up again and again. The ideas and words of the first President of Tanzania, and Father of the Nation, have indeed been summoned to either legitimize one group's position concerning changes in the Constitution, or to delegitimize the stand and argument of the other factions. Nyerere's speeches and decisions have been used not only as a moral authority but also as a justification to debate the country's destiny, and most notably the structure of the Union government. This chapter gives a brief account, with examples, of the use of the figure of Nyerere in the ongoing debates about the constitutional review. It presents how different parties involved in these debates have appropriated Nyerere to support their arguments or to dismiss others' arguments. The chapter highlights the living legacy of Nyerere that is still vividly influential on the country's destiny 15 years after his death.

Background

Following the re-introduction of a multiparty system in Tanzania in the early 1990s, concerns have grown over the slowness of Tanzania's opposition to effectively challenge the ruling party and former single party, Chama Cha Mapinduzi (CCM, the Party of the Revolution). CCM has won all elections since the first multiparty general election in 1995, thus commanding the majority from the levels of village authorities to the levels of Parliament and the Executive.

As a result, the opposition has been complaining and arguing that its failure to take power is due to structural factors, most of them instituted in the country's Constitution. They complain that Tanzania's 1977 Constitution gives the President too much power, including the power to select the Chairman of the National Elections Commission (NEC). The enactment of the Political Parties Act (1992) and the consequent constitutional amendments led to the establishment of NEC in 1993 as an autonomous government body under Article 74 (1) of the Constitution. According to it, the President appoints NEC members. One of the most important roles of NEC is to supervise and co-ordinate the conduct of the presidential and parliamentary elections.[3] The opposition political

---

2   The CA includes all Members of Parliament and 201 Members appointed by the President from different groups in Tanzanian society.

3   See NEC website at http://www.nec.go.tz/index.php

parties have thus been demanding for a review of the 1977 Constitution as far back as 2001.⁴ This demand created public pressure that President Kikwete decided to heed. In 2011 he announced that he would form a commission to collect public views on a new Constitution.

The second draft of the Constitution taken to the Constituent Assembly on 18ᵗʰMarch 2014 addresses several topics that have been the subject of debates since then. These include the structure of the Union government, Tanzanian citizenship (dual or single), the appointment of Cabinet Members and eligibility criteria, and presidential powers. However, the topic of attention has so far been the structure of the Union between Tanzania mainland (former Tanganyika) and Zanzibar. It has been a burning issue which has divided the CA along the lines of party affiliations. The central question revolves around how the Union should be structured in the new Constitution. At the moment, the Union is organized in a two-tier government arrangement. This includes the main government (also called the Union government) and the government of Zanzibar (or Revolutionary Government of Zanzibar). The main government takes care of the Union matters, including all of the mainland governance, while the government of Zanzibar is in charge of the Isles⁵ governance. According to the government's official website, "the Government of the United Republic of Tanzania is a unitary republic… All state authority in the United Republic is exercised and controlled by the Government of the United Republic of Tanzania and the Revolutionary Government of Zanzibar. Each Central Government has three organs: the Executive; the Judiciary; and the Legislature that have powers over the conduct of public affairs".⁶ This description states that the government is unitary yet explains the functions of two separate governments. This confusion is reflected in today's constitutional review debates. As a result, a new institutional arrangement is being debated.

Three different type of structures have been under scrutiny by different groups, each of them making use of the figure of Julius Nyerere to ground their views.

---

4 See http://www.panapress.com/Opposition-parties-rally-for-a-new-constitution--13-561812-18-lang2-index.html. Earlier efforts to modify the Constitution took place since 1977 but never led to a thorough constitutional review.

5 The archipelago of Zanzibar is composed of two main islands, Pemba and Unguja, commonly referred to as "the Isles" (*visiwa* in Swahili).

6 See http://www.tanzania.go.tz/home/pages/1

The first type is to keep the status quo by maintaining the current two-tier government. Its promoters are led by CCM as a political party and by President Kikwete as its Chairman. It makes use of Nyerere literally, quoting Nyerere's political discourses in which the former President showed as an unflinching defender of a two-government structure, the government of the Union and the government of Zanzibar. To this group, maintaining the existing system is seen as the only way to preserve the Union.[7]

The second structure that some CA members advocate for is a three-tier government. This second group includes members of the Constitutional Review Commission. Their vision is represented in the draft Constitution defending the creation of a government of Tanganyika alongside the government of Zanzibar and the Union government. They argue that Nyerere's stand with regard to the Union structure should not be frozen and that the three-tier government is the only structure that will maintain what Nyerere had initiated – a true Union. This group, therefore, argues that Nyerere was a progressive and that Tanzanian politicians should walk in Nyerere's progressive footstep by adapting the Constitution to present needs.

The third type of structure discussed, defended by the opposition group Umoja wa Katiba ya Wananchi (UKAWA, the Coalition for People's Constitution), is a modified three-tier government. UKAWA gathers members of the strongest opposition parties in the country, including CUF (Civic United Union), CHADEMA (Chama cha Demokrasia na Maendeleo, Party for Democracy and Progress), and NCCR-Mageuzi (National Convention for Construction and Reform-Changes). This third group is critical of Nyerere. Questioning the legitimacy of the Union, they requested to see the original Articles of the Union, that is, the Union agreement document signed on 22nd April 1964 by the President of Tanganyika, Julius Nyerere and the President of the People's Republic of Zanzibar and Pemba, Abeid Amani Karume. UKAWA even questioned the authenticity of the two heads of state's signatures on the document. As a response, the Government Chief Secretary, Mr. Ombeni Sefue, announced during a 14th April 2014 press conference that the government would release the Articles to the public for the first time in the history of the Union.[8] He then showed the

---

7 See "Constitution should reflect Nyerere's principles", *The Guardian*, 14 October 2014.

8 "Revealed: The Articles of the Union", *The Citizen*, 16 April 2014, accessible at http://www.thecitizen.co.tz/News/Revealed--The-Articles-of-the-Union/-/1840392/2281240/-/11w3km6/-/index.html

document to the journalists.⁹ *The Citizen* newspaper cited Mr. Sefue's statement that "the move was to show the proof of the existence of an agreement by Mwalimu Nyerere and Sheikh Karume to establish one sovereign country contrary to claims by some members of the CA that it did not exist".¹⁰ Yet the question of the authenticity of the signatures, especially Karume's signature that appeared to some as a fake, has remained unresolved, and still looms over current debates at the CA. I will now present in greater detail the position of each of these three factions currently involved in the current heated debates about the Tanzanian Union structure, and give insight into how they appropriate – or sometimes reject – the legacy of Nyerere to both advocate for and legitimize their views.

'Nyerere said this… and so it should stay that way'

The first group composed mainly of CCM as a political party has been using Nyerere to support their argument of maintaining the status quo of the Union structure. For them, the existing two-tier government should remain as it is because both former Presidents Nyerere and Karume carefully pondered its creation and put a lot of thought into it when it was adopted in 1964. The fact that this structure has survived for 50 years, and that it has fostered national unity and peace, are brandished as signs of the Union's good health. The Union between former Tanganyika and the Isles of Zanzibar is also seen as a successful outcome of efforts towards unity on the African continent, which had accompanied the early postcolonial times, and therefore a symbol of Pan-Africanism. Discussions on social media networks, in particular tweets by pro-CCM people, reverberate Nyerere's statement that we were all born Tanzanians. In 1995, Nyerere wrote: "[t]he reality is that the vast majority of the present citizens of our country were born and brought up in Tanzania – a country now 30 years old. No one has ever lived in an independent and 'sovereign' Tanganyika for more than 29 months, or an independent 'sovereign' Zanzibar for more than five months. There is no evidence at all that in either part of the Union they are dissatisfied with the Union; there is much evidence that they are dissatisfied with very many economic and social matters" (Nyerere, 1995: 6).

---

9   Shekighenda L. "Articles of the Union in House Today." IPP Media, 15 April 2014, accessible at http://www.ippmedia.com/frontend/?l=66910

10 http://www.thecitizen.co.tz/News/Revealed--The-Articles-of-the-Union/-/1840392/2281240/-/11w3km6/-/index.html

It is noticeable that the proponents of a two-tier government have challenged the statistics about the Union structure that resulted from the public consultations conducted by the Constitutional Review Commission in 2013. They did so by asserting that these statistics, which were publicly presented by the Commission, would not represent the real picture of citizens' opinion.[11] People both from the mainland (39,000 in total) and Zanzibar (38,000 in total) participated in the polls on the Union. According to the Commission, in the mainland 3,510 (13%) preferred one government, 6,480 (24%) two governments, and 16,470 (61%) three governments. In Zanzibar, 25 persons (0.001%) wanted one government, 11,400 (60%) wanted a contract government, and 6,460 (34%) wanted two governments. According to political scientist from the University of Dar es Salaam (UDSM), Sabatho Nyamsenda, the total number of Tanzanians who want either one or two governments (to which he includes people who have not expressed any opinion about the structure of the Union, for not mentioning it can, in his views, be equated with approving the structure as it is) exceeds the total of those who want a three-tier government (27,800 people out of the total 77,000 Tanzanians surveyed on the Union). Nyamsenda also argued that the sampling was not valid, saying: "[t]here isn't any scientific research which shows that a sample of 16,000 (people) can represent the opinion of 45 million Tanzanians".[12] On the heated issue of the sampling, Kitila Mkumbo, an associate professor at UDSM also insisted that the data collection sampling was not scientific. He contended that the 47,820 citizens who the Commission claimed to have surveyed on the question of the Tanzanian government structure were not systematically or randomly sampled; rather, they were people who voluntarily attended the public consultation sessions. He argued that the method used, which he calls "convenience sampling", is not an acceptable method in scientific survey or opinion polls.[13] On their side, CCM has been arguing that their position in maintaining the current structure of the Union is the strongest at the national level because the party has wide membership across the country. Nyerere himself had

---

11 http://udadisi.blogspot.com/2013/12/mlizingatia-maoni-ya-nani-jaji-warioba.html

12 See Nyamsenda, Sabatho. "Mlizingatia Maoni ya Nani, Warioba?" 31 December 2013, available http://udadisi.blogspot.fr/2013/12/mlizingatia-maoni-ya-nani-jaji-warioba.html. The original Swahili quotation is: "Pia hakuna utafiti wowote wa kisayansi unaoonyesha kuwa sampuli ya watu 16,000 inaweza kuwakilisha maoni ya Watanzania million 45."

13 See Mkumbo K. "Uhalali wa Kitafiti wa Maoni ya Wananchi Tume ya Warioba." 25 March 2014 available http://www.wavuti.com/2014/03/mkumbo-uhalali-wa-kitafiti-wa-maoni-ya.html

strong opinions about the validity of nationwide popular consultations. In his book, *Our Leadership and The Destiny of Tanzania* published in 1995, Nyerere argued that "[t]he 'sample' of citizens who expressed their views through CCM machinery is so very much larger than the 'sample' taken in the more fashionable 'Public Opinion Polls' (most of which ignore the majority who live in the rural areas) that the less random nature of the interviewees is completely outweighed" (Nyerere, 1995: 6). Although challenges to the Commission's statistics are made in relation to two different scientific bases (one concerned with scientific representativeness through sampling, the other focused on the total number of people surveyed), both scholars and CCM members point to the same conclusion: the statistics of the Commission are not powerful enough to support the creation of a three-tier government structure.

Apart from heated debates about the methods used by the Commission to conduct the public consultations and produce statistics, the reliance on the figure of Nyerere has been a strategy to defend the position that the current structure of the Union should not be modified. Some of the statements in the Constituent Assembly made by January Yusuf Makamba,[14] a CCM Member of Parliament (MP) and also Deputy Minister for Science and Technology, capture this group's use of Nyerere. Makamba is one of the vibrant upcoming CCM politicians who portrays himself as modern young CCM member but at the same time highly faithful to the values and ideas cherished by the party. On 15th April 2014, during a session of the Constituent Assembly, Makamba declared: "we (CCM) have been blamed here for quoting Nyerere too much... but he is one of the founders of the Union, and he wrote a book about the Union... so I do not know who else we are supposed to cite?" He then added that although some say that Nyerere's ideas had changed over time and that Nyerere himself admitted some of his mistakes, "there (was) one thing certain: it is that when he died he was still a member of CCM, and when he died he had not changed his ideas on a two-tier Union structure."[15] By these words, Makamba was underlining that the

14 Before becoming an MP in 2010, Makamba was President Kikwete's speechwriter. He has often claimed that President Kikwete is his political mentor. In his tweeter account and blog, Politics, Society, and Things, Makamba often posts pictures of him and Kikwete as well as entries on his time as a Foreign Affairs staff under Kikwete's leadership (when Kikwete was then Minister) and as Kikwete's speechwriter when Kikwete became president in 2010 (see notably "Times in the Presidency: The Teleprompter Magic", 29 July 2013, by Makamba, available http://taifaletu.blogspot.fr/2013/07/times-in-presidency-teleprompter-magic.html). On 2nd July 2014, in a BBC Swahili DIRA TV program, Makamba announced his intention to run as a CCM presidential candidate in the 2015 elections.

15 https://www.youtube.com/watch?feature=player_embedded&v=sCJGL9GZog8. The original Swahili quotation is: "Tunaambiwa kwamba Mwalimu Nyerere alikuwa hana mawazo

CCM has the right to refer to the ideas Nyerere had stood for because these ideas were the legacy he had left to Tanzanians.

President Kikwete himself strategically, and in a convoluted way, used the figure of Nyerere to legitimize his position on the draft Constitution. When he delivered his controversial opening speech to the CA on 19th March 2014, President Kikwete had invited Mama Maria, Julius Nyerere's widow, to attend the session. According to the observer and critic of Tanzanian political life Chambi Chachage, Tanzania's President did so to give his main argument insistence, legitimacy, authority, and power.[16] Interestingly, different political factions have been trying to relate to Mama Maria in attempts to show solidarity or closeness to Mwalimu Nyerere's family and ideals. These efforts to, in a way, appropriate Mama Maria are exemplified by a tweet by January Makamba. Makamba posted a picture of CHADEMA's leaders Dr. Willbrod Slaa (Secretary General) and Mr. Freeman Mbowe (Chairman) sitting with Mama Maria, to which he added the caption 'Subliminal'.[17] In the picture Mama Maria wears a green dress while Slaa and Mbowe are wearing the CHADEMA's attires (*gwanda*). The caption is indicative that Makamba thinks the opposition is not entitled to associate with Mama Maria; that they try to do so is, to him, laughable.

Source: https://twitter.com/JMakamba/status/459239658866892800/photo/1
From left to right: Freeman Mbowe, Maria Nyerere, Willbrod Slaa.

---

mgando, alikuwa anabadilisha mawazo, alikiri makosa. Ni kweli. Lakini jambo moja la uhakika ni kwamba alikufa akiwa bado ni mwana CCM, na alikufa akiwa hajabadili mawazo yake kuhusu muundo wa serikali mbili..." (from 9 min 10 sec).

16 Chachage, Chambi. "Uhalali wa Hotuba na Uzito wa Hoja ya Rais." UDADISI Blog, 23 March 2014 http://udadisi.blogspot.com/2014/03/uhalali-wa-hotuba-na-uzito-wa-hoja-ya.html

17 See https://twitter.com/JMakamba/status/459239658866892800/photo/1

'Nyerere cannot be frozen... he was progressive'

The Constitutional Review Commission led by retired Judge Joseph Warioba composes the majority of the group advocating for the establishment of a three-tier government. Some CA members who have not identified themselves with any political party also belong to this group. This group, in particular some commissioners, have been accused of betraying Nyerere for saying he was progressive. Thus, Captain John Komba, a retired army officer and CCM MP, lamented that "Why do I categorically charge the trio (that is: Joseph Warioba,[18] Salim Ahmed Salim,[19] and Joseph Butiku[20])? They were among the closest aides of Mwalimu Nyerere… they applauded Mwalimu before anyone… they ate *ugali* and bread and drank tea with him… they know exactly Mwalimu died believing in the two-government system. How on earth are they abandoning it".[21] In response to such accusations and in defence to their position, Warioba, who also worked closely with Mwalimu Nyerere and is a Board member of the Mwalimu Nyerere Foundation (MNF) led by Joseph Butiku, replied: "Nyerere did not have frozen ideas, he followed time and those who are saying that we have betrayed him are the ones who have betrayed him. Mwalimu left the Union government intact; he left when there was one Union parliament, when there was one Union judiciary with complete authority; he left when only one president was saluted, but now it is two presidents. The Union government that Mwalimu left has been disrupted. Mwalimu should not be used like *hirizi*.[22] Are they doing what Mwalimu wanted them to do? Mwalimu was protecting the Constitution".[23]

---

18 Joseph Warioba served in various high government positions during Nyerere's administration, notably as Attorney General in 1976-1983 and Minister of Justice 1983-1985. He also served as Prime Minister under President Ali Hassan Mwinyi's administration. Under President Benjamin Mkapa, he chaired the Anti Corruption Commission famously known as 'Warioba Commission'.

19 Salim A. Salim is a renowned diplomat. Under Nyerere's administration he served as Tanzanian ambassador in various countries and also in the UN. In 1981 he bid for the UN Secretary General. He also served as Prime Minister in the last two years of Nyerere administration between 1984 and 1985. He was the Secretary General for the Organization of African Union (OAU) from 1989 to 2001.

20 Joseph Butiku is the Executive Director and Trustee of Mwalimu Nyerere Foundation. He was President Nyerere's Personal Research Assistant and Chief of Staff and Personal Envoy. He also served as Principal Private Secretary and Chief of Staff under President Mwinyi.

21 Mtulya, A. "Komba vows to embark on a rebellion if proposal sails through in assembly." The Citizen, 25 April 2014, available at http://www.thecitizen.co.tz/News/Komba-vows-to-embark-on-a-rebellion-if-proposal-/-/1840392/2292492/-/14c623b/-/index.html.

22 *Hirizi* is the Swahili word for charm or amulet.

23 https://www.youtube.com/watch?v=1p7AS_MeVuw: "Mwalimu hakuwa na mawazo mgando… alikuwa anafata wakati ulivyo. Hao wanaosema hivyo ndio wamemsaliti Mwalimu…

With these words, Warioba argued that with the changes that already took place in Zanzibar,[24] Mwalimu would not – if he was still alive – defend conceptions of the Union structure similar to those he had in his lifetime. The Union structure he left is undeniably different from the one in place today. The argument put to the fore here is that Nyerere was not adamant about his ideas. Indeed, experience has proven that Nyerere was ready to change whenever seemed appropriate or inevitable. For instance in the early 1990s he supported the reintroduction of a multiparty system, which he had opposed earlier on the basis that when a fledging nation-state is in the very first steps of taking shape, it cannot take the risk of internal contest and dissension. Indeed, Nyerere had long viewed a one-party state as a means for protecting Tanzania from factionalism. To him, fully open competition between rival parties could open the way to ethnic, racial, regional divisions, arguing that "[t]his is our time of emergency, and until our war against poverty, ignorance and disease has been won, we should not let our unity be destroyed by a desire to follow somebody else 'books of rules'" (Nyerere, 1961). On this, Prof. Mohabe Nyirabu observed that "in February 1990, Nyerere, the architect of one-party rule, made an acrobatic U-turn and proclaimed that it was no longer treasonable to discuss the introduction of multi-party politics. Tanzania, like the rest of the world, would be affected by the democratic changes sweeping across the globe and thus he advised his party and government to be primed for the changes" (2002).[25] He cites Nyerere's statement that "When you see your neighbour being shaved, wet your head to avoid a dry shave. The one party is not Tanzania's ideology and having one party is not God's will. One-party has its limitation". In 1992, Nyerere pushed CCM arguing "CCM can and should welcome the opportunity to give a lead in yet another major peaceful political transition in our country. We have an opportunity to ensure that this change happens democratically under rules to provide for genuine democracy. This is a moment when Tanzania under CCM can choose to change and oversee that change, rather than be made to

---

Mwalimu ametuachia Muungano ambapo Bunge la Muungano lilikuwa na madaraka kamili, mahakama ilikuwa na madaraka kamili, aliacha nchi moja wakati anaondoka Mwalimu mizinga ilikuwa inapigiwa rais mmoja lakini sasa ni wawili.... Mwalimu alikuwa analinda katiba. Nilisema Mwalimu asitumiwe kama hirizi..." (mins 26:38 to 28:57).

24 In 2010 Zanzibar amended its Constitution to give the Isles increased autonomy within the Union. Zanzibar now has its own flag, national anthem, and a government with its Constitution. These were not in the 1964 agreements. Also listen to Warioba explaining the changes in https://www.youtube.com/watch?v=1p7AS_MeVuw (from mins 27:32 onwards).

25 See also "Nyerere Calls for Multi-Party System", *Daily Nation*, 23 February 1990.

change".[26] Similarly, his ideas on farming cooperatives changed over time – he abolished all farming cooperatives in 1976 only to bring them back in 1982 (Savage, Guderyon and Jordan, 1982).[27]

'Nyerere cannot be used in the current situation… He is not relevant'

The third group is led by UKAWA, a coalition of opposition parties (CHADEMA, CUF, and NCCR). UKAWA has boycotted debates at the Constituent Assembly. The group walked out one week before the last CA session and has refused to go back in the second session that resumed on 5th August 2014. There have been attempts and mediations efforts to bring back UKAWA to the Assembly. The mediation efforts have included faith leaders and a prominent lawyer from Nairobi, Professor Patrick Lumumba. This group argues that Nyerere's ideas are no longer relevant today and that Nyerere had not always been right. Tundu Lissu, an outspoken CHADEMA MP, the Party's chief whip and UKAWA's main spokesperson –is a known trained lawyer with reputable experience in working with the civil society in legal issues on areas of tax and natural resources. He has cited Nyerere's booklet, titled *Tujisahihishe* (1962) in which Nyerere spoke about the importance of acknowledging mistakes. To add on that, Lissu also referred to Nyerere's words that "CCM is not my mother". He further observed that "the Father of the Nation was a human being, he was not a god, neither an angel, and he is not yet a saint[28]… he recognized Biafra and he was wrong".[29] To say that the Father of the Nation was wrong, citing the Biafra case, is unprecedented in the Tanzanian Assembly.

There have been a few Tanzanian political figures, such as Reverend Christopher Mtikila, Chairman of the Democratic Party (DP), who have openly and harshly criticized Nyerere. During the CA session, Mtikila often asserted that the Union between Zanzibar and Tanganyika was never legitimate and that Tanganyika should be on its own.[30] Yet,

---

26 "Address to CCM Extra-Ordinary Congress", *Daily News*, 29 February 1992 (Nyirabu, 2002).

27 See also Mbowe's speech at Parliament: https://www.youtube.com/watch?v=n1c1IIX2ZOo (mins 5:50-6:10).

28 There is a process of canonization of Nyerere underway, which started in 2007 as announced by Cardinal Pengo, see http://thepatrioticvanguard.com/spip.php?article1082

29 https://www.youtube.com/watch?v=4Yvp-8AKWgc. "Baba wa Taifa aliyekuwa mwenyekiti mwanzilishi wa CCM alisema, 'CCM si mama yangu'… Baba wa Taifa alikuwa binadamu, hakuwa Mungu, hakuwa malaika, na hajawa mtakatifu bado… Baba wa Taifa aliwahi kuunga mkono Jamhuri ya Biafra, alikosea, hakuwa Mungu, alikosea" (from mins 1:12-2:11).

30 See for example Juma, M. "Mtikila: Warioba kanirahisishia kazi ya kuifufua Tanganyika", Mwananchi, 21 April 2014.

Lissu's statement came as a shock to many. Even his party chairman, Freeman Mbowe, had to clear this matter up by stating that what they were questioning is why the government did not bring the Articles of the Union to the Assembly while committee members were demanding it?[31] In the same speech Mbowe explained that the Father of the Nation, whom everyone refers to a lot, acknowledged his mistakes such as to abolish cooperative societies and local governments.[32] CHADEMA fears it might be labelled as a party opposed to Nyerere's legacy. It could be politically counter-productive and even a threat to their political survival, seeing how much Nyerere is remembered and recalled in a positive way in Tanzania mainland (Askew, 2006; Fouéré, 2014 and in this volume), in spite of existing dissent (Becker, 2013). To remedy Lissu's controversial statement, an UKAWA delegation led by CHADEMA's Secretary General, Dr. Willbrod Slaa, visited Mama Maria Nyerere at her home in Butiama, where Nyerere's mausoleum is built, in 21st May 2014. During this visit, Dr. Slaa warned that people should not use Nyerere hypocritically. He argued that in the Constitutional Review Process, people should uphold Nyerere's ideals by actions through writing a Constitution that respect people's will and the nation's interests.[33] On 6th July 2014, in an interview with *Mwananchi* newspaper, Dr. Slaa again mentioned Mwalimu Nyerere in an effort to support UKAWA's position. He cited a speech by Nyerere in June 1965, stating: "It will be stupid if people believe that the Constitution is unchangeable, even if it has been established that it does not serve the citizens' need at that time".[34] He thus questioned the CCM's basis for rejecting change in the Constitution if Mwalimu himself had insisted, as early as 1965, that a Constitution can be changed to reflect the will and needs of citizens.

---

31 https://www.youtube.com/watch?v=n1c1IIX2ZOo: "Mheshimiwa Mwenyekiti natoa ufananuzi huu.... kwa umuhimu wa Hati hii na kwa umuhimu wa mjadala huu... tunahoji tu ni nini kimeizuia serikali isilete taarifa hiyo mapema tangu imedaiwa na vikao vya Bunge" (mins 1:39-3:10).

32 https://www.youtube.com/watch?v=n1c1IIX2ZOo: "Baba wa Taifa ambaye tunamrefer sana katika mazungumzo na uwasilishaji wetu mahali hapa... alikuwa na tabia ya kukiri ukweli, Baba wa Taifa alikiri tulifanya makosa kuua vyama vya ushirika, Baba wa Taifa alikiri kuwa tulifanya makosa kuuwa serikali za mitaa" (mins 5:50-6:15).

33 See http://ukomboz.blogspot.com/2014/05/ukawa-wakutana-na-mama-maria-nyerere.html

34 Yamola, I. and E. Kachenje, "Slaa: Rais Kikwete ana rungu la Katiba Mpya", Mwananchi, 6 July 2014, available at http://www.mwananchi.co.tz/habari/Kitaifa/Slaa--Rais-Kikwete-ana-rungu-la-Katiba-Mpya/-/1597296/2373664/-/item/1/-/gnytmg/-/index.html: "Itakuwa upumbavu kama watu wataamini kwamba katiba haibadiliki, hata kama imedhihirika kuwa haitoshelezi tena haja ya wananchi kwa wakati ule."

He also challenged CCM politicians, asserting that they cannot ground their views on the Union structure on the basis of Mwalimu's ideals.[35]

The cartoon by Masoud Kipanya, a reputed Tanzanian cartoonist, aptly captures the centrality of Nyerere in the CA debates. The depiction that they will not accept anybody's call to return to the Assembly expect if it comes from Nyerere is a clear indication of how 'alive' Mwalimu Nyerere is in the ongoing Constitutional Review process.

Source: Masoud Kipanya, 6/7/2014, published in Mwananchi Newspaper, http://www.mwananchi.co.tz/Picha/-/1597602/2367674/-/3nmg4tz/-/index.html#leaf

Conclusion

The debates between the three factions advocating for a different Union structure in the CA debates underline the centrality of Mwalimu Nyerere and his ideas in the Constitutional Review Process. Although only one group takes Mwalimu's ideas literally, the remaining two groups are also engaging with his ideas – whether to appropriate them or to contest them. This leads us to what Marie-Aude Fouéré (2014, and in this volume) says of Nyerere being used as a "moral toolbox" in which people draw ideas, values, notions to debate about politics and morality in contemporary Tanzania. Every group attempts to show that they revere Nyerere and his ideas more than the others. This explains why Warioba asked: "Who is betraying Nyerere between them (the other groups) and

---

35 Ibid.

us?"[36] Similarly, CCM seeks to show that changing the Union structure from a two-tier to a three-tier government would be betraying Nyerere. Thus Nyerere becomes the moral mirror through which these debates find legitimacy. It is important, however, to underline that the parties in the debates are using Nyerere only as an 'object' of justification. Each of them, in particular CCM and UKAWA, has its own political interests in defending a certain type of Union government. In this light, Nyerere is only used to provide moral and political legitimacy for the attainment of prosaic political interests. All in all, the legacy of Nyerere as a moral leader, as the Father of the Nation, and a point of reference in key national decisions is still alive.

References

ASKEW, Kelly M. "Sung and Unsung: Musical Reflections on Tanzanian Postsocialism." *Africa* 76, no. 1 (2006): 15–43.

BECKER, Felicitas. "Remembering Nyerere: Political Rhetoric and Dissent in Contemporary Tanzania." *African Affairs* 112, no. 447 (2013): 1–24.

FOUÉRÉ, Marie-Aude. "Julius Nyerere, Ujamaa and Political Morality in Contemporary Tanzania." *African Studies Review* 57, no. 1 (2014): 1–24.

NYERERE, Julius K. *Africa Today and Tomorrow*. Dar es Salaam: Mwalimu Nyerere Foundation, 2000 (2nd ed.).

NYERERE, Julius K. *Our Leadership and the Destiny of Tanzania*. Harare: Zimbabwe Publishing House, 1995.

NYERERE, Julius K. *Tujisahihishe*. Dar es Salaam, 1962 [Let's Correct Ourselves].

NYIRABU, Mohabe. "The Multiparty Reform Process in Tanzania: The Dominance of the Ruling Party." *African Journal of Political Science* 7, no. 2 (2002): 99–112.

SAVAGE Job K., Newton J. GUDERYON and Harold P. JORDAN. "Review of Cooperative Development in Tanzania as it Relates to Agriculture." Dar es Salaam: ACDI, December 1982.

---

36 See https://www.youtube.com/watch?v=1p7AS_MeVuw when Warioba talks about the constitutional review commission's statistics and the changes in Zanzibar while defending the findings and the arguments for a three-tier government structure (from mins 12:04- 15:04).

PART 4:

Julius Nyerere & His Critics

Chapter 7

Julius Rex: Nyerere through the Eyes of His Critics, 1953-2013

James R. Brennan

> But when I tell him he hates flatterers, He says he does, being then most flattered.
> *Julius Caesar*, II.1.208

Upon his death on 14th October 1999, a wave of fulsome obituaries praised the life and work of Julius Kambarage Nyerere, Tanzania's first president and "father of the nation" (*Baba wa Taifa*). South Africa's ANC declared Nyerere "an outstanding leader, a brilliant philosopher and a people's hero – a champion for the entire African continent".[1] The journalist Richard Gott described him as "an extraordinarily benign and charismatic figure unequalled on the world stage".[2] Western leaders were only slightly less effusive. Bill Clinton declared Nyerere "a pioneering leader for freedom and self-government in Africa"; Tony Blair described him as "a leading African statesman of his time" and credited Tanzania's peace as "in large part a tribute to Mwalimu". Among frequent descriptors were *modest, untainted, idealistic, honest, tireless, bright, wise,* and *compassionate*. Yet most writers also acknowledged Tanzania's dire economic difficulties.

---

* This text was first published in the *Journal of Eastern African Studies*, vol. 8, no. 3 (2014), pp. 459–477. It is reprinted with permission. The author wishes to thank Marie-Aude Fouéré, Tom Molony, and the anonymous reviewers of *Journal of Eastern African Studies* for their helpful comments.
1 African National Congress statement on the death of Julius Nyerere, 14 October 1999, *ANC* Department of Information and Publicity, at Nyerere Foundation website www.juliusnyerere.info, accessed on 19 February 2013.
2 Letter of Richard Gott, *Guardian*, 18 October 1999.

The *Times* best summarized what remains today the conventional wisdom on Nyerere:

> As a statesman Nyerere achieved a reputation for personal incorruptibility and principled dealings which made him stand out among post-independence African leaders. But his experiment in agricultural socialism, with its collectivization of traditional farming methods, was over-ambitious and ultimately disastrous.[3]

Not all obituaries were sympathetic. Conservatives indicted Nyerere's political philosophy by stressing the authoritarian wreckage that his policies had wrought. David Frum, later infamous for coining the phrase 'axis of evil' as George W. Bush's speech-writer, judged that Nyerere's moniker, the "conscience of Africa", was "overgenerous praise for a man who presided over a one-party dictatorship, plunged his country into socialist poverty and built a corruption-plagued bureaucracy, but everything is relative".[4] However, one obituary stands out for its unrestrained hostility. Anthony Daniels, a British psychiatrist and conservative commentator better known by his pen name Theodore Dalrymple, wrote:

> JULIUS Kabarege [sic] Nyerere, for 25 years the president of Tanzania, has died aged 77 of leukaemia in London... Despite a poor education [sic], he was cultured enough to translate Shakespeare's Julius Caesar and The Merchant of Venice into Swahili. But, though he was widely admired and even revered as a secular saint in the West, his influence was almost wholly evil and pernicious... He was able to preserve his reputation for wisdom and saintliness in the West because he shrewdly realized that, to assuage its guilt for its slave-trading and colonial past, the West had need of an African hero. He also recognized that his audience would be far more interested in what he said than in what he did and had no interest at all in the reality of the Tanzania he had created. Nyerere was an African spin doctor. Even Tony Blair was taken in.

Daniels belittles Nyerere's honorific title, *Mwalimu* ("Teacher"), as "certainly a Professor of Poverty", and concludes that the best that can be said for him was "that he could have been worse . . . [c]apable of

---

3 Obituary of Julius Nyerere, *Times*, 15 October 1999.

4 David Frum, "Nyerere's failed vision leaves lasting debt", *National Post* (Ontario), 16 October 1999.

ruthlessness, he was nevertheless not bloodthirsty, and in the context of postcolonial Africa that was no small virtue".[5]

By dramatically dissenting from the positive consensus, Daniels' obituary resonates with an unstudied but significant body of Nyerere criticism that dates from the mid-1950s. Moreover, such heated attacks have not disappeared in the years since his death, as Nyerere's political legacy continues to come under broad challenges informed by the thought and writings of his critics, ranging from the pettily personal to the robustly philosophical. The stakes of that debate are high, not only for those who oppose Tanzania's embrace of economic liberalization, which Nyerere deplored, but also because contemporary political debate continues to conflate Nyerere, as 'father of the nation', with Tanzania's larger national character.

This article examines and contextualizes three distinct groups of Nyerere critics – paternalist Anglo-American elites who sought to influence the path of Tanzania's decolonization; a later generation of Western anti-socialist writers; and exiled or imprisoned Tanzanian political opponents. This is far from an exhaustive survey, for it omits other foreign critics, in particular those from rival African states, as well as internal critics who ranged from university radicals to mid-level party intellectuals to peasant farmers.[6] What binds together the groups studied here is a shared sense of frustration with the signature hallmarks of Nyerere's personality – the humble intellectual and unbending moral champion of the oppressed – that inevitably prefaced and shaped their wider criticisms. The substance of their criticisms also reflects the nature of political debate with Nyerere, who as teacher and president put great stock in the need for consensus through debate, but who in practice served as Tanzania's lone authorized critic.

Anglo-American de-colonizers as Nyerere critics, 1955-1970

In the early years of his career, Nyerere distinguished himself from other African nationalists by the efforts he made to showcase his own comparative reasonableness. His acts of careful intellectual deliberation, in which he was seen to be weighing both sides of an issue, drew in most of his foreign admirers, who saw more than a little bit of themselves

---

5 Anthony Daniels, "Nyerere, the leader who achieved by cunning what Idi Amin achieved by force", *Daily Mail*, 15 October 1999.

6 For starting points on internal dissenting groups, see, respectively, Hirji (2010); Hunter (2012); Giblin (2005); and Feierman (1990).

in Nyerere. He secured crucial American diplomatic support early on by befriending William 'Red' Duggan, consulate head in Dar es Salaam (1958-62) who found Nyerere an intellectual equal. Projecting his discomfort with 'typical' African nationalists, Duggan explained that Julius was "too modern, too disciplined mentally, too sophisticated to find companionship among more rabid, chaotic, gangster-type African political leaders". Duggan's biggest concern was with Nyerere's softness, treating local extremists like a school master instead of a political leader.[7] He later rhapsodized that Nyerere "lacks most vanities and conceits of the world's great. He is able to laugh at his own mistakes. He is never arrogant" (Duggan and Civille, 1976: 42).

Nyerere faced a more skeptical audience among British colonial officers, none greater than Governor Edward Twining (1949-58). Though scornful of the Tanganyika African National Union (TANU), Twining saved his greatest critical energies for discussing Nyerere, whom he regarded "as a rather conceited would-be prophet".[8] He elaborated his view to the Colonial Office:

> Julius Nyerere, who took a pass degree in history after four years in Edinburgh, considers himself to be a sort of prophet and sees in himself a second Nkrumah. He has no business head but undoubtedly has the gift of the gab and a quick brain.[9]

Reflecting this wariness, the British administration code-named Nyerere "Rhubarb",[10] half palatable, half poisonous. Tanganyika's Special Branch drew a particularly alarmist portrait, declaring that the TANU leader displayed "a strong racial prejudice" upon his return from Edinburgh in 1952, and was "a sensitive person quick to take offence and easily swayed by outside influences".[11] But in London, the Colonial Office welcomed the reasonableness that seemed to typify Nyerere. "[Nyerere] made a good impression on me", East Africa Department head W.A.C. Mathieson, explained. "I felt that he was quite sincere and anxious to promote harmony in Tanganyika provided the African got a reasonably

---

7 United States National Archives and Records Administration (NARA), College Park MD, Record Group (RG) 59 778.13/10-2561, Duggan to Department of State, 25 October 1961.

8 NARA RG 59 778.00/4-2156, notes of conversation held on 19 January 1956 between Miss Margaret Bates and Sir Edward Twining, enclosed in McKinnon to Department of State, 21 April 1956.

9 United Kingdom National Archives (UKNA), Colonial Office (CO) 822/859/f.33, Twining to Lennox-Boyd, 31 October 1955.

10 UKNA CO 822/859, minute of Macpherson to Hare, 17 September 1956.

11 UKNA Foreign and Commonwealth Office (FCO) 141/17912, Tanganyika Special Branch study of Julius Kambarage Nyerere, August 1957, 6.

square deal".¹² Mathieson's boss William Gorell Barnes concurred that Nyerere "is rather an attractive person . . . [h]e seems to me to be at one and the same time subtler and very much less unpleasant than Mr. Tom Mboya of Kenya. On the whole I would not expect him ever to resort deliberately to violence".¹³ Mathieson ultimately recommended that "Nyerere is probably capable of being a moderate and sensible chap, liable to tailor his opinions to his audience, but nevertheless worth sweeping into the fold".¹⁴

Yet in 1957, owing to his deteriorating relationship with Twining, Nyerere was abruptly swept out of the fold. "[I]n his present megalomaniac mood," Twining speculated, "[Nyerere] is piqued that he is not being treated as a great national leader who, whenever he toots his trumpet, makes the walls of Jericho fall down. He is obviously in a bit of a mental and emotional muddle".¹⁵ Practically alone among Colonial Office staffers, F. D. 'Max' Webber grasped Nyerere's essential radicalism, which almost single-handedly shifted the dates of constitutional reform across East Africa from decades to years. Webber stated bluntly that "I do not believe that Nyerere is a moderate and I think that once he gets control the Europeans and Asians will have a very bad time of it".¹⁶ Nyerere had left Colonial Secretary Alan Lennox-Boyd cold, but his successor Iain Macleod found that he "formed an immediate liking for Julius Nyerere... [h]e had, I think perhaps more than any other African leader a peculiarly not just Western, but British, sense of humour, which is an odd sort of quirky thing".¹⁷ In Tanganyika, more than a few rank-and-file administrators were impressed by Nyerere's "sincerity and rationality".¹⁸ Richard Turnbull, Twining's successor, saw Nyerere through the expedient lens of limited alternatives. "It is essential for us to use Nyerere whilst he is still powerful", he explained, warning that "[i]f we got into a shooting match, Nyerere would quickly be displaced, and instead of him we should have a group of hairy men demanding 'Africa for the Africans'."¹⁹

---

12 UKNA CO 822/859, minute of Mathieson to Gorell Barnes, 7 September 1956.
13 UKNA CO 822/859, minute of Gorell Barnes to Macpherson, 12 September 1956.
14 UKNA CO 822/912/f.30, Mathieson to Twining, 28 December 1956.
15 UKNA CO 822/1362/f.162, Twining to Lennox-Boyd, 21 December 1957.
16 UKNA CO 822/1449, minute of Webber to Gorell Barnes, 10 June 1959.
17 Rhodes House, University of Oxford (RH) MSS Afr.s.2179, Colonial Records Project interview with Iain Macleod, 29 December 1967.
18 RH MSS Afr.s.2089, Timothy Mayhew, "Reminisces" (1965–68), 139.
19 UKNA CO 822/1450/f.246, Turnbull to Crawford, 9 July 1959.

Nyerere was a transformative rather than a transactional leader. "One of his Nyerere's greatest political gifts", John Iliffe argues, "was to react *creatively* to situations which pressed on him, not merely satisfying demands but by his response transforming a political context to his own advantage" (Iliffe, 1979: 511). British and American admirers grasped this core point, and in the process were captured by Nyerere's own improbability. They shared both optimism and disbelief. Visiting Butiama a year after independence, Judith Listowel described the wild juxtaposition of world statesman and his humble home:

> I saw the rondavel in which Julius Nyerere was born, under a flat boulder on which sacrifices (not human, only animal) are still being held; when I met his brother, Chief Edward who has nine wives and 23 children, (I could go on...) I realized what a miracle it is that Julius Nyerere has become such a remarkable man, probably the most outstanding political leader in Africa.[20]

Listowel, née Judith de Marffy-Mantuano, a Hungarian-born, British-based journalist who traveled in the social circles of colonial elites, attributed a similar incredulity to African elders across Tanganyika, in front of whom Nyerere had first appeared, "wearing the shortest shorts ever seen, leaning on a tall stick", for how could he possibly vanquish the British, who themselves had "defeated the seemingly invincible Germans".[21]

Nyerere's prophetic and utopian streaks grew clearer after independence. When the first American ambassador William Leonhart expressed his favorable impression of Tanganyika's road construction progress, Nyerere lit up:

> He had been relaxed; he was suddenly galvanized; his face came alive; his eyes shone; he jumped up and down as he spoke. Pointing his finger, the little man said, 'Oh those big machines, I love them. Every time I saw one today I felt good all over. Machines are what we need, big ones. Roads and big machines are the answer. Give us big machines, and I will make a new world'.

"The man has the quality of enthusiasm and conviction", Leonhart concluded, at last understanding "the irresistible appeal of Nyerere".[22]

---

20 Listowel Papers (LP) Box 1 File 8, Listowel to Sister Maria Renata, 22 November 1962. I thank Lord Richard Grantley for providing my access to the privately held papers of his grandmother.

21 Judith Listowel, "Tanganyika's Chances", *The Tablet*, 15 December 1962.

22 NARA RG 59 778.00/10-2262, memorandum of conversation, Julius K. Nyerere and William Leonhart, 5 October 1962, Kilombero, Rusha Valley, enclosed in Leonhart to Department of State, 22 October 1962.

Other admirers took comfort that Nyerere's own modesty licensed them to heap on praise that might go to the head of lesser African leaders. Douglas Willys, BBC's East Africa correspondent in the early 1960s, commented that "[o]ne hesitates to praise him; one withdraws from embarrassing him or his views for acceptance is already general, and the gap between admiration and flattery is so narrow that is can only embarrass the modest, and Nyerere is the most modest and unassuming of men".[23] Yet these Anglo-American de-colonizers, proud to have transferred power to a figure so humble yet capable, also feared the growing gap between fragile idealism and the grubby realities of managing an African state. Britain's successful decolonization had become worryingly dependent on a Gandhi-like figure who seemed to value convictions over results. "There's a shadow of a death wish in him", Turnbull told Nyerere's best biographer, *Time* correspondent William Edgett Smith. "He likes to follow a principle to its logical end rather than its realistic end" (Smith, 1973: 30). Whitehall analysts worried that Nyerere was "by temperament, a philosopher not an administrator and he often fails to enforce his will on his more ambitious ministers even when they adopt courses of which he proposes to disapprove". They also noted something new, that "[d]espite this he is not without an authoritarian streak".[24]

In retrospect, Nyerere's state visit to Washington in July 1963 marked the high point of official Anglo-American Tanzaphilia. Two year earlier, Kennedy was briefed by the CIA that Nyerere "is widely regarded as the ablest native leader in British Africa and as one of the most impressive nationalist figures on the African continent", while highlighting Nyerere's concern for excessive executive power among newly-independent African states, his dislike of violence and racialism, and generally modest disposition.[25] By 1963, Nyerere was still reckoned a "force for moderation and racial harmony in his own country", and stood out for being "among the most respected and influential leaders of the new nations of Africa". His modesty was now more carefully noted – he was a "tireless worker who seldom has time for recreation, he is mild-mannered and unassuming, with a ready wit and a good sense of humor.

---

23 RH MSS Afr.s.1604, memorandum entitled "Tanganyika: Church and Political Situation 1961" by Sydney Clague-Smith to Lionel Greaves.

24 UKNA Dominions Office (DO) 213/209/f.4, Dominions Office note on Julius Nyerere, n. a., July 1963.

25 John F. Kennedy Presidential Library, Boston MA (JFKL) Presidential Office File (POF) 124-013, biographic entry of Julius Nyerere, July 1961, CIA Office of Central Reference.

He has little use for pomp and usually prefers to dress in a bright sport shirt. A chain smoker, Nyerere likes an occasional Scotch and soda or gin and tonic. He is a devout Catholic".[26]

Yet happy incredulity soon yielded to circumspection and disappointment. Anglo-American observers who looked upon Nyerere with cherished hopes from 1955 to 1963 grew wary after the Zanzibar revolution and army mutinies of early 1964, and began to fully abandon him following the nationalizations that accompanied the 1967 Arusha Declaration. The journalist Anthony Sampson deeply regretted the humiliation that the army mutiny – during which time Nyerere had gone into hiding – had inflicted. "He has two especially important qualities", Sampson explained. "He detests violence and anything which smacks of it; and he has always disliked the extreme crudities of nationalism. He has insisted, against his political advantage, in attacking black racialism as much as white, and this undoubtedly has added to his peril".[27] Listowel, who had just authored *The Making of Tanganyika* (1965), a sympathetic and influential popular history of TANU and Nyerere, was already changing her tone:

> It looks as though President Julius Nyerere, the man who went grey after the mutiny last February, has lost his grip. When some of his Ministers are on a world tour he speaks like an echo of his former self, but as soon as the 'satraps' are back he becomes their mouthpiece again. One feels sorry for the man who, a couple of years ago, wanted to light a torch on the peak of Mount Kilimanjaro to show the world a country of racial harmony. Hard-working, idealistic, honest but soft, he finds himself lost among the turmoil of world political intrigue.[28]

Long-whispered rumors of family madness grew louder. Shortly after the Arusha Declaration, Listowel explained to ex-Governor Turnbull that Nyerere's "nervous system is beginning to give way".[29]

Such disappointed observers tended to interpret Nyerere's actions through two contradictory lenses. The first focused on Nyerere's personal virtues and foibles; the second, on his guileless role as tool of Cold War puppeteers. The sharp deterioration of relations in 1965, beginning with the expulsion of American diplomats and culminating in the break in relations with Great Britain following Rhodesia's UDI, were viewed by

---

26 JFKL POF 124-13, biographic entry of Nyerere, n. a., dated 10 July 1963.
27 Anthony Sampson, "Personal tragedy of Julius Nyerere", *Observer*, 26 January 1964.
28 "The Delicate Balance", *The Tablet*, 6 February 1965, 148.
29 LP Box 1 File 9, Listowel to Turnbull, 7 April 1967.

British and American conservative media as the work of the USSR and China.³⁰ Nyerere's unabashed enthusiasm for Maoist China as political ally and role model following his state visit that same year alarmed Anglo-American de-colonizers. Intellectual agency had to be external. Listowel attributes Nyerere's official embrace of socialism in 1967 with the Arusha Declaration to his reading of the French agronomist René Dumont's *False Start in Africa* (1966), which decried capital-intensive 'neo-colonial' policy continuities, called for stripping African rulers of all privileges and luxuries, and recommended that African states instead concentrate resources "on agricultural development since over 80% of all Africans are poor farmers".³¹ Yet erstwhile optimistic liberals also saw Nyerere's uncompromising stance against South Africa and willingness to accept Soviet and Chinese support as revealing hitherto hidden qualities. "With quiet but purposeful fanaticism", Listowel explained, Julius Nyerere was prepared "to pay any price to achieve the supreme end: the liberation of all Africa," though now he needed only the backing of a "small but important group of African intellectuals" and not "the Tanganyikan masses, desperately poor and still largely illiterate".³²

As both an ex-spouse of a colonial governor and a working journalist, Judith Listowel best typifies this elite Anglo-American shift to a resigned criticism of Nyerere as inevitable dictator. Her livelihood depended on the general reader's interest. She explained to a friend the paradoxical effects of the continent's growing instability in the later 1960s – "for the British public is getting not only disinterested but bored and annoyed with the Africans".³³ By this time, a new journalism of detached Afro-pessimist malaise, succored by the buffoonery of Emperor Bokassa and Field Marshall Amin, as well as the cloak-and-dagger mischief of Frederick Forsyth, was beginning to displace a decade of engaged journalism that viewed British politics in tandem with those of Africa's new nations.³⁴ After surviving a wave of political crises in the immediate years that followed the Arusha Declaration, Nyerere nonetheless, according to Listowel, had:

---

30 See, *inter alia*, "Nyerere's Integration Problem", *Daily Telegraph*, 28 August 1967.

31 LP Box 1 File 9, "Socialism in Tanzania" by Judith Listowel, BBC script for transmission on 17 May 1967.

32 Judith Listowel, "President Nyerere's Fight for Unity", *Times* (London), 9 April 1965.

33 LP Box 1 File 9, Listowel to Bullock, 17 April 1967.

34 On British journalism and political engagement in 1960s Tanzania, see especially Hunter (2004).

retained his sense of humour and his charm, which is enhanced by his hair having turned grey at the early age of 47. But he has hardened; toughness is no longer an effort for him. The cynics say that he has come to terms with the utterly irremediable poverty of his country and has wisely decided that since there is no hope of the peasant farmer having a better life, no one else shall have one either. What they forget is that in this case Nyerere's principles coincide with Tanzania's realities.

She concluded with a soothing anecdote to justify Western disengagement. "There is a story that many years ago Julius Nyerere told a friend", Listowel explained. "'I am going to try British democracy, but I know that it will not work. Then I am going to apply the system of our chiefs – after all, my father was one too – and that will work better. The rest will depend on luck'. He has had the luck and Tanzania the results."[35]

Foreign critics of *Ujamaa*-era Nyerere, 1970-1985

By the 1970s, outsiders no longer viewed Nyerere as someone to be molded, and accepted that he had become a fully committed socialist sworn to the causes of non-alignment and southern African liberation from minority rule. Western leftists continued to fete "Mwalimu," projecting onto him their own hopes of what Ujamaa or African rural socialism should be, even as the failures and abuses of Tanzania's villagization project grew difficult to ignore.[36] Meanwhile, older Anglo-American de-colonizers had yielded to a more realist-minded generation of policy-makers who viewed Nyerere as neither ally nor enemy, but as indispensable sovereign actor on Africa's diplomatic chess board, to be courted with both energy and caution. For them, Nyerere's primary value was based on his enduring control over a stable and strategic country. Britain's FCO concluded that, though there was some disquiet among rightist 'liberals' upset with state overreach, and among 'left-wing theorists' who sought a more doctrinaire socialism, neither "have any organized identity and loyalty to Nyerere is overriding".[37] Nyerere's impeccable moral stature and political savvy led Washington policy-makers to conclude that diplomatic settlements in southern Africa could not be achieved without his full inclusion. A deeply impressed Henry Kissinger regarded him as "a seductive interlocutor…

---

35 Judith Listowel, "Tanzania and her future: problems of building African socialism", *The Round Table*, July 1970, p. 284.

36 For an early appreciation, see Mazrui (1967); for villagization, see Jennings (2008).

37 UKNA FCO 31/1764, draft of FCO briefing for the Prime Minister's meeting with President Nyerere of Tanzania, 15 September 1974.

capable of steely hostility," but above all as "the key to the front-line states" (Kissinger, 1990: 932, 936). It was left to the rock-ribbed, anti-socialist Cold Warriors who opposed the defeatism of détente to land the sharpest rhetorical blows against Nyerere, as he grew into the role of elder African statesman. *Reader's Digest*, the most popular venue for this perspective, editorialized that "Julius Nyerere, President of Tanzania, denounces racial injustices in South Africa, but keeps black people under lock and key without trial, some for eight years now".[38] In Britain, this group was best represented organizationally by the Monday Club, a far-right coterie of Conservative Party members who opposed Britain's abandonment of its settler colonies, as well as the sharp rise in Commonwealth immigration (McNeil, 2011). Its members publicized Tanzania's role in facilitating Chinese subversion in Africa (Greig, 1977, 132–133), and supported Nyerere's exiled enemies (see below).

But it was more cerebral conservative writers, whose goal was to discredit the socialist convictions that undergirded projects of Nyerere and Western leftists alike, who would develop the most searching criticisms of *ujamaa*-era Nyerere. This marked an important shift in two ways. First, this new generation of foreign critics had not come to their subject through a direct relationship with an accessible former school-teacher, but rather stood at a distance from the one-party state leader who had formulated his own doctrine of African socialism and with it collectivized rural agriculture. Second, their core objection to Nyerere was ultimately philosophical rather than personal and temperamental, and thus they took his intellectual work rather more seriously.

Anthony Daniels, author of the provocative obituary above, best typifies this group. Having worked in Tanzania as a village doctor during 1984-86, Daniels distills Mwalimu's rival elements of modesty and power into a tale of hypocrisy. In his travelogue *Zanzibar to Timbuktu*, Daniels conjures a scene in Dodoma where Nyerere arrives to greet various party and government figures:

> While I stared into the marvelously starry sky, a yellow Mercedes drew up. Mwalimu Nyerere had come for a chat with some of the Ndugu ['comrades']. How natural he was! How without affectation! Just another man, in fact. Of course, he has made something of a career of modesty in a continent famous for its ostentation and corruption. But if he is so modest, I wondered, how can he go round the world – in a special jet – telling it how it ought to be organized? And if he is such an egalitarian, how

---

38 David Reed, "Freedom's Rocky Road", *Reader's Digest*, February 1973.

is it that when his daughter is mildly indisposed she goes to an expensive London clinic rather than to her local dispensary? I stared once more into the starry sky. The universe has many mysteries (Daniels, 1988: 27).

Daniels developed a fuller criticism of socialist Tanzania in his lampoon novel Filosofa's Republic. Writing under the pseudonym of Thursday Msigwa, Daniels fictionalizes Tanzanian socialism as the 'Human Mutualism' of the state of Ngombia, led by 'Cicero B. Nyayaya'. 'Filosofa' (i.e., 'Mwalimu') Nyayaya is a rather distant figure in this village-set novella, though his 'Human Mutualism' aphorisms, unvaryingly hubristic and naïve – "Under Human Mutualism there will be no wealth and no poverty. All social distinctions will cease" (Ibid: 44)– preface each chapter. Nyayaya's exhibitionist use of his own humility ("humility was a favourite word of Filosofa's", Ibid: 4) delivers the satire's strongest commentary. Bishop Herbalgoode, a caustic caricature of Bishop Trevor Huddleston, remains a spiritual adviser to Nyayaya, travelling "frequently to Ngombia from his slum diocese to console Filosofa for the travails of power" (Ibid: 121). Herbalgoode winds up giving a long encomium to Filosofa at a British university conference that ends up, once more, celebrating Filosofa's modesty, that he "should openly have questioned his ability to lead at a time when no-one else entertained such doubts" (Ibid: 122).

Daniels' critique of Nyerere's Ujamaa is a classically conservative one– that socialism is doomed to fail because it denies both the value of tradition and the individual acquisitiveness of human nature. Nyayaya's humbleness, whether personally authentic or not, cleverly masks the underlying socialistic conceit to divine everyone's best interest, as well as to ensure the material privileges of a political elite while leaving the rest to navigate the black market realities that sustained village life. This perspective had already been gaining adherents, even among former fellow travelers. The *Guardian*'s Xan Smiley reported in 1980 that:

> Even today, remarkable play is made of his austerity. Unseduced by flashy cars, glossy airports and skyscrapers that are often *de rigueur* in other parts of Africa, Nyerere pays himself little, dresses simply, and earns praise from Western journalists for his engaging habit of admitting mistakes. He is taken seriously. Yet nowadays in Tanzania, *ujamaa* itself is hardly ever mentioned… it has been eclipsed by another catch-all Swahili phrase, *magendo* (black market).[39]

---

39 Xan Smiley, "How smugglers ended Nyerere's dream", *Guardian*, 10 August 1980.

The most stinging of all the socialist-era Nyerere critics is Shiva Naipaul, a Trinidadian and younger brother to Sir V. S. Naipaul. In his travelogue *North of South*, based on a tour of Kenya, Tanzania, and Zambia in the late 1970s, Shiva Naipaul finds a poignant intellectual hopelessness in Ujamaa Tanzania, which flows from the unidirectional teachings meant to connect Nyerere to his supporters. Naipaul describes Nyerere as inhabiting "a special place in the moral firmament for himself, his policies, and by extension his country", primarily because he "is just about the only African head of state one can contemplate without immediate sensations of outrage or embarrassment" (Naipaul, 1979: 197–198). He explores the subterranean psychology that cosmopolitan observers might share when contemplating Nyerere's Tanzania:

> Even Tanzophobes will pause at [Nyerere's] name and dole out the ritual praise. Nyerere is a good man. Nyerere is a sincere man. Nyerere does not feather his nest. See how simply he dresses. See how simply he lives. The 'Mwalimu" (Teacher) reinforces faltering faith; he makes it possible to believe – if only for a little while – that African can be taken seriously, that Africa really wants to 'liberate' itself (Ibid: 198).

Tanzania, he continues, similarly stimulates "the fantasies of a certain type of outmoded European socialist – men and women of a somewhat pastoral and utopian turn of mind – whose socialism fades by imperceptible degrees into a kind of benevolent, condescending patronage of the backward and deprived" (Ibid: 199).

Yet it is Naipaul's interactions with the man-on-the-street, a taxi driver named Abdallah, that fully develop his criticism – a criticism which flows not from conservative political conviction as with Daniels, but from despair at the disconnection between words and meaning. Abdallah debates with Naipaul using the omnipresent socialist language of national enemies – exploiters, capitalists, reactionaries, revisionists– who are besieging and undermining what would otherwise be a prosperous society. "The pat words, the pat phrases, unleavened by thought, came pouring out of Abdallah's mouth. In this society he could qualify as an 'intellectual'" (Ibid: 271), the narrator regrets. Abdallah, also a local ten-cell party leader, comes to share the narrator's despair:

> "I try to be an idealist. Mwalimu wants all of us to be idealists."
>
> "But not many are?"
>
> "That is the trouble," Abdallah said. "Human nature – it is a terrible thing. Many pretend to be idealists but few are"
>
> (Ibid: 273).

Naipaul concludes by suggesting that "in Tanzania, where performance consistently negates intention, where every commodity – butter, meat, milk, cheese, fish, chocolate, knives, forks, spoons, cups, saucers, baby diapers – is in short supply, the socialist revolution is being built with words" (Ibid: 282). Naipaul finds Nyerere's largest fault not in his readiness to imprison foes, or even to hypocritically display his material humbleness while insisting that the less privileged do likewise. Rather, it is that Nyerere is a teacher who brooks no disagreement and engages in no genuine debate, and thus his words – most paradoxically, given Nyerere's uniquely wide and ambitious publications and speeches on political philosophy – mainly carry the power to dull public discourse.

Nyerere's Tanzanian critics: irony, exile, imprisonment

Outsiders like Daniels and Naipaul approached Nyerere through abstractions like socialism and justice, which they juxtaposed with the ironic realities of an impoverished and hierarchical society. The most vocal Tanzanian critics, by contrast, approached Nyerere through their own visceral experience of his autocratic power. Nyerere's earliest internal detractors came to resent the upstart's lightning success. These figures were more firmly established, either through age (Hassan Suleiman, Seleiman Takadiri), royal lineage (Abdullah Fundikira, Thomas Marealle), or commercial success (John Rupia, the Sykes and Aziz families). Nyerere was widely seen among this group as the obvious choice to lead the Tanganyika African Association – which in 1954 reinvented itself as the Tanganyika African National Union (TANU)– because of his superior education (Edinburgh MA), command of English, and formidable debating skills. Except for the outspoken Takadiri, who was expelled from TANU in 1958 after attacking Nyerere for favoring Christians over Muslims, this group muted their criticisms after Nyerere's ascent to power (Iliffe, 1979: 507–576; Said, 1998: 110–147, 233–260). His retirement in 1985 and the country's return to multi-party elections, however, unleashed a wave of pent-up, bitter commentary and historical revisionism. Criticism while Nyerere was in office mainly took the indirect form of subtle and ironic wordplay. Direct barbs were aimed not at him but at his lieutenants, who represented one or other ideological faction within the party or government.[40]

The most consequential of these oblique insults was the peculiar trajectory of the term *Mwalimu* itself. Nyerere had not yet become

---

[40] For examples of this indirect style in Dar es Salaam, see Brennan (2006); for factionalism among political elites, see Hartmann (1985).

Mwalimu in the 1950s, and instead endured a host of embarrassing but mercifully short-lived praise names – 'our Savior', 'the Immaculate', and 'the Most Honourable' – that would be enthusiastically embraced by other nationalist leaders (Lowenkopf, 1961: 140). *Mwalimu* means 'Teacher', and this became Nyerere's quasi-official designation in 1962, sometime between February when he resigned as Prime Minister and November when he returned to office elected as President, and would remain his principal praise name thereafter. If its suitability is straightforward – Nyerere was employed as a teacher until 1954, and embraced a theatrically didactic approach to political leadership – its history as political moniker remains less clear. One intriguing account comes from the political scientist John Nellis, who argues that *Mwalimu* was first created in 1962 as a gentle rebuke against the man who embraced compromise and racial moderation at no apparent cost to himself, while others were forced to await Africanization. Nellis does not identify the insulters, though it seems likely that they would have included the above-mentioned established figures who had viewed Nyerere as a fortunate outsider to nationalist politics. Nellis does explain that these critics had realized:

> that an open attack upon such a revered public figure would be suicidal, and noting Nyerere's habit of using public platforms to lecture his followers and colleagues, rather than serve up bombastic political harangue, the few detractors coined the nickname 'Mwalimu'. This was meant to connote, mildly, it must be remembered, a slight tendency towards pedagogic pomposity on Nyerere's part.

Be it by dullness or political miracle, mocking irony transubstantiated into numinous authority. "[B]oth Nyerere's supporters and the mass of the people took the title as a compliment", Nellis continues. "Nyerere's close associates began to use the title in a praiseworthy sense," because it not only connotes a "tendency towards pomposity, towards empty moralization, towards patronization" but also "intelligent concern about scholarly authority".[41]

Nyerere's real opposition came from within TANU, as the short-lived formal opposition parties – the Tanganyika African National Congress (ANC) and the All-Muslim National Union of Tanganyika (AMNUT)– were ludicrously unsuccessful. Speaking of Nyerere at Karl Marx University in Leipzig, ANC leader Zuberi Mtemvu could only weakly

---

41 Letter from John Nellis to John Richard Crutcher, 16 November 1966, quoted in Crutcher (1968: 287, footnote 30).

muster that "when so many praises are sung about a nationalist in the capitalist metropoles then you know that in the leader you may have another TSHOMBE"[42] – the Katangan leader whose secession from Congo and acceptance of Western support made his name a byword for imperial sellout. These parties largely disappeared with Nyerere's overwhelming 1962 presidential victory; after the 1964 army mutiny, stray remnants of organized opposition disappeared in the face of certain imprisonment (Brennan, 2005). As Tanzania embraced a more rigorous socialism following the Arusha Declaration in 1967, those who stayed within the political system could offer only muffled, off-the-record criticisms. Paul Bomani confided to Listowel that he thinks that "Julius is out of his mind", and told her, three times no less, that "we will not live under a crazy Nyerere dynasty".[43] Open criticism required either the panoplies of deeply abstracted theory, as typified debates over socialism at the University of Dar es Salaam, or the foolhardy posturing of politicians willing to risk jail. Most remarkable of this latter group are the writings of Grey Mattaka and John Life Chipaka, who in 1968 anonymously published the vituperative newspaper, *Ukweli*.[44] One issue of *Ukweli* ('Truth'), which figured in a subsequent treason trial, proclaimed rather wildly that Nyerere was a madman, an exploiter, and a thief (*kichaa, mnyonyaji, mwizi*), and elaborated that he horded stolen cash in a Swiss bank account, enjoyed funding from the CIA, Aga Khan, and wealthy local Asians such as Amir Jamal, Andy Chande, and Abdulkarim Karimjee. The writers saved their harshest attacks for Nyerere's relationship with white women, alleging that his two strongest supporters were Lady Chesham, a American 'CIA agent', and Joan Wicken, Nyerere's British personal assistant and *hawara* (mistress).[45]

Most direct criticisms of Nyerere were voiced from exile or prison. Among the latter, Amnesty International estimated that there were between 1,500 and 2,000 detainees being held without trial on the mainland in 1977.[46] Three major waves of political displacement had produced these imprisoned and exiled critics, each wave marking a significant event in the country's postcolonial history. The first came with the Zanzibar Revolution, that saw thousands flee into exile to Oman,

---

42 NARA RG 59 778.00/4-1861, Duggan to DOS, 18 April 1961.
43 LP Box 1 File 9, Listowel to Turnbull, 13 April 1967.
44 They were connected to the paper in a subsequent treason trial that followed their arrest in 1969 for plotting a coup attempt.
45 *Ukweli*, 28 July 1968, copy in Lady Chesham Papers, Box 4, Borthwick Institute, University of York.
46 Xan Smiley, "How smugglers ended Nyerere's dream", *Guardian*, 10 August 1980.

Kenya, mainland Tanganyika, and the United Kingdom, the latter to which the overthrown Sultan himself and his entourage emigrated. The second followed in 1967 following the fall from grace and departure of Oscar Kambona, Nyerere's most prominent rival. The final wave followed assassination of Zanzibar President Abeid Karume in April 1972, when several ex-Umma party figures were imprisoned or made to flee.

Unsettling Nyerere's popular global standing became the primary goal of the *Free Zanzibar Voice* (FZV), a publication of the Zanzibar Organisation edited by Ahmed Seif Kharusi from Southsea, England. Zanzibaris suffering imprisonment and torture in Zanzibar and on the mainland were identified as victims of Nyerere's autocratic and abusive tendencies. Appealing to the anti-communist sensibilities of their ideal readers and potential patrons, items in the *Free Zanzibar Voice* rarely failed to mention that Zanzibar's prison wardens were schooled in the torture tactics of the communist octopus stretching from East Germany and 'Red China' into Tanzania and across East and Central Africa. Even before Karume's assassination, Nyerere had become the paper's principal target. "He poses to the outside world as an angel", the paper explained, "while at home he is a devil-incarnate. He seems to play the role of Dr. Jekyll and Mr. Hyde".[47] The most arresting content of FZV was letters smuggled out of prisons to indict the hypocrisy of Tanzania's positive humanitarian image. *I Was Nyerere's Prisoner*, a short book authored by former ZNP leader Ali Muhsin al-Barwani and published by Kharusi, typifies this genre.[48] The work drips with bitterness toward Nyerere – unsurprisingly, given it was penned after a decade of imprisonment on mainland Tanzania without charge. Nyerere, Muhsin contends, had intervened to prevent the murder of ZNP ministers in order to secure the new regime's legitimacy, "[b]ut slow, silent, sure murder years afterwards", through imprisonment and control orders, "would evoke little comment" (Muhsin, 1975: 11). Nyerere's liberal use of imprisonment, Muhsin argued, was "calculated merely to terrorise the populace and to make them conscious all the time that there is on top of them an arbitrary power that brooks no interference, no criticism" (Ibid: 16). Muhsin also neatly summarized the sense of institutional frustration that he other opponents shared, by contending that everything Nyerere does "is whitewashed with British liberalism and Roman [C]atholicism" (Ibid: 26).

---

47 "A Challenge to Nyerere", *Free Zanzibar Voice*, July/August 1971.
48 Sections were later incorporated into Muhsin's self-published memoir (2000).

With the same bitter effectiveness employed by foreign critics, FZV juxtaposed the idealism of Nyerere's writings with political conditions on the ground. Nyerere's stated opposition to mobilizing development through force, outlined in his pamphlet *Freedom and Development*, was rendered meaningless by his decision to repatriate Zanzibaris to Karume's prisons. FZV called Nyerere's own conscience into question, which somehow allowed him "to live in peace as the Head of a State when it is he who condones the injustices and atrocities perpetrated by the cut-throat authorities in Zanzibar to the helpless people, while Zanzibar is part and parcel of the State he rules".[49] Nyerere had moved from distaste for Karume immediately after the revolution to indifference, and then to 'something worse' by 1968, when he handed over Kassim Hanga and Othman Sharif, accused of treason on the islands, to Karume and thus to their certain deaths. Following Karume's 1972 assassination, Nyerere had continued to comply with the requests of Karume's successor, Aboud Jumbe.[50] Nyerere had made Zanzibar "his vast concentration camp with its torture chambers and the lot".[51] Indeed, the idea of 'Afrabia', which presupposes a harmonious Zanzibar undone by Nyerere's meddling (see below), was already being nurtured by FZV exiles during the 1970s. In a rhetorical questionnaire constructed for Nyerere, FZV editors asked:

1. Was Julius Nyerere given instructions to unite the African and Shirazi Associations to form a party to oppose the ZNP?

4. Why did the ASP leaders pay frequent visits to see him in Dar-es-Salaam when efforts were underway to unite ASP and ZNP?

10. Apart from other known sources of help, who helped the ASP to stage a bloody coup d'etat?

12. Why did he [Nyerere] despatch Tanganyika Troops to Zanzibar less than 24 hours after the coup started? Was it to keep law and order or to reinforce the coup?[52]

FZV embraced Amnesty International, which it hoped might finally damage Nyerere's moral credibility. His international reputation remained frustratingly high, they argued, "only amongst those who do not want to see the man as he really is. To those who know him, he is merely a hypocrite and a humbug. Time only will remove the sheep's clothing to show us the naked wolf".[53]

---

49 "Does Nyerere Practise What He Preaches?", *Free Zanzibar Voice*, September/October 1971.
50 "The Duty that lies West of Zanzibar", *Free Zanzibar Voice*, March 1973.
51 "Nyerere vs. Jumbe: a legal tug-of-war", *Free Zanzibar Voice*, April 1973.
52 "The Freedom of Zanzibar: A Questionnaire for Nyerere", *Free Zanzibar Voice*, April 1973.
53 "Prisoners should be freed", *Free Zanzibar Voice*, July/August 1973.

Full book-length criticisms of Nyerere by Tanzanians only came after he had stepped down from office in 1985. The three most significant were Barwani's memoir (self-published in 2000 but circulating in the mid-1990s), Ludovick Mwijage's *The Dark Side of Nyerere's Legacy* (1994); and Mohamed Said's *The Life and Times of Abdulwahid Sykes* (1998). Each book was written to elicit a response from Nyerere. Mwijage mailed his book directly to Nyerere in 1994, without reply.[54] Said's book at least caught the attention of Haroub Othman, who told Said that he had told Nyerere to respond directly to Barwani and Said with a written account of his own, a challenge Nyerere never took up.[55] In all three accounts, Nyerere stands as a distant rather than familiar figure, internationally loved abroad while imprisoning opponents for spurious or sinister reasons at home.

Writing in the vein of liberal human rights critic, Mwijage shares FZV's focus of unlawful imprisonment and security service abuses. Mwijage himself had left Tanzania after multiple arrests for Swaziland, where he was seized by Frelimo security in 1983, handed over to Tanzanian intelligence, and returned to Dar es Salaam for internment. He was eventually released and rusticated, slipped out of the country to Rwanda, and received asylum in Denmark. From Copenhagen Mwijage published the serial *Tanzania Argus* (later *Africa Argus*) between 1989 and 1995 – a platform, often highly personalized, for ex-filtrated prisoner letters and political criticisms of post-Nyerere Tanzania. As author of the dystopian African political novel *Of Magic and Mutiny* (2001), Mwijage offered criticisms of a fictionalized Tanzania ('Kanyinya') that suffered through the authoritarian rule of the country's first president, the socialist Andreas Goudas, who happily used a private jet to attend ideological conferences denouncing North-South inequality, as well as mobilizing a para-militarized Youth Wing and one-party apparatus to eliminate political opposition, at least until his unexpected military overthrow (Mwijage, 2001).

---

54 As recounted in Mwijage's updated version of the same book, retitled *Julius K Nyerere: Servant of God or Untarnished Tyrant?* (2010), p. 11. The original was published as Mwijage, *The Dark side of Nyerere's legacy* (1994), and later widely distributed as a text document on a variety of websites.

55 Communication with Mohamed Said, 31 March 2011.

But it is as narrator of his own imprisonment and exile– an experience which Mwijage connects to Nyerere's larger history of autocratic rule and quickness to imprison opponents – that gives his memoir uncommon rigor and pathos. Mwijage concludes with a rights-based argument for African self-reliance, which includes confronting Tanzania's dictatorial past with both self-awareness and honesty.

Mohamed Said's book, by contrast, presents a useable counter-narrative of Tanzanian nationalism that has gained a significant and largely Muslim public constituency. Nyerere remains at the narrative center, no longer the benevolent philosopher king but now a diabolic despot who carries out the will of larger, malevolent, and opaque institutions – alternatively the U.K., the United States, the Vatican, China, and Soviet Union. Said's underlying foundation is not a critique of human rights like Mwijage, but an often tendentious argument of deliberate religious marginalization. Said's Nyerere not only elbows aside an earlier generation of Muslim nationalists to usurp control of the movement in 1953-54, but is also the post-colonial dismantler of the East African Muslim Welfare Society, a civil society organization that sought to propagate Islam through construction of mosques and schools. Its banning in 1968, according to Said, marks the culmination of Nyerere's efforts to guarantee Christian hegemony in Tanzania (Said, 1998: 282–315). The most recent contribution in this vein of useable counter-narrative is Harith Ghassany's history of the Zanzibar Revolution, *Kwaheri Ukoloni, Kwaheri Uhuru!* (2010), which calls for the reconciliation of 'Afrabia', i.e., the 'African' and 'Arab' elements that comprise Zanzibar. This formulation deliberately embraces the ZNP and its rival 'African' Afro-Shirazi Party (ASP), whose competition set in motion the Zanzibar Revolution, and by extension embraces both the Chama Cha Mapinduzi (CCM) and its rival Civic United Front (CUF) in Zanzibar today. By using the language of reconciliation and inclusion, Ghassany's work offers broad appeal in Zanzibar, but as history it relies on portraying Nyerere as mastermind of the Zanzibar Revolution, who led an unforgiveable mainland invasion in which the ASP plays the role of forgivable pawn. The formidable counter-narratives of Said and Ghassany are important as works of remembrance and political meta-narrative crafting, but are also profoundly flawed as works of history. But they at least shift attention to the history of those political figures whose transgressions left them imprisoned or in exile; traitors who in earlier narratives figured, if at all, as short-lived vectors of reactionary intrigue.

Nyerere's most threatening critic was Oscar Kambona, who fled Tanzania in July 1967 for London after having fallen out with Nyerere over *ujamaa* and anticipating imminent arrest. Kambona drafted but never published a memoir, yet made something of an exile's career writing pamphlets and letters. In 1971 after much lobbying, Kambona persuaded the strongly pro-Nyerere *Guardian* to publish a letter that attacked Nyerere for removing all separation between the party and the government. Although Kambona himself had supported this position while in government, from his London exile he lambasted Nyerere for transforming the party "into a subservient organ of the regime and its clique at the top."[56] Yet even on this most visible of public stages, Kambona failed to elicit a response from Nyerere, who determinedly ignored all of his exiled critics. Using the name of the "Co-ordination Committee for Freedom and Democracy in Tanzania" from a Kensington address shared by other organizations receiving Monday Club support, Kambona later offered a more scurrilous pamphlet that summarized, crudely if effectively, both his personal and public disagreements with Nyerere and Trevor Huddleston, his most fervent British backer, in a broadside attack of the recently-formed Anglo-Tanzania Committee (today's Britain-Tanzania Society) in 1974. One section entitled 'Do You Know?' suggested that:

> For 30 bags of maize Nyerere sells Mandela, Sebukwe, Sithole, Nkomo and Nujoma
>
> That Nyerere is a mental case . . .
>
> Nyerere is a new Tshombe
>
> That Nyerere's days are numbered . . .

The pamphlet also referenced two alleged extra-marital affairs – first, rather opaquely by asking Amon Nsekela, then Tanzania's High Commissioner in London and co-founder with Huddleston of the Anglo-Tanzania Committee, who the real High Commissioner was, him or "Mrs. Howell", in reference to Lucille Howell, long-standing staffer at the High Commission and long-alleged Nyerere paramour; and second, more directly, by asking Nyerere 'Isn't Maria jealous of Joan?', in plain reference to Nyerere's wife and private secretary, respectively. Kambona went on to allege that Nyerere "has turned all the youth and all the schools in Tanzania as a means of his personal glorification on Mao's style", and that Nyerere was not a citizen of Tanzania for his parents had come from Kenya during the First World War. Kambona attacked Nyerere's

---

56 Letter of Oscar Kambona, *Guardian*, 7 April 1971.

exhibitionist modesty, not for its gamesmanship to psychologically disarm opponents that disturbed foreign critics, but rather more directly for its simple hypocrisy. The Nyerere family, Kambona alleged, enjoyed "luxurious international hotel with swimming pool and sauna bath" at the "so-called Butiama Ujamaa Village," and Nyerere's "corrupt brother Joseph, with six wives, gets a salary of 7,000 shillings, makes him the second highest paid" person in Tanzania next to the president himself.[57] Kambona would long dine out on stories of Nyerere and Mao, whose first meeting he marks as the key event in Nyerere's turn to authoritarianism. "On the way back to Tanzania", he later wrote about their February 1965 trip to Beijing that they had taken together, "Nyerere talked about how development had been possible in China only because of one leader. He said that ministerial portraits in the ministries in Tanzania were confusing the loyalties of the civil servants, and henceforth only his picture should appear there".[58]

By the mid-1970s, prison writing had become a recognizable Tanzanian literary genre characterized by a skilled professionalism, particularly in the letters of Abdulrahman Babu, who was convicted of involvement with Karume's assassination, and had already made a long career as journalist, essayist, and cabinet member, not to mention revolutionary.[59] These works featured in the journal *Habusu* ("Prisoner"), which sought to attract human rights activists and anyone opposing Nyerere. At their most inventive, these writers attacked Nyerere where he was strongest, on his liberation struggle credentials and demand for African dignity. One anonymous letter explained:

> One day, while in detention in Ukonga prison Dar es Salaam, we came across a copy of the government owned "DAILY NEWS" which showed how our African brothers were being humiliated in South African prisons – the humiliation being a naked search of the prisoners. My first reaction was to ask if that picture so boldly displayed by the "DAILY NEWS" had not in fact been taken at Ukonga, Keko or any other Tanzanian prison. For not only are prisoners daily paraded in the nude, as anyone who has access to the big prison yard between 2 p.m. and 4 p.m. will be able to testify; not only did condemned people have to submit to most humiliating exposure in front of us every morning

---

[57] Co-ordination Committee for Freedom and Democracy in Tanzania pamphlet entitled 'Anglo-Tanzania Committee', n. d. [circa 1974], in Ahmed Seif Kharusi papers, privately held.

[58] Oscar Kambona, "The Time I Met Mao", *Salisbury Review*, June 1991, 19.

[59] There is no adequate biography; for helpful overviews, see Othman (2001).

and afternoon, but hardly a week passed without we ourselves, detainees, being lined up in the nude – for the stupid excuse that we may have cigarettes.[60]

These were stinging inversions of Tanzania's sterling anti-colonial image, an image that was both well-earned and carefully burnished. The contemporary impact of these writings of Zanzibari and other political prisoners featured in *Habusu* and *Free Zanzibar Voice* seems to have been minimal within Tanzania. But outside, such writings did gradually erode Nyerere's standing over the 1970s, at least among an emerging group of internationalist activists who eschewed collectivist utopias represented by Ujamaa in favor of the individualist utopia of human rights law.[61]

Conclusion

After retiring in 1985, Nyerere's relationship with his own political legacy grew increasingly fraught. He defended the union between Tanganyika and Zanzibar in adamant, even alarmist terms (Nyerere, 1995). Yet he also raised doubts about the viability and desirability of the one-party state, explaining that the lack of competition led to complacency.[62] CCM officials had grown distant from the grass roots – if parish priests could visit small congregations and pray with the faithful, then Nyerere "saw no reason why political party officials adhering to the policy of socialism should not do the same".[63] In his final years, Nyerere grew to respect the tenacity of tradition, and declared Ujamaa collectivization a grave mistake. "You can socialize what is not traditional", he told an American reporter visiting his Butiama farm in 1996. "The *shamba* can't be socialized".[64] Nyerere was famously exercising the right to change his mind. Yet if he was his own fiercest critic, it was at least partly because he long had the luxury of being his only public critic within Tanzania.

The production of counter-mythologies that invert the heroes and villains of nationalist mythology is the common practice of opposition movements. In Tanzania this process was led by critics who inverted

---

60 "How I became a State Guest", n. a., *Habusu* 6 (1976), Northwestern University Library.

61 Amnesty International's annual reports on Tanzania over the 1970s increasingly stress the thousand-plus cases of detention without trial. In general see Moyn (2010).

62 "Nyerere's reported doubts about the one-party system in Africa", 11 June 1986, BBC Monitoring Summary of World Broadcasts.

63 "Nyerere denounces party's 'incompetence'", 20 January 1987, BBC Monitoring Summary of World Broadcasts.

64 James McKinley, "African Statesman Still Sowing Seeds for Future", *New York Times*, 1 September 1996.

Nyerere's cardinal virtue, his humility, into either a savvy psychological tool used to manipulate credulous supporters, or simply a ruse to disguise human rights abuses or even outright theft. Today, understandings of Nyerere, critical or otherwise, become inevitably bound together with the subsequent impact of neo-liberal reforms enacted over his objections in the years since he left power. A resulting genre has emerged of favorable academic reflections on Nyerere squarely framed as protests against neo-liberalism (see, e.g., Chachage and Cassam (2010) and McDonald and Sahle (2002)). Such neo-liberal reforms have ushered in an age of taboo-free corruption that would be unrecognizable to visitors from Ujamaa-era Tanzania. Contemporary Tanzanian eulogies of Nyerere stem from the pain that has accompanied this recent absence of public moral norms to guide political discourse (Fouéré, 2011). Such lionizations are more than just about the man himself, for Nyerere serves "as a reference point for debates over participation, privilege, and entitlement" (Becker, 2013: 261). His political personage remains an object of envy among politicians of many stripes. Willbrod Slaa, leader of Tanzania's main opposition party CHADEMA, campaigned against the ruling CCM party in 2010 by promising to emulate Nyerere's struggle against corruption. He and other party leaders later made a highly publicized pilgrimage to Nyerere's grave at Butiama and befriended his family.[65] Yet those who understandably embrace Nyerere's legacy for its many virtues – discouraging gross inequality, publicly shaming corruption and ethnicity-based patronage, just to name a few – should not conclude that such a system was also the product of dialogical political debate. It came about by doing as the teacher says.

---

[65] "Slaa amtumia Nyerere kummaliza Kikwete", *Raia Mwema*, 6 October 2010; "Can Opposition Demonstrations Oust the Government?", *The Citizen* (Dar es Salaam), 1 March 2011.

References

BECKER, Felicitas. "Remembering Nyerere: Political Rhetoric and Dissent in Contemporary Tanzania." *African Affairs* 112, no. 447 (2013): 238–261.

BRENNAN, James R. "The Short History of Political Opposition and Multi-Party Democracy in Tanganyika, 1958-1964." I*n Search of a Nation: Histories of Authority and Dissidence in Tanzania*, ed. Gregory H. MADDOX and James L. GIBLIN, 250–276. Oxford: James CURREY, 2005.

BRENNAN, James R. "Blood Enemies: Exploitation and Urban Citizenship in the Nationalist Political Thought of Tanzania, 1958-1975." *Journal of African History* 47 (2006): 221–246.

DUGGAN, William R., and John R. CIVILLE. *Tanzania and Nyerere: A Study of Ujamaa and Nationhood*. Maryknoll: Orbis Books, 1976.

CHACHAGE, Chambi and Annar CASSAM. *Africa's Liberation: The Legacy of Nyerere*. Nairobi: Pambazuka Press, 2010.

CRUTCHER, John Richard. "Political Authority in Ghana and Tanzania: The Nkrumah and Nyerere Regimes." Unpublished PhD Diss., University of Notre Dame, 1968.

DANIELS, Anthony. *Zanzibar to Timbuktu*. London: John Murray, 1988.

FEIERMAN, Steven. *Peasant Intellectuals: Anthropology and History in Tanzania*. Madison: University of Wisconsin Press, 1990.

FOUÉRÉ, Marie-Aude. "Tanzanie: la nation à l'épreuve du postsocialisme [Tanzania: The Nation Put to the Test of Postsocialism]." *Politique africaine* 121 (2011): 69–85.

GHASSANY, Harith. *Kwaheri Ukoloni, Kwaheri Uhuru! Zanzibar na Mapinduzi ya Afrabia* [Goodbye Independence, Goodbye Colonialism! Zanzibar and the Revolution of Afrabia]. Raleigh NC: Lulu Publishing, 2010.

GIBLIN, James L. A *History of the Excluded: Making Family a Refuge from State in Twentieth-century Tanzania*. Oxford: James Currey, 2005.

GREIG, Ian. *The Communist Challenge to Africa: an analysis of contemporary Soviet, Chinese and Cuban policies*. Richmond: Foreign Affairs Publishing Co. Ltd., 1977.

HARTMANN, Jeannette. "The Arusha Declaration revisited." *African Review* 12 (1985): 1–11.

HIRJI, Karim. *Cheche: Reminiscences of a Radical Magazine.* Dar es Salaam: Mkuki na Nyota, 2010.

HUNTER, Emma. "British Tanzaphilia, 1961-1972." Unpublished M.A. Diss., University of Cambridge, 2004.

HUNTER, Emma. "'The History and Affairs of TANU': Intellectual History, Nationalism, and the Postcolonial State in Tanzania." International *Journal of African Historical Studies* 45 (2012): 365–383.

IlIFFE, John. *A Modern History of Tanganyika.* Cambridge: Cambridge University Press, 1979.

JENNINGS, Michael. *Surrogates of the State: NGOs, Development and Ujamaa in Tanzania.* Bloomfield CT: Kumarian Press, 2008.

KHARUSI, Ahmed S. *Zanzibar, Africa's First Cuba: A Case Study of the New Colonialism.* Richmond: Zanzibar Organisation, 1967.

KISSINGER, Henry. *Years of Renewal.* New York: Simon & Schuster, 1999.

LISTOWEL, Judith, *The Making of Tanganyika.* London: Chatto and Windus, 1965.

LOWENKOPF, Martin. "Political Parties in Uganda and Tanganyika." Unpublished MSc. Diss., University of London, 1961.

MAZRUI, Ali. "Tanzaphilia: a diagnosis." *Transition* 31 (1967): 20–26.

McDONALD, David A. and Eunice Njeri SAHLE. *The Legacies of Julius Nyerere: Influences on Development Discourse and Practice in Africa.* Trenton: Africa World Press, Inc., 2002.

McNEIL, Daniel. "'The Rivers of Zimbabwe Will Run red With Blood': Enoch Powell and the Post-Imperial Nostalgia of the Monday Club." *Journal of Southern African Studies* 37 (2011): 731–745.

MOYN, Samuel. *The Last Utopia: Human Rights in History.* Cambridge MA: Belknap Press, 2010.

MSIGWA, Thursday. *Filosofa's Republic.* London: Pickwick Books, 1988.

MUHSIN, Ali al-Barwani. *I Was Nyerere's Prisoner.* Southsea: Zanzibar Organisation, 1975.

MUHSIN, Ali al-Barwani. *Conflicts and Harmony in Zanzibar, Memoirs.* Dubai (self-published), 2002.

MWIJAGE, Ludovick S. *The Dark Side of Nyerere's Legacy.* London: Adelphi Press, 1994.

MWIJAGE, Ludovick S. *Of Magic and Mutiny.* Leeds: Wisdom House Publications Ltd., 2001.

MWIJAGE, Ludovick S. *Julius K. Nyerere: Servant of God or Untarnished Tyrant?* Leeds: Wisdom House Publications Ltd., 2010.

NAIPAUL, Shiva. *North of South: An African Journey.* New York: Simon and Schuster, 1979.

NYERERE, Julius K. *Our Leadership and the Destiny of Tanzania.* Harare: African Publishing Group, 1995.

OTHMAN, Haroub. *Babu: I Saw the Future and It Works: Essays Celebrating the Life of Comrade Abdulrahman Mohamed Babu 1924-1996.* Dar es Salaam: E&D Limited, 2001.

SAID, Mohamed. *The Life and Times of Abdulwahid Sykes: The Untold Story of the Muslim Struggle against British Colonialism in Tanganyika.* London: Minerva Press, 1998.

SMITH, William Edgett. *Nyerere of Tanzania.* London: Victor Gollancz, 1973.

Chapter 8

Recasting Julius Nyerere in Zanzibar: The Revolution, the Union and the Enemy of the Nation

Marie-Aude Fouéré

In present-day Zanzibar, the figure of the first president of Tanganyika (1961-1963) and Tanzania (1964-1985), Julius Kambarage Nyerere, is being recast in collective debates over sovereignty, belonging and nationhood. Fiery discussions about Zanzibar's self-rule with their array of legalistic arguments about the Union, work migration and borders control, as well as about Zanzibari cultural distinctiveness and civility increasingly conjure up the figure of Nyerere. These debates explore the political role of Nyerere in the major events that have shaped the history of the archipelago since 1964, as well as his intentions and personal sentiments, to speculate about the past and make sense of the present.

Whilst there is no single narrative about Nyerere, one constant theme of debates on his relation to Zanzibar's history is that Nyerere is at the centre, and the origin, of the islands' present-day predicaments (Harding, 2003). While in mainland Tanzania, he is regarded as the Father of the Nation and presented as embodying political morality, in Zanzibar Nyerere is increasingly vilified for impoverishing and dividing the population along racial and religious lines through the control of its political elite. As one interlocutor put it during an informal discussion in a café of the capital city Stone Town, "Nyerere is by no means the Father of the Nation (*Baba wa Taifa*): he is the Enemy of the Nation (*adui wa taifa*)". Such negative rhetoric about the Enemy of the Nation has become increasingly widespread since democratization in the mid-1990s.[1]

---

* This text was first published in the *Journal of Eastern African Studies*, vol. 8, no. 3 (2014), pp. 478–496. It is reprinted with permission. I presented a first version of this paper at the conference 'Citizenship, Belonging & Political Community in Africa' organized on 11–12 July 2012 at the British Institute in Eastern Africa (BIEA), Nairobi, Kenya by Emma Hunter from the Centre of African Studies of the University of Cambridge. Many comments and questions made on that day have been useful when revising this paper. My deep thanks also go to the

This article explains the production, dissemination and contemporary uses of this derogatory narrative of Nyerere in Zanzibar. It does so by exploring the various tropes of that narrative, its actors and places of production, as well as its reception and appropriation. In particular, it looks to two key episodes in the history of Zanzibar which feed into current imaginaries of today's Zanzibari polity, namely the Revolution, and subsequent Union. Both events are cast as strategic means to deprive Zanzibar of its sovereignty, and destroy the economic strength, social fabric, cultural specificity and religious integrity of the Isles.

This narrative has been produced through a wide array of materials since 1964, by authors whose own political convictions are known to their readership. Yet, the founding writings of these "homespun intellectuals", to borrow from Derek Peterson (2004), or "amateur historians", who each aimed at editing a single story of the role of Nyerere are themselves strongly multi-vocal and characterized by inter-textuality. They are re-appropriated by their readers orally not only through countless mundane street-corner discussions, formal debates in public forums or fickle rumours, but also through written excerpts reprinted in newspapers or tracts, publications and Internet postings. New home-grown intellectuals concerned with their past, whether they are people of authority in the community or anonymous citizens, have thus entered into the continuous debate over Nyerere, with readers becoming producers themselves. Using the language of everyday political discourses, they do not simply pass on this narrative in its original form, but reshape it, select certain aspects while ignoring others, and add to it other sources of knowledge such as family recounts, popular memories or street stories.

These local architects and brokers of history and memory operate a "compositional work" (Ibid.) or assemblage of motifs to create a new product. It is a process which echoes the "work of narrative configuration" depicted by philosopher Paul Ricoeur who, discussing memory narrative, asserts that "one can always narrate differently, by deleting, by shifting focuses of importance, by re-featuring differently the protagonists of the action at the same time as the contours of the action" (Ricoeur, 1990: 579). In view of this ongoing "creative writing" (Peterson, 2004), it is an illusion to pretend to fully disentangle production and reception.

---

two reviewers of the journal for their challenging comments. Last, I am indebted to the French Institute for Research in Africa (IFRA) for its continuous support since 2010.

Popular perceptions of Nyerere and the Union have varied over the years. Rather positive in the 1960s, a shift occurred in the 1970s when promises of social and economic development failed to materialize. The researcher has to work with a composite or hybrid narrative made of multiple intertwined strands of collective memories, rumours, individual remembrance, memoirs and autobiographies, conspiracy theories, political and historical amateur essays and academic works of history. These materials, both oral and print, sometimes visual, are not to be explored as mere "literary topoi", but must be "anchored in the process of their production, in the orbits of connection that give them life and force" if one aims at producing a heuristic analysis (Comaroff and Comaroff, 1992: 34).

Such growing anti-Nyerere views must be explained by taking into account the specificity of the history of the Isles and their relation to mainland Tanzania. Although it will hint at some aspects of political economy and demographic history, this study situates within the framework of the history of ideas in contemporary Zanzibar. It therefore focuses on the circulation of vernacular historical knowledge and how such knowledge mirrors preoccupations typical of the time of its composition. Moreover, the objective of this article is not to assess the adequacy between critical discourses on Nyerere and historical reality, or to measure the veracity of the rewriting of history. Rather it explores how such discourses operate in the present; or to put it differently, how they conceptualize the political space and aim to act upon it by opening a dialogue between the past and the present. How the negative narrative of Nyerere is deployed, in what circumstances is it used, what claims people make of it and how it contributes to defining certain conceptions of Zanzibariness consequently matters more than drawing the line between the historically veridical and the fictional.

It will be shown that the figure of Nyerere works as a negative "place of memory" (Nora, 1997) mostly pioneered by the patriotic home-grown literati of the Isles and relayed through various political and cultural brokers. This is why we can define this negative narrative of Nyerere as a "politicized historical memory" (Werbner, 1998). Deployed in the political arena when its promoters seek to influence competition for power, it relates in fine to a sense of collective belonging, whether shared or contested, deeply anchored in specific representations of the past.

The Zanzibari Exception in Tanzania

Unlike many African countries where Fathers of the Nation have been contested or debunked, Tanzania still holds in high esteem its former president. In mainland Tanzania, Mwalimu (the teacher), as Nyerere was affectionately called, is regarded as a genuinely wise and well-intentioned political leader. Since his death on 14th October 1999, he has been memorialised as embodying an array of moral principles – humility, integrity and incorruptibility – variously mobilized by the state, politicians and ordinary citizens in contemporary political and social struggles. The repertoire of values which Tanzania's "Titan" (Mazrui, 2002) now symbolizes is appropriated to define and construct conceptions of political morality and Tanzanianness (see notably Askew, 2006; Fouéré, 2011a, 2014; Becker, 2013; Chachage and Cassam, 2010). The prominent presence of the idealized figure of Nyerere in the public space does not mean, however, that there is no alternative perspective. Among such alternative narratives, Nyerere's central role in shaping the politics of his time is cast in a derogatory light and rhetoric.

This pejorative discourse varies between the different circles and networks amongst which it is heard, and varies in the tropes used to express it. Three main factors help explain these differences. First, party affiliations strongly matter, with a strong division between members of the ruling Chama Cha Mapinduzi (Party of the Revolution, CCM), and the main opposition party in the islands, Civic United Front (CUF). Second, identity positioning, primarily cast not only along ethnic or racial lines, but also between people from Unguja and people from Pemba, also informs reception of the derogatory narrative about Nyerere. Such identity positioning only partly superimposes political loyalties. Third, religious fervour also plays its role, notably amongst Muslim activists committed to the propagation of Islam, who adhere to this narrative.

However, ethnographic materials derived from fieldwork conducted in different periods between 2008 and 2013 and within a large array of social groups testify that the mainland's iconic image of Nyerere is strongly opposed today not only among the urban Zanzibari activists of the opposition parties and their ordinary sympathizers but also among the many disappointed supporters of the ruling party, whether they continue to vote for this party or not. These opinions are widespread not only among the CUF intelligentsia but also within CCM, amongst the educated and the less educated alike, and are expressed by journalists and independent intellectuals who claim their free speech and independence from any political party. In spite of the limitation of the research undertaken for this article that targeted more town-dwellers than villagers, more CUF hard-line supporters than CCM partisans, more men than women, more educated than illiterate, we contend that the negative version originally pioneered by nationalist or separatist patriots has become if not fully ubiquitous, at least increasingly visible in the public space in contemporary Zanzibari society, thus leaving little room for the public expression of more positive statements. This construction has become a tool for political mobilization. Consequently, the figure of Nyerere is set in a discursive configuration whose understanding is inseparable from a political and social strategy. The politically committed Zanzibari community in diaspora, the educated of the opposition in Zanzibar and Muslim activists play a fundamental role in disseminating it.

It is notable that, in the portrayal of Nyerere as an Enemy of the Nation, the term 'nation' does not refer to Tanzania as a whole but to Zanzibar only, though the Isles are not sovereign. Since 26th April 1964, the date of the passing of the Treaty of the Union between the Republic of Tanganyika and the People's Republic of Zanzibar, Zanzibar has only had a semi-autonomous status within the United Republic of Tanzania.[2] Yet such institutional status has been highly controversial, due to conflicted conceptions of the Nation, or nationalisms, in the islands: African nationalism and Zanzibari nationalism (Glassman, 2011).[3] By nationalism, we do not just mean state ideology or political mobilization by the state, but any dynamics, be they organized or spontaneous, elitist or popular, ordinary or extraordinary, which asserts the existence of a national entity imbued with a sense of collective belonging.[4]

---

2 The islands have a government and a House of Representatives in charge of internal affairs.

3 Today's nationalisms, however, only partially meet past trends described by Glassman (2011), which he refers to as "African nationalism" and "civilizational nationalism".

4 The idea of the nation as understood in Zanzibar since at least the 1950s combines a territory of defined boundaries, a sovereign polity and a common culture. This resonates with the definition of nationalism by authors such as Anderson (1983), Gellner (1983) and Hobsbawm (1990).

Such nationalisms, expressed along political, cultural and racial lines, are strongly rooted in the long-term history of Zanzibar. In the nineteenth century, this island world was the centre of a powerful commercial empire under the rule of a Sultan. Its economy was mainly based on trade (spices, ivory and slaves) throughout the Western Indian Ocean, and its creolized population was the outcome of incessant migration from Africa, the Arabian Peninsula, India and the Indian Ocean islands. Today's grievances against the mainland, which the angry rhetoric against Nyerere mediates, owe to the present situation characterized by growing disenchantment in the face of unfulfilled promises of self-rule and economic development within the Union – a reality that appears even more bitter in the face of the revisited past golden age of Zanzibar (Bissell, 2005). The well-known and oft-repeated saying that 'when the pipes are played on Zanzibar, all Africa east of the Lakes must dance' was heard again and again during fieldwork.[5]

Last, although Nyerere-bashing is mostly expressed in the realm of politics, it is reinforced by arguments of a cultural order that, among others, targets Nyerere's use of Swahili language. Supporters of the representation of Nyerere as an enemy of the Zanzibari Nation often assert that Nyerere tortured Swahili because he did not speak Zanzibari Swahili, characterized by its Arab borrowings, but mainland Swahili.[6] For instance, one interlocutor mentioned that Nyerere introduced words taken up from ethnic languages of the mainland. He declared that nobody had ever heard the term *kung'atuka* before Nyerere used it in 1985 to announce his withdrawal from office, saying "I am leaving (*ninang'atuka*) power but I still believe that without a strong CCM, our country will falter".[7] Because language is a marker of identity mobilized to define national belonging and citizenship, anti-Nyererism serves representations of coastal chauvinism and cultural distinctiveness promoted by the Isles' educated patriots, which resonates with 'the geography of ethnic difference' built upon a religious and cultural

---

5 Quoted in Smith (1971: 90). A simplified version is more commonly in use: 'When the pipes play at Zanzibar, they dance at the lakes'.

6 Contrary to this view, many publications present Nyerere not only as a promoter of Swahili for the purpose of nation building but also because he was himself a lover of this language. For instance, Nyerere translated two plays of Shakespeare into Swahili, *Julius Caesar (Juliasi Kaisari*, 1963) and *The Merchant of Venice (Mabepari wa Venisi*, 1969). He also worked on the translation of the Gospels. He wrote his political writings and gave all his public political discourse in Swahili.

7 'Ninang'atuka lakini ninaendelea kuamini bila CCM imara nchi yetu itayumba'. The term *kung'atuka* made a lasting impression because it is constantly used by the CCM when asserting that it should remain the political keystone of Tanzania.

paradigm that distinguishes between the civilized Muslim nobility of the Coast (*wastaarabu*) and the barbarian unbelievers of the mainland (*washenzi*) (Glassman, 2011: 34–39).

Revisiting the 1964 Revolution

The historical episode recorded in state history and official discourses as the 1964 Revolution refers to the overthrow, on the night of 11-12th January 1964, of the constitutional monarchy of Zanzibar, just one month after it gained independence from the authorities of the British protectorate on 10th December 1963.[8] During that night and in the following days, the insurgents committed significant violence against members of the ousted government, people of Arab origin and other groups considered alien and close to the political power, namely Indians and Comorians.[9] The actual facts of this armed takeover are still an "enigma" (Shivji, 2008: 62)[10] because of the authoritarian nature of the revolutionary regime (Clayton, 1981; Martin, 1978). Opponents and those recalcitrant to the new men in power, under the presidency of Abeid Amani Karume, were imprisoned or assassinated. Public freedom was harshly restricted, popular social spaces controlled, the flourishing pre-revolutionary press disappeared and history as a subject banned in school. In other words, public channels of memory and history transmission were blocked. In this context of memories that were publicly silenced and therefore driven underground, making of the Revolution an open secret muted yet still privately discussed, the state imposed its own single historical version of events through pro-government publications or Swahili novels made required readings in secondary schools (Myers, 2000).

First, according to this account, the Revolution was founded upon ideological convictions articulated by the Afro-Shirazi Party (ASP), the political party formed in the late 1950s that advocated for narrowly defined African nationalism imbued with racialism. Second, the Revolution was cast as a popular uprising supported by the Afro-Shirazi 'autochthones' of the Isles (who made up the demographic majority).[11]

---

8 In this constitutional monarchy, inspired by the British system, the Sultan was the head of State but his powers were mostly honorific and advisorial.

9 The last census before the Revolution, in 1948, gives the racial distribution of the population, counting 264,059 inhabitants: 16.9% Arabs, 5.8% Indians, 1.1% Comorians and 75.7% Africans (24% from the mainland; 74% native). See Lofchie (1965: 71).

10 As stated by the historian Glassman (2011: 284), "the full story of the revolution has still to be written".

11 Populations identified as 'Shirazi' claim their ancestors came from the city of Shiraz in Iran. They were the targets of attacks by Karume who did not regarded them as 'African'. In

Finally, the Revolution was said to have precipitated the overthrow of a tyrannical power supposedly in the hands of 'alien' Omani Arabs, by Afro-Shirazis who had been denied their right to sovereignty for centuries – hence its definition as "the logical outcome of centuries of oppression and subjection of the African people" (Mapuri, 1996: 1). In this view, the 1963 monarchy was not a legitimate regime but the continuation of Omani power under the guise of legality. In this historical master-narrative, the independence of the islands is canonically referred to as 'false independence' (*uhuru bandia*). The revolutionary regime built its legitimacy to rule on the Revolution credentials. Today, in CCM public meetings, the historical reference to the 'Glorious', 'Sacred' or 'Great' Revolution is still chanted as a slogan (*Mapinduzi*! Revolution!) to which the crowd responds in unison: *Daima*! (Forever!).

It is as the founding myth of the Zanzibari Nation, however, that the Revolution is increasingly contested today. Although the CUF decries the decay of the post-revolution period and its corrupt politicians rather than the Revolution as a founding event, other minor political currents go as far as to contest the legitimacy of the Revolution. This counter-narrative downplays the single event of the Revolution in the creation of the Zanzibari independent state.[12] Independence from British rule and the establishment of an elected government in December 1963, rather than the armed takeover of 1964, is seen as the foundation event of the Zanzibari nation. The adoption of a national flag bearing the image of a clove and the granting of a UN seat are held up as symbols of this internationally recognized sovereignty – whose visual archives are notably put online or on Facebook by separatist activists.[13] Today's political commitment of these separatist groups in Zanzibar is grounded on the idea that the Isles' independence is the product of a century of slow maturation, throughout the nineteenth century, of a body politic rooted in a clearly delimited island territory.

The nature of the authority of the pre-independence Sultanate is redefined accordingly. Far from being a foreign and colonizing power, the pre-revolutionary regime is granted the status of a legitimate autochthonous power. Culturally, Zanzibar, seen as the cradle of Swahili culture (Caplan, 2007), is defined as a cosmopolitan and mixed-blood

---

the early 1970s, they were required to publicly reject their identity (Amory, 1994).

12 As stated earlier, the political proponents of a contested version of the great national narrative are numerous. This explains why only certain elements of this version are highlighted according to the interlocutors interviewed.

13 These visual archives are, among others, footage of the ceremony of independence on 10 December 1963, the Zanzibari delegation to the UN, photographs of the national flag, etc.

society united by a single language, Swahili and the practice of Islam.[14] In short, Zanzibari nationalism is deployed in the face of the African nationalism that animated the revolutionaries and whose traces still permeate today's official ideology. Such Zanzibari nationalism asserts itself on the basis of historical, political, cultural and religious references associated with a real or imagined Arabness from which today's Zanzibariness would be derived, and which is strongly permeated with the local deep-rooted "racial thought" developed on the Isles (Glassman, 2011; see also Loimeier, 2006).

Nyerere, Mastermind of the Revolution?

Contest over the official history of the Revolution also resorts to the rereading of the role Nyerere played during the revolutionary event. Whether Nyerere knew about the armed coup d'etat before it occurred remains debated in academic historiography. According to Issa Shivji (2008: 46), "it was not clear if the Tanganyikan leadership knew or was involved in any way. It is conceivable though that by Friday [one day before the overthrow] Hanga or Babu could have informed Kambona or Nyerere or both".[15] However, individual testimonies on the actual involvement of Nyerere in the Revolution and consequent role in the Isles' loss of autonomy have circulated in a clandestine way in Zanzibar since 1964, which some academic publications make reference to.[16] The gradual diffusion of these testimonies in society was operated through the many biographies, memoirs, political essays and rewriting of history produced by exiles of the Revolution settled in Europe or in the Arabian Peninsula, and circulated among the educated politicized Zanzibaris, notably among the opposition (Babakerim, 1994; Fairooz, 1995; Muhsin, 2002).

---

14 The possession of these linguistic and religious attributes defines the entry into civilisation (ustaarabu), and distinguishes the civilised/educated (waungwana) from the unbelieving and illiterate savages (washenzi). Former strategies of reclassification, with regard to these cultural, linguistic and religious markers, reflect the influence of this high culture on the definition of Zanzibariness. See notably Fair (2011).

15 Kassim Abdallah Hanga, an ASP uncompromising leftist intellectual, became the vice president of Zanzibar after the Revolution. Mohamed Abdulrahman Babu, leader of the Marxist Umma Party, was made Zanzibar Minister of Foreign Affairs and Trade. Oscar Kambona was, in 1964, the Tanganyika Minister of Foreign Affairs and Defence and the confidant of Nyerere.

16 See for instance Bakari (2001: 104, 105): "a group of plotters was apparently working with the support of Tanganyika"; "some unconfirmed sources suspected that the uprising had been well planned from the mainland".

The latest work in this array of rewriting of history is a book by a Zanzibari scholar living abroad, Harith Ghassany (2010), entitled *Kwaheri ukoloni, Kwaheri uhuru*! (Goodbye colonization, Goodbye independence!). It supports the theory of the organisation of the Revolution by Nyerere and his right-hand man, Oscar Kambona. Written in Swahili, the book targeted a Zanzibari audience and aimed at intervening in popular political debates.[17] It succeeded well in its objectives, being mentioned in most interviews conducted during fieldwork since its publication in July 2010, most specifically among CUF activists or sympathisers but also among the CCM elite – it was said that the then President, son of Abeid Amani Karume, had it by his bedside – whether to praise or decry it.[18] The book, which presents a collection of personal testimonies never put in print before, made waves even though its core argument was not fundamentally new, reflecting the earlier nationalist writings mentioned above.[19] The author reveals, through the voice of eyewitnesses or actors of the insurrection, that Nyerere plotted the Revolution, sending his loyal henchmen to organize the mobilisation of sisal workers in Tanganyika, in Tanga region, for armed combat, with the help of some mainland immigrants settled in Zanzibar.[20] The book seeks to make a stand in the local historical battle, with its title ironically suggesting that the departure of the British rulers made way to a new colonizer, Tanganyika, reducing hopes for sovereignty to nothing.[21]

---

17 Ghassany (2010 : xiv): "(...) kitabu hichi kimeandikwa kwa lugha ya Kiswahili ili watumiaji wa lugha hiyo waweze kufahamu namna gani historia ya Zanzibar ilivyopotoshwa na wachangiye kujenga harakati mpya (...)" (this book is written is Swahili language so that the users of this language may understand how much the history of Zanzibar was distorted, and contribute to building a new movement).

18 The few books that were put on sale in Zanzibar were sold out in a few days in July 2010. They circulated from hand to hand (personal communication).

19 If the book presents itself as academic historiography, the veracity of the collected testimonies is not only disputed within academia but also among the educated population of the Isles.

20 See for instance p. 65: "Nyerere ndie alokuwa akifanya organisation (mipango) yote na kuweza kuwafanya watu wapinduwe serikali ya Zanzibar. Yeye Nyerere" ("It was Nyerere who did all the organisation and made it possible for people to overthrow the government of Zanzibar. Nyerere himself"). See also testimonies in chapters 5 and 6.

21 In a similar vein, see also the book by Nasser Abdulla Al Riyami, an Omani of Zanzibar origin, recently translated into English (2012), that cast the Revolution as an 'invasion', notably 147–48.

More recently, independent media has also contributed to presenting hitherto silenced testimonies and disseminating this patriotic version of history. Among them, the first independent Zanzibari weekly newspaper since 1964, *Dira* ('Vision' in Kiswahili), published in 2002-2003, was a key player.[22] The article 'Nyerere is not an angel' published in the first edition and written by the newspaper's Chief Editor, Ali Mohamed Nabwa, was clearly intended to dismantle the idealised image of Nyerere upheld in mainland Tanzania. The author depicts Nyerere as a condescending and disloyal politician who would have resorted to all sorts of intrigues to get to the top of the state. It suggests that Nyerere would have regarded the Arabs of Zanzibar as a colonizing and enslaving power, hence as a power to be removed. According to the article, Nyerere masterminded the Revolution in order to impose, on the islands, the Black African culture of the mainland. In this version of history, the Revolution is nothing more than an 'invasion', at times even an 'ethnic cleansing' or 'genocide'. This echoes a terminology increasingly in use within nationalist circles in Zanzibar or abroad through which Nyerere is cast as the wily imperialist who extended his empire on Zanzibar, making it a colony to be exploited for the benefit of the mainland.

Nyerere, Colonizer of Zanzibar?

In the nationalist version of the history of Zanzibar that the anti-Nyerere rhetoric mediates, the first step in the control of the islands (the Revolution) was followed by a second step aimed at ensuring the total submission of Zanzibar: the establishment of the Union between Tanganyika and Zanzibar 100 days after the Revolution. At that time, however, the Union was welcome by politicians and the population, for it was seen as a constitutional arrangement[23] that could ensure economic and social development in the Isles, as well as a symbol of pan-Africanist ambitions to foster regional unity. As reminded by Jonathon Glassman, "champions of the union in its current form like to depict it as a singular triumph of pan-African solidarity".

---

22 *Dira* was banned by the state in 2003, one year only after it was launched, because the newspaper was resurfacing alternative memories of the Revolution and produced counter-narratives of state history considered a threat to civil order. For details, see Fouéré (2012).

23 Zanzibar retains an independent government but cedes to the Union sovereign affairs such as the police, the defence, the interior, foreign affairs and customs.

Yet, over the years, the island populations and the political elite have become increasingly angered by the encroachment of the Union in the internal affairs of Zanzibar, and its critics now "deny the significance of pan-African ideals and instead regard (the union) as the product of a cynical power play imposed by mainland politicians" (Glassman, 2011: 292–294). Today's opponents of the Union or citizens dissatisfied with its current state (Othman and Peter, 2006; Rawlence, 2005) harshly denunciate the political and economic marginalization of Zanzibar within the United Republic, often resorting to the terms 'colonization' or 'imperialism' to describe what they consider as the annexation of the Isles by ex-Tanganyika.

More than any other book, Ali Muhsin's memoirs, *Conflict and Harmony in Zanzibar*, was repeatedly mentioned during interviews with the literati of the opposition. This author, the "de facto leader" (Glassman, 2011: 6) of the 1963 December government, condemns the appalling destruction of Zanzibar both by the revolutionary leaders who "stooped lowest to rob their subject", making Zanzibar "the laughing stock of the world" (Muhsin, 2002: 282) and by mainland politicians. Nyerere is made responsible for most evils, even compared to Adolf Hitler:

> Nyerere has destroyed everything that he has ever handled. Hitler built then destroyed everything by his mania. But this man [Nyerere] is worse. (...) He has destroyed Zanzibar and all its fine orchards and plantation of clove trees and coconut palms (...) (Ibid: 162)

Nyerere's famous statement about Zanzibar, "[i]f I could tow that island out into the middle of the Indian Ocean, I'll do it" (Smith, 1972: 48) came up again and again during my research in support of Ali Muhsin's narrative.[24]

In this perspective, the history of the Union is again reread in the light of the role played by its main protagonists, the president of Tanganyika and the president of Zanzibar. Nyerere and Karume, being re-featured through their relational but opposed positioning, respectively embody Tanganyikan imperialism and Zanzibari nationalism. It is said that the wrongs of Nyerere were to have imposed the Union onto Karume by force and by guile. Karume who had established his power through

---

24 In this regard, another biography in mainland Tanzania is also frequently mentioned, *The Dark Side of Nyerere* by Ludovick Mwijage (1996). This text about the author's persecution and imprisonment is often cited to support the theory that Nyerere schemed and assassinated to get rid of any form of protest, whether in Zanzibar or on the mainland.

force and fear until his assassination in 1972 and was described as a charismatic public speaker, is portrayed as lacking competence in institutional, legal and administrative issues. A former seaman who had travelled a lot, he was indeed barely educated and ill at ease with English. He feared the local educated employed in his government and public administration, who could have formulated well-argued critiques or organized his overthrow (Martin, 1978) Seen as political rivals, many among the Zanzibari intelligentsia were eliminated or forced into exile between 1964 and 1972, for he had "no mercy for his enemies" (quoted in Myers, 2003: 51).

However, because of his supposed reluctance to sign the Union Treaty[25] and his subsequent efforts to increase the autonomy of Zanzibar, Karume is today increasingly upheld as symbol of resistance to what is presented as the insidious annexation of the Isles, as well as for his grand vision for Zanzibar's social and economic development. As Issa Shivji asserts:

> official historiography repeats ad nauseam that Karume was a Union enthusiast. Nothing could be further from the truth. If there is one thing that Zanzibaris venerate Karume for, in spite of his despotic rule, it is Karume's Zanzibariness and his dogged resistance to get integrated into the Union and loose Zanzibari autonomy (Shivji, 2008: 123–124).

My interlocutors repeated at will the phrase attributed to Karume that "the Union is like a coat, if it's too tight you can take it off" in order to underscore Karume's contempt for the Union. The other oft-repeated famous line by Karume that "the Arusha Declaration stops at Chumbe", an island at the entry of Zanzibar Town, also points to Karume's resistance to adopt the path of socialist development followed in the mainland.[26]

Interestingly, Karume's foreign origin, his defence of parochial Africanness as opposed to Zanzibar's cosmopolitan dhow culture, his absence on the night of the Revolution, his authoritarianism and

---

25 However, Haroub Othman (1995: 173) says that "according to Nyerere, Karume immediately agreed to the idea (of a union) and suggested that Nyerere should be the president of such a nation".

26 The Arusha Declaration of 1967 established African socialism, or Ujamaa, as a development path for Tanzania based on the communitarisation of the labour force, collectivisation of the means of production, nationalisation of enterprises and establishment of free public services. Zanzibar followed a somehow different path: the left-leaning social and economic grand vision embraced by Karume was implemented in agriculture, education, housing and health but was only partially accomplished and suffered from authoritarian power.

arbitrary power, the deprivation caused by the ban on food imports into the Isles from the late 1960s, the racist invectives that he held against so-called foreigners such as the Asians and Comorians, and finally his lifestyle in conflict with Muslim precepts[27] – in short, a whole set of elements that are summoned in today's popular discussions – are glossed over when the passing of the Union is debated. Karume is then portrayed as Nyerere's helpless victim. When the assassination of Karume is recalled,[28] it is much less to remind that it hastened the end of a regime in which "political thuggery was a virtue" (Othman, 1995: 175) than to assert that Nyerere was the one who had armed Karume's murderers. It is said that Karume was, at that time, on the point of severing the Union (Shivji, 2008; Chachage, 2004). Karume's violence and lawlessness, denounced internationally, also constituted a real burden on Nyerere, as such attitudes were detrimental to the image of Tanzania on the international scene.[29] Last, it is often recalled, in the talks and debates of the patriotic intellectuals, that Nyerere was mentioned under the nickname of 'Mister X' in the trial of the alleged conspirators of the assassination of Karume (Chase, 1976). Undeniably, Nyerere is castigated as the ultimate instigator of this crime and once again portrayed as a shrewd manipulator.

Ending 'Nyerere's Dictatorship'

Current public discussions on the revision of the Constitution of the United Republic of Tanzania – a process launched after the last general elections of October 2010 – illustrate the pervasiveness of these negative tropes about Nyerere and their use in the political realm. This recent phase of political turmoil actually started in the lead-up to last election, when, in August 2010, the House of Representatives amended the Constitution of Zanzibar and adopted the principle of power sharing between the elected party and the opposition, which was to be applied after the elections (Bakari and Makulilo, 2012; Matheson, 2012; Fouéré, 2011b) This coalition government was expected to end 15 years of tensions between CCM and CUF.[30] The amendment was also a first

---

27 For a depiction of Karume lifestyle and personality, see notably Burgess, "Karume the Terrible" (2009).

28 Karume was assassinated at the ASP headquarters on 7 April 1972.

29 The case of forced marriages between members of the government and young Arab girls was highly publicised internationally (Martin, 1978: 69–71; Burgess, 2009: 205). Amnesty International also mobilised to demand the release of political prisoners and to protest against the use of torture in prisons.

30 Since the reintroduction of multiparty politics in 1992, all elections took place in a deleterious environment. Electoral fraud culminated in police and military violence, which,

symbolic step towards greater autonomy for the Isles because it included the principle that the Isles were a *nchi*, a Swahili word meaning 'country' but also 'homeland' or 'nation'.

The outraged reactions from the mainland show that these constitutional changes were seen as a major threat to the integrity of Tanzania. Several political or legal organizations of the mainland as well as independent lawyers spoke out, saying that such amendments needed to be in accordance with the Constitution of Tanzania. They feared that this thinly veiled claim to sovereignty might lead to the dismantling of Tanzania. In this mainland outcry, the demand for increased autonomy by Zanzibar was vilified as an attack on the memory of the Father of the Nation and a betrayal of the legacy of unity and peace he had left to the country. Nyerere's well-known political speeches on unity and against parochialism, especially with regards to Zanzibar, were again quoted, reprinted and broadcast to champion the respect of the Union.

Public debates organized in Zanzibar since 2011 have resonated with deep-rooted anti-Nyererism. Various Zanzibari institutions gathered to launch such public debates with the declared aim of countervailing the usual technocratic monopoly on legal and institutional issues. During February and March 2011, the research institute Zanzibar Indian Ocean Research Institute (ZIORI) in partnership with legal organisations (ZLSC, Zanzibar Law Services Centre, and ZLS, Zanzibar Law Society) and Muslim organisations such as JUMIKI, commonly referred as Uamsho (Jumuiya ya Uamsho na Mihadhara ya Kiislamu, the Association for the awakening and propagation of Islam) and JUMAZA (Jumuiya ya Maimamu Zanzibar, the Association of Imams in Zanzibar) held several meetings, under the umbrella of BAKAZA (Baraza la Katiba Zanzibar, the Zanzibar Constitution Council). Beginning with speeches by well-known professionals and academics who discussed the legal dimension of the revision of the constitution, they were an opportunity for the public to make their voice heard. The audience was largely made up of active homespun patriotic intellectuals, who are readers of the nationalist texts discussed above. Legalistic arguments were relentlessly recalled to remind all that the original document of the Union Treaty, which needed to be signed by both parties to be valid, does not exist or that Karume did not sign it. It was also recalled that the agreement was validated neither by members of the government nor by the then Attorney General Wolfgang Dourado. Most of the views expressed revisited the history of the formation of the Union by putting

---

in 2001 and 2005, caused between 30 and 60 deaths and hundreds of injured (Rawlence, 2005).

a significant emphasis on the manipulation of Karume by Nyerere and Nyerere's animus towards Zanzibar.

During a meeting held on 5 March 2011, a journalist, former sympathizer of the Marxist party Umma Party and also a former team member of the weekly newspaper *Dira*, argued that the Union was the result of a secret agreement between two men only, Presidents Nyerere and Karume, which was held against the great political figures of the Zanzibar Government of 1964, even less approved by the people of Zanzibar:

> What I would like to say here is that, that day [of the Union] I was with the late Abdallah Kassim Hanga. And for your information, that day, the Vice President of Zanzibar, Kassim Abdallah Hanga, was not aware of this Union. (...) I spoke with Abdulrahman Babu more than a dozen times, and he said that in all the recommendations on the making of the Union, he and other ministers were not involved.[31]

The presumption of a conspiracy organised by Nyerere and assertions that Karume was an incompetent leader clearly sustained claims for a popular debate over the revision of the Union Treaty and the Constitution.

In another meeting, held on 9 April 2011 by the government of the islands and intended to collect citizens' views on an initial version of a draft text of the new Constitution, the atmosphere was charged and the crowd chanted in unison 'We do not want the Union', before the leader of JUMAZA ripped the draft stating that the 'dictatorship of Nyerere' (*udikteta wa Nyerere*) was over. Stone Town's baraza[32] echoed these heated constitutional debates, especially among CUF sympathizers. As a middle-aged Zanzibari employed in an educational non-governmental organization (NGO) declared to me a few days later while we were sipping a coffee in the CUF stronghold of Jaws Corner, "that is exactly what was needed to be said: this is the end of Nyerere's dictatorship, which has deprived us of our rights since 1964". Zanzibari nationalism, even separatism, unquestionably feeds into the disrepute of Nyerere, the latter being turned into a scapegoat in the long series of social, political and religious ills faced by the islands since independence.

Since the beginning of 2012, not only the radicalization of JUMIKI/ Uamsho's political stand with regard to the Union, but its increasing

---

31 Ecrotanal building, author's translation from her recording of the meeting, 5 March 2011.

32 *Baraza* are stone benches built along the outside walls of houses, where people like to sit and chat. The term metonymically refers to places of daily sociability. See Loimeier (2007).

visibility and popularity among both the urban and rural populations clearly revealed how much the association between Nyerere, as a negative political figure, and the fight for sovereignty in the Isles has become part of Zanzibari conventional wisdom. In one of their earliest public sermons of 2012 in the suburbs of Zanzibar Town, Uamsho's leaders declared their political agenda, saying: "The path is very long to claim for the independence of our country. We need patience and cooperation so as to ensure that our islands will be free. The decision is ours, Muslims".[33] The 'colonization' which they claim to be fighting for the sake of sovereignty both resonates, in their politically discourses, with what they see as the destructive politics of Nyerere and his heirs, and the subsequent increasing presence of mainlanders, accused of 'invading' the islands.[34] Today's use of anti-Nyererism in the realm of patriotic activism clearly mediates anxious concerns about cultural distinctive- ness and religious integrity in Zanzibar.

Nyerere's crusade against Islam?

Broader political determinants are discussed by Zanzibaris when they explore the role that Nyerere played during 1964. The context of the cold war, during which Americans feared that Zanzibar might become the 'Cuba of Africa' (Wilson, 1989; Hunter, 2010; Kharusi, 1967) is often used to highlight how the influence of the international superpowers was central in Nyerere's decision to establish the Union. However, it is striking that, in the anti-Nyerere rhetoric, the decisions taken at that time by the head of the state are not simply regarded as political tactics aimed at, for instance, controlling political opposition, muzzling collective protest or retaining power, but are said to be rooted in prejudices and feelings deeply anchored in Nyerere's heart.

Such accounts assert that as a devout Catholic,[35] Nyerere would have hated Islam; as a native of mainland Africa, he is castigated for his 'Arab-bashing' in relation to Arabs' participation in the slave trade and slavery. Nyerere's objective in pushing the Union is said to be to impose a mainland African regime in the Isles and, even more, to destroy an economy of transnational trading networks and a culture too Arabicized

---

33 Kibanda Maiti, author's translation from her recording of the public sermon, 4 March 2012.

34 See their recent pamphlet, Mipango ya Kuritadisha Zanzibar, distributed during their 2012 public sermons. Fears of uncontrolled immigration and mainland secret agenda of invasion feature in Uamsho's discourse since the early 2000s, see Loimeier (2011).

35 It is said that, when he was a student at Makerere University, Nyerere considered becoming a priest but he was dissuaded to do so by his friend, the White Fathers priest Richard Walsh. See Ludwig (1999: 78, 80, note 5); Civille and Duggan (1976: 43).

for his liking based on endless discrimination against the Africans. Thus, Nyerere's role in the history of the islands is, today, positioned along the lines of his supposed hostility to Arabs and, by extension, to Islam. It does so by drawing upon personal anecdotes, putting the emphasis on some of Nyerere's words that might raise suspicion, and resorting to the scientific backing of academic literature on religious preference and discrimination during Nyerere regime. A book by the Catholic priest John Sivalon (1992) about Christian–Muslims relations and the Tanzanian state is recurrently used as a reference to support this angry Muslim rhetoric. As reminded by Frederick Ludwig, this publication "has often been referred to as supporting the thesis of the suppressors of Islam (in Tanzania), though this was probably not the intention of the author and publisher" (1992: 230).

The idea that Nyerere was animated by his hostility to Islam gained momentum in 1998 with the publication *The Life and Times of Abdulwahid Sykes: The Untold Story of the Muslim Struggle against British Colonialism in Tanganyika* by Mohamed Said (1998). In this polemical essay, the author revisits the history of nationalism in Tanganyika to capture the essential contribution, erased from official history, of a circle of educated Muslims in Dar es Salaam led by the Sykes family.[36] He brings to light how these Muslim townsmen, who were founders of the first nationalist organisation, took Nyerere to the summit of power, for he was then perceived as "a highly educated person with admirable debating skills" (Ibid: 111). The book depicts how a conspiracy against Islam was set in motion after Nyerere turned against those who co-opted him to favour his fellow Christian politicians.

The theme of Nyerere's animus towards Islam also gained visibility following the growing expression of politicized Islam in the media.[37] The press has been a key player in such politically active Islam. Excerpts of Mohamed Said's and Harith Ghassany's works are often reprinted in the pages of the weekly newspaper An-*Nuur*, thus giving increased visibility to the Muslim question in the public space. During and after the 2010 election, *An-Nuur* provided wide coverage of a set of

---

[36] Kleist Sykes is the founder of the African Association, a political movement engaged in the struggle against colonialism. He was the Mayor of Dar es Salaam. His son, Abdulwahid Sykes, Secretary General of the Dockers Union, took over from him and founded TANU.

[37] Internet also contributes strongly to this dissemination. See 'Nyerere against Islam in Zanzibar and Tanganyika', accessed 4 June 2011, http://victorian.fortunecity.com/portfolio/543/nyerere_and_islam.htm; or 'Suppressing Dissent: The Crackdown on Muslims in Zanzibar" accessed 4 June 2011, http://www.ihrc.org.uk/attachments/7772_PROOF01mar12ZanzibarReport.pdf(a).

declarations by Muslims of the mainland against what is referred to as the 'Christian system' (*mfumo wa Ukristo*), accused of dominating Tanzania and discriminating the country's Muslims. It recurrently resorted to terms such as contempt (*dharau, uonevu*), discrimination (*ubaguzi*), humiliation (*dhulma*), hatred (*chuki*) or religious bias (*udini*) to describe this Christian system. In such politicized Islam, Nyerere embodies anti-Islam almost single-handedly. Given that in Muslim activism, religious affiliation is equated with national identity, Nyerere is portrayed simultaneously as an enemy of Islam and of the Zanzibari nation.

There were times when *An-Nuur* quoted Nyerere's words in positive terms, for example, when it recalled his discourses on the necessity of the struggle against colonial oppression. In its edition of 18-20 January 2011, for instance, an article cited Nyerere's "words of wisdom" according to which "the oppressed, if he does not fight his oppressor, will continue to suffer while his oppressor lives comfortably and peacefully"[38] to justify that Muslims, identified with the figure of the humiliated and the oppressed, may fight their Christian oppressors. But more than often Nyerere is vilified as a destroyer of Islam, with the support of the Catholic Church of Tanzania, through the use of "strategies to ensure the preferential treatment of Christians and discrimination of Muslims" (Ibid.). In this politicized Islamic discourse, the canonization process of Nyerere launched by the Catholic Church of Tanzania since 2006 is interpreted as the reward of the advantages Nyerere granted to the Church in his lifetime and his fight against the power and spread of Islam.[39] Today's canonization process is therefore perceived as proof of the existence of the said Christian preferential system.

---

38 "Anayedhulimiwa asipopambana na huyo dhalimu, yeye ataendelea kuteseka wakati dhalimu atastarehe kwa amani" (An-Nuur, 18-20 January 2011).

39 An-Nuur, 21–27 October 2011. On the canonization process, see notably Mesaki and Malipula (2011).

Conclusion

The 1964 Revolution has fuelled polarized imaginations of national identity. Whether it was the beginning of the Zanzibari Nation or of a new era of colonization of the Isles is a debate that remains unpacified. Together with the Union, remembered as the final step in Zanzibar's loss of sovereignty, it constitutes a collective "chosen trauma" (Glassman, 2011: incessantly placed at the basis of conceptions of identity, citizenship and nationhood. Among patriotic home-grown intellectuals committed to the Isles' increased autonomy, if not independence, Nyerere-bashing is increasingly mediating local conceptions of Zanzibari-ness. Although grievances against Nyerere's destructive politics are varied and can be expressed in different ways according to the people, moments and objectives of their mobilisation, the views that Nyerere was the Enemy of the Nation have become a widespread political discourse which is used to negatively define who is a Zanzibari, and to claim for change in the institutional status of the Isles.

From the partisan vantage point of these patriotic homespun historians, Nyerere is broadly cast in the reversed traits of the idealized Zanzibari: he is the invader who came from mainland Africa as opposed to a maritime civilization open to distant horizons; the Christian hater of Arabs and Muslims in a society that celebrates Arabness and Islam; the ignorant from the African bush as opposed to the island Swahili and Arab highly educated scholars. In this highly pejorative narrative deployed within nationalist circles, victimisation is a manifest and operates at different levels: naive Karume is the victim of cunning Nyerere; the Muslims are the victims of a Christian conspiracy hatched against them; the Arabs are the victims of the bloodthirsty passions of African assassins; and finally the islands of Zanzibar are the victims of the neocolonial appetites of mainland Tanzania. Given the memory trajectory of Nyerere in mainland Tanzania, characterised by a constant increase in official deference, Zanzibari growing anti-Nyererism variously fuelled by patriotic discourses therefore stands as an exception.

Certainly, one can still hear respondents admit that Nyerere's influence was beneficial to mainland Tanzania, evoking the formation of a sense of collective belonging on which the cohesion and unity of the people of the mainland would be built today. This sense of belonging is seen as the product of the spread of Swahili and the weakening of ethnic distinctions in former Tanganyika. In other words, the major themes underlying the official public memory of Nyerere as disseminated in mainland Tanzania are acknowledged by some Zanzibari critics of Nyerere. Yet they do so only when these themes are applied to the population of mainland Tanzania, not of Zanzibar. In other words, in Zanzibar, the figure of Nyerere can combine the attributes of a *Baba wa Taifa* with those of an *adui wa taifa* because the term *taifa* refers, in each phrase, to two separate entities: mainland Tanzania on the one hand; Zanzibar on the other hand.[40] On islands where the official narrative of the nation is not fully shared, the figure of Nyerere works as a negative 'place of memory' from which the patriotic literati can pioneer contemporary conceptions of belonging and nationhood.

References

AL-RIYAMI, Nasser Abdulla. *Zanzibar. Personalities and Events (1828–1972)*. Cairo: Beirut Bookshop, 2012.

AMORY, Deborah Peters. "The Politics of Identity on Zanzibar." PhD diss., Stanford University, 1994.

ANDERSON, Benedict. *Imagined Communities: Reflections on the Origin and Spread of Nationalism*. London: Verso, 1983.

ASKEW, Kelly. "Sung and Unsung: Musical Reflections on Tanzanian Postsocialisms." *Africa* 76, no. 1 (2006): 15–43.

BABAKERIM. *The Aftermath of Zanzibar Revolution*. Muscat Printing Press (self-published), 1994.

BAKARI, Mohammed A. *The Democratization Process in Zanzibar: A Retarded Transition*. Hamburg: Institut für Afrika-Kunde, 2001.

BAKARI, Mohammed, and Alexander Makulilo. "Beyond Polarity in Zanzibar. The 'Silent' Referendum and the Government of National Unity." *Journal of African Contemporary Studies* 30, no. 2 (2012): 195–218.

BECKER, Felicitas. "Remembering Nyerere: Political Dissent Rhetoric and Dissent in Contemporary Tanzania." *African Affairs* 112, no. 447 (2013): 238–261.

BISSELL, William C. "Engaging Colonial Nostalgia." *Cultural Anthropology* 20, no. 2 (2005): 215–248.

---

40 In this regard, the designation of the territorial entities that make up the Union posits the speakers on the political spectrum: officially, these two entities are referred to as 'Mainland Tanzania' *(Tanzania bara)* and 'Island Tanzania' *(Tanzania visiwani)*, but in Zanzibar, the mainland is often called 'Tanganyika'. The use of colonial names symbolically erases the establishment of the Union.

BURGESS, Thomas G. "Karume the Terrible." In *Race, Revolution, and the Struggle for Human Rights in Zanzibar*, ed. Thomas G. Burgess, 202–209. Ohio: Ohio University Press, 2009.

CAPLAN, Pat. "'But the Coast, of Course, Is Different'. Academic and Local Ideas about the East African Littoral." *Journal of Eastern African Studies* 1, no. 2 (2007): 305–320.

CHACHAGE, C. L. S. *Environment, Aid and Politics in Zanzibar*. Dar es Salaam: Dar es Salaam University Press, 2004.

CHACHAGE, Chambi, and Annar CASSAM. *Africa's Liberation. The Legacy of Nyerere*. Nairobi, Kampala: Pambazuka, Fountain Publishers, 2010.

CHASE, H. "The Zanzibar Treason Trial." *Review of African Political Economy* 6 (1976): 14–33.

CIVILLE, John R., and William R. DUGGAN. *Tanzania and Nyerere: A Study of Ujamaa and Nationhood*. Maryknoll: Orbis Books, 1976.

CLAYTON, Anthony. *The Zanzibar Revolution and its Aftermath*. London: C. Hurst & Company, 1981.

FAIR, Laura. *Pastimes and Politics. Culture, Community and Identity in Post-Abolition Urban Zanzibar, 1890–1945*. Oxford: James Currey, 2001.

FAIROOZ, Amani T. *Ukweli ni huu (kusuta uwongo)* [This Is the Truth (Challenging the Lie)]. Dubai (self-published), 1995.

FOUÉRÉ, Marie-Aude. "Chronique des élections de 2010 à Zanzibar [A Chronicle of the 2010 Election in Zanzibar]." *Politique africaine* 121 (2011): 127–145.

FOUÉRÉ, Marie-Aude. "Julius Nyerere, Ujamaa and Political Morality in Contemporary Tanzania." *African Studies Review* 57, no. 1 (2014): 1–24.

FOUÉRÉ, Marie-Aude. "Reinterpreting Revolutionary Zanzibar in the Media Today: The Case of *Dira* Newspaper." *Journal of Eastern African Studies* 6, no. 4 (2012): 672–689.

FOUÉRÉ, Marie-Aude. "Tanzanie: la nation à l'épreuve du postsocialisme [Tanzania: The Nation Put to the Test of Postsocialism]." *Politique africaine* 121 (2011): 69–85.

GELLNER, Ernst. *Nations and Nationalism*. Oxford: Blackwell, 1983.

GHASSANY, Harith. *Kwaheri Ukoloni, Kwaheri Uhuru! Zanzibar na Mapinduzi ya Afrabia* [Goodbye Independence, Goodbye Colonialism! Zanzibar and the Revolution of Afrabia]. Tring, Herts: Anno Domini, 2010.

GLASSMAN, Jonathon. *War of Words, War of Stones. Racial Thought and Violence in Colonial Zanzibar*. Bloomington and Indianapolis: Indiana University Press, 2011.

HARDING, Leonhard. "Nyerere in Neuem Licht. Interpretationen in den Lebensgeschichten von Sansibaris." In *Unser Leben vor der Revolution und danach–Maisha yetu kabla ya Mapinduzi na baadaye. Autobiographische Dokumentartexte sansibarischer Zeitzeugen*, ed. Sauda al-Barwani, Regina Feindt, Ludwig Gerhardt, Leonard Harding and Ludger Wimmelbücker, 493–577. Köln: Köppe Verlag, 2003.

HOBSBAWM, Eric. *Nations and Nationalism since 1780: Programme, Myth, Reality*. Cambridge: Cambridge University Press, 1990.

HUNTER, Helen-Louise. *Zanzibar. The Hundred Days Revolution*. Santa Barbara: ABC-CLIO, 2010.

KHARUSI, Ahmed S. *Zanzibar: Africa's First Cuba. A Case Study of the New Colonialism*. Richmond: Zanzibar Organisation, 1967.

LOFCHIE, Michael F. *Zanzibar: Background to Revolution*. Princeton: Princeton University Press, 1965.

LOIMEIER, R. "Memories of Revolution: Zur Deutungsgeschischte einer Revolution (Sansibar 1964)." *Afrika Spectrum* 41, no. 2 (2006): 175–197.

LOIMEIER, R. "Sit Local, Think Global." *Journal for Islamic Studies* 27 (2007): 16–39.

LOIMEIER, R. "Zanzibar's Geography of Evil: the Moral Discourse of the Ansar al-sunna in Contemporary Zanzibar." *Journal for Islamic Studies* 31 (2011): 4–28.

LUDWIG, Frieder. "After Ujamaa: Is Religious Revivalism a Threat to Tanzania's Stability?" In *Questioning the Secular State: The Worldwide Resurgence of Religion in Politics*, ed. D. Westerlund, 216–236. London: Hurst, 1992.

LUDWIG, Frieder. *Church and State in Tanzania, Aspects of A Changing Relationships, 1961–1994*. Leiden-BostonKöln: Brill, 1999.

MAPURI, Omar. *The 1964 Revolution: Achievements and Prospects*. Dar es Salaam: Tema, 1996.

MARTIN, Esmond B. *Zanzibar: Tradition and Revolution*. London: Hamish Hamilton, 1978.

MATHESON, Archie. "Maridhiano: Zanzibar's Remarkable Reconciliation and Government of National Unity." *Journal of Eastern African Studies* 6, no. 4 (2012): 591–612.

MAZRUI, Ali A. *"The Titan" of Tanzania: Julius K. Nyerere's Legacy*. Binghamton: The Institute of Global Cultural Studies, 2002.

MESAKI, Simeon, and Mrisho MALIPULA, "Julius Nyerere's Influence and Legacy: From a Proponent of Familyhood to a Candidate for Sainthood." *International Journal of Sociology and Anthropology* 3, no. 3 (2011): 93–100.
MUHSIN, Ali al-Barwani. *Conflicts and Harmony in Zanzibar*. Memoirs. Dubai (self-published), 2002.
MWIJAGE, Ludovick S. *The Dark Side of Nyerere's Legacy*. London: Adelphi Press, 1996 [1994].
MYERS, Garth A. "Narrative Representations of Revolutionary Zanzibar". *Journal of Historical Geography* 26, no. 3 (2000): 429–448.
MYERS, Garth A. *Verandah of Power. Colonialism and Space in Urban Africa*. Syracuse, NY: Syracuse University Press, 2003.
NORA, Pierre. *Les lieux de mémoire* [Places of Memory]. I, II, III. Paris: Gallimard, 1997.
NYERERE, Julius Kambarage. *Juliasi Kaisari* [Julius Caesar]. Nairobi: Oxford University Press, 1963.
NYERERE, Julius Kambarage. *Mabepari wa Venisi* [The Merchant of Venice]. Dar es Salaam: Oxford University Press, 1969.
OTHMAN, Haroub, and Chris M. PETER. *Zanzibar and the Union Question*. Zanzibar: Zanzibar Legal Services Centre, 2006.
OTHMAN, Haroub. "The Union with Zanzibar." In *Mwalimu. The Influence of Nyerere*, ed. Colin Legum and Geoffrey Mmari, 170–175. Oxford, Dar es Salaam, Trenton NJ: James Currey, Mkuki na Nyota, Africa World Press.
PETERSON, Derek R. *Creative Writing. Translation, Bookkeeping, and the Work of Imagination in Colonial Kenya*. Portsmouth, NH: Heinemann, 2004.
RAWLENCE, Ben. "Briefing: The Zanzibar Election." *African Affairs* 104, no. 416 (2005): 515–523.
RICOEUR, Paul. *La mémoire, l'histoire, l'oubli* [Memory, History, Forgetting]. Paris: Seuil, 2000.
SAID, Mohamed. *The Life and Times of Abdulwahid Sykes: The Untold Story of the Muslim Struggle against British Colonialism in Tanganyika*. London: Minerva Press, 1998.
SHIVJI, Issa G. *Pan-Africanism or Pragmatism? Lessons of Tanganyika–Zanzibar Union*. Dar es Salaam: Mkuki na Nyota/Addis Abeba: OSSREA, 2008.

SIVALON, John. *Kanisa Katoliki na Siasa ya Tanzania Bara 1953–1985* [The Catholic Church and Politics in Tanzania Mainland]. Ndanda: Ndanda, 1992.

SMITH, William E. *We Must Run while They Walk. A Portrait of Africa's Julius Nyerere*. New York: Random House, 1972.

WERBNER, Richard. "Beyond Oblivion: Confronting Memory Crisis." In *Memory and the Postcolony: African Anthropology and the Critique of Power*, ed. Richard Werbner, 1–17. London: Zed Books, 1998.

WILSON, Amrit. *US Foreign Policy and Revolution: The Creation of Tanzania*. London: Pluto Press, 1989.

PART 5:

Politics & Poetry

Chapter 9

Tanzanian Newspaper Poetry: Political Commentary in Verse

Kelly Askew*

Swahili poetry, recognized as one of the world's distinctive poetic traditions (Greene et al, 2012), emerged in the coastal regions of Kenya and Tanzania. It subsequently developed into an East African regional form, thanks to the widespread usage of Kiswahili as a *lingua franca*. Whilst written examples of Swahili poetry date to the early sixteenth century, Swahili poetic traditions (which include both oral and literary, composed and improvisatory, sung and recited forms) are believed to be considerably older (Mulokozi, 1975; Mulokozi and Sengo, 1995). Over the centuries, poets composing in Kiswahili have generated and still typically adhere to a canon of compositional rules concerning meter (*mizani*), rhyme (*vina*), strophe (*beti*), refrain (*kibwagizo*), and the division of lines (*mishororo*) into line segments (*vipande*).[1] Wide variation in form can be found, as well as in topic, but common throughout is a passion for subtlety and artful deployment of language. One common subgenre is that of praise poetry, a famous example of which is the earliest dated manuscript (1517 AD): the *Swifa ya Mwana*

---

* This text was first published in the *Journal of Eastern African Studies*, vol. 8, no. 3 (2014), pp. 515–537. It is reprinted with permission. The research on which this essay is based was funded by the University of Michigan Office of the Senior Vice Provost for Academic Affairs (OSVPAA) in two grants (2012, 2013). My deep thanks go to Senior Vice Provost Lester Monts for his support. This essay was written while the author was a fellow at the Wissenschaftskolleg zu Berlin (2012–2013). Support of the institute is gratefully acknowledged, with special thanks for the opportunity to work with master poet Abdilatif Abdalla on the translations of the poems discussed herein. To Abdilatif Abdalla I offer my deep gratitude for long discussions, shared translation labors, and a cherished friendship. Early drafts received critical input from the "African Print Cultures" network, especially Karin Barber, Rebecca Jones, Stephanie Newell, Derek Peterson, David Pratten, and Kate Skinner; and from participants at the Humboldt-Universität zu Berlin Afrikakolloquium, especially Lutz Diegner, Vital Kazimoto, and Howard Stern. My thanks as well go to the two anonymous reviewers who offered very insightful suggestions for improvement. All errors and infelicities are my own.

1 For more on the varying traditions and structures of Swahili poetry, see Abedi (1954); Biersteker (1996); Harries (1956, 1962); Komba (1976); Maw (1999); Miehe et al. (2004); Mulokozi and Sengo (1995); Njogu (2004); Saavedra Casco (2007); Shariff (1988). A modernist school of Swahili poetry rejecting the traditional rules of composition and advocating free verse did emerge in the 1970s (Madumulla et al, 1999) but this has not proved popular.

Manga ("Ode to Mwana Manga") attributed to Fumo Liyongo, a warrior prince of the northern Swahili coast who is believed to have lived sometime between the ninth and twelfth centuries (Mulokozi and Sengo, 1995; Miehe and Abdalla, 2004). Another subgenre is epic "war poetry" associated with the German colonial period and analyzed in great depth by Biersteker and Shariff (1995), Miehe et al. (2002), and Saavedra Casco (2007).

When newspapers emerged in the late nineteenth century under German colonial administration of what was then Deutsch-Ostafrika, they offered a new venue for Swahili poetry. By the 1910s, Swahili poetry constituted a regular feature of newspapers, whether state or missionary productions. Poetry could be found alongside news about local events; international news; editorials; explication of government policies; announcements; agricultural, educational and public health advice; advertisements; obituaries; and letters to the editor (Scotton, 1978; Kezilahabi, 2008). Its popularity grew with independence, and further yet when socialism was institutionalized in 1967, paralleling the privileged position poetry assumed within the cultural policy of the new nation (Askew, 2002). The growth of the press from 20 print periodicals before the start of World War I (11 in German, 6 in Swahili, and 3 in other African languages), to 50 in 1954 and to 119 in 1986, took a sudden leap when liberalization of the media took root in the 1990s, with over 323 periodicals (the vast majority in Swahili) registered by 1996, including nine daily newspapers (Sturmer, 1998: 42–45, 65, 178; see also Kezilahabi, 2008). Newspapers hit the pavements from Zanzibar to the Western borders on the Great Lakes, and most sought poetry to include within their pages. This essay will present and analyze praise poems from newspapers in what was Deutsch-Ostafrika, then Tanganyika, then Tanzania: (1) German colonial-era poems about Kaiser Wilhelm II; (2) British colonial-era poems about King George V; and (3) post-independence poems about first president Julius Nyerere published at various points in his political career and following his death. By examining them within their political and historical contexts, a history of newspaper poetry emerges and with it an exploration of the poetics of popular expectations and assessments of governance.

Swahili Newspaper Poetry in Deutsch-Ostafrika

The earliest Swahili newspapers in the former Deutsch-Ostafrika (Tanzanian mainland) and the British Protectorate of Zanzibar were Universities' Mission to Central Africa (UMCA) Anglican missionary publications: *Msimulizi* ("The Storyteller") launched first in Zanzibar in 1888, the short-lived *Mtenga Watu* ("The Converter") on the mainland from 1890 to 1892, and the newspaper widely viewed as the first true newspaper on the mainland *Habari za Mwezi* ("News of the Month"), which ran from 1894 to World War I and reached a monthly print run of 6000 copies per issue (Lemke, 1929; Sturmer, 1998). These likely did not feature any Swahili poetry since according to Sturmer:

> At the very beginning, *Habari za Mwezi* ran only religious articles, but after negative responses from the readership, secular items were printed, too. Nevertheless, its contents often were of European origin and did not serve the needs of the indigenous population (Sturmer, 1998: 30).

The first secular Swahili newspaper was *Kiongozi* ("The Leader") launched in 1904 at the Government School in Tanga, Deutsch-Ostafrika's first state and first secular school. Tanga School had been established in 1892 by Governor Julius Freiherr von Soden, and aimed to produce Swahili-speaking African bureaucrats to facilitate colonial administration and commercial trade in the territory (Askew, 2002: 43f). *Kiongozi* was to support this by being a source of information for Africans and to promote government agendas. It was subsidized by the government and after acquiring a high-speed press in 1905, issues were released monthly, reaching a print run of 3000 copies and becoming the most influential newspaper of the period (Lemke, 1929; Sturmer, 1998; Geider, 2002).

Poetry became a regular feature of *Kiongozi*, transferring into massmediated format the Swahili passion for verse. In her 1929 doctoral thesis on *Swahili Newspapers and Journals in German East Africa*, Hilda Lemke comments, "In almost all newspapers, poetry plays a big role. The Swahili can express everything in their poetic language... and newspaper editors always succeeded in acquiring one or more poets for their papers." (Lemke, 1929: 44). One finds in the pages of *Kiongozi* poems of praise for the Kaiser on his birthday and for his might in quashing the Maji Maji "rebellion". Thus was the praise poem, especially of political leaders, established as a regular feature of newspaper poetry. German colonial editors appreciated Swahili praise poetry and would sometimes commission Swahili poets to compose poems (Saavedra Casco, 2007). On occasion, according to Lemke, these poems would be translated into German and published together for readers to be able to compare the two and try to teach themselves either Swahili or German. One Swahili poet, Hamisi Auwi who composed a poem entitled "Who Has the True Authority If Not the Kaiser?" was even rewarded with a trip to Germany to meet the Kaiser, who "richly rewarded" him (Lemke, 1929: 44; Velten, 1907: 343–349; Miehe and Abdalla, 2004: 471–477).

Inexplicably, the first German missionary publications did not appear until nearly two decades after German missionaries arrived in East Africa. In 1904 (the same year that *Kiongozi* was launched), Lutherans produced periodicals in the Chagga and Shambala languages but it was not until the German Evangelical missionary began publishing *Pwani na Bara* ("Coast and Hinterland") in Swahili in 1910 that a religious alternative to the "godless" *Kiongozi* was offered. Swahili poetry found a place within this publication as well, an example of which is the 1911 praise poem for Kaiser Wilhelm II entitled *Shukrani za Africa* ("Thanks from Africa") composed by Jakobo Ngombo. *Shukrani za Africa* is an acrostic, with each line beginning with a successive letter in the Roman alphabet, demonstrating the Swahili passion for word play (Maw, 1999).[2] It features a loose poetic structure composed of rhymed couplets and triplets with hemistiches that do not adhere to a strict syllabic count. It is heavy-handed in its praise, extolling the Kaiser's might in extinguishing the Bushiri and Maji Maji uprisings and issues a warning to any who would dare challenge the Kaiser. It urges residents to pay their taxes and to pray for the Kaiser's continued existence. Missionary Pastor Delius who knew the poet and his poetic output commented:

> Even finer and more artistic is a "Song of Thanks from Africa" which Jakobo composed as a greeting on the Kaiser's birthday, and which has already been published in *Pwani na Bara*. With its noble language it appears like a psalm from the Old Testament (Lemke, 1929: 43).

---

2 Another example of an acrostic, which was published in the newspaper *Mambo Leo*, is the poem "A.B.C.D." by Omari Sebu of Tabora (in *Mashairi ya Mambo* Leo, vol. 1, no. 23, 1966 [1946]). This is an innovation building from an earlier Swahili poetic genre of composing acrostics based on the Arabic alphabet. My thanks to an anonymous reviewer for pointing this out.

Shukrani za Africa ("Thanks from Africa")[3]
Jakobo Ngombo
Pwani na Bara (January 1911)

Afrika furahi, mshukuru sana Kaisari wee;	Rejoice, Africa, be very grateful to Kaiser
Baraka na amani kakupa Kaisari yee!	Blessing and peace the Kaiser has given to you!
Jina lake la sifa na lenyi ufahari.	His name is glorious and full of fame
Kumbuka waasi wafanywavyo ni Kaisari	Remember how rebels are treated by the Kaiser
Chuma pendo, umpende sana Kaisari saa;	Gather love that you may love dearly the Kaiser
Dola yake ni kubwa, miji yote kaiwasha taa!	The empire is big: in all towns he has lit lamps![4]
Eleza ya kale kama sasa yakufaa,	Tell of the past and if the present is useful to you
Fundisha watoto wako wapate kumtii.	Teach your children so that they obey him
Ginsi gani wafanya matata wala hutulii?[5]	Why do you cause trouble instead of being calm?
Hura, hura umwigie, umwombee na uhai,	Shout 'Hurrah, hurrah!' for him and pray that he have a long life
Itokeapo hatari, aikingiyae ni yeye tai,	When danger threatens, it is he, the eagle, who protects[6]
Jina lake la sifa na lenyi ufahari.	His name is glorious and full of fame
Kumbuka waasi wafanywavyo ni Kaisari,	Remember how rebels are treated by the Kaiser
Lazimu umwogope wala usimkosee,	You must fear him and not go against him
Mheshimu sana na kodi umletee,	Respect him and pay your taxes to him

---

3 Lemke (1929: 49–50), trans. A. Abdalla and K. Askew.
4 Likely a metaphorical phrase indicating that he has dispensed darkness in many places.
5 The correct term is *jinsi* but to maintain the acrostic form, the poet instead substituted a 'G'
6 Brandenburg eagle, symbol of the Prussian state.

Nani aondoaye shida zako kila pahali?	Who else removes all your troubles everywhere?
Nguvu hizi ni za watu walio wakali,	This is the strength of fierce people.
Ona ujue, ya kwamba hii serkali,	See and know very well that this is a government.
Palipo na vita aendaye ni yeye shujaa,	Where there is war it is he, the hero, who strides forth
Raiya wote salama katuondolea mabaa,	All citizens are safe. He has removed all danger
Salaam Bwana wetu wee, na baada ya salaam:	'Hail to you, our Lord!' and after greetings:
Shujaa mkuu ndiwe, wote twakufahamu.	'You are the greatest hero. We all recognize you.
Tangu Bushiri na majimaji akusubutuye nani?	Since Bushiri and Maji Maji who dares rise against you?
Umewatibu kwa nguvu wala huwezekani	You dealt with them with unmatched force.
Vuruguvurugu waondoa kwa watu wakaidi,[7]	You eradicate disorder caused by stubborn people.'
Wakristo mwombeeni maisha, aishi azidi,	Christians, pray that he be blessed with a long life.
Yeee, Mungu azidi kumpa nguvu na uzima,	Oh, God, continue to grant him strength and health.
Ziondolewe shida zote za hapa Afrika daima	That he may continue so that all of Africa's troubles are dispelled forever.

Colonial-era newspaper poetry also commented on contemporary events in a manner still characteristic of Swahili newspaper poetry today. The following ode to the Kaiser on the occasion of his birth is more a depiction of the unfolding of World War I than a birthday commemoration. With its 13 stanzas, *Kwa Siku Kuu ya Kaiser Wetu* ("On Our Kaiser's Birthday") exemplifies the most popular poetic form of nineteenth-century Swahili poetry (Harries, 1956; Miehe et al, 2002) and the one most typical of newspaper poetry past and present: the 16-syllable per line quatrain (called *shairi* form). According to Lemke,

---

7 Corrected *wahaidi* to the correct *wakaidi*, the former being a nonsense word.

Kiongozi's editors published this poem side by side with a German translation so that all readers could enjoy it.

Kwa Siku Kuu ya Kaiser Wetu ("On Our Kaiser's Birthday")[8]
Ramazan Saidi
Kiongozi (February 1915)

(1) August ni mwanzo, wa kuenezewa vita.	In August began the spread of the war
Yakatujia mawazo, nyoyo zetu zikijuta.	Ideas came to us while regret filled our hearts
Adui mzo kwa mzo, kuja kwetu kutupita.	Many enemies came to dominate us
Mungu atawalani, kwa baa la kujitakia.	May God curse them for bringing calamity upon themselves.
(2) Wote tukastaajabu, Wangereza watakani?	All of us were amazed: what do the English want?
Watajitia aibu, kwa nguvu za jermani.	They'll embarrass themselves against German might
Wajuwao kuzurubu, wakiingia utamboni.[9]	Because [the Germans] know how to fight a war
Mungu atawalani, kwa baa la kujitakia.	May God curse them for bringing calamity upon themselves.
(3) Maadui wengi sana, walijazana Ulaya.	Many enemies gathered in Europe
Wakataka kupigana, kuyaeneza mabaya.	They wanted to fight and spread evil
Dola kupunguziana, [missing hemistich]	to reduce each other's empires
Mungu atawalani, kwa baa la kujitakia.	May God curse them for bringing calamity upon themselves.

---

8 Lemke (1929: 46–48), trans. A. Abdalla and K. Askew.
9 *Kuingia utamboani* is an idiomatic phrase meaning "to fight".

(9) *Wangereza wasikiri, araza ya jermani.*
The English failed to heed the Germans' warning

Walizani mahodari, jamii ulimwenguni.
Thinking themselves the world's finest

Kumbe, ni chao kiburi, pambo lao mwilini.
But it is only their arrogance that they decorate themselves with

Mungu atawalani, kwa baa la kujitakia.
May God curse them for bringing calamity upon themselves.

(10) *Wadachi wakauzika, wakaanza kuwapiga:*
The Germans got angry and started fighting them

Taveta wakaiteka, pamwe na muji wa Vanga;
They captured Taveta and the town of Vanga;

Hata Gasi wamefika, mnyororo kuwatunga.
They even reached Gasi, shackled and chained them!

Mungu atawalani, kwa baa la kujitakia.
May God curse them for bringing calamity upon themselves.

(11) *Hata Ulaya jamaani, kuna mashujaa sana.*
My friends, even Europe has many heroes.

Wamewapiga yakini, kwa pigo la kiungwana.
They have really fought them with noble attacks

Huko kwao Berlini, mateka wamejazana.
There in their capital Berlin, they've taken many prisoners of war.

Mungu atawalani, kwa baa la kujitakia.
May God curse them for bringing calamity upon themselves.

(12) *Sasa ni mwezi wa sita, hisabu nawaambia!*
It is now the sixth month—I'm counting it for you!

Na wale walioteta, sasa wamejinamia.
And those who fought now bow down

Majeshi waliyoleta, yamekwisha angukia.
The army they brought has surrendered

Sasa wanajutia, kwa baa la kujitakia.
Now they regret bringing calamity upon themselves.

(13) Kaiser wetu mpole, mshujaa wa wadachi.	Our Kaiser is calm, hero of the Germans
Uishi wewe milele, jamia kila nchi.	May you live forever, in all countries
Kokote utawale, uzistawishe nchi.	May you rule everywhere, developing the countries
Siku yako kufika, salam nakuletea.	On this your birthday I bring you greetings.

In this example, poet Ramazan Saidi employs a refrain (*kibwagizo* or *kipokeo*) repeated as the final line of each stanza (*beti*), which serves to emphasize his main point. While it is normally the case that a refrain is sustained throughout the entire poem, in this instance the poet abandons it in the final two verses. In verse 12, he shifts emphasis slightly but significantly from "God will curse [the English] for bringing calamity upon themselves" to "Now they regret bringing calamity upon themselves." And it is only in the final line of the entire poem that the poet at last makes reference to the Kaiser's birthday, the putative subject of the poem. This poem would be more accurately described as an analysis of the war as it played out in the East African theater, and this is acknowledged by *Kiongozi*'s editors, albeit in the paternalistic fashion of the time:

> This translation of the poem is as literal as possible in order to make it easier for interested German readers to translate it in reverse. For this reason it will often appear clumsy and inelegant which is not, however, the case in the original text. The recurring rhyme in fact has been chosen and modified with great skill. The whole things shows that our natives completely understand the course of events and shows that even the events leading up to the war are completely clear to them (Lemke, 1929: 48f).

Scholars of Swahili poetry highlight the long-standing deployment of verse for praise and political commentary, such as the famous Fumo Liyongo texts, and the use of metaphor and innuendo to convey subtexts. Thus we have, for instance, from Zache (1897) and Miehe et al. (2002) the following example of a double-edged epic poem (*utenzi* style), titled *Uimbo wa Kaizari* ("Song for the Kaiser"). The poet Mbaraka bin Shomari employs a performative style reminiscent of West African griots, whose public declarations about the generosity of a potential patron are intended to induce said patron to be generous, often to great effect.

---

10 Miehe et al (2002), trans. Miehe et al.

Uimbo wa Kaizari ('Song for the Kaiser')[10]
Mbaraka bin Shomari (c.1897)

(1) Salam kwa wetu bana, Kaisari wa Virhamu,	(1) Greetings to our Lord Kaiser Wilhelm.
Bana mkubwa na sana, maarufu hatta Shamu.	He is our great Lord well known even in Syria.
Sisi takupenda sana, wadogo hatta harimu:	We like you very much both young and old:
Hapana tena hapana, wewe ndio Kaizari!	There is nobody else. You are the Kaiser!
(2) Wewe ndio Kaizari, mtoto wa Virhamu;	(2) You are the Kaiser, son of Wilhelm[11]
Jina lake mashuhuri, sote tunalifahamu	His famous name, we all know it:
Ulaya na Zingibari, na Mrithi hatta Amu	From Europe to Zanzibar, and from Egypt to Lamu:
Hapana tena hapana, wewe ndio Kaizari!	There is nobody else. You are the Kaiser!
(3) Wewe ndio Kaizari, hatta na wazee wako!	(3) You are the Kaiser. Even your forefathers!
Tumezipata habari, kwa huku mbali tuliko.	We've got the news, far away, where we are.
Una wengi askari, wahesabiwa lukuku	You have a lot of soldiers. They number in hundreds of thousands.
Hapana tena hapana, wewe ndio Kaizari!	There is nobody else. You are the Kaiser!
(4) Kaizari ya Wadachi, na barra ya Afrika.[12]	(4) Kaiser of the Germans, and of the African continent
Nakusifu, bwana wangu, upate kunipulika	I praise you, my lord, that you may hear me.
Niletee langu fungu, nipate kufurahika	Give me my share, so that I may be happy:
Hapana tena hapana, wewe ndio Kaizari!	There is nobody else. You are the Kaiser!

---

11 Kaiser Wilhelm II was the son of Friedrich III, not Wilhelm I.

12 *Wadachi* does not fit the rhyme scheme for this verse, but as an anonymous reviewer suggested, it was likely an editor's substitution for *Wazungu*, which would have indeed fit.

This poem, published significantly not in a newspaper but in an academic collection in its original Arabic orthography, transliterated into Roman orthography, and with German translation (Zache, 1897: 133–137) is instructive in multiple ways. First, it exemplifies how a stark political claim ("Give me my share") can be cloaked in praise ("I praise you, my lord") and in implicit critique ("that you may hear me") – for the Kaiser may not read or listen to a poem if not framed as laudatory. In contrast to the above newspaper poems, it offers an example of "poetic license", namely the articulation of discontent, dissent, and/or critique through artful deployment of language, which is tolerated to varying degrees by those in power. As Vail and White argue "poetry in sub-Saharan Africa [is] licensed by a freedom of expression which violates normal conventions... in ways that the prevailing social and political codes would not normally permit, so long as it is done through poetry" (Vail and White, 1991: 43).[13] In these Kaiser poems, however, the heavy appearance of exaltation bespeaks a carefully choreographed dance with the colonial state, which expected and demanded obeisance and glorification from its subjects.[14] Mbaraka bin Shomari complied but in his final stanza meta-discursively drew attention both to what he was doing and the discrepancies in status and power between himself and the subject of his poem (Miehe et al, 2002: 479).

(9) *Wakatabahu khadimu, Mimi kijitu fakiri.*	(9) This was written by a servant, I'm an unimportant, poor person
Jina langu mwalimu, Mbaraka bin Shomari.	My name is Mwalimu, Mbaraka bin Shomari.
Nimesifu mwazzimu, Mfalme akhiyari	I've praised the Great, the beloved Kaiser —
Hapana tena hapana, wewe ndio Kaizari!	There is nobody else. You are the Kaiser!

Mbaraka bin Shomari died from smallpox in 1897, the year his poem was published by Zache. He had written a number of poems that have been preserved in German collections, including one on the German bombardment of Zanzibar that won him particular praise from colonial authorities and scholars (Velten, 1907; Saavvedra Casco, 2007). An Islamic teacher and jurist, he had assisted colonial authorities in their

---

13 For more examples, see Askew (2002, 2003); Finnegan (1970); Gunner (1994); Mitchell (1956); Scott (1990); Tracey (1948).

14 For a rich analysis of Swahili poetry during the German colonial, see Saavedra Casco (2007).

work even serving as a scribe and translator in the court martial and conviction of rebel leader Hassan bin Omari. That ought to seal Shomari's fate in the historical record as a "collaborator". Yet in assessing his poetic output, both Saavedra Casco and Miehe et al. independently find him to have penned veiled critiques of German colonialism: "Going through the lines one is inclined to call them eulogies. A closer look reveals that they contain a lot of criticism" (Saavvedra Casco, 2007: 1943f; Miehe et al, 2002: 92).

To summarize, poems in praise of Kaiser Wilhelm II place a solid emphasis on praise, even appearing at times sycophantic accolades. Just as Kaiser Wilhelm inculcated his reputation as a military man, so too do these poems focus on militaristic themes of battles won, honor secured, and enemies soundly defeated. In reviewing these colonial-era poets, Kezilahabi dismissed them as "bootlickers" who betrayed their people in glorifying the colonial oppressors (Kezilahabi, 1973: 64). Yet this is to deny the real potential for repercussions were poets to openly articulate anti-colonial sentiments, especially directed at a triumphant German state that had won the Abushiri war (1888-1889), the Hehe wars (1891-1898), and the Maji Maji wars (1905-1907), hanging or beheading rebels to reiterate their supremacy. Instead, one must seek the subtle mechanisms by which discontent and dissent were conveyed (Arnold, 1973; Mulokozi, 1975; Biersteker, 1996). As highly public records, newspapers were (and are still) dangerous venues for the expression of dissident sentiment. It is thus not surprising that of the examples presented here, it is the one from an academic collection that reveals the most critique, though still opaque and allusive. As Hunter notes (2012: 9).

> while it is tempting to see such newspapers as offering a rare and valuable source for African intellectual history, this is a particular kind of colonial intellectual history, one shaped by the power dynamics which produced the newspapers and by the forms of engagement proposed within them.

Swahili Newspaper Poetry during British Colonial Period

World War I brought a temporary cessation to the Swahili press in East Africa, with not one of the above-mentioned publications surviving the war.[15] A hiatus of a decade would pass before the now British-

---

15 *Pwani na Bara*, which initially ran from 1910-1916, was relaunched in 1978 and apparently still prints today. A new Kiongozi completely unrelated to the Tanga School newspaper was launched in 1950 as the main publication of the Catholic Church and also continues today. See Sturmer (1998).

administered Education Department launched *Mambo Leo* ("Current Affairs") in 1923 in Dar es Salaam. A monthly, it included poetry and proved to be a highly popular periodical, though always remaining a mouthpiece for the colonial government. According to both Hunter and Geider, *Mambo Leo* featured submissions primarily from local authors and "was intended to respond to demands for a newspaper from the African population of Tanganyika, evident from the fact that its circulation rose from 6,000 in 1923 to 15,000 by 1938, and that demand always outstripped supply" (Hunter, 2012: 285; Geider, 2002: 263-268).

Mambo Leo would follow in the tradition established by the German colonial press of publishing poetry praising the ruler of the empire, in this case, King George V. However, whereas praises for the German emperor focused primarily on his military prowess and might, King George was commemorated for the pageantry and spectacle of empire, exemplified by symbols of authority like crowns and grand birthday celebrations. The following poem by an unnamed poet who identifies himself only by the pen name *Kaniki Nguo ya Kale* (meaning "Coarse Clothing from Long Ago") describes the King's birthday celebration to take place in the absence of the king (who remained in Europe). The only personal attribute attributed to King George is that he liked his subjects. Hints of trouble and dissatisfaction with the colonial order are implied by the many references to the forces on hand to keep the peace, the frequent (seemingly forced) exhortations to be joyful, and a refrain that encourages readers to show the king due respect on this special occasion.

Heshima ya King George V ("Respect for King George V")[16]

Kaniki Nguo ya Kale, Dar es Salaam

Mambo Leo (c.1923-36)

(1) Leo siku ya tatu katika mwezi wa Juni	(1) Today is the third day in the month of June
Kazaliwa Bwana wetu King George Sultani	When was born our lord and sultan King George
Jamii ya wote shime andameni Mkongeni	Everyone hurry up and proceed to Mkongeni
Tukatazame heshima ya maulana King George.	So we see respect paid to His Highness King George

---

16 *Mashairi ya Mambo Leo*, vol. 1, 28–29 (1966 [1946]), trans. A. Abdalla and K. Askew.
17 *Asad* is Arabic for "lion."

(2) King George ni mwana wa King Edward	(2) King George is the son of King Edward
Amezaliwa Ulaya nchi ya upande wa kaskazi	He was born in Europe in a country to the north
Kama tujuavyo yeye ni pekee asadi[17]	As we know he is a special lion
Tukatazame heshima ya maulana King George.	So we see respect paid to His Highness King George
(3) Watakutana mabwana wakubwa na wadogo	(3) The noble and the lowly will participate
Hapazuiwi kijana akuambiaye ni mrongo	No youth will not be denied; whoever tells you otherwise is a liar
Wala fujo hapatakuwa ya mafimbo na magongo	Nor will there be disturbances with sticks or clubs
Tukatazame heshima ya maulana King George.	So we see respect paid to His Highness King George
(4) Siku hiyo ni siku ya furija na anasa[18]	(4) This day is a day of celebration and entertainment
Atakayejaliwa kwenda furaha hatakosa	Whoever attends will certainly be happy
Kwani ni siku ya idi bashasha yatupasa	For it is a holiday and we are expected to be joyful
Tukatazame heshima ya maulana King George.	So we see respect paid to His Highness King George
(5) Atahudhuria Gavana bwana wa Tanganyika	(5) His Lord the Governor of Tanganyika will attend
Siku hiyo mwenye nishani itampasa kupachika	On this day whoever has medals should wear them
Asiyekuwa na mwana hata jiwe ataeleka[19]	The one without children should carry a stone
Tukatazame heshima ya maulana King George.	So we see respect paid to His Highness King George

18 *Furija* is colloquiual Arabic for celebration.
19 Reference to the Swahili saying: *Asiyekuwa na mwana aeleke jiwe* ("She who doesn't have a child should carry a stone on her back"), meaning everyone should participate, and come in big numbers (bringing even fake children).

(6) Akina Bwana Askari hupanda wao farasi	(6) The soldiers will mount their horses
Mwendo wao taratibu kama mwendo wa papasi	They will pass slowly by, at the speed of a tick
Kuwaonyesha raia mambo yasiyo kiasi	To show the citizens extraordinary things
Tukatazame heshima ya maulana King George.	So we see respect paid to His Highness King George

(7) Tazameni ibura ya Mfalme kuwa Ulaya	(7) Look at this extraordinary celebration for a king who is in Europe
Huko mambo mbayana kama amehudhuria[20]	There [at Mkongomeni] things will be celebrated as though he were attending
Jamaa ukaidi wani mbona mtaangamia[21]	What's the point of being stubborn lest you be destroyed?[22]
Tukatazame heshima ya maulana King George.	So we see respect paid to His Highness King George

(8) Kuna wingi wa Polisi wazuiao hatari	(8) There are many police to prevent danger
Wapitisha kwa kiasi zote pia motakari	They only allow selected motorcars to pass
Hiyo ndiyo dunia wala nyingine haiwi	That is indeed how the world is. It cannot be otherwise
Tukatazame heshima ya maulana King George.	So we see respect paid to His Highness King George

(9) Mfalme King George wote mnamjua	(9) Sovereign King George all of you know him
Kwa alama za mataji mara utamjua	By the symbol of his crowns you'll immediately recognize him
Na utakapo ya zaidi soma utajua	And if you want to know more, read about him
Tukatazame heshima ya maulana King George.	So we see respect paid to His Highness King George

---

20 *Mbayana* means "openly, in an open fashion," meaning no restrictions, no one will be banned from attending.
21 *Wani* = shortened form of *wa nini*.
22 This line has no seeming connection to what preceded it. Likely forced for the sake of rhyme.

(10) King George ana sifa kupenda wake raia	(10) King George is known for liking his subjects
Walio bora na hafifu wote twamfurahia	The upper and lower classes we all are happy for him
Tumwombee Rabuka huruma amzidishie	Let us pray to God will show more mercy to him
Tukatazame heshima ya maulana King George.	So we see respect paid to His Highness King George
(11) Sifa hapa zimekoma mwaka huu najaribu	(11) The praises end here, this year I am trying
Labda nitapata yangu huwa bahati nasibu	Perhaps I will have my luck
Sikukaa nasimama nangoja yangu matulubu[23]	I am not sitting, I stand, waiting to get what I expect
Tukatazame heshima ya maulana King George.	So we see respect paid to His Highness King George

The following example of another birthday poem for King George composed by a poet with the pen name "Komagi bin Sansa",[24] spends numerous stanzas describing the King's many health problems and praising him for overcoming them. This poem is even more loaded with back-handed compliments than the previous example, such as the King is "secretive", surrounded by "rich people", had to develop the quality of bravery, and had to be rescued from near death by his doctors. This is hardly the image of an indomitable and omnipotent ruler as we saw in the poems praising Kaiser Wilhelm.

---

23 *Matulubu* = that which you are expecting to receive.
24 Meaning of this pen name unknown.

Sikukuu ya Kuzaliwa Mfalme ("King's Birthday")[25]
Komagi bin Sansa, Tabora
Mambo Leo (c.1923-36)

(1) Wenzangu nawahubiri, sikukuu imefika!	(1) My fellows, I'm preaching to you: the birthday is here!
Sote tukae tayari, tuadhimishe ushirika!	We should all be ready to celebrate together
Wala siyo kukasiri, raia tumefurahika,	And we shouldn't be angry. We citizens are happy
King George mtajika, Mfalme tunayemkiri!	The renowned King George is the king we accept!
(2) Tunamtakia heri nyingi, na baraka,	(2) We wish him best wishes and blessings
Mfalme mashuhuri, ambaye twamtaka	The famous king, whom we want
Atutawale dhahiri, na milele apendeke!	May he rule us well and be forever loved
King George mpendeka, mwema mwenye siri!	The beloved King George, good and secretive!
(3) Pasiwe na ghururi, Mungu amemsimika,	(3) Let there be no deceit, God has installed him
Awali na aheri, hakika ni sikukuu,	From start to finish, truly it is a holiday
Leo hakuna shauri, afisi zimefungwa,	Today there'll be no government work, the offices have closed[26]
King George hakika ana wengi matajiri!	Truly King George has many rich people!
(4) Ni furaha ya fahari, Mfalme anatukuzika!	(4) It is a great joy that the king is praiseworthy
Raia na askari, wamejishika pamoja,	The citizens and armed forces are united
Tajiri na maskini, huungwa na mamlaka,	The wealthy and the poor are joined by the authority
King George amefika, hali ya ujasiri.	King George has reached a state of bravery...

---

25 *Mashairi ya Mambo Leo*, vol. 3, 56–60 (1966 [1946]), trans. A. Abdalla and K. Askew.
26 *Bwana shauri* was the title given to colonial administrators. So on this day no "advice" will be available.

(7) *Kwa yakini nasadiki, ugonjwa ulivyoshika,*	(7) With certainty I believe illness attacked him
Mfalme kwa dhahiri, maradhi yalimshika,	The king apparently was overtaken by disease
Katibiwa na madaktari, na ugonjwa ukatibika!	He was treated by doctors and his ailment cured
King George amevuka, maradhi yaliyokuwa hatari.	King George overcame the dangerous disease.
(8) *Alipatwa na hatari, sasa ameokoka,*	(8) He faced danger but now has been saved
Nasi sote kadiri, himaya ilimofika,	And we all are able to accept the extent of his rule
Siku zote twamkiri, Mfalme wa mamlaka,	We always accept him as a king with authority
King George Afrika, kaitawala dhahiri.	King George has transparently ruled Afrika.
(22) *Salaam nyingi tayari, nafasi zinapunguka,*	(22) Many greetings already. Space is running out
Mambo Leo mashuhuri, pokea chakula shika,	Famous *Mambo Leo*, take the food[27]
Gazeti letu zuri, busara hukutanika;	Our newspaper is good, wisdom collects here
Maulana ajuika, King George dhihiri.	His Highness is famous. King George appear to us!
(23) *Mtengenezaji habari, Mungu akupe baraka,*	(23) News editor, may God bless you
Umetutoa kiburi, gizani pia tumetoka;	You removed our arrogance and we came out of the darkness
Twakusalimu dhahiri, na wengine kadhalika;	We greet you openly and the others as well
Maulana hakika, King George kadiri.	Truly His Highness King George is the able one.[28]

---

27 Food in this context means the poem, since a newspaper is made of words.
28 The term *kadiri* here is one of the praise names for God and typically not used outside of that context.

(24) *Kaditamati shairi, kalamu ninaiweka,*	(24) I bring the poem to a close and set down my pen
Nawaambia kwa dhamiri, Inshalla nikifika,	I'm telling you that my intention, God willing, is to continue
Hoja kuwa na umri, kutunga na kuandika,	To compose [poems] and to write as long as I live
Kwa heri nasimika, King George wa fahari.	I bid you farewell, King George the Proud.

These poems honoring King George V are notably different in character from those described earlier praising his first cousin Kaiser Wilhelm. Colonialism had matured by this point in the 1920s, and so too had African subjects who had witnessed, and in some cases participated in, the defeat of one colonial power by another. King George, who only became king due to the unexpected death of his older brother, was forced into World War I due to Wilhelm's aggressive militarism. Even before the war ended and Germany had been defeated, King George distanced himself from his shared origins with Kaiser Wilhelm II by Anglicizing the family name, renaming the British royal house the "House of Windsor". Soon after the war's end, one ailment after another beset the king, until he died in 1936. Poems about King George take a more nuanced position relative to his rule, saying actually very little of what, if anything, he contributed to the colony. Notably, the newspaper *Mambo Leo* itself also receives the poet's praises – as a repository of collective wisdom offering poetic food for readers.

Post-independence Swahili Newspaper Poetry: An Efflorescence

After Tanganyikan independence in 1961 and through the 1990s, newspapers quadrupled in number and varied extensively in their frequency, with some published on a daily or nightly basis, and others issued weekly, biweekly, or monthly. This led to a concomitant demand for more poetry, now an established element of the medium. Hence the effusion of poetic output that marks this period. Poems covered a wide range of topics from the personal to the local, the national and the international, and filled the pages of newspapers. In this period, editors began the practice of setting aside dedicated poetry sections to accommodate the flurry of artistic activity.

Newspaper	Poetry Section
Baraza ('Council')	*Mashairi Yenu Matamu* ('Your Sweet Poetry')
Dira ('Compass')	*Bustani ya Washairi* ('Garden of the Poets')
Heko ('Hurrah!')	*Washairi Wetu* ('Our Poets')
Kusare	*Mashairi* ('Poetry')
Majira ('Season')	*Tungo* ('Compositions')
Mshindi ('The Victor')	*Ukumbi wa Washairi* ('Forum for Poets')
Mwafrika ('The African')	*Mawaidha ya Washairi* ('Poets' Advice')
Mwananchi ('The Citizen')	*Wasemavyo Washairi* ('What the Poets Say')
Nipashe ('Tell Me')	*Mashairi* ('Poetry')
Uhuru ('Freedom')	*Maoni ya Washairi* ('Poets' Opinions')
Zanzibar Leo ('Zanzibar Today')	*Bustani ya Washairi* ('Garden of the Poets')

Among these poems, one finds poets addressing in verse topics found discussed in prose in the same papers, for example, description and commentary on national and local events/news; and description and commentary on international news. Just as Hunter has argued in her analysis of *Mambo Leo*, international news in verse:

> gave a strong sense of an increasingly connected world, in which the people of Tanganyika needed to know the affairs of far distant places as much as people of coastal Tanganyika needed to know the news of up-country areas. There was a sense too of an emerging international society (Hunter, 2002: 287).

There were more praise poems for politicians and other community leaders (as subsequent examples will show). In addition, there were poems that constituted obituaries, editorial-like addresses on social issues (e.g., moral decline or corruption), "Dear Abby"-like calls for advice, and even poetic personal ads seeking a spouse. Newspaper poetry also, however, featured (and still features today) topics not typically found in newspaper format. These include prayers and poems of thanks to God for prayers answered; enigma poems, in which a conundrum is posed and fellow poets challenged to resolve it (Harries, 1956); and love poems.

Like most of the Swahili press of the immediate post-independence period, nationalist and socialist-themed poems proved especially popular. This was not by chance nor only an outpouring of public support for Nyerere and the socialist policies he introduced via the *Azimio ya Arusha* ("Arusha Declaration"), the *Mwongozo* ("Guidelines"), and his many writings on Ujamaa na Kujitegemea ("Socialism and Self-Reliance") – though it was certainly also that. Harries reports how on 6 June 1968, Nyerere invited a group of Tanzanian poets to the State House and specifically requested that they "use their talents in order to promote a better understand by the people of the land (wananchi) of national politics, and particularly of the responsibilities of the citizen resulting from the implementation of the Arusha Declaration" (Harries, 1972: 52).

Nyerere Poems: A Collective Biography in Verse

As the foundational figure of Tanganyika and the United Republic of Tanzania that followed, as its first president, leader of its ruling party, commander-in-chief, philosopher-in-chief, and "father of the nation" (Baba wa Taifa), Julius Kambarage Nyerere is the subject of countless newspaper poems that span the late colonial period to his death in 1999 and beyond. While many examples exist that trace the contours of his political career in the expected honorific manner of political praise like that shown for Kaiser Wilhelm II, as his popularity fell in the midst of extreme economic crisis in the 1980s, a disarmingly blunt view emerges. By the time of his death, however, his popularity had resurged in the face of widespread corruption and abuse of political office by his successors. Not surprisingly, the lamentation poems canonize him and his achievements on behalf of the nation he brought into being.

In an early example, published in *Mwafrika* in January 1963 (just over a year after Tanganyika achieved independence in December 1961), the poet grapples with Nyerere's decision to spurn honorific titles that would become the rage among African leaders. In contrast to, for instance, the particularly egregious title that would be adopted by "His Excellency, President for Life, Field Marshal Al Hadji Doctor Idi Amin Dada, VC, DSO, MC, Lord of All the Beasts of the Earth and Fishes of the Seas, Conqueror of the British Empire in Africa in General and Uganda in Particular, and Uncrowned King of Scotland", Nyerere wanted to be known as nothing other than Mwalimu ("Teacher"). Trained as a teacher before embarking on his graduate education in Europe, a devout Catholic, and committed socialist, Nyerere eschewed pomp and ostentation. But is "Mwalimu" fitting for Tanganyika's first president, asks Mohamed Ali of his fellow poets?

Nyerere Kuitwa Mwalimu Mwasemaje Washairi?[29]

("Poets, What Do You Say about Calling Nyerere *'Mwalimu'*)

Mohamed Ali (Mwanafunzi -"Student"), High Court, Box 9004, Dar es Salaam

Mwafrika (22 January 1963)

(1) Ninashikia kalamu, ilosafika nyinyiri	(1) I take hold of this totally purified pen
Niwaulize kaumu, vipi wanatafakari	That I may ask the multitudes what they think:
Jina hili la Mwalimu, kwa Raisi Mashuhuri	This name of 'Teacher' for our renowned president—
Mwasemaje washairi, Nyerere kwitwa Mwalimu?	Poets, what do you say about calling Nyerere 'Teacher'?
(2) Nyerere kwitwa Mwalimu, mimi sitii dosari	(2) For Nyerere to be called 'Teacher', I don't consider that a shortcoming
Bali huwa mahamumu, na kuingiwa na ari	Instead I become excited and full of enthusiasm
Kwani ninavyofahamu, sio jina la fahari	For as I understand it, it's not a pompous title
Mwasemaje washairi, Nyerere kwitwa Mwalimu?	Poets, what do you say about calling Nyerere 'Teacher'?
(3) Majina ya kuzaliwa, hayataki kutabiri	(3) Names assigned at birth do not need guessing
Walakini ya kupewa, twatazama tafsiri	But for acquired names we need to examine their meanings
Iwapo ya kubeuwa, hatuwezi kuikiri	If they are derogatory, we cannot accept them
Mwasemaje washairi, Nyerere kwitwa Mwalimu?	Poets, what do you say about calling Nyerere 'Teacher'?

---

29 Translated by Abdilatif Abdalla and Kelly Askew, February 2013, Berlin.

(4) *Tulisikia ghafula, jina likatanawari*	(4) Suddenly we heard the title widely used
Hatukupewa muhula, tukapata kufikiri	We weren't given time to contemplate it
Sasa hatunayo hila, kimepwelewa kihori	Now we have no tricks, the canoe is beached
Mwasemaje washairi, Nyerere kwitwa Mwalimu?	Poets, what do you say about calling Nyerere 'Teacher'?
(5) *Mwalimu ni jina bora, kwa mahalipe dhahiri*	(5) 'Teacher' is a good name if properly used
Hakika litatukera, livishwapo na johari	Yet surely it will bother us when garlanded with jewels
Hivi kaniki ya jora, yafunikiwa mimbari?	How can a pulpit be covered with a plain black cloth?
Mwasemaje washairi, Nyerere kwitwa Mwalimu?	Poets, what do you say about calling Nyerere 'Teacher'?
(7) *Wanambia vyadamana, kwa jina lilokithiri*	(7) They tell me they suit each other perfectly with a name well-known
Kupewa wetu Mungwana Raisi wa Jamhuri	To be given to our noble president of the Republic
Na suna yapatikana, jina lilotakarari[30]	And there is precedent for a name oft-repeated
Mwasemaje washairi, Nyerere kwitwa Mwalimu?	Poets, what do you say about calling Nyerere 'Teacher'?
(10) *Beti kumi ninatuza, mimi sio jemadari*	(10) I end with ten verses, I'm not a field commander
Msijenisusuwaza, mkamba ni machachari	Don't shame me saying that I am incoherent
Ndisa nanze kutawaza, ningali ni mwanamwari[31]	I have just started to be kept in seclusion because I am a virgin
Mwasemaje washairi, Nyerere kwitwa Mwalimu?	Poets, what do you say about calling Nyerere 'Mwalimu'?

---

30 *Suna* refers to knowledge about the Prophet from secondary sources, stories, accounts. Also used to mean "precedent" or something normally done
31 *Kutawaza* is to be in seclusion. The poet's reference to being in seclusion is metaphorical for still being a novice poet.

Unlike the panegyric odes for Kaiser Wilhelm, or even the more muted, more critical but still sycophantic poems for King George, Mohamed Ali does not wax rhapsodic about President Nyerere's many talents and attributes. Instead, he limits himself to the incongruence between the simplicity desired by Nyerere and the augustness of his position as first president. Ali concludes that although one would not ordinarily cover a pulpit with a black cloth, in this case, the man and the title suit each other perfectly. He ends by emphasizing his own humble status, a "virgin" poet with little experience whose pen name *(lakabu)* is Mwanafunzi ("Student") – a particularly apt and doubly meaningful choice for this poetic exposition on the suitability of "Mwalimu".

After 1967, numerous newspaper poems appeared addressing and assessing Nyerere's introduction of "African socialism" or Ujamaa, in which the commanding heights of the economy were nationalized and a socialist ethic promulgated. The following poem by J.I. Farahani (pen name Simba Kuu – "Great Lion") assures President Nyerere that the citizens support both the 1967 Arusha Declaration and the 1970 *Mwongozo* ("Guidelines"). He further describes how these policies caused many capitalist exploiters (bloodsucking "ticks") to run away and frustrated foreign powers.

Rais Nyerere ("President Nyerere")[31]
J. I. Farahani (Simba Kuu – "Great Lion")
Baraza (6 April 1972)

(1) Baba Nyerere Raisi, Raisi wa Tanzania	(1) Father [of the Nation] President Nyerere, President of Tanzania
Akujalie mkwasi, Rabbi Rassuli Jalia	May almighty and generous God protect you
Upate nyingi nemsi, dua tunakuombea	May you be abundantly honored. We offer prayers for you
Mola akupe afia, Raisi Baba Nyerere	May God grant you health, President Father [of the Nation] Nyerere

---

31 Translated by Abdilatif Abdalla and Kelly Askew.

(2) Baba Nyerere Raisi, Mwalimu mwenye sharia	(2) Father [of the Nation] President Nyerere, our lawful Teacher
Usiwe na wasi wasi, tuko imara raia	Do not be worried, we the citizens are strong
Ataeleta ufyosi, tayari kumvamia	We will attack the one who brings chaos
Mola akupe afia, Raisi Baba Nyerere	May God grant you health, President Father [of the Nation] Nyerere
(3) Baba Nyerere Rais, kiongozi mwenye nia	(3) Father [of the Nation] President Nyerere, a motivated leader
Azimio limepasi, makupe wamekimbia	The Declaration passed; the ticks have run away[32]
Limewatoa kamasi, wa kule wamechukia[33]	It caused them great hardship. Those far away [Western countries] are furious
Mola akupe afia, Raisi Baba Nyerere	May God grant you health, President Father [of the Nation] Nyerere
(4) Baba Nyerere Raisi, Mola akupe afia	(4) Father [of the Nation] President Nyerere, may God grant you health
Hapo hukusema basi, Mwongozo ukatongoa	You didn't say: "Enough", you clearly explained *The Guidelines*
Majumba yakala lasi, ya lai yalofikia[34]	[Meaning unclear, likely having to do with the prohibition against government officials holding rental properties for additional income]
Mola akupe afia, Raisi Baba Nyerere	May God grant you health, President Father [of the Nation] Nyerere

---

32 In his speeches, Nyerere often used the metaphor kupe ("ticks") for "capitalists" or "exploiters". See Hunter (2008) and Brennan (2006).
33 *Limewatoa kamasi*, literally "it has caused them to produce snot," is a colloquialism for something causing hardship.
34 The meaning of *majumba yakala lasi ya alai yalofikia* escapes us. But since the *Mwongozo* was just mentioned, it could reference the prohibition against having second homes for rental income.

(5) Baba Nyerere Raisi, beti tano naishia	(5) Father [of the Nation] President Nyerere, I've completed five verses
Edita Bwana Khamisi, shairi langu pokea	Editor Mr. Khamisi, receive my poem
Litafutie nafasi, hata pemba sawa pia	Seek out a spot for it, even a corner will suffice
Mola akupe afia, Raisi Baba Nyerere	May God grant you health, President Father [of the Nation] Nyerere

By the start of the 1980s, Tanzania was in a severe economic crisis due to a potent combination of factors spanning debts from the 1978–1979 war to unseat Idi Amin, support for liberation struggles south of the border, inefficiencies in the parastatal sector, a series of droughts that badly affected agricultural production, plus an alarming foreign exchange deficit stemming in large part from the international oil crisis. Nyerere was pressured to abandon his resistance to International Monetary Fund (IMF) conditional-ities to access much needed loans. He refused to concede his principles, anticipating rightly that opening the doors to free trade would undermine the previous two decades' efforts to build up Tanzanian agricultural and commercial strength. But structural adjustment proved inescapable and so in 1985 Nyerere stepped down from the presidency to allow President Ali Hassan Mwinyi, a known advocate of reform, to oversee liberalization of the economy and political system. He retained his post as chairman of the ruling party Chama cha Mapinduzi or CCM until 1990, before also passing that on to President Mwinyi.

Following the abandonment of socialist policy, Nyerere suffered a fall in his popularity. Some openly blamed him for the economic woes of the country, the high rates of poverty, and lack of development (especially compared to neighboring Kenya). In 1998, poet Rajabu Njembwe came to his defense, asking that people show the first president respect. He praises Nyerere for delivering education and being full of wisdom, but the degree to which he pleads with his audience to respect Nyerre and stop "publicly deriding him", to "not belittle him and ruin his reputation," illustrates that Nyerere had become – in some circles – an object of scorn. In 1998, Nyerere was an elder of 76 years old. Committed still to addressing the plight of the poor and bringing peace to trouble spots on the continent, Nyerere spent his later years promoting South-South cooperation and serving as chief mediator in the Burundi conflict, something obliquely acknowledged by Njembwe: "The world knows and respects him."

Tumuheshimu Mwalimu ("Let's Respect Mwalimu")[35]
Rajabu Njembwe, P.O. Box 33353, Dar es Salaam
Mfanyakazi, 20 June 1998

(1) Tumuheshimu Mwalimu, kiumbe mwenye fahamu	(1) We should respect Mwalimu, a person with great knowledge
Tuache kumlaumu, ameokoa kaumu	Let's stop blaming him. He saved the nation
Katufundisha elimu, katuachia[36]	He educated us; he has bequeathed us
Dunia yamfahamu, tena inamheshimu	The world knows and respects him.
(2) Nasema kitaadhima, huyu mtu ni mpevu	(2) I say this with honor: this person is enlightened
Natutunuku heshima, kwa kuwa huyu mwelevu	And let's give him respect because he is knowledgeable
Sitaacha kuwasema, kumtusi si welevu	I'll never stop admonishing them, because insulting him is not a wise thing to do
Hamna hata haiba, kumnanga hadharani[37]	You show disrespect by publicly deriding him
(3) Leo nami naeleza, huyu kwetu ndiyo baba	(3) So today I'm telling you that to us he's a father
Na mimi nawabwatiza, nyinyi kwetu ni viroba	I am scolding you: to us you are robbers
Sisi tumewapuuza, nawajazia kibaba[38]	We ignore you but in responding I'm giving you credit that you don't deserve
Tumuheshimu Mwalimu, nawaeleza kwa heshima	We should respect Mwalimu, I respectfully argue

---

35 Translated by Abdilatif Abdalla and Kelly Askew.
36 Newsprint smudged; word unclear
37 The meaning of *kunanga* is unknown to us; we infer "to deride" from the context.
38 Before foreigners introduced Western measurements of kilograms and pounds, *Swahili* used to measure in *kibaba* and *pishi* measurements. There's also a *Swahili* saying: *Haba na haba hujaza kibaba*, meaning literally, "Grain by grain, the *kibaba* will be filled" or "Little by little...."

(4) Hamna hata haiba, kumnanga hadharani	(4) You show disrespect by publicly deriding him
Nawaeleza kwa mahaba, tumuheshimu jamani	I inform you out of love, let us respect him, people
Nawajazia kibaba, huyu mtu ni makini	I'm adding yet more: this person is steadfast
Tumuheshimu Mwalimu, nawaeleza kwa heshima	We should respect Mwalimu, I respectfully argue
(5) Nawaeleza kwa heshima, Nyerere tumthamani	(5) I respectfully argue that we should value Nyerere
Ni mtu mwenye heshima, ametutowa gizani	He is someone deserving great respect who delivered us from darkness
Ni mtu aliyezama, kwenye kina baharini	He delved deeply into the waters of the ocean[39]
Dunia yamfahamu, tena inamheshimu	The world knows and respects him.
(6) Dunia yamfahamu, tena inamheshimu	(6) The world knows and respects him.
Huyu mtu ni Mwalimu, mengi anayafahamu	This person is a Teacher, who knows a lot
Watu wote mufahamu, huyu kwetu ni muhimu	You should all understand that he is important to us
Tumpe vigelegele, vilivyojaa imani	Let's cheer him from the heart
(7) Kambarage maarufu, anavuma duniani	(7) The famous Kambarage of world renown
Habari zake ni ndefu, zimejaa vitabuni	Books are full of information about him
Tusimpake udhaifu, ili ashuke thamani	Let us not belittle him and ruin his reputation
Tumuheshimu Mwalimu, nawaeleza kwa heshima	We should respect Mwalimu, I respectfully argue

The year after Njembwe's poem signified a vexed relationship between the nation and its first president, the news was released that Nyerere had died of leukemia in a London hospital on 14 October 1999. Crowds took to the streets, a 30-day period of national mourning was announced, and a poetic outpouring of lamentation filled the newspapers and airwaves (Askew, 2006).

---
39 The metaphor here signifies someone who is not superficial but gets to the heart of the matter.

One example published in March 2000 was composed by a youth named Kassim Kibwe ("The Musician-Poet"). Embedded within the poet's expression of sorrow is a critique of efforts by politicians to revise the constitution so as to undermine further the policies championed by Nyerere, now rehabilitated and viewed as moral exemplar and champion of the powerless.

Twakulilia Nyerere ("We Cry For You Nyerere")[40]

Kassim J. S. Kibwe (*Mwanamuziki Mshairi* - "The Musician-Poet") National Youth Forum, S.L.P. 9354, Dar es Salaam

Mfanyakazi (1 March 2000)

(1) Kwa jina lake karimu, donge langu nalitoa[41]	(1) In the name of God, I must unburden myself of this weight
Litiki ewa muhimu, niwaeleze jamaa[42]	I need to explain this to you friends
Binafsi nalaumu, katiba kuichezea	Personally I blame those who are playing with the constitution
Kweli kufa kupotea, twakulilia Mwalimu	Truly to die is to disappear. We cry for you Mwalimu
(2) Twakulilia Mwalimu, kweli kufa kupotea	(2) We cry for you Mwalimu. Truly to die is to disappear
Hujambo si marehemu, kiza kimetunamia	You are fine, not deceased. Darkness envelops us
Tungekupigia simu, ili uje tukemea	We would telephone you so you could come and tell us off
Kweli kufa kupotea, twakulilia Mwalimu	Truly to die is to disappear. We cry for you Mwalimu

---

40 Translated by Abdilatif Abdalla and K. Askew
41 *Donge* means a clump of something. So refers to something clumped up in one's heart or soul. *Nitatoa donge langu* = colloquialism for unburdening yourself of something; saying what's bothering you.
42 *Litiki ewa* is not Kiswahili. Meaning unknown.

(3) *Katiba si kama ndimu, kila mwaka inazaa*

   Kwa zama au msimu, kuichafua chafua

   Ila kisa maalumu, kitakachopelekea

   Kweli kufa kupotea, twakulilia Mwalimu

(3) A constitution is not like a lime tree that fruits every year

   In turn or by season, continually revising it and messing it up

   Only a special incident should provoke review

   Truly to die is to disappear. We cry for you Mwalimu

(4) *Chafuko kila sehemu, viongozi waanzia*

   Katiba hawaheshimu, ndipo lazuka balaa

   Kwa madaraka matamu, hivyo nguvu watumia

   Kweli kufa kupotea, twakulilia Mwalimu

(4) Trouble in every corner, stirred up by leaders

   They don't respect the constitution, creating strife

   From privileged positions they use their power

   Truly to die is to disappear. We cry for you Mwalimu

(5) *Katika hii awamu, wengi waifurahia*

   Katiba waihujumu, wapate kuendelea

   Twaomba yako mizimu, Nyerere kutuepua

   Kweli kufa kupotea, twakulilia Mwalimu

(5) Many are happy about our current government

   They are sabotaging the constitution for private gain

   We plead for your spirits, Nyerere, to heal us

   Truly to die is to disappear. We cry for you Mwalimu

(6) *Ni jambo la kidhalimu, japo mtanichukia*

   Muhalalishe haramu, ili vitini kukaa

   Mwisho mtamwaga damu, Rabbi kwa hili tengua

   Kweli kufa kupotea, twakulilia Mwalimu

(6) It is a matter of cruelty even if you'll hate me for it

   You legalize that which is forbidden in order to occupy the seats [of power]

   In the end you'll spill blood, let this not happen, O God

   Truly to die is to disappear. We cry for you Mwalimu

(7) *Beti saba nasalimu, kwa wote Watanzania*

   Tuonyeshe urahimu, vyovyote itavyokua

   Ghadhabu tuzihukumu, busara kuzitumia

   Kweli kufa kupotea, twakulilia Mwalimu

(7) With seven verses I greet all Tanzanians

   Let us show gentleness, whatever it takes

   Let us abandon anger and apply wisdom

   Truly to die is to disappear. We cry for you Mwalimu

Here the poet contrasts the period of Nyerere's governance with that of the current regime, which he accuses of revising the nation's constitution to facilitate plundering of the state. The peace and unity that Nyerere championed and devoted himself toward establishing in Tanzania are being sabotaged and the nation runs the risk of violent upheaval. Would that they could telephone Nyerere to ask for his guidance once more, but "to die is to disappear. We cry for you Mwalimu."

October has remained a month of mourning ever since with newspapers, politicians, and musicians honoring the anniversary of Nyerere's death with poetry, speeches, exhortations, songs, and editorials of remembrance. A final example, one focused more on the man and the legacies he left his nation, is the poem composed by Athanas George Masao ("Power Strike") on the first anniversary of his death.

Nyerere Tunakukumbuka ("Nyerere, We Remember You")[43]

Athanas George Masao (*Power Mkongoto* -"Power Strike")

Mfanyakazi, 28-31 October 2000

(1) *Nyerere tunakukumbuka, wa kudumu muhisani*	(1) Nyerere, we remember you, our eternal benefactor
Mema yako twakumbuka, mengi yasiyo kifani	We recall your unparalleled goodness
Twakuombea Rabuka, uwe kwake namba wani	We pray that God makes you his number one
Nyerere kipenzi chetu, bado tunakukumbuka	Our dear Nyerere, we still remember you
(2) *Ilikuwa kama ndoto, na leo hii ni mwaka*	(2) It seems like a dream yet today a year has passed
Vyetu bado moto, nyoyo bado zinawaka	Things are still tough, our hearts still on fire
Kifo kweli ni kiboko, umetwacha nyakanyaka	Death really is a blow.[44] You have left us in a sorrowful mood
Nyerere kipenzi chetu, bado tunakukumbuka	Our dear Nyerere, we still remember you

---

43 Translated by Abdilatif Abdalla and Kelly Askew.
44 *Kiboko* is a whip made of hippo hide, which deals heavy blows. I credit a reviewer for this insight.

(3) *Kukumbukwa unapaswa, wewe wa kisawasawa*
    Butiama hata Maswa, popote tumepagawa
    Kukuenzi tunapaswa, kwa mema uliyogawa
    Nyerere kipenzi chetu, bado tunakukumbuka

(3) You deserve to be remembered, you the righteous one
    From Butiama to Maswa, everywhere we are overwhelmed
    To honor you we must forward the goodness that you shared
    Our dear Nyerere, we still remember you

(4) *Nani asosikitika, kwa pengo uliloacha*
    Mbuyu umekatika, na wa uhakika ticha
    Darasani umetoka, hutorudi hata kucha
    Nyerere kipenzi chetu, bado tunakukumbuka

(4) Who doesn't regret the void you left behind?
    A baobab has fallen. And it is certain, teacher
    That you have left the classroom, never to return
    Our dear Nyerere, we still remember you

(5) *Elimu umetwachia, pia wingi wa hekima*
    Amani umetwachia, pia wingi wa heshima
    Upendo umetwachia, wala siyo wa kupima
    Nyerere kipenzi chetu, bado tunakukumbuka

(5) You left us education, and lots of wisdom
    You left us peace, and lots of respect
    You left us love, a love beyond measure
    Our dear Nyerere, we still remember you

(6) *Utulivu umetwachia, kwenye anga kama njiwa*
    Umoja umetwachia, tena ni wa kusifiwa
    Vyote hatutaachia, hata kwa kughilibiwa
    Nyerere kipenzi chetu, bado tunakukumbuka

(6) You left us calm, in the air like a pigeon
    You left us unity, a unity worthy of praise
    We'll not abandon any of it, not even by deception
    Our dear Nyerere, we still remember you

(7) *Na alaaniwe hasa, atakayetuvuruga*
    Yote uliyotuasa, ni mwiko kuyavuruga
    Tutayalinda kabisa, hata kwa ngoma kupiga
    Nyerere kipenzi chetu, bado tunakukumbuka

(7) Curses on anyone who would mess us up
    All your warnings should not be neglected
    We shall abide by them, even playing the drum
    Our dear Nyerere, we still remember you

(8) *Kaditama muhisani, ujumbe wangu fikisha*	(8) Here I end. O benefactor, send my message[45]
Usije nitia kapuni, nikabaki kuchekesha	Don't put my poem in the wastepaper basket, lest I be laughed at
Nyerere namba wani, jemadari wa kutisha	Nyerere is number one, a fearsome warrior
Nyerere kipenzi chetu, bado tunakukumbuka	Our dear Nyerere, we still remember you

Conclusion

Swahiliphone newspaper poetry offers an incredibly rich repository of popular political debate. These examples translated by Kenyan master poet Abdilatif Abdalla and myself give but a mere glimpse into the vast quantity of poems that have been produced by ordinary people over the twentieth century and into the twenty-first century, spanning the full geography of what is now Tanzania. Famous poets also published poems in newspaper format, a notable example being Shaaban Robert's *Utenzi wa Vita vya Uhuru*, "Poem of the War for Independence", which was serialized from 1942 to 1944 in *Mambo Leo*, or at least 726 of its 3000 stanzas (Geider, 2002: 276). Yet by far, the majority of poems in the vast untapped sea of swahiliphone newspaper poems were composed by nonelite citizens. They have not received serious attention because of this, since literary scholars tend to deride this corpus as the work of amateurs and thus unworthy of analysis. For as Barber has noted, the popular arts "are usually disregarded by the formal educational and cultural apparatus" (Barber, 1987: 11). And yet it is this very fact of popular production in the sense of "the populace" that makes swahiliphone newspaper poetry such an important archive for understanding engagements with political processes by ordinary citizens whose opinions are difficult to access otherwise, especially for periods in the past.

This essay has offered an exploration of the historical, structural, topical, and contextual contours of Swahili newspaper poems about leaders spanning three eras: German colonial Deutsch-Ostafrika, British colonial Tanganyika, and independent Tanganyika/Tanzania. These poems expose significant developments in political praise poetry with levels of critique increasing in directness over time, from the homophonic panegyric odes about Kaiser Wilhelm to the contrapuntal passive-aggressive poems "honouring" King George to the polyphonic, complex and nuanced poems about Nyerere.

Kaiser Wilhelm II was widely viewed as ruthless, impetuous, bombastic, prone to violent outbursts, and insistent on his superiority in all matters but especially military ones. In newspaper poems, the Kaiser received praise for his military prowess, his might, his ability to put down rebellions, and defeat his enemies. He emerges as a single-faceted figure, unsurprisingly so given that the experiences colonial subjects had of their German overlord were primarily of military domination. Indeed, in a July 1900 speech he gave to troops being sent to the colonies, Kaiser Wilhelm exhorted them to "administer violence and to repress brutally any form of resistance" (Conrad, 2012: 83). Poetic allusions to resistance under German colonialism are thus understandably hidden and indirect. When Britain acquired Tanganyika in post-World War I negotiations, the militaristic mode of praise characterizing poems for Kaiser Wilhelm no longer suited the circumstances of rule under King George. Famous not for military prowess but for chronic illnesses, King George is memorialized in the newspaper poems reviewed here for the pageantry his administrators performed in the colony. These poems offer a curious mix of uninspired praise and back-handed compliments for the politically and physically weaker British monarch.

In the era following independence, by contrast, undiluted praise, pride, and patriotism characterize early poems about Tanzania's first president. The combination of socialist rhetoric about people's empowerment and an increasingly liberalized media enabled the publication of a wide variety of opinions about him in verse. Nyerere's praises range from his success in bringing independence to Tanganyika, his humility in rejecting grandiloquent titles, and his policies against capitalist parasitism to his wisdom, his educational policies, his advocacy for the poor, and his legacies of peace and national unity. He is memorialized as a hero of the people who waged battle with the twin legacies of colonial and capitalist economic relations. However, as unrealistic expectations of the eradication of poverty, ignorance, and disease failed to be realized over his 24-year presidency, newspaper poets expressed growing popular disillusionment with Nyerere. By relinquishing the presidency and later control of the ruling party, he would be interpreted by many as a tragic figure, defeated by a world system focused on economically driven individuals, not philosophically driven communities. This would evoke in some quarters feelings of contempt toward him and his socialist policies, inciting one poet to plead that he be shown respect. Yet derision would be replaced by eulogy upon Nyerere's death. His legacy and principles, so recently cast in negative light, would once more be championed as the standard to be emulated. Poets have not, however, returned to the panegyric and uncritical style with which the Kaiser was memorialized nearly a century earlier. Instead, they acknowledge that Nyerere made mistakes but contrast his policies and principles to those of current politicians, many of whom have lost legitimacy in the eyes of citizens and are viewed as placing self-interest ahead of the needs of the nation.

In her rich analysis of the agency of texts, Karin Barber argues that:

> As well as being social facts, however, texts are commentaries upon, and interpretations of, social facts. They are part of social reality but they also take up an attitude to social reality. They may criticize social forms or confirm and consolidate them: in both cases they are reflexive. They are part of the apparatus by which human communities take stock of their own creations. Textual traditions can be seen as a community's ethnography of itself (Barber, 2007: 4).

Swahili newspaper poems constitute one form through which Tanzanians assess their political institutions and the faces of those institutions: the leaders who give voice to and shape the nature of these institutions. The violent nature of the German colonial state as figured in the man of Kaiser Wilhelm is thus fundamentally different from the spectacle of the British colonial state under King George, which in turn is wholly distinct from the independent Tanganyikan/Tanzanian state figured in the philosopher-teacher Julius Nyerere. The poems analyzed here articulate these differences in artful language and in so doing offer poetic ethnographies of the Tanzanian state even as they offer partial biographies of a German emperor, a British king and an African president.

References

ABEDI, K. Amri. *Sheria za Kutunga Mashairi na Diwani ya Amri* [Rules of Poetry Composition, by Diwani Amri]. Nairobi: East African Literature Bureau, 1954.

ARNOLD, Rainer. "Swahili Literature and Modern History: A Necessary Remark on Literary Criticism." *Swahili* 42, no. 2; 43, no. 1 (1973): 68–73.

ASKEW, Kelly. *Performing the Nation: Swahili Music and Cultural Politics in Tanzania*. Chicago: University of Chicago Press, 2002.

ASKEW, Kelly. "As Plato Duly Warned: Music, Politics and Social Change in East Africa." *Anthropological Quarterly* 76, no. 4 (2003): 609–637.

ASKEW, Kelly. "Sung and Unsung: Musical Reflections on Tanzanian Postsocialism." *Africa* 76, no. 1 (2006): 15–43.

BARBER, Karin. *The Anthropology of Texts, Persons and Publics: Oral and Written Culture in Africa and beyond*. Cambridge: Cambridge University Press, 2007.

BARBER, Karin. 1987. "Popular Arts in Africa." *African Studies Review* 30, no. 3, pp.1–78.

BIERSTEKER, Ann. *Kujibizana: Questions of Language and Power in Nineteenth- and Twentieth- century Poetry in Kiswahili*. East Lansing: Michigan State University, 1996.

BIERSTEKER, Ann, and Ibrahim Noor SHARIFF. *Mashairi ya Vita vya Kuduhu: War Poetry in Kiswahli Exchanged at the Time of the Battle of Kuduhu*. East Lansing: Michigan State University Press, 1995.

BRENNAN, James R. "Blood Enemies: Exploitation and Urban Citizenship in the Nationalist Political Thought of Tanzania, 1958–1975." *Journal of African History* 47, no. 3 (2006): 389–413.

CONRAD, Sebastian. *German Colonialism: A Short History*. Cambridge: Cambridge University Press, 2012.

FINNEGAN, Ruth. *Oral Literature in Africa*. Nairobi: Oxford University Press, 1970.

GEIDER, Thomas. "The Paper Memory of East Africa: Ethnohistories and Biographies Written in Swahili." In *A Place in the World: New Local Historiographies from Africa and South Asia*, ed. Axel Harnet-Sievers, 255–288. Leiden: Brill, 2002.

GREEN, Roland, Stephen CUSHMAN, Clare CAVANAGH, Jahan RAHAZANI and Paul ROUZER. *The Princeton Encyclopedia of Poetry and Poetics*. Princeton: Princeton University Press, 2012 (4th ed.).

GUNNER, Liz. *Politics and Performance: Theatre, Poetry, and Song in Southern Africa*. Johannesburg: Witwatersrand University Press, 1994.

HARRIES, Lyndon. "Cultural Verse-Forms in Swahili." *African Studies* 15, no. 4 (1956): 176–187.

HARRIES, Lyndon. *Swahili Poetry*. Oxford: Clarendon Press, 1962.

HARRIES, Lyndon. "Poetry and Politics in Tanzania." *Ba Shiru* 4, no. 3 (1972): 52–54.

HUNTER, Emma. "Revisiting Ujamaa: Political Legitimacy and the Construction of Community in Post-colonial Tanzania." *Journal of Eastern African Studies* 2, no. 3 (2008): 471–485.

HUNTER, Emma. "'Our Common Humanity': Print, Power, and the Colonial Press in Interwar Tanganyika and French Cameroun." *Journal of Global History* 7, no. 2 (2012): 279–301.

KEZILAHABI, Euphrase. "The Development of Swahili Poetry: 18th–20th Century." *Swahili* 42, no. 2; 43, no. 1 (1973): 62–67.

KEZILAHABI, Euphrase. "The House of Everydayness: Swahili Poetry in Tanzanian Newspapers." In *Beyond the Language Issue: The Production, Mediation and Reception of Creative Writing in African Languages*, ed. Anja Oed and Uta Reuster-Jahn, 191–197. Köln: Rüdiger Köppe Verlag, 2008.

KOMBA, S. M. *Uwanja wa Mashairi* [The Field of Poetry]. Dar es Salaam: Longman, 1976.

LEMKE, Hilde. "Die Suaheli-Zeitungen und -Zeitschriften in Deutsch-Ost-Afrika [Swahili News- papers and Journals in German East Africa]" Ph.D. thesis, University of Leipzig, 1929.

MADUMULLA, Joshua, Elena BERTONCINI, and Jan BLOMMAERT. "Politics, Ideology and Poetic form: The Literary Debate in Tanzania." In *Language Ideological Debates*, ed. Jan Blommaert, 307–341. Berlin and New York: Mouton de Gruyter, 1999.

Mashairi ya Mambo Leo: Swahili Poems from the Swahili Newspaper "Mambo Leo", Vol. 1. London: The Sheldon Press, 1966 [1946].

Mashairi ya Mambo Leo: Swahili poems from the Swahili Newspaper "Mambo Leo", Vol. 3. London: The Sheldon Press, 1966 [1946].

MAW, Joan. *Fire and Lightning: Language, Affect and Society in 20th Century Swahili Poetry*. Breiträge zur Afrikanistik, Band 63. Wien: Institut für Afrikanistik und Ägyptologie der Universität Wien, 1999.

MIEHE, Gudrun, Katrin BROMBER, Said KHAMIS, and Ralf GROSSERHODE. *Kala Shairi: German East Africa in Swahili Poems*. Archiv afrikanischer Manuskripte, Vol. 6. Köln: Rüdiger Köppe Verlag, 2002.

MIEHE, Gudrun, and Abdilatif ABDALLA. *Poems Attributed to Fumo Liyongo*. Archivafrikanistischer Manuskripte, Vol. 7. Köln: Rüdiger Köppe Verlag, 2004.

MITCHELL, J. Clyde. *The Kalela Dance: Aspects of Social Relationships among Urban Africans in Northern Rhodesia*. Manchester: Manchester University Press, 1956.

MULOKOZI, Mugyabuso M. "Revolution and Reaction in Swahili Poetry." *Swahili* 45, no. 2 (1975): 46–65.

MULOKOZI, Mugyabuso M., and Tigiti S. Y. SENGO. *History of Kiswahili Poetry* [AD 1000–2000]. Dar es Salaam: Institute of Kiswahili Research, University of Dar es Salaam, 1995.

NJOGU, Kimani. *Reading Poetry as Dialogue: An East African Literary Tradition*. Nairobi: The Jomo Kenyatta Foundation, 2004.

SAAVEDRA Casco, José ARTURO. *Utenzi, War Poems, and the German Conquest of East Africa: Swahili Poetry as Historical Source*. Trenton: Africa World Press, 2007.

SCOTT, James C. *Domination and the Arts of Resistance: Hidden Transcripts*. New Haven: Yale University Press, 1990.

SCOTTON, James F. "Tanganyika's African Press, 1937–1960: A Nearly Forgotten Pre-Independence Forum." *African Studies Review* 21, no. 1 (1978): 1–18.

SHARIFF, Ibrahim Noor. *Tungo Zetu: Msingi wa Mashairi na Tungo Nyinginezo* [Our Compositions: Fundamentals of Poetry and Other Compositional Forms]. Trenton, NJ: Red Sea Press, 1988.

STURMER, Martin. *The Media History of Tanzania*. Tanzania: Ndanda Mission Press, 1998.

TRACEY, Hugh. *Chopi Musicians, Their Music, Poetry, and Instruments*. London: Oxford University Press, 1948.

VAIL, Leroy, and Landeg WHITE. *Power and the Praise Poem: Southern African Voices in History*. Charlottesville: University Press of Virginia, 1991.

VELTEN, Carl. *Prosa und Poesie der Suaheli*. Berlin: self-published by the author, 1907.

ZACHE, Hans. "Beiträge zur Suaheli-Litteratur [Contributions to Swahili Literature]." *Zeitschrift für afrikanische und oceanische Sprachen* [Journal for African and Oceanic Languages] 3 (1897): 131–139, 250–267.

Chapter 10

The Poetry of an Orphaned Nation: Newspaper Poetry and the Death of Nyerere

Mary Ann Mhina*

I arrived in Tanzania in September 1999 to take language classes at the Institute of Kiswahili and Foreign languages in Zanzibar. On 14 October, the first president of Tanzania, Julius Nyerere, died in a London hospital. Thereafter President Benjamin Mkapa declared 30 days of national mourning. The 'Father of the Nation' had been ill for sometime and was known to be in hospital. I had noticed since I first arrived in Zanzibar that there had been a growing awareness amongst the general public of his worsening health and lively discussion about when he might die; some people hoped for a swift recovery, others that he would die soon, still others claimed he was already dead but that his death was being concealed.

After Nyerere's death was confirmed and the mourning period had begun everybody seemed to be more forgiving of their former president. The television stations devoted themselves to constant coverage; the mass which was held in Westminster cathedral, the body arriving back in Tanzania, the funeral and the burial proceedings were all televised, interspersed with speeches Nyerere had made whilst alive and various tributes to him, often in the form of song. Sometimes the singers became hysterical, began to cry and fell to the ground in grief. For those 30 days, news other than that of Nyerere's death was minimal. Dancing and listening to music were officially forbidden and sports events were cancelled.

---

*This text was first published in the *Journal of Eastern African Studies*, vol. 8, no. 3 (2014), pp. 414–537. It is reprinted with permission. The translations of the poems are my own and reflect my own comprehension. I am grateful to Farouk Topan and Erik Bakilana for their patient help with words or expressions I was not familiar with when I originally translated them, as an undergraduate at the School of Oriental and African Studies, London, in 2000. The poetry used in this article has been sourced from the *Uhuru* newspaper, Tanzania.

Within a week Nyerere's body was returned to Dar es Salaam and the funeral procession paraded through the streets of the city as people watched and some wept. Then the body was taken to the national stadium, where it was placed in a specially erected glass building through which people could pass and view the open coffin and see the face of the 'Father of the Nation' for the final time. Leaders from many countries around the world came to pay their respects to a man who was often considered the only African statesman of his generation to have held to his principles. Once they had filed past the body, the wider public was invited to do the same. Finally, Nyerere's body was transported to his home at Butiama in northwestern Tanzania, where it was again driven through the streets. Nyerere was buried there, next to his father and mother, on 23 October 1999. All of this was viewed widely on national television, a medium which Nyerere had during his Presidency resisted establishing in the country (Sturmer, 1998: 191). It was therefore, perhaps the first local event of its kind of this size and scale (Askew, 2006) and I and the Zanzibari family with whom I was staying at the time watched it with interest.

In this article, I review the specific form of Swahili readership poetry printed in a specific Tanzanian newspaper, *Uhuru*, as an instance in which 'poetics may illuminate representations of ethnographic phenomena' (Caton, 1990:20). The poetry it concentrates upon was all published during the mourning period for President Nyerere in *Uhuru* (Freedom/ Independence), a newspaper established by the CCM (*Chama Cha Mapinduzi*, the Party of the Revolution) political party that has ruled Tanzania since independence. These poems were originally written in Swahili and are also here translated into English. The translation of language itself presents a challenge, which is never wholly surmountable; to understand the meaning of language for the author and the readers of the texts one is working with. However, as Steiner explains, language is communication through translation even within any given language: "inside or between languages, human communication equals translation" (Steiner, 1975: 47). The poems have become part of my text and compliment my voice. They appear in this project in my own English translations of them alongside the original Swahili versions. Whilst the original poems respect the rhyming form of *shairi* which is explained below, my translations of course do not.

This very specific kind of poetry leads me to consider the place of a dominant discourse in the maintenance of Nyerere's powerful position as 'Father of the Nation' in contemporary Tanzania. The media was one important factor in the creation of that discourse and I show how poetry played its part in that. The discourse by which Nyerere is 'Father of the Nation' is one that makes him central to the conceptualisation and imagining of that post-independence nation (Anderson, 1991). I use the term discourse here, and elsewhere in this article sense to describe sets of signs, images, notions and metaphors shared by politics and, in this case, literature to 'imagine' the nation. The intensity of the period of mourning makes the salience and utility of that discourse apparent. Some of the poems also use Nyerere's pivotal position in discourse as a means to try to obtain power for the party, CCM and Mkapa as its leader and the nations reigning president after his death.

Uhuru Newspaper

The newspaper *Uhuru*, launched on Independence Day on 9 December 1961, was the successor to the TANU (Tanganyikan African National Union) party publication '*Sauti ya Tanu*' (the voice of TANU) (Sturmer, 1998: 103). It became a daily issue in 1964 (Mzee, 1995: 79). This made *Uhuru* the first African national newspaper to be established by a post-independence governmental party. In 1980, when it was still the only daily Swahili newspaper in Tanzania, 100,000 copies of *Uhuru* were printed every day. This made it the paper with the highest publication rate at the time (Ng'wanakilala, 1982: 15) and in fact it "dominated the Tanzanian press sector for a period of over 30 years" (Sturmer, 1998: 265). The key local language publication for the duration of Nyerere's direct leadership of Tanzania, its circulation reduced substantially following the proliferation of non-state media that emerged during the nineteen-nineties (Grosswiler, 1997). Still selling 80,000 copies a day in 1991, circulation figures for *Uhuru* had dropped to 26,000 by 1996 three years before Nyerere died (Sturmer, 1998: 140, 178). This article concentrates on poetry from *Uhuru* and accepts that it is known to be restricted to reporting the one-sided party line of CCM – the successor party to TANU which was formed in 1977 when TANU was united with the Zanzibari Afro-Shirazi Party (ASP) (Grosswiler, 1997). The first reason for concentrating on poetry from *Uhuru* is pragmatic; the poetry from *Uhuru* newspaper was available for review. The second is that it offers an opportunity to explore how poetry was presented during the mourning period and played its part in portraying that 'party-line'.

Swahili Newspaper Poetry

Swahili poetry has what are normally known as a set of rules (Abedi, 1954) that date back some time. On the coast, where Swahili is a first language and Swahili poetry has been written down (initially in Arabic script) for at least four centuries (Knappert, 1979; Biersteker, 1996), these prosodic rules are regarded as indispensable to the writing of *shairi*. *Shairi* is the Swahili word usually translated as 'poem' but it often refers to the specific fixed form of verses of four lines of sixteen syllables each, which rhyme internally, and with a repeated refrain at the end of each verse which rhymes with all the other final lines in the verse of the poem.[1]

In the context of newspaper poetry, the invitation for readers to contribute their compositions for publication sets up a potential forum for debate on issues relevant to the readers and in which locally written literature can be circulated in a country with a limited publishing industry. Such poetry has been printed in Tanzanian newspapers for some time (Biersteker, 1996: 13). Chalamanda points out that newspapers may be shared by three or four different readers and poems may even be read to those who are unable to read themselves thereby increasing the actual circulation beyond that suggested by distribution figures (Chalamanda, 2001). Readership poetry is an opportunity for a named but invisible citizen to pass comment on events and issues and enter into a 'national' discursive realm with their ideas. Debates often emerge on readers' poetry pages concerning topics such as the role of women, the importance of education or the role of language.

We will cry for our father

The party-control of the press in Tanzania during Nyerere's presidency (Sturmer, 1998) was an important force in the maintenance of a discourse that revered Nyerere as 'Father of the Nation', and it continued to do so when he died. This poem was printed in *Uhuru* on 26 October:

---

1 Called *kituo bahari* which means the sea coming back again; it returns again and again.

Baba Tutamlilia ("We will cry for Our Father")
Saidi A. Likongine
Uhuru, 29 October 1999

(1) *Pongezi yangu ya dhati, Redio Tanzania,*
Kazi zenu madhubuti, Mola atawajalia,
Pamoja na magezeti, ya chama na jumuia,
Baba tutamlilia, ingawa hatumpati.

(1) Congratulations to you Radio Tanzania
On your honest work, God bless you
Together with the newspapers of the party and the people
We will cry to our father even though he isn't there

(2) *Ingawa hatumpati, baba tutamlilia,*
Katu hatufurukuti, shimo tumedidimia,
Mwananchi gani kiti, atakae kikalia,
Baba tutamlilia, ingawa hatumpati.

(2) Although we cannot see him, we mourn our father
We cannot sleep, we have sunk into a deep hole
Upon which chair will the people sit to cry?
We will cry to our father even though he isn't there

(3) *Juhudi ya Barakati, uhuru kupigania,*
Tamaa aliishiti, mali kulimbikizia,
Akitetea umati, wengi ni wala bamia,
Baba tutamlilia, ingawa hatumpati.

(3) It was a blessed project to fight for freedom
He hoped that he could build up wealth
He defended the underprivileged masses
We will cry to our father even though he isn't there

(4) *Tangu kwenya utafiti, landani kujitibia.*
Radio kila wakati, hali mkifuambia.
Hivi sasa kwa bahati, hali yake yaridhia.
Baba tutamlilia, ingawa hatumpati.

(4) Since he went for the consultation in London
The radio has been telling us how he is all the time
And now that his condition is confirmed
We will cry to our father even though he isn't there

(5) *Mara ikaja ripoti, mambo yalipozidia.*

Kwamba yuko mahututi, pumzi ina mwishia.

Usingizi awapati, wana Mama Maria.

Baba tutamlilia, ingawa hatumpati.

(5) A Report came saying that things were more serious

Saying he was ill and his breath was near to its end

Give them rest Mama Maria and her children

We will cry to our father even though he isn't there

(6) *Ukasitushwa umati, Mkapa kutuambia.*

Baba Mwalimu maiti, mpendwa katukimbia.

Waume na mabinti, nyuso tuko jinamia.

Baba tutamlilia, ingawa hatumpati.

(6) The masses were shocked when Mkapa announced

That the body of the beloved Teacher had left us

Men and women, we stand together

We will cry to our father even though he isn't there

(7) *Tumepoteza yakuti, ni kati kuti na njia.*

Mgumu huu wakati, wenye tekenolojia.

Nani atakunja goti, njia kuifatilia.

Baba tutamlilia, ingawa hatumpati.

(7) We have lost a gem, the gem which lit our way

It is hard in this time of technology

Who will bend their knees to follow the way

We will cry to our father even though he isn't there

(8) *Televisheni kidhati, nayo haikutulia.*

Moyo mhjizatiti, yote kutuandalia

Yaliopita maiti, hadi walipozikia.

Baba tutamlilia, ingawa hatumpati.

(8) Sincerely the television hasn't stopped showing it

They put their hearts into it to show us

The body passing, even the burial

We will cry to our father even though he isn't there

(9) *Nimefikia tamati, natunga huku nalia.*

Kumvumilia sipati, twamuombea jalia,

Akae pema janati, milele bila udhia,

Baba tutamlilia, ingawa hatumpati.

(9) I have reached the end, this composition makes me cry

I cannot bear it, we pray he will be blessed

That he may rest in a good place forever without trouble

We will cry to our father even though he isn't there

Likongine wonders what will happen in Nyerere's absence. Nyerere, the 'jewel' has gone, his body has left the people of Tanzania and there is nobody now to light their way. He continues 'in this time of technology, who will bend their knees to follow the way?' These lines suggest that the poet sees Nyerere as a person from a time before technology. It is as if Nyerere is being seen as a bridge from a pre-colonial 'imagined' past,[2] into a technological world. He sees the contemporary world 'of technology' as preventing anyone else who would be like Nyerere emerging again. In a sense Nyerere, as the first president of Tanzania, is irreplaceable – no one else can be first. No one else is seen to have contributed to bringing about independence as Nyerere is. In many ways too, given what we now know about the potential of technologies to challenge autocracy, there is much truth in this sentiment. A modern day Nyerere, restricting the availability of television and information as he did in the 1960s and 70s, yet retaining the love of his people, seems an unthinkable political 'animal' now.

This poet also pays tribute to the media for their reporting of Nyerere's death. The response to Nyerere's death, which we see in Likongine's poem and which we will continue to see in poems from *Uhuru* was paralleled in many other local newspapers and was also echoed by the international media.

Revered in death

Nyerere referred to himself as 'Mwalimu', the Swahili word for teacher,[3] and it was used repeatedly to refer to him in the poems of mourning. A poem called 'Farewell Teacher' (*Buriani Mwalimu*) published in *Uhuru* on 16 October was based upon the metaphor of Nyerere as educator of the nation. In it he is described as the ideological leader of his people who taught them the way to go:

---

2   In many speeches and articles, Nyerere espoused the idea of a return to 'traditional African' ways of life as a means for Africa, and particularly Tanzania, to recover from the damage inflicted by colonialism (Nyerere, 1967, 1968).

3   Nyerere said that he preferred the title Mwalimu to anything more ostentatious since he had himself briefly been a teacher.

(2) Hayupo Mwalimu wetu, wanafunzi tuna shaka,	(2) Our Teacher is gone, we the students are in trouble
Na nani darasa letu, wa kutufunza kwandika	Who will take the class, who will teach our lessons,
Mawazo ya kila mtu, mbali sana yamefika.	Everyone's thoughts are far away
Mwalimu ametutoka, daras letu na nani!	Our teacher has left us, who will teach us?

In this poem Bibi Nasrah N. Nyoka asks "Who will teach us now?" She also suggests that 'Bad people will come and seek to destroy the peace' and asks how, without Nyerere, they will be put off? She again describes Nyerere as a person who gave light, and has hope that a "good person will emerge to be like Nyerere and shine over our country".

Another poem entitled simply "Nyerere" (*Nyerere*) and published in *Uhuru* on 15 October 1999 is a prayer like petition to God that Nyerere might rest in peace. The author of the poem, Abdallah R. Chekanae also prays that, when he dies, Nyerere be waiting in heaven:

(7) Mbele yake nyuma yangu, Yarabi unisikie,	(7) Before him behind me, Hear me God
Ikifika zamu yangu, Nyerere anipokee,	When my turn comes, may Nyerere receive me
Nimejawa na uchungu, acha nisiendelee.	I am filed with sadness so I shall end here
Mlaze mahali pema, Julius Kambarage	Rest in Peace, Julius Kambarage

Here the request that Nyerere should be waiting for the poet in heaven to receive him seems to suggest that Nyerere has a personal and spiritual relationship with his people. Such assertions seem to confer upon Nyerere saint-like qualities and seek to cement his super-human legacy.

The poem "He lays in a good place in heaven" (*Kalale Pema Peponi*), by Fedelis Manyota also explicitly takes its theme from the speech in which Mkapa declared a period of national mourning, reminding the reader that in death Nyerere's legacy should be respected:

(2) Kimetupata kikuli, Mkapa akatumka	(2) Mkapa said that it was a tragedy
Ya kwamba wetu halili, Kambarage msifika	That our beloved, the praised Kambarage
Kama taa ya kadili, Mwalimu ametuzimika.	Like the light of a candle, Mwalimu was extinguished
Kalale peema peponi, mpendwa wetu Nyerere	Sleep peacefully in heaven, our beloved Nyerere

Clearly that this should happen was not only testament to Nyerere but was also politically important for Mkapa, president and leader of CCM at that time, whose position was apparently challenged by Nyerere's death. Mkapa needed to capitalise on Nyerere's death in a certain way in order to try to negate a loss of stability in its aftermath. In this context, the near God like achievements attributed in the poem to Nyerere are also intended to consolidate Mkapa's position:

(5) Utumwa metutoa, mkoloni kaondoka	(5) You freed us from slavery, and got rid of the colony
Uhuru tukapokea, bila damu kumwagika	We got our freedom, without blood being shed
Kiti ukakikalie, kakujalia Rabuku.	You occupied the seat, God granted it to you
Kalale pema peponi, mpendwa wetu Nyerere	Sleep peacefully in heaven, our beloved Nyerere

The poem "Nyerere has left us" (*Nyerere Ametutoka*) by Rajabu M. Kianda gives Nyerere a plethora of different titles and descriptions. In the second verse he is called a 'general':

(2) Katutoka JEMEDARI kote aliyesifika	(2) He has left us our praised general
Aliyekuwai MAHIRI wa siasa Afrika	Who was skilled in the politics of Africa
Tumegubikwa na hori, nimuhali kutoweka.	Who led us out of the darkness
Mola amghuhrie, ametutoka Nyerere	God help us, Nyerere has left us

Thereafter he is described as both the Founder and Teacher, while in the fifth verse he is referred to as 'Glorious':

(5) *NYERERE ni maarufu, kota alifahamika*	(5) Nyerere is famous everywhere he is known
Ni sawa na mtukufu, jina lilivyotajika	He is like a Glorious one wherever he is known
Leo amekuwa mfu, daima tamkumbuka.	Today he lives no longer, we will always remember him
Mola amghuhrie, ametutoka Nyerere	God help us, Nyerere has left us

In the eighth verse he is likened to a 'light':

(8) *Hakuonyeshwa kmvaa, kila mtu kumshika*	(8) He wasn't disgusted to be touched by anyone
Kweli alikuwa taa, tuliona ikawaka	Truly he was a light we saw shining
Nuru yake iling'aa, kila pembe ilifika.	His beam shone everywhere that it reached
Mola amghuhrie, ametutoka Nyerere	God help us, Nyerere has left us

In the final verse, verse 20, he is 'Our pilot President' (*Rais RUBANI Wetu*). It is worth noting that all of these analogies also appear in poems reproduced in the poetry collection about the Arusha Declaration published in 1971 (Kamenju and Topan, 1971). Therefore, while they are being reiterated in death, these analogies are not new. They cannot be viewed merely as the positive descriptions necessitated by mourning, but must also be seen as a continuation of an existing discourse. "A grief like this", emphasises the immense sorrow felt at Nyerere's death, which the author compares to a big ulcer; "Grief has gripped us, like a big ulcer". The poet asks that people remember the positive legacy of Nyerere rather than the things he did which were controversial. In doing so, the poems contribute not only to the sense of national mourning, but also the silencing of that which is controversial which is so critical for the maintenance of Nyerere's political legacy. The apparent necessity of sombre and reverential mourning again leads to a call for political stability in the present. In this way, poetry plays a part in imagining the nation and consolidating Nyerere's legacy as a fundamental part of that (Anderson, 1991).

We should concentrate on the future

Finnegan suggests that praise poetry was often 'an essential part in rites of passage' because it celebrated what had been and marked status for the future (Finnegan, 1970). Some of the poems in *Uhuru* more blatantly used the mourning for Nyerere as a time to recollect and to plan for the future. The poem "Farewell Teacher" (*Buriani Mwalimu*) by Saidi Nyoka uses the first section of the Swahili proverb: 'That which is past is past; we should concentrate on the Future'.[4] His poem focuses on how the nation has now lost its teacher Nyerere, but also advocates looking to the future in search for someone who can be his replacement.

In another poem published on 16 October 1999, Nyoka mobilises the same proverb again and compares Nyerere to a Lion:

Mwana wa Simba ni Simba ("The Child of a Lion is a Lion")
Saidi Nyoka
Uhuru, 16 October 1999

(1) Kufariki kwa Mwalimu, kuna watu wanatamba	(1) There are those who assert that because of the death of Mwalimu
Kwamba sasa CCM, utata itaikumba	That CCM will now be plunged into trouble
Na Mkapa hali ngumu, itamfanya kayumba	And this situation will cause Mkapa to sway
Mwana wa simba ni simba, hababaishwi na nyani	The child of a lion is a lion, he is not threatened by a baboon
(2) Wanasema Ikulu, mageuzi itasomba	(2) They say State house, it will handle the changes
Kwa sasa watafaulu, amekwishakufa mwamba,	For now they will succeed, he has already died the courageous one
Kifo hiki kwao lulu, kana kwamba waliomba	This death for them a pearl, what they had prayed for,
Mwana wa simba ni simba, hababaishwi na nyani	The child of a lion is a lion, he is not threatened by a baboon

---

4 I refer to the proverb '*Yaliyopita si ndwele, tugange yaijayo*'. In the poem, only the first half (*'Yaliopita si ndwele'*) is used.

(3) Nyerere amefariki, hii kazi ya Muumba,

Kwa sasa watfaulu, amekwishakufa mwamba

Kifo hiki kwao lulu, kana kwamba waliomba

Mwana wa simba ni simba, hababaishwi na nyani

(3) Nyerere has died, it was the work of the Creator

For now they will succeed, the courageous one is already dead

For them this death is a diamond, that they had prayed for

The child of a lion is a lion, he is not threatened by a baboon

(4) Tuongelee msiba, ulio katika nyumba.

Tunamzikaje baba, sio mengine kuomba

Tumzike kwa mahaba, tushikana sambamba,

Mwana wa simba ni simba, hababaishwi na nyani

(4) We should grieve this calamity which is in our houses

Is it too much to ask

That we should bury our father with love, together side by side,

The child of a lion is a lion, he is not threatened by a baboon

(5) Hababaishwi na nyani, Mwana wa simba ni simba,

Utulivu na amani, kila pembe utawamba

CCM tambueni, imeshika namba moja

Mwana wa simba ni simba, hababaishwi na nyani

(5) He's not threatened by a baboon, the child of a lion is a lion,

Calm and peace, it will spread in every corner,

This CCM recognise, it is the most vital matter

The child of a lion is a lion, he is not threatened by a baboon

(6) Kampeni zenu mbovu, mazishini zitafumba

Na kwamba ni upumbavu, Ikulu! Ikulu! Kwimba,

Ni wenu sio werevu, kichwani umewapamba,

Mwana wa simba ni simba, hababaishwi na nyani

(6) Your dirty tricks campaign won't spoil the burial

It is stupid to call out State House,

You have not been clever, it is written on your faces

The child of a lion is a lion, he is not threatened by a baboon

This poem's repeated refrain draws on an image of Nyerere as a lion and connects Mkapa to him as his direct descendent by also referring to him as a lion. In seeing Mkapa as a direct descendant of Nyerere, the author perhaps asserts that, just as Nyerere held CCM strong so will

Mkapa. He might also have been instead suggesting that Mkapa was not worthy to succeed Nyerere. Nyoka implies in this poem that there was an opposition group,[5] hoping to pounce on the opportunity to contest Mkapa's position in the wake of Nyerere's death. He refers to those who seek to make trouble as "baboons", a characterisation, which implies that people who like to scorn and laugh at others do not realise that they have the same faults (Ndalu and King'ei, 1989: 153). Nyoka suggests then that people who contest the leadership of CCM are foolish and idiotic.

Certainly there was also speculation in the press that Nyerere's death would signal an end to political stability in Tanzania (*The Guardian*, 23 October 1999; *The Daily Nation*, 16 October 1999). Nyoka scorns those who sought to take advantage in the wake of Nyerere's death, he asks instead in verse four "that Nyerere be buried with love by a population united – united in grief". The message of this poem is that those who saw Nyerere's death as a signal for change should leave things to be and bury Nyerere in peace. He advocates a unified memory for the nation's father to solidify the role of his successor. By seeing the right leader for CMM as Nyerere's child the poet suggests a kind of natural lineage between Nyerere and the current leadership, more akin to a monarchy than a political leadership. This reifying of Nyerere and by implication his successors seeks to link them to Nyerere not just as leader but also as a liberator, teacher and father of the Tanzanian nation.

In her study of *Oral Literature in Africa*, Finnegan charts a development in praise poetry from oral traditions to modern praise poems for political leaders and party candidates (Finnegan, 1979: 90). She looks at traditions of praise poetry composed for kings and chiefs in the kingdoms which existed in pre-colonial times in parts of Africa. Oral poetry was recited by men who were employed as bards by the courts (Ibid: 116), and was sanctioned and commissioned by rulers as a means through which they could reiterate their importance, power and legitimacy. As Finnegan says, praise poetry can 'validate status', stress 'accepted values' and draw 'attention to one's achievements, preserving accepted versions of history' (Ibid: 120). The author has studied a long tradition of such praise poetry amongst what she describes as the Southern Bantu (Ibid: 129). Analysing texts from across East and Central Africa Finnegan identifies praise poetry, which shares many of the characteristics of the poetry in newspapers about Nyerere. As in the

---

5 The poem does not appear to refer to a specific group of people who might be a threat to political stability.

poetry here she notes in her analysis the use of comparisons between the object of praise and various concepts of greatness (as in 'Nyerere has left us') as well as comparing them with animals (as in 'The Child of a Lion is a Lion') and inanimate objects (such as a light and a jewel in the poems above). This form also used repetitive refrains and similar prosody and structure to that observed in these newspaper poems.

The poem 'Advisors of the Nation' by Saidi Nyoka, published on 23 October 1999, links Nyerere with a number of major political figures in CCM:

Washauri wa Taifa ("Advisors of the Nation")
Saidi Nyoka
Uhuru, 23 October 1999

(1) Tulikuwa na Mwalimu, Kawawa, Jumbe na Mwinyi	(1) We had Mwalimu, Kawawa, Jumbe and Mwinyi
Na washauri muhimu, la kinyume hamfanyi	It is the important advisors who got things right
Mwalimu ni marehemu, nguzo zetu sasa nyinyi.	Mwalimu is deceased, you are our shield now
Washauri wetu nyinyi, baada kufa Mwalimu	After Mwalimu's death you are our advisors
(2) Mwalimu amekwachia, Kawawa huu upenyi	(2) Mwalimu left Kawawa with wisdom
Tutapo tingwa na njia, kuja hatujikanganyi	When the road ahead is shaky, we won't hesitate
Haraka tutakujia, twaamini hutusonyi	To come to you for the help we believe you will give us
Washauri wetu nyinyi, baada kufa Mwalimu	After Mwalimu's death you are our advisors
(3) Mwalimu kakwacha jumbe, watoto hututawanyi	(3) Mwalimu left a message, that we should not be divided,
Tutakuja tukuombe, ushauri hutubinyi	We will come to you for advice
Mwazo bora tupumbe, nasi hatuparuganyi	To get good ideas so that we don't ruin things
Washauri wetu nyinyi, baada kufa Mwalimu	After Mwalimu's death you are our advisors

(5) Palipo kinga na kinga, moto haujigawanyi	(5) Where there is defense and protection, Fire doesn't divide itself
Utatoa kila mwanga, wala haufinyi finyi	You will give out light, and it will not decrease
Hazina tumeipanga, vyema hatuitapanyi	The treasurer is arranged, hopefully it won't be dispersed
Washauri wetu nyinyi, baada kufa Mwalimu	After Mwalimu's death you are our advisors

Now that Nyerere is gone, the poet suggests Mwinyi (Tanzania's second president from 1985-1995), Kawawa (prime minister in 1962 and again 1972-1977), and Jumbe (second president of Zanzibar under whose control, in 1977, the Afro-Shirazi Party merged with TANU to become CCM) should replace him as the nation's advisors. Kawawa returned to Tanzania from London after it became clear that Nyerere would die but had been with him before that. Perhaps that is why in verse two the poet emphasises Kawawa's role in carrying forward Nyerere's wisdom. On the day of Nyerere's death *The Daily News* published comments about Nyerere by some, whom they called his "close associates". One of those featured was Kawawa who commented on Nyerere's determination to use an African language and his passionate belief that education was more important than wealth. He ends his tribute with the words: "If you cannot grow up (*kukomaa*) under Mwalimu Nyerere, you cannot make it elsewhere."

Kawawa suggests that, anyone who could not mature under the government of Nyerere could not have matured and grown well anywhere. This is the ultimate tribute to Nyerere. Apparently Kawawa felt that Nyerere provided everything the Tanzanian people needed. The idea that Nyerere somehow provided all that was needed reflects the discourse we have explored; Nyerere is the best option, the most honest, he has integrity and ultimately the inference of all of these texts is that he was and is the only option.

These last two poems reiterate the importance of following on from Nyerere. They certainly do not contest his power but view him as a legitimising force in the power of others. The discourse that views Nyerere as fundamental for Tanzania is being extended to others in his death. Nyerere is canonised to legitimate and affirm the credibility of the continuation of CCM as the only credible – and even possible –

party to lead Tanzania. In post-Nyerere Tanzania, to have Nyerere on your side and to claim him as your 'ancestor' is to gain a place in the legitimising discourse of the nation of Tanzania. Phillips has shown how the image of Nyerere as the 'Father of the Nation' has indeed continued to have salience since (Phillips, 2010). Observing the 2004-2005 election campaign of the incumbent President Jakaya Kikwete's, she identifies the use of Nyerere praise songs and the political impact of CCM's continued use of the Nyerere 'myth' in which there is a party lineage from Nyerere to Kikwete through the party and in which the party remains "institutionally senior to the government" (Ibid: 117).

Nyerere as Discourse

Through the poems of mourning published in *Uhuru*, I have begun here to sketch a picture of Nyerere as discourse. Our impression of Nyerere, and the mourning for him, has been mediated by the dominant discourse articulated in the poetry itself. This discourse was not just seen in the poetry; on the contrary it pervaded all reporting about and reflections on Nyerere's death. Nevertheless examining the poetry in this way has allowed us to explore a view of Nyerere which can help understand his place as 'The Father of the Nation' of Tanzania as a source of power which legitimised his rule, the authority of his successors and the state's conception of national identity in Tanzania. The possession and use of this pervasive discourse in Tanzania society, it seems, can remain powerful even after Nyerere is dead.

Barthes recognised that the 'claim to "decipher" a text' was futile since once the author has committed text to page he is no longer there (Barthes, 1986). The text, he says, stands alone ready for interpretation. The texts in this project stand alone, their authors remain absent in all but name. My analysis however, is embedded in a discussion of the particular situation that the poets were writing for and about. We must read this poetry with an awareness of the social, political and historical context in which it was originally created. The necessity to do so becomes evident when we realise that the tropes of respect and reverence which appear in the poetry of mourning are also echoed in various other mediums: for instance, the *Daily News*[6] led on 14 October 1999 with the comment, "Nyerere was a towering figure; endeared to his Tanzanian people and acknowledged by people in the rest of the world as a unique statesman". *The African*, another daily newspaper in Tanzania, explained on the 15 October 1999: "So, when we today mourn his death, we are not alone.

---

6   The *Daily News* is *Uhuru's* English language sister-publication.

Thousands of people – the world all over – who shared Mwalimu's vision of a friendly and just world, feel the poorest without him. They share with us the deep grief we feel – of losing an internationalist and defender of the defenceless and voice of the voiceless. At this saddest moment of our nation, we join our fellow compatriots to pray that may our nation stick to the ideals that Mwalimu believed in sacrificed his life for".

As we have seen the term Mwalimu, the Swahili word for teacher is recurrently used when referring to Nyerere. Many newspapers also carried condolence messages from their advertisers. One for example placed in *The Guardian* by Vodacom (then one of the two main cell-phone companies) simply reads: "We extend our deepest sympathy to the Tanzanian nation for the loss of Mwalimu" (*The Guardian*, 23 October 1999). The sympathy extended is to a whole nation who called Nyerere their teacher. Speaking to a teacher whose school had closed when they heard news of Nyerere's death a reporter from *The African* was told: "The pupils were disturbed after hearing the sad news, adding that they regard Mwalimu Nyerere as their grandfather" (*The African*, 15 October 1999). Everywhere the message echoes; a nation grieving the loss of its teacher, father, and even grandfather; champion of independence, peace and stability. There may have been those who were not so keen to celebrate Mwalimu but their voices were not heard in the media during the mourning period.

Biersteker explains that poetry composed in Swahili is usually in "response to another poem and/or to elicit a poetic response" (Biersteker, 1996: 12). As further evidence of poetry 'as praxis' or debate, Biersteker mentions a book of poems published in newspapers in the 1960s on the subject of the Arusha Declaration (Ibid: 113). The editors Kamenju and Topan introduce their book as follows:

> Kiswahili literature is now a literature of the farmers and the workers of Tanzania...The socialist revolution which is being carried out in this country fuels the spread, development and establishment of a Kiswahili literature (Kamenju and Topan, 1971: ix).

For them, readership poetry was about giving a voice to the grass-roots organic intellectuals who had, they suggest, been empowered by Ujamaa (their socialist revolution) to create a popular literature for the masses. Yet, it is striking that this supposed 'literature of the masses' uniformly sings the praises of Nyerere and his party. One poem from the book entitled *The Policy of Ujamaa* refers to Nyerere as a 'brave president', who gives 'good leadership' which the people approve of. There are many other poems expressing similar sentiments in their book and all of them are written in prosodic form. It is striking to note the way in which the poems reproduced in their book, collected from newspapers published in the 1960s, revere Nyerere in a similar way to the poems which were published when he died in 1999. Were these poems of the 1960s really the literature of the 'farmers' and the 'workers' establishing a literary form which they could understand and find meaningful? Did the people of Tanzania all really think that Ujamaa was a wonderful idea, and that Nyerere and his party were to be praised for everything they were doing? Or, was that party, with Nyerere at its head, and the discourse that surrounded it in fact losing touch with the 'workers and farmers' it claimed it had freed from oppression? Is it possible that these poems rather than facilitating a literature of, and for, the masses as the editors claimed, in fact facilitated the dissemination of a dominant ideology espoused by the government? As Hunter explains, the presentation of Ujamaa at the time was a 'new narrative (...) presented as an all- encompassing package of solutions' (Hunter, 2009: 479), but as she points out, the narrative had limits and was only partly successful in creating the post-colonial nation of Nyerere's imagining. Clearly the poems selected for publication in the 1960s, like those published in *Uhuru* after Nyerere died were part of the creation of this new narrative.

Indeed Nyerere himself wrote poetry, as well as often being the subject of it. Biersteker analyses a poetic debate which took place in the 1960s with Kandoro, which Kandoro himself published in and anthology called *Mashairi ya Saadani* (The Saadani Poems) in 1972 (Kandoro, 1972). Kandoro was an important writer and politician.[7] In the poetic debate, they discussed the principles of Ujamaa. She claims that their debate illustrates Ujamaa as 'praxis'; a practical exercise (as opposed to a purely theoretical one) in which they 'struggled to create a progressive discourse based in mutual respect and equality' (Biersteker, 1996: 134). Biersteker implies that the dialectical nature of poetry shows that Ujamaa was open and debatable as a concept. Biersteker views the apparent internal debate between Nyerere and Kandoro, as evidence of the potential for dialogue about Ujamaa ideology (Ibid: 137). Yet,

---

7 Saadani Kandoro was, at one time a member of the governing council of CCM; he was "a leading activist in the nationalist movement and a very prolific poet" (Biersteker, 1996: 98). His government positions since independence have included being TANU secretary and Area Commissioner of Mafia and then Bagamoyo (Ibid: 30).

Nyerere and Kandoro were, by the time they engaged in this poetic debate between 1964-69, both powerful members of a ruling party that controlled post-colonial Tanzania. The ideologies of equality and freedom from domination which they debated were, paradoxically, continually legitimising their actual power.

Poetry and debates

Bloch has explored the ways in which forms of political oratory often limit what can be said. He is writing about speech and language when he says: "as soon as you have accepted a form of speaking in an appropriate way you have begun to give up, at a bewilderingly rapid rate, the very potential for communication..." (Bloch, 1975: 15). Bloch sees formalised speech as a means of restricting what can be said. In the context of poetry recognised forms of prosody, terminology and the form of the medium in which something is published might in fact act in a similar way. In the case of prosodic poetry published in the party newspaper *Uhuru*, to what extent might it be possible to ask: how else the poets could have written? The discourse initiated by Mkapa's declaration of mourning (which took its inspiration from a discourse surrounding Nyerere in life) informed the reporting of Nyerere's death and also established the thematic and linguistic parameters to which the poems of mourning can all be said to conform.

The apparent presence of a dialogue does not necessarily amount to justice and equality because it does not amount to the same thing as freedom of dialogue. The fact that poetry in the Swahili context can be a discursive medium does not mean that it cannot simultaneously be a medium for disseminating a dominant ideology. A form in which the potential for debate is assumed to be present can actually be a restrictive form, in Bloch's sense, which sustains and legitimises a dominant idea. In the context of these poems and, when considering the part they have to play in a wider discourse about Nyerere, it is very likely that the apparent equality and openness of the discourse was, in fact, a major political tool in maintaining a dominant party-line. In many ways too the poetry of mourning represents a continuation of this discourse controlled by a party line even after Nyerere had died.

Weden describes "daily state-controlled newspapers in Syria" as "functional tablecloths, rather than respected records of current events" (Weden, 1999). We might think of *Uhuru* in this way, too. One reason for nevertheless choosing poems from *Uhuru* is that it simply published more poetry and had indeed done so since publication commenced sometimes containing as much as 25% poetry in a section called 'Your Poems' (*Mashairi Yenu*). Initially poems "paid tribute to Nyerere, praised the nation and attacked colonialism" (Sturmer, 1998: 109). Secondly, even as a 'tablecloth', *Uhuru* remains an important instrument for the dissemination of discourse and in this context it merits analysis. Looking at this poetry allows an investigation of the discourse creating that party line and Nyerere's place in it even in death. Moreover, as I have described during the mourning period, *Uhuru* was not particularly unique in its celebration of Nyerere's life and in the way that the poems it chose to publicly eulogise him. The poetry in the period after Nyerere's death, however, did not engage in a debate. Mourning was not a topic that was 'up for discussion'.

My subject matter is political and value-loaded. Nyerere may have been the nation's father. He may be publicly praised and revered and in this poetry he is most often portrayed as inhumanly perfect. I nevertheless retain a desire to believe in Nyerere and this desire is perhaps a consequence of my partial acceptance of the discourse which I describe in this article. My attempt to be a 'participant in the discourse' has led me to believe that our view of discourse, as is well illustrated by Scott and by Weden, must not neglect the ability people have to penetrate, transcend or ignore it (Scott, 1985, 1998; Weden, 1999). Often perhaps discourse is accepted not because it is conceived of as categorically true, but because people either want to believe it or because for some reason it is beneficial to appear to believe it. Now that Nyerere has died it makes sense to allow him to continue to be revered in popular discourse, partly because he is no longer there to use or abuse that 'heroicism'. Power for the future, however, rests in the ability of an individual or party to appropriate that discourse for their own.

The eulogisation of Nyerere seems to suggest that criticism of him is unacceptable. Cannadine looks at ways in which ruling elites:

> try to make alternative and subversive modes of thought seem off limits and even unthinkable, and seek to present what is in fact only one particular way of ordering, and organising society as authoritative and God-given (Cannadine, 1992: 2).

Consider, for example, if the eulogising of Nyerere had in fact contrasted him with Mkapa how different the options for our understanding of the relationship between them and their place in CCM might seem. As Weden has claimed of the cult surrounding the Syrian leader Assad it is not that everybody thinks he is always wonderful that makes the image of him 'effective and powerful' but rather that those who agree and those who do not 'alike, come increasingly to share the common experience of (the) vocabulary' that reveres him (Weden, 1999: 30). The vocabulary respecting and revering Nyerere was shared by all the newspaper reports on his death, by all the television reports (on the mainland and Zanzibar) and by the many people who turned out to pay their last respects to the 'father of the(ir) nation'. It was unthinkable perhaps not to pay one's respects to him, no matter what one actually thought of him.

Conclusion

Like me, Chalamanda writing about readership poetry in Malawian and South African newspapers makes the link between these oral forms and readership poetry which debates topical issues and she observes their use too in times of transition when 'a nation and its key figures are being re-imagined' (Chalamanda, 2002: 120). She observed of the call for poems following Malawi's independence in 1963 that 'the express aim of reader-contributions seems to be to demonstrate that readers truly absorb and celebrate the authority of the ruling power' (Ibid: 160). As we have seen the readership poetry in *Uhuru* newspaper played a part in the creation of Nyerere's power in the newly independent Tanzania during the 1960s and 1970s and the maintenance of his power thereafter. In death it revered him and supported the passing on of political power from Nyerere to those who followed him. The death of Nyerere was a significant national event in Tanzania politically, culturally and socially and one which necessitated a kind of transition of sorts from a nation with a living 'Father' to one which remembered him as its 'Founding Father'.

In particular, in the context of a party newspaper like *Uhuru* the poets are creating texts which legitimate rule and emphasise a dominant national version of history. These texts are commissioned by the paper not the court – but in many ways a party publication is part of the modern 'court' in the Tanzanian context. In this context I would suggest that the elite surrounding Nyerere, including amongst others the sympathetic editors of party publications were engaged in producing media which would continually seek to reinforce his legitimacy and in doing so, perpetuate their influence and power as well.

The constant repetition in the mourning poems of Nyerere's role as the bringer of light and independence reinforces the notion that it was he alone who was instrumental in bringing independence to Tanzania. The discourses which legitimise nations often rely upon a dominant history, which excludes the multiple histories and realities of the people within them. Geiger's analysis of women's involvement in TANU suggested that women's instrumental role in the independence struggle has not been recognised after independence (Geiger, 1997). Women then, were one of the casualties of a 'nationalist discourse' created by historians, authors, journalists and politicians, which has undoubtedly been successful in the construction of the idea of what, at least until he died in October 1999, can be seen as predominantly 'Nyerere's Tanzania'. Equally official histories minimised the role of Muslim political activists in the heritage of independence, thereby 'Christianising' the independence movement (Said, 1998: 330). The nationalist discourse is that Tanzania was neither 'benevolent' nor 'oppressive' (Anthias and Yuval-Davies, 1993: 29), but rather constructed upon a synthesis of these positions. Often, what was framed as benevolence was in fact a means to exert control and power. A nation of children protected by Father Nyerere? The insufficiency of this protection evidenced by the catastrophes of economic reality, villagisation and a country, which has since seemed to be playing catch up with the capitalist economy which grew around it during Nyerere's rule seems to have had minimal effect in destroying the idealisation of Nyerere. His resignation in 1985 certainly must have helped to perpetuate his iconisation. It is one of the facts frequently cited by commentators from Tanzania and abroad as proof of Nyerere's honesty and integrity (Pratt, 1999).

Nyerere was mourned nationally and internationally because the discourse that revered him was, to some extent, translatable. Not only Tanzanians and the media in Tanzania but the international media as well accepted for the most part the claim of the discourse; Nyerere, despite his faults was, at heart, a good man.

References

ABEDI, Kaluta Amri. *Sheria za Kutunga Mashairi na Diwani ya Amri* [The Rules of Swahili Poetry and the Poems of Amri]. Dar es Salaam: The Eagle Press, 1954.

ANDERSON, Benedict. *Imagined Communities: Reflections on the Origin and Spread of Nationalism*. London: Verso, 1991.

ANTHIAS, Floya, and Nira YUVAL-DAVIS. *Racialized Boundaries: Race, Nation, Gender, Colour and Class and the Anti-racist Struggle*. London: Routledge, 1993.

ASKEW, Kelly M. "Sung and Unsung: Musical Reflections on Tanzanian Postsocialisms." *Africa* 76 (2006): 15–43.

BARTHES, Roland. "The Death of the Author." In *The Rustle of Language*, ed. Roland Barthes, 49–55. Oxford: Basil Blackwell, 1986.

BIERSTEKER, Ann Joyce. *Kujibizana–Questions of Language and Power in Nineteenth- and Twentieth-Century Poetry in Kiswahili*. East Lansing, MI: Michigan State University Press, 1996.

BLOCH, Maurice. *Political Language and Oratory in Traditional Society*. London: Academic Press, 1975.

CANNADINE, David. "Introduction: Divine Rights of Kings." In *Rituals of Royalty. Power and Ceremonials in Traditional Societies*, ed. David Cannadine and Simon Price, 1–19. Cambridge: Cambridge University Press, 1992.

CATON, Steven Charles. *'Peaks of Yemen I Summon' Poetry as Cultural Practice in a North Yemeni Tribe*. Berkley, CA: California University Press, 1990.

CHALAMANDA, Fiona J. "'Pressing Literary Expressions': Reading Transitions in Malawian Press Poetry." *Interventions: International Journal of Postcolonial Studies* 3, no. 3 (2001): 376–390.

CHALAMANDA, Fiona J. "'Interpretations in Transition': Literature and Political Transition in Malawi and South Africa in the 1990s." PhD diss., University of Stirling, 2002.

CHEKANAE, Abdallah R. "Nyerere" [Nyerere]. *Uhuru*. 15 October 1999.

FINNEGAN, Ruth. *Oral Literature in Africa*. Oxford: Clarendon Press, 1970.

GEIGER, Susan. *TANU Women: Gender and Culture in the Making of Tanganyika Nationalism, 1955–1965*. Portsmouth, NH: Heinemann, 1997.

GROSSWILER, Paul. "Changing Perceptions of Press Freedom in Tanzania." In *Press Freedom and Communication in Africa*, ed. Festus Eribo and William Jong-Ebot, 101–119. Lawrenceville, NJ: Africa World Press, 1997.

HUNTER, Emma. "Revisiting Ujamaa: Political Legitimacy and the Construction of Community in Post-Colonial Tanzania." *Journal of Eastern African Studies* 2, no. 3 (2009): 471–485.

KAMENJU, Grant, and Farouk TOPAN. *Mashairi ya Azimio la Arusha* [The Poetry of the Arusha declaration]. Dar es Salaam: Longman Tanzania, 1971.

KANDORO, Saadani Abdu. "Mashairi ya Saadani" [The Poetry of Saadani]. Dar es Salaam: *Shirika ya Magazeti ya Chama*, 1972.

KIANDA, Rajabu M. "Nyerere Ametutoka" [Nyerere Has Left Us]. *Uhuru*. 28 October 1999.

KNAPPERT, Jan. *Four Centuries of Swahili Verse*. London: Heinemann, 1979.

LIKONGINE, S. A. "Baba Tutamlilia" [We Will Cry for Our Father]. *Uhuru*. 26 October 1999.

MANYOTA, Fedelis. "Kalale Pema Peponi" [He lays in a good place in heaven]. *Uhuru*. 28 October 1999.

MZEE, Hassan. "Uhuru na Mzalendo Katika Kuendeleza na Kukuza Kiswahili [Freedom and Nationalism in the Growth and Development of Swahili]." In *Kiswahili na Vyombo vya Habari* [Swahili and the Media], ed. Shaaban Ali Kachenje Mlacha 71–85. Dar es Salaam: TUKI, 1995.

NDALU, Ahmed E., and Geoffrey Kitual King'ei. *Kamusi ya Methali za Kiswahili* [Dictionary of Swahili Proverbs]. Nairobi: East African Educational Publishers, 1989.

NG'WANAKILALA, Nkwabi. *Mass Communication and Development of Socialism in Tanzania*. Dar es Salaam: Tanzania Publishing House, 1981.

NYERERE, Julius Kambarage. *Uhuru na Umoja* [Freedom and Unity]. Dar es Salaam: Oxford University Press, 1967.

NYERERE, Julius Kambarage. *Ujamaa–Essays in African Socialism*. Dar es Salaam: Oxford University Press, 1968.

NYOKA, Saidi. "Mwana wa Simba ni Simba" [The Child of a Lion Is a Lion]. *Uhuru*. 16 October 1999.

NYOKA, Saidi. "Washauri wa Taifa" [Advisors of the Nation]. *Uhuru*. 23 October 1999.

NYOKA, Nasrah N. "Buriani Mwalimu" [Farewell Teacher]. *Uhuru.* 16 October 1999.

PHILLIPS, Kristin. "Pater Rules Best. Political Kinship and Party Politics in Tanzania's Presidential Elections." *PoLAR: Political and Legal Anthropology Review* 33, no. 1 (2010): 109–132.

PRATT, Cranford. "Julius Nyerere: Reflections on the Legacy of his Socialism." *Canadian Journal of African Studies* 33, no. 1 (1999): 137–152.

SAID, Mohamed. *The Life and Times of Abdulwahid Sykes, 1924-1968. The Untold Story of the Muslim Struggle against British Colonialism in Tanganyika.* London: Minerva Press, 1998.

SCOTT, James C. *Weapons of the Weak. Everyday Forms of Peasant Resistance.* New Haven: Yale University Press, 1985.

SCOTT, James C. *Seeing Like a State: How Certain Schemes to Improve the Human Condition Have Failed.* New Haven: Yale University Press, 1998.

STEINER, George. *After Babel. Aspects of Language and Translation.* New York: Oxford University Press, 1975.

STURMER, Martin. *The Media History of Tanzania.* Ndanda: Ndanda Mission Press, 1998.

WEDEN, Lisa. *Ambiguities of Domination. Politics, Rhetoric and Symbols in Contemporary Syria.* Chicago: University of Chicago Press, 1999.

PART 6:

Post-Mwalimu Education?

Chapter 11

The University of Dar es Salaam: A Post-Nyerere Institution of Higher Education? Legacies, Continuities and Changes in an Institutional Space (1961-2012)

Olivier Provini

In 2008, the Council of the University of Dar es Salaam (UDSM) approved the appointment of Professor Issa G. Shivji to the Mwalimu Julius K. Nyerere Professorial Research Chair in Pan-African Studies. The Chair was officially launched on 15th April to coincide with the birthday of the first President of Tanzania (12th April 1922). Since then, a Julius Nyerere Intellectual Festival has been organized every year in the month of April during which a renowned academic personality – the Distinguished Nyerere Lecturer – is invited to deliver a conference on a topic of his/her choice.[1] This festival is supported by the Mwalimu Nyerere Foundation (MNF), an organisation established in June 1996 by Nyerere himself and which, today, pays him a permanent tribute by disseminating his political thought through various media and the publication of his speeches.[2] This festival is also the occasion to publicly debate Mwalimu's political philosophy and thoughts on education and more generally on the socio-political space in Tanzania. For instance, the "Second Julius Nyerere Intellectual Festival" (12th-15th April 2010) was

---

*I wish to thank Marie-Aude Fouéré who provided significant scientific feedback, constructive comments and advice during the writing process. I am grateful to IFRA for supporting my research from 2011 to 2013. Finally, my thanks go to Hélène Provini, Hugh Dowding, Thierry Perronnet and Sina Schlimmer as my text is all the better for their comments and corrections.

1 See the website of the Chair: http://nyererechair.udsm.ac.tz/. For instance, during the "Third Julius Nyerere Intellectual Festival" (April 2011), there were communications about "Pan-Africanism and the Challenge of East African Integration" (Issa G. Shivji), "Tanzanian Socialism and Africa's Future: Mere Footnote or First Step on a Long March" (John Saul) and "Nkrumahism and Consciencism in the Struggle for African Emancipation in Contrast to Senghor's Negritude" (Dani W. Nabudere). See the publication *Chemchemi. Mwalimu Nyerere Professorial Chair in Pan-African Studies* no. 4, 2011.

2 See MNF's website: http://www.nyererefoundation.org.

conceived as a week of reflection on the Arusha Declaration, advertised with these words by Nyerere reprinted on a large banner hung on the Administration Hall of the university: "We have been oppressed a great deal, we have been exploited a great deal, we have been disregarded a great deal... Now we want a revolution" (Nyerere, 1969: 235). The fourth festival programme, held in 2012 from 12-13th April, bore again several quotations by Nyerere on the importance of culture for nation-building, such as: "A country which lacks its own culture is no more than a collection of people without the spirit which makes them a nation",[3] which resonates with other reprinted quotations by Frantz Fanon and Amilcar Cabral along the same lines. On these occasions, books by or about Nyerere are on sale at the entrance of UDSM's Nkrumah Hall where the festival takes place.

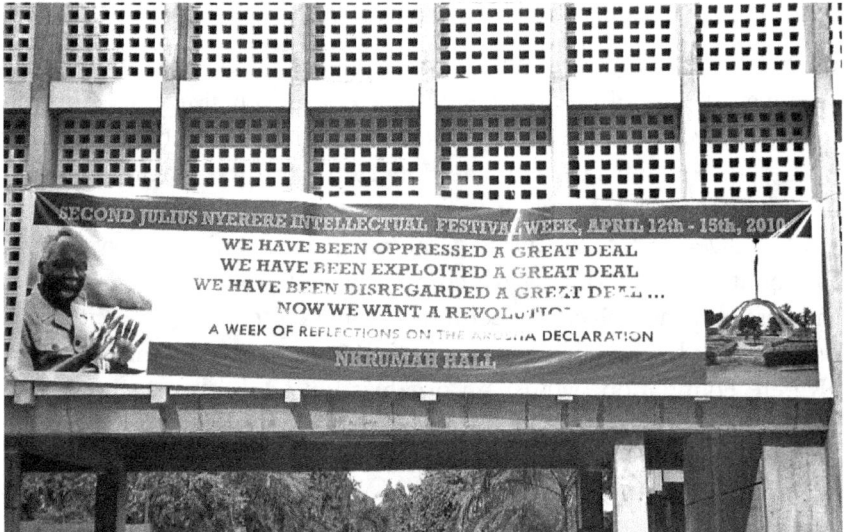

Banner of the Second Julius Nyerere Intellectual Festival, 2010 (by Olivier Provini, 24th April 2010)

In the face of the impact of the neoliberal turn on Tanzanian policies since the end of the 1980s, Nyerere's words on exploitation, revolution and nation-building, but also on Ujamaa (socialism) and Kujitegemea (self-reliance) – the catchwords of Tanzania's African socialism – may seem outmoded.

---

[3] UDSM, "Fourth Julius Nyerere Intellectual Festival, Programme" (2012: 6) (quotation from Nyerere, 1966: 186).

Yet, rather than seeing the recurring references to Nyerere and his views on higher education as an anachronism that may soon disappear, I contend that the university space reflects the imbrication of opposing dynamics. Indeed, from its initial path informed by Tanzania's brand of socialism (Bjerk, 2010) to its adaptation to the market economy since the mid-1980s, the University of Dar es Salaam – the historic, oldest and biggest university in the country – is a unique model of evolution of public policy in a neoliberal context, informed both by the past and the present.[4] "Constructed as a showpiece of Tanzania's new postcolonial era" (Ivaska, 2011: 124), UDSM owed its early reputation to the tremendous efforts and high hopes placed in it by the fledgling Tanzanian state. Nyerere himself, in an address opening the University College Campus on 21st August 1964, stressed that the ultimate objective of the University was to "contribute to the raising of the standard of living of the mass of the people", notably by training a cohort of loyal and high-level Tanzanians at the service of the national project for modern socialist development (Ivaska, 2011: 127–129). The Hill, as UDSM was referred, also owed its regional repute and attractiveness to the many intellectuals, notably leftist expatriates, who theorized and taught development and historical socialism in the 1960s-1970s, embraced under the term of "Dar es Salaam school" (Shivji, 1993: 77–88, 129).[5] Yet, with the neoliberal revolution of the late 1980s and its watchwords of "good governance" and "efficiency", the socialist past may seem far away today. The vision and mission of higher education developed in the 1960s have been altered, disrupting balances put in place after independence and generating new social and political spaces. However, it is striking to see that this neoliberal turn has not entirely transformed practices and representations. Julius K. Nyerere's shadow is not merely present as a tutelary figure through his pictures on administration offices' walls, nearby those of incumbent President Jakaya Mrisho Kikwete. The pervasive presence of Nyerere in the public space through his images, his words and the reverential tributes paid to him (Fouéré, 2009, 2011, 2014; see also Askew, 2006; Becker, 2013), alongside those actual changes in policies, highlights the specific situation of Tanzania, as a "post-socialist" space (Pitcher

---

4 The term 'neoliberalism' is used to understand and underline the pregnancy of the state in the process of shifts and reforms through advent of a new distantly governmental mode (Dardot and Laval, 2009: 13–15).

5 The university, geographically located on a hill outside Dar es Salaam, was "one of the few in Africa where debates and discussions have been a hall-mark of academic life" (Shivji, 1993: 129). In the 1960-1970s, intellectuals played a major role in the decision-making process of education policies through their reflections.

and Askew, 2006; Fouéré, 2011). Analysing the current university configuration through this post-socialist paradigm that "seeks to address theoretically and empirically the current state of formerly socialist African countries by privileging post-socialism as its frame", and asking "what institutional and discursive legacies has socialism left behind, and how might they inform current processes?" (Pitcher and Askew, 2006: 3) help understand the interlocked pattern of a priori antagonist models in higher education. In "post-socialism", the prefix "post-" does not entail that the socialist horizon has totally disappeared, but rather, points to institutional legacies, symbolic frameworks and individual or collective strategies stemming from the socialist past. The presence of the past in the present, though much reframed and reshaped in sometimes deeply ambiguous ways, explains why it is necessary to adopt a historical perspective to explore the intricacies of higher education reforms in contemporary Tanzania, notably in view of the mobilisation of the figure of Nyerere in the contemporary Tanzanian public space. Can we identify legacies of the socialist past in the present? How do such legacies – whether as conceptions of what education should be, or as actual bureaucratic practices – intermingle with and impact upon today's reforms, shaping Tanzania's singular trajectory in the present?

In my view, the post-socialist paradigm has much in common with the notion of 'path dependence' used today in the public policy approach. Indeed, the path dependence concept is heuristic to apprehend spaces where several opposed dynamics cohabit and intermingle, and to understand why there are limited breaks or changes in political structures (Pierson, 2000). According to Levi (1997: 28), "path dependence has to mean, if it is to mean anything, that once a country or region has started down a track, the costs of reversal are very high. There will be other choice points, but the entrenchments of certain institutional arrangements obstruct an easy reversal of the initial choice. Perhaps the better metaphor is a tree, rather than a path. From the same trunk, there are many different branches and smaller branches. Although it is possible to turn around or to clamber – and essential if the chosen branch dies – the branch on which a climber begins is the one [it] tends to follow". This conception of transition points to the idea that institutional configurations may progress slowly or marginally. The actors who wish to implement reforms face resistance in the form of bureaucratic routines, collective action, etc. which may lead to negotiated change or even status quo (Dupuy and Thoenig, 1985; Fontaine and Hassenteufel, 2002). In the case of UDSM, similar dynamics can be seen, notably through the role of the students' organisation. As will be discussed further below, students play a crucial role in conciliation, for instance in consciously using Mwalimu's shadow and symbol to contest the financial participation of the students to the university costs.

Thus, we argue that UDSM is situated in an in-between space set between transition, through the implementation of a new neoliberal agenda, and continuity, with the maintaining of representations and practices related to a socialist-oriented approach of education, notably in relation to the financial engagement of the state in UDSM global budget. Even if transformations are manifest, in particular in university research, the higher education system remains widely subsidized by the Tanzanian government. Negotiations delay the implementation of an actual cost-sharing policy and advent of the privatisation of UDSM, unlike in the neighbouring universities of Kenya and Uganda.

The University of Dar es Salaam: An Institution for National Development

UDSM was first established in 1961 as a college of the university of London. In 1963, it became a constituent college of the University of East Africa.[6] A clear division of labour was introduced between colleges: Makerere was a pre-eminent institution in East Africa with an established strength in Medicine and great reputation in Liberal Arts and Agriculture; Nairobi concentrated on Engineering and Business; and Dar es Salaam got specialized in Law and Development Studies. In July 1970, it became an independent national university (Cooksey, Levey and Mkude, 2003: 1). During this time, the mission and vision upon which UDSM was to develop were formulated. As early as 27th June 1966 Nyerere emphasized in his opening speech to the World University Assembly in Dar es Salaam that "the university in a developing society must put the emphasis of its works on subjects of immediate moment to the nation in which it exists, and it must be committed to the people of that nation and their humanistic goals" (Nyerere, 1969: 183). This quotation reminds us of the ambiguous and complex relations between political power and universities. Conceived as a symbol of sovereignty and independence, universities stood as a nationalist emblem against

---

6 From the 1920s, Britain started formulating educational policy for its African colonies. In 1936-1937, the publication of the De la Warr Commission Report set the process of establishing the federal University of East Africa, which was finally inaugurated in June 1963. It was perceived as a regional asset; the University of East Africa Act did not only set up the institution, but also reminded the people of East Africa that regional cooperation was extending its boundaries beyond specificities (Mngomezulu, 2004: 114–181).

the former colonial state (Hargreaves, 1973:26-36). Universities had a global mission in the construction and the development of the new state through the production of a new independent national elite (Charton and Owuor, 2008: 108-109) committed to the national project – whom Ivaska, in the case of Tanzania, calls the "servants of the nation" (Ivaska, 2011: 126-127). Paradoxically, universities were also recipients of European legacy. The use of English as the official language in higher education,[7] or the ceremonies of graduation with their usual clothes and rites are symbols of such narrow links with the colonial past. Since they were established, universities have been hybrid and consequently often controversial, constructions of past and present practices.

Higher education and the new ideology

The development of a "socialist attitude of mind" (Nyerere, 1962: 1), a prerequisite for building the new Tanzanian socialist society and citizen subjectivities, was notably to be accomplished through government education institutions. The Arusha Declaration of February 1967 was the moment when Julius Nyerere fully committed Tanzania to this socialist project under the development path of Ujamaa na Kujitegemea, or "socialism and self-reliance".[8] Interestingly, an event that influenced the Declaration was, in 1966, the opposition of the students of the University College to be compelled to National Service. They also rejected the imposition of what they called "political indoctrination during the National Service program" (Bienen, 1974: 427; Ivaska, 2005). The students' stand in opposition to Nyerere's conception of dedication to the social state resulted in stronger control on the university, notably through the creation of youth organisations affiliated to the single party,

---

7 The language policy in Tanzania generates a lot of debates, especially because of the transition between primary and secondary education. Swahili is used in primary education while English is the medium of instruction at the secondary and post-secondary levels. Under the headline "Education for self-reliance", Tanzania transformed the educational system into a force for the common good (Ivaska, 2011: 147-148). The establishment of Swahili as a national language was instrumental in the move towards self-reliance in general. But despite Nyerere's desire to reimagine the education system through this new paradigm, English remained the language used in secondary and higher education. However, there is a gap between theory and practice, in the sense that nowadays, many university courses and informal discussions between teachers and students are in Swahili. Swahili often becomes the de facto language of instruction because secondary schools students are not adequately prepared to use English as a medium of instruction.

8 Strictly speaking, the Arusha Declaration refers to a specific declaration and policy resolutions adopted in February 1967 at a Conference of the National Executive Committee of TANU held in the town of Arusha in northern Tanzania (Msekwa and Maliyamkono, 1979: 20-37). The term Ujamaa "proposed that socialism was native to Africa, and as such was not the socialism of Europe that was built on class conflict" (Bjerk, 2010: 285-286).

the Tanganyika African National Union (TANU). TANU was indeed charged, along with the Ministry of Education, to introduce the guidelines laid down in the Arusha Declaration into the education program.[9] This episode is the first of a long negotiation process – sometimes marred by violent action – between students, state and university administration authorities over the means and ends of higher education which can still be observed today.

Mwalimu always asserted that universities in East Africa could no longer afford to be disinterested parties in the task of nation-building. The university had to be developmental, and to be so it had to meet the standards of higher education like everywhere else in the world while at the same time being active in building the nation (Robertson, 1979: 34–45). Its curriculum, syllabus, research, personnel, moral code and philosophy had to be created in view of individual and collective involvement in developing Tanzanian society. One crucial aspect was to make a real break in the education content inherited from the colonial period: "The third action we have taken is to make the education provided in all our schools much more Tanzanian in content. No longer do our children simply learn British and European history. Faster than would have been thought possible our University College and other institutions are providing materials on the history of Africa" (Nyerere, 1973: 49). The national university was considered a crucial tool for emancipation. As the newly independent state depended heavily on expatriates to staff the middle and upper cadres of the civil service, the government implemented a new training programme leading to the Africanization of the workforce: "Very often facts are extremely unpleasant... Those of our people who were denied a chance of education [are not] more competent to be doctors, engineers, teachers or administrators simply because we want to replace expatriate servants by local ones".[10]

From speeches to facts: The implementation of University policies

The principles of equality, freedom and unity developed by Nyerere were put in action through concrete political and social reforms in the country which affected all sectors, higher education included. The five-year period from 1968 to 1973 marked the first stage of the implementation of Nyerere's ideology. The policy of self-reliance in education was implemented in at least three ways: i) the abolishment

---

9 In 1965, TANU Youth League sections were introduced into secondary schools; they became more active at the University College in 1966.

10 Opening speech of the university college campus, Dar es Salaam, 21st August 1964 (Lema, Mbilinyi and Rajani, 2004: 18).

of racial distinctions, ii) an expansion of educational facilities, and iii) the Africanization of education contents and teachers. Education was by far the largest social service costs. During the "First Five Year Plan", introduced in 1964, priority was given to the expansion of opportunities for secondary and higher education (Bienen, 1974: 281–306).

When the college of the University of East Africa became an independent national university, the head of state became its titular Chancellor. It was a way for the government and the party to control the day-to-day administrative and academic affairs of the university. This centralized plan had great impacts in the management of the university, to the point of changing admissions conditions (Cooksey, Levey and Mkude, 2003: 1). For instance, with the Musoma resolution in 1974, students were eligible for higher education only if they had completed one year of compulsory national service and had a minimum of two years of work experience.[11] This was a radical departure from past practices established in the British Commonwealth where admission was based on Advanced level performance.

There were also directives to review curricula in order to make adjustments to the needs and aspirations of the new state. During his speech at the inauguration of the University of Dar es Salaam in 29th August 1970 Julius K. Nyerere explained that "the aim of the university of Dar es Salaam must be service to the needs of developing socialist Tanzania. This purpose must determine the subjects taught, the content of the courses, the method of teaching, and the manner in which the university is organized, as well as its relations with the community at large" (Schutte, 1972: 75). According to him, it was unnecessary to teach students by drawing examples from Europe. Considering that the university was an African institution, it had to reflect its African character by Africanizing its curricula, syllabi and staff (Mngomezulu, 2004: 266–311). In this way, a course called "Development studies" was introduced at UDSM to enable students to theorize and understand innovative alternative development strategies.[12] The department of history was also famous for its several schools of thoughts (Slater, 1986).

---

[11] In November 1974, the National Executive Committee met in Musoma to review Tanzania's progress in its policies of socialism and self-reliance. UDSM implemented the resolution from the 1975–1976 academic year until the government reversed the Resolution and removed student's pre-requisite conditions of admission.

[12] Some new units charged with development issues were created: the Economic Research Bureau (ERB), the Bureau of Resource Assessment and Land Use Planning (BRALUP), the current Institute of Resource Assessment (IRA), the Institute of Kiswahili Research and the Institute of Adult Education (Cooksey, Levey and Mkude, 2003: 2–3).

It was a place where scholars debated the historical roots of Tanzanian egalitarianism, mass nationalism, or the role of the elite and popular forces in post-independence Africa (Ranger, 1971). The development of Marxist theory in UDSM was an original trait in the region and accounts for the university's reputation regionally, if not internationally. Renowned leftist thinkers taught there for some years, among them Walter Rodney between 1966-1967 and 1969-1974 (Ivaska, 2011: 126).

The Neoliberal Turn: a Quiet Revolution[13]

During recent years Tanzania has been upheld as a champion of structural reforms in all its sectors. This is being reflected in relatively high growth rates and the stabilization of macro-economic parameters. This neoliberal shift was made under the presidency of Benjamin Mkapa (Havnevik and Isinika, 2010: 1–18).[14] The 1980-1995 period was a transition between the Ujamaa model and an economy under transformation spearheaded by the international organisations (Mollel, 2005).

Shift in UDSM's mission

In the 1980-1990s, the Tanzanian government initiated global reforms (Kelsall, 2002) to answer political and economic crises. The education sector in Tanzania faced major constraints arising out of economic hardships, particularly the war against Idi Amin Dada's Uganda, the sharp increase in prices of petroleum products and the drastic fall in volume and prices of agricultural product exports (Luhanga, 2009). During that period, UDSM started major transformations through the implementation of financial and managerial reforms labelled the Institutional Transformation Programme (ITP) which were achieved in 1991. It was argued that infrastructures, governance and curricula did not correspond to the new political, social and economic realities. This process of transformation was widely spread by UDSM publications produced by reformers.

---

13 The "quiet revolution" is an expression used by D. Court to describe reforms in Makerere in a World Bank report (Court, 1999).

14 The former President Benjamin Mkapa (1995-2005) was partisan champion of privatisation. To him, the privatisation process was adopted not because it was the cure for all economies woes the country was facing, but because the former economic system had proved a failure: "privatisation does not mean that we have found a cure for our problems. I want to remind you that every new strategy has its pros and cons. Privatisation likewise, has its advantages and disadvantages". See Guardian Reporter, "Mkapa Defends Privatisation", *The Guardian*, 1 June 1992, p.1.

This neoliberal turn can be seen in the evolution of the missions of UDSM, as a comparison between the Official Act of 1970 and the 2003-2008 Strategic Plan brings to light. Tremendous changes in the lexical field of education point to the fact, more generally, that a "quiet revolution" (Court, 1980) was taking place in the conception of the university role. Whilst the Official Act of 1970 associated higher education with "national development", the "needs of the nation", or efforts to create a "sense of public responsibility" among students, the Strategic Plan of 2003-2008 underlines the regional and international "competitive environment" in higher education and research, and the necessity for the university to become a "major actor" in the region. It advocates "global competitiveness", "vocational training" and "entrepreneurship" to adapt to the market. The recent reforms therefore prompted and resulted in a decisive shift in the mission of the university from development-oriented to market-driven ends. In 1999, the former President Benjamin Mkapa underlined this globalized and competitive context, saying: "Recognizing that the world of the 21th century will increasingly be globalized, we must devise new and more stringent strategies in initiating and managing change in African universities. Of necessity, African universities will have to strive to improve further the quality of their output if they are to continue to maintain even their current share of the local and international labour market" (Cooksey, Levey and Mkude, 2003: 13).

Evolution of UDSM's mission in official documentation

Missions of the university according to the Official Act of 1970	Missions of the university according to the 2003-2008 Strategic Plan
– To preserve, transmit and enhance knowledge for the benefit of the people of Tanzania in accordance with the principles of socialism accepted by the people of Tanzania – To create a sense of public responsibility in the educated and promote respect for learning and pursuit of truth – To prepare students to work with the people of Tanzania for the benefit of the nation – To cooperate with the Government of the United Republic of Tanzania and the peoples of Tanzania in the planned and orderly development of education in the United Republic – To stimulate and promote intellectual and cultural development of the United Republic for the benefit of the people of Tanzania	– To assume a leading role in the responsibility of University education and to make provision for centres and places of learning education, professional or vocational training, and research – To promote continuing education to Tanzanians in order to maintain labour productivity and global competitiveness – To excel in knowledge and human resource capacity building by ensuring a balance between quality and quantity – To provide, promote and maintain centres of excellence and management exemplary in knowledge creation, skill development and entrepreneurship – To stimulate students to engage in productive services and entertainment activities in and outside the University – To establish mutually negotiated, beneficial and durable links within institution(s) of learning and research nationally, regionally and globally

The current conception of higher education is linked with new recommendations made by international organisations (Brock-Utne, 2003). The university's mission is harnessed to governmental priorities implying a state-planned organisation. The neoliberal turn underlines the advent of collective and individual competition as a structural norm and rationality, which has to regulate all behaviours (Dardot and Laval, 2009).

Reintroducing cost-sharing policy

During the period between 1975 and 1985, the higher education sector faced a serious financial crisis in terms of both recurrent and capital development budgets. For instance, the number of government fellowships available was very limited. The public system of higher education was caught between declining governmental revenues and a growing demand. The development of primary and secondary education, which had been encouraged by international institutions, had generated a greater demand for higher education. In response, Tanzania turned to private revenue. A policy of cost-sharing,[15] whereby costs are shared by governments, parents and students, was implemented in three phases. In phase 1 (1992-1993), students and parents were required to cover transportation, application registration, entry examination and union fees; in phase 2 (1993-1994), they had to pay for food and accommodation only; in the last phase (2004-2005), they were required to pay tuition and examination fees, books, stationary costs and medical insurance (Ishengoma, 2004: 105–106).

Such a policy is premised on the assumption that cost-sharing makes students and their families more discerning consumers and universities more cost-conscious providers – what is called "producer responsiveness" (Ishengoma, 2004: 104). The other argument is that it increases the independence of university structure and actors, as they no longer depend on government budget exclusively. Obviously, these reforms generate a new definition of the university. Knowledge becomes a private good, which must be profitable in the short term. The university becomes a service provider, and students are seen as consumers. A member of the top administration and lecturer in humanities in his sixties explained to me the radically different situation of students in the 1970s as compared with today: "In the beginning, students just came here to study and they paid no costs except just their own fares. Books were provided. In my first years, I just paid my fare. As soon as I arrived in the campus, all was free. I go to the cafeteria. I go to the bookshop [...]. All books were paid by the university, even books that we found outside the university, in the city. You gave your receipt, and they paid back your

---

15 The policy of cost-sharing in higher education is not new in Tanzania. It existed during the colonial period and post-independence Tanzania until 1967, when the government implemented Ujamaa. During the colonial period and even after Independence, students in higher education institutions paid tuition fees. In 1967, the Tanzanian government decided to grant scholarships to all students admitted to UDSM, which was then the only public university. Cost-sharing in higher education was officially reinstated in January 1992 (Ishengoma, 2004: 105).

books [...]. At this time, higher education was only for few people. The government says that this situation is not possible. So, I think also, that we have been pushed by the World Bank and development partners, outside the country".

The budgetary outsourcing in University research: the end of self-reliance

The policy of cost-sharing was not the only strategy applied to save money. The government also drastically reduced its investment in the research sector. The university research has long been strongly subsidized by the Tanzanian state (Harrison, Mulley and Holtom, 2009: 271-298), but since the 2000s, the research sector has mainly been financed by external public organisms. External agencies contribute up to 99% to UDSM research sector in 2000-2005. The main donors were the Swedish agency Sida/SAREC, the Norwegian organism NORAD and the US institution Carnegie.

Budget in research sector at UDSM (1999-2004)

Academic year	Budget allocated by the government for research sector (US $)	Budget allocated by donors for research sector (US $)	Others (US $)	Total (US $)	Percentage of funds allocated by donors in budget for research sector (%)
1999	526,529	2,306,958	0	2,833,488	81
2000	12,580	2,519,871	0	2,532,451	99
2001	10,395	1,832,944	0	1,843,339	99
2002	11,747	1,120,230	535,285	1,667,262	99
2003	12,861	2,178,537	399,743	2,591,141	99
2004	13,163	2,822,569	285,830	3,121,562	99

Reference: UDSM (2005: 54)

Donors invested in staff training, scholarship, infrastructure and the research sector. Relations between donors and UDSM can be developed through two channels, either by direct relations between an external agency and a faculty, or by indirect relations between donors and the university central administration. In this case, it is the university, with the agreement of a given donor, which reallocates money to several faculties. These modalities of financing reveal the unequal market-attractiveness of faculties. The university report entitled "Self-Evaluation of the Sida/SAREC Bilateral Research Cooperation Programme 1998-2008" shows that social sciences are the "losers" of those investments (UDSM, 2007: 43–63). Moreover, the key transformation brought about by external funding is the withdrawal of the government from the research sector. This huge dependence can generate perverse effects for curricula and, more generally, is a danger for research as it is dependent on the internal reorganisations taking place in these foreign donor institutions. For instance, the Norway Embassy through its agency NORAD/Oslo, recently reduced its investments, especially in humanities departments, for the reason that its development strategy would now focus on climate and energy (Havnevik and Isinika, 2010: 57–70). NORAD/Oslo has developed a partnership with another state university, Sokoine University of Agriculture (SUA) in Morogoro. This new configuration directly impacts on the global functioning of faculties, and more generally, on the university.

Furthermore, Sida/SAREC support accounts for about fifty per cent of the donor funding to the University of Dar es Salaam. This support has lasted for over thirty years. For UDSM, the challenge is to ensure that Sida/SAREC maintains, increases and diversifies its support. This interference is harmful to the independence and autonomy of the university in the short- and mid-term. Even though ideals of self-reliance did not fully translate into actual practices under Nyerere, as socialist Tanzania paradoxically depended upon donor aid – especially stemming from Scandinavian countries –, today's open call to outside agencies is a huge break with past conceptions of national sovereignty and autonomy. Present-day dependence of higher education upon external donors fully goes against Nyerere's warning of "eternal vigilance" vis-à-vis foreign aid: "The Arusha Declaration says: To govern yourself is to be self-reliant [...]. The International Monetary Fund is not a friend of Tanzania or of any poor country. It is an Institution used by the imperialist countries, which govern it to control the economy of a poor country and destabilise the governments of countries they do not like. Tanzania is one of those countries, and we must not forget it – or allow people to think that we have forgotten it. It has been said that the price of freedom is eternal vigilance. So, let us be vigilant! If you agree to give them a goat they will demand a camel!" (Nyerere, 1969: 12).

The Ideological Legacy: From Memories to Practices

The reintroduction of a cost-sharing policy, the implementation of a new language about higher education competitiveness in the face of the market demand, and the retreat of the state from research budgets are concrete examples of a political, social and economic shift that reflects neoliberal transition in Tanzania. However, traces of the conceptions and practices of higher education as implemented during Nyerere's times still shape today's functioning of the university, thus pointing to the uniqueness of the system of higher education in Tanzania in the region A comparison with neighbouring universities in East Africa will better highlight the peculiar trajectory of UDSM, revealing how much Tanzania follows the track of path dependence. It is indeed a trajectory of resistance to privatisation processes via negotiated continuity.

The ongoing though insufficient financial involvement of the state

A study of UDSM budgetary evolution shows an increase in funding allocated by the government from 7,797,373 US$ in 1987-1988 to 26,468,208 US$ in 2006-2007. This investment, although it is on the rise, is nonetheless insufficient compared to the increasing number of students enrolled. In other words, there is a manifest inadequacy of the budget when matched with needs of the university, all the more so as the latter is compelled to create new faculties and curricula to answer an increased demand for higher education. The decrease in the amount allocated by the Tanzanian government to one student clearly reveals this inadequacy: from 2,697 US$ in 1987-1988, it dropped to 1,279 US$ in 2006-2007 (Provini, 2012a).

In addition, the government still sponsors the great majority of students. A hybrid model of scholarship and student loan has been put in place. Since the academic year 2002-2003, the government has imposed quotas for scholarships which cover all university fees. Concerning the system of student loans, introduced in 2005-2006 to partly cover tuition fees, other academic fees, room and board, it finances the great majority of student in B.A. At the end of their studies, students have to repay their loans but many do not. This situation produces considerable economic damage for the state. In brief, the state is not absent, but its role changes: there is not a clear-cut privatisation process.

The cost-sharing policy has been a symbol and an instrument used by international institutions to promote the marketization of higher education in Africa. The failure of the implementation of a complete cost-sharing policy in Tanzania requires new insight into the current, and singular, state of higher education in this formerly socialist country in order to understand the formation of a hybrid model of bureaucratic and discursive practices at the university. A reconfiguration of new spaces and ways of intervention has taken place, which implies negotiations between public and private, and between inside and outside actors.

University Actors and Negotiated Continuity

The two main university associations, DARUSO (Dar es Salaam University Students Organisation) and UDASA (University of Dar es Salaam Academic Staff Assembly), played a significant role in mediating university crises during the implementation of reforms (Luhanga et al., 2003: 70–71). The example of the student association provides a good vantage point to identify actors involved in limiting the neoliberal change and to understand that UDSM had a leftist contingent legacy which "was essential in establishing the university's reputation across Africa and the world as an important nodal point of socialist thought and activism. Indeed, the radicals, as they were often called in Dar es Salaam, managed to achieve a visibility far beyond their numbers" (Ivaska, 2011: 147). DARUSO strategy was to protect the economic status of students. Several demonstrations took place to particularly contest the new cost-sharing policy. In 1992, a long process of discussion and balance of power began between students and both the central administration and the government. In February, a statement signed by two students threatened the government of unspecified action if it did not scrap the new cost-sharing proposal for higher education. The statement "has given the Government three days (…) to implement the students demands", and the students warned they would "take action against anyone trying to interfere with education in any way".[16] This threat eventually led to a boycott demanding the suspension of the cost-sharing scheme in education.[17] More generally, from the beginning of the 2000s and the launch of the third phase of the cost-sharing policy, the academic years had been punctuated by many demonstrations and strikes across UDSM campuses.[18]

---

[16] Daily News Reporter. "Students Threaten Action Against Government." *Daily News*, 5 February 1992, p. 1.

[17] *Daily News Reporter*. "Go Back to Classes, Senate Tells Students." *Daily News*, February 13 1992, p. 1 and *Daily News Reporter*. "Students End Class Boycott." *Daily News*, 18 February 1992, p. 1.

[18] See for instance: Cosato, Chumi. "Government Allays Fears to D'Salaam University Freshers." The Guardian, 28 September 2002, p. 4; Daily News Reporter. "Dar Varsity Students Want More Boom." *Daily News*, 29 April 2006, p. 2; Mwasumbi, Jonas. "Students Implore Full Govt Sponsorship." *Daily News*, 15 August 2006, p. 3; Kasiba, Sabato and Mambo, David. "UCLAS

UDSM students chant as they went on strike. Their messages are often made of direct attacks against the central administration and incumbent President. On the left, we can read: "Higher education is mandatory. Travels abroad, ostentatious cars are a luxury and a shame"; and on the right: "The problem is not the loan board… It is with this government of Kikwete's buddies".[19]

In this contest, Mwalimu's legacy is frequently used by students' leaders as a tutelary figure to foster student mobilisation. For instance in January 2007, "students from all constituents of the University of Dar es Salaam had assembled at the Nkrumah Hall of the University of Dar es Salaam at 9.00 am yesterday from where they marched to Jangwani grounds. Once at Jangwani, they listened to their leaders, who said that the government should emulate Mwalimu Nyerere's example of prioritizing education for all eligible students, rather than making it a privilege of

---

Students Boycott Still on." *The Guardian*, 24 February 2007, p. 3; Navuri, Angel. "UDSM Explodes Again Over Studies Stipend." *The Guardian*, 17 April 2007, p. 12; Joseph, Hillary. "Varsity Student Boycott Smacks of Political Undertones." *The Guardian*, 24 April 2007, p. 9; Kitabu, Gerald. "Dialogue at the Hill Should Take Centre Stage to Resolve Boycotts." *The Guardian*, 29 April 2008, p. 11; Mushi, Deogratias. "Planned Students Strike Illegal, Says Prof. Maghembe." *Daily News*, 4 November 2008, p. 3; Saiboko, Abdulwakil. "UDSM Students Boycott Classes." *Daily News*, 11 November 2008, p. 2; *Daily News Reporter*. "UDSM Students Sent Packing." *Daily News*, 13 November 2008, p. 1; *Daily News Reporter*. "UDSM College Students Go Home Too." *Daily News*, 14 November 2008, p. 1; Mbashiru, Katare. "Calm Returns to UDSM After Failed Demonstrations." 5 February 2011; Wa Simbeye, Finnigan. "UDSM Students Defiant as Govt Pledges Allowance Review." *Daily News*, 7 February 2011; Kagashe, Beatus. "UDSM Students Protest, Clash with Police in Dar." *The Citizen*, 4 February 2011; *Daily News Reporter*. "Demonstration Another Strike Looms at UDSM." *The Citizen*, 10 January 2011 and Mchome, Erick. "Taking a Hard-Line on Student Protests." *The Citizen*, 17 January 2012.

19 *The Guardian*, April 17 2007, p. 1.

the well-to-do lots".[20] The students used this reference to Nyerere and his education policy as a political legitimate language to make their claims and better bring out the irony of the government's discourse when it promotes higher education reform today, at the same time defending the marketization of higher education while pretending to honour and carry on Nyerere's legacy. In fact, the Tanzanian government often plays a double game in these negotiation processes. This was the case in 2002 when the government assured students of higher learning institutions that it would continue to be their major financier through providing loans and scholarships to students whereas the policy of cost–sharing was reintroduced ten years before. The former Permanent Secretary in the Ministry of Science, Technology and Higher Education, Ruth Mollel, declared that fears that government might abdicate its responsibility are not valid: "I would like to allay fears expressed by many that by introducing cost–sharing in higher education the government intends to abdicate its responsibility as the main provider of this constitutional rights to every Tanzanian". She added that "due to economic disparities, the Government recognised that not all students could raise enough funds for their studies". [21] Another example is when the former Ministry for Science, Technology and Higher Education, Dr Pius Ng'wandu, explained that university fees had to be regulated: "after hearing many complaints from MPs, we feel the fees are high and cannot be afforded by the majority of the Tanzanians".[22] With this strategy of double discourses, the Tanzanian government opted for appeasement on campuses and agreement with international recommendations at the same time. Negotiations between students and the government led to a process of negotiated change and translated into budgetary reforms that did no fully embrace the neoliberal model originally supposed to be adopted.

The example of the partial implementation of cost-sharing policy show that we should not underestimate the weight of university actors to appreciate how structures, modalities and configurations emerged in UDSM and are subject to debates and compromises through words and actions. This provisional situation about cost-sharing eventually satisfied all actors: i) DARUSO students, whose struggle against cost-sharing policy has been the basis of their legitimacy in negotiations,

---

20 Guardian Reporters. "Students March Against Loan Scheme." *The Guardian*, 29 January 2007, p. 1.

21 Cosato, Chumi. "Government Allays Fears to D'Salaam University Freshers." *The Guardian*, 28 September 2002, p. 4.

22 Mukiza, Darius. "Govt hands Tied Over Tuition Fee Hike." *Daily News*, 30 July 2009, p. 3.

and was therefore reinforced; ii) university lecturers and professors, who even though they may denounce the privatisation of research and the decline of the quality of teaching, find alternative ways to improve their wages and publish their researches by resorting to consultancies; iii) the Tanzanian government, which is striving to save public money through its financial withdrawal to answer donors' requirements while trying to maintain some of its specific practices as well as social stability on campuses with a cost-sharing policy incompletely and unclearly implemented. We can say that, constantly mediating between internal and external actors and faced with the necessity to adapt to the new political, social and economic context while meeting with resistance anchored in past practices and representations of how higher education should be, UDSM has adopted a "cosmetic market doctrine" (Provini, 2012b). The peculiarity of the situation of UDSM is even more manifest if we compare it with the neighbouring universities of Kenya and Uganda.

A comparison with Nairobi and Makerere

Tanzania's neighbouring East African states of Kenya and Uganda have been used as models to drive higher education reforms at UDSM since the late 1980s (Kimambo, 2003: 231–50). A regional area was put in place through which new knowledge and "good practices" could spread throughout East Africa. This process was facilitated by common administrative heritage and routine between the universities of Nairobi, Dar es Salaam and Makerere associated with the University of East Africa which had educated regional elites to succeed the colonial administrators at independence (Kithinji, 2012). It was also stimulated by the East African Community (EAC) and its major institution for higher education, the Inter-University Council for East Africa (IUCEA). This council aims to facilitate regional education interactions and cooperation, and "promotes comparable higher education standards and systems for sustainable development".[23] It is in this context that a regional process of harmonisation of higher education reforms has been conducted until today. Nevertheless, we can argue that regionalisation in theory does not match with regionalisation in practice; or in other words, efforts to drive harmonisation of higher education reforms at the East African level has not fully entailed a standardisation of concrete practices.

A good example of this is the opportunity to admit privately sponsored students which is the headlight policy of international organisations'

---

23 See website http://www.iucea.org/welcome-to-joomla.

requirements. Makerere is the first university in the region to have reorganized its financial system and governance. This explains why, in the 1990s, donors took to touting the experience of Makerere as the model for driving reform elsewhere in East Africa (Court, 1999: 5). Thus, in 2002, it is the first time that the university global budget mostly depended on the budget generated by private students (52%). In the same way, since 2003 – even if there is an exception in 2006 – the University of Nairobi (UoN) has also been principally subsidized by self-sponsored programs (Modules II and III) because the majority of students are private students. For instance, in 2011 58% of the global budget depended on private funds, namely on private students and activities. At UoN, a joke circulates between Kenyan lecturers to make fun of these mixed public–private systems, as explained to me by a lecturer in history: "We are the oldest university in Kenya. We are the largest public university in Kenya. And we are also the largest private university in Kenya". Despite the existence of privately sponsored programs in Tanzania since 1996, the admissions of such privately sponsored students have remained very low in public universities. In 2002-2003, privately sponsored students on UDSM's main campus numbered only 13%. Compared to the Makerere University 'success story' of privately sponsored students from the point of view of donor institutions – a success put into question by some renown scholars (Mamdani, 2007) – the Tanzanian new policy for higher education, characterized by resilience and negotiation that have hindered a strict application of neoliberal reforms, can be seen as a failure. The specificity of the Tanzanian path with regards to higher education reforms is made more relevant in comparison with its neighbouring universities. While Makerere university and the University of Nairobi embraced a total based-market model, the University of Dar es Salaam is situated, at least until today, in an in-between space, set between transition, through the implementation of a new neoliberal agenda, and continuity, with the maintaining of socialist legacies of higher education in institutional practices and visions of education.

Makerere University privatisation process (1995-2005)

Academic year	Budget allocated by the government (US $)	Budget generated by private students (US $)	Global budget (US $)	Percentage of the global budget issued of the budget generated by private students (%)
1995	19,786,481	3,971,286	23,757,767	17
1996	19,813,610	7,280,117	27,093,727	27
1997	19,612,939	8,201,686	27,814,625	29
1998	19,023,730	11,110,096	30,133,826	37
1999	17,210,572	10,369,145	27,579,717	38
2000	14,336,748	10,743,010	25,079,758	43
2001	15,831,974	10,939,046	26,771,020	41
2002	15,912,704	17,017,619	32,930,323	52
2003	14,449,973	17,344,090	31,794,063	55
2004	20,282,740	20,702,567	40 985,307	51
2005	19,779,135	30,196,108	49,975,243	60

References: Kasozi (2009: 164); Court (1999: 5-7); Makerere University (2010: 5)

The University of Nairobi privatisation process (2000-2011)

Academic year	Budget allocated by the government (US $)	Budget generated by private students (US $)	Budget generated by the other private activities (US $)	Global budget (US $)	Percentage of the private funds in the global budget (%)
2000	19,793,303	5,027,381	4,224,813	29,045,497	32
2001	20,748,796	7,619,429	9,544,134	37,912,359	45
2002	20,787,437	11,856,293	6,275,537	38,919,267	47
2003	21,911,787	16,938,558	9,897,859	48,748,204	55
2004	25,003,673	19,990,060	6,654,650	51,648,383	52
2005	35,553,823	26,295,406	8,908,707	70,757,936	50
2006	50,983,813	31,873,197	10,155,798	93,012,808	45
2007	48,963,964	36,360,501	12,911,949	98,236,414	50
2008	50,569,652	36,572,457	15,638,625	102,780,734	51

2009	46,827,016	44,960,785	13,103,530	104,891,331	55
2010	47,066,847	49,690,906	18,826,532	115,584,285	59
2011	52,235,429	56,140,151	16,368,117	124,743,697	58

References: Budgetary Control Section, University of Nairobi; University of Nairobi (2000-2011)

A Post-socialist University? USDM as an Institutional Space of Transition and Continuity

Transformations implemented at UDSM symbolize political, economic and social changes which have affected Tanzania since the end of the 1980s, geared towards the future but also looking back to the past. As Pitcher and Askew said, "in short, socialism has left institutional, aesthetic, psychological and discursive legacies that African peoples and their governments have rejected, appropriated and reconfigured in order to reflect on the past and to negotiate the terrain of contemporary life" (Pitcher and Askew, 2006: 11). Indeed, the government is currently requested to compose with internal and external actors in order to build a new higher education system. The university reforms have created a new market where students, teachers, faculties, public and private universities are in competition. Donors and international institutions believe that the most effective way to promote market forces within the university is to give maximum freedom to academic units. However, the more these reforms disintegrate the decision-making process, the more the academic units reorganize their activities in response to the market. In that sense, the university of Dar es Salaam is a good reflection of contemporary Tanzania: it is a space of individualist competition, where neoliberalism increasingly shapes actors' behaviours; but it is also a space of continuity, where certain manifestations of the nature and mission of education embodied in Julius K. Nyerere and the socialist-inspired national project for nation-building and national development, as well as certain bureaucratic and state functioning put in place in the 1960s-1970s, also orientate practices.

The main question remains of how long this hybrid situation will be maintained. Indeed, this mixed system of transition within continuity results from the co-presence of two generations on the campus. Unsurprisingly, the difference in discourses on the mission and workings of education is highly significant between old generations of lecturers, brought up in socialist times and whose conceptions of education conflate with Nyerere's; and the new generation of lecturers who, having integrated the new language of standards, competitiveness and good governance, tend to think that the old ideology is no longer adapted to the new socio-economic context. This suggests that, if the Tanzanian state and its elite continues to promote market forces and distances itself from the ideologies of the past, the new generational renewal of scholars will likely complete the neoliberal transition on the campus soon.

References

ASKEW, Kelly M. "Sung and Unsung: Musical Reflections on Tanzanian Postsocialism." *Africa* 76, no. 1 (2006): 15–43.

BIENEN, Henry. *Tanzania. Party Transformation and Economic Development*. New Jersey: Princeton University Press, 1974 (1970).

BJERK, Paul K. "Sovereignty and Socialism in Tanzania: The Historiography of an African State." *History in Africa* 37 (2010):275–319.

BOESEN, Jannik, Birgit Storgard Madsen and Tony Moody. *Ujamaa. Socialism From Above*. Uppsala: Scandinavian Institute of African Studies, 1977.

BROCK-UTNE, Birgit. "Formulating Higher Education Policies in Africa: The Pressure from External Forces and the Neoliberal Agenda." *JHEA/RESA* 1, no. 1 (2003): 24–56.

Budgetary Control Section. *University of Nairobi*. Nairobi: University of Nairobi, 2012.

CHARTON, Hélène and Samuel OWUOR. "De l'intellectuel à l'expert. Les sciences sociales africaines dans la tourmente: le cas du Kenya." *Revue internationale d'éducation Sèvres* 49 (2008): 107–119.

COOKSEY, Brian, Lisabeth LEVEY and Daniel MKUDE. *Higher education in Tanzania: A Case Study*. Dar es Salaam: University of Dar es Salaam Press, 2003.

COURT, David. "The Development Ideal in Higher Education: The Experience of Kenya and Tanzania." *Higher Education* 9, no. 6 (1980): 657–680.

COURT, David. "Financing Higher Education in Africa: Makerere, the Quiet Revolution." Working Paper: The World Bank and The Rockfeller Foundation, 1999.

DARDOT, Pierre and Christian LAVAL. *La nouvelle raison du monde. Essai sur la société néolibérale*. Paris: La Découverte, 2009.

DUPUY, François and Jean-Claude THOENIG. *L'administration en miettes*. Paris: Fayard, 1985.

FONTAINE, Joseph and Patrick HASSENTEUFEL. "Introduction. Quelle sociologie du changement dans l'action publique? Retour au terrain et "refroidissement" théorique" In *To Change or not to Change? Les changements de l'action publique à l'épreuve du terrain*, ed. Joseph Fontaine and Patrick Hassenteufel, 9–29. Rennes: Presses Universitaires de Rennes, 2002.

FOUÉRÉ, Marie-Aude. "J. K. Nyerere entre mythe et histoire: Analyse de la production d'une culture nationale en Tanzanie post-socialiste [J. K. Nyerere Between Myth and History: An Analysis of the Production of a National Culture in Post-socialist Tanzania]." *Les Cahiers d'Afrique de l'Est* 4 (2009): 197–224.

FOUÉRÉ, Marie-Aude. "Tanzanie: la nation à l'épreuve du postsocialisme Tanzania: The Nation Put to the Test of Postsocialism]." *Politique Africaine* 121 (2011): 69–86.

FOUÉRÉ, Marie-Aude. "Julius Nyerere, Ujamaa, and Political Morality in Contemporary Tanzania." *African Studies Review* 57, no. 1 (2014): 1–24.

HARGREAVES, J. D. "The Idea of a Colonial University." *African Affairs* 286, no. 72 (1973): 26–36.

HARRISON, Graham, Sarah MULLEY and Duncan HOLTOM. "Tanzania: A Genuine Case of Recipient Leadership in the Aid System?" In *The Politics of Aid: African Strategies for Dealing with Donors*, ed. Whitfield Lindsay, 271–298. Oxford: Oxford University Press, 2009.

HAVNEVIK, Kjell and Aida C. ISINIKA. *Tanzania in Transition: From Nyerere to Mkapa*. Dar es Salaam: Mkuki na Nyota Publishers, 2010.

ISHENGOMA, Johnson. "Cost–Sharing in Higher Education in Tanzania: Fact or Fiction?" *JHEA/RESA* 2, no. 2 (2004): 101–133.

IVASKA, Andrew M. "Of Students, "Nizers", and a Struggle over Youth: Tanzania's 1966 National Service Crisis." *Africa Today* 51 (2005): 83–107.

IVASKA, Andrew M. *Cultured States: Youth, Gender, and Modern Style in 1960s Dar es Salaam*. Durham: Duke University Press, 2011.

KASOZI, A. B. K. *Financing Uganda's Public Universities. An Obstacle to Serving the Public Good*. Kampala: Fountain Publishers, 2009.

KELSALL, Tim. "Shop Windows and Smoke–Filled Rooms: Governance and the Re-Politicisation of Tanzania." *Journal of Modern African Studies* 4, no. 40 (2002): 597–619.

KIMAMBO, Isaria N. *Humanities and Social Sciences in East and Central Africa: Theory and Practice*. Dar es Salaam: Dar es Salaam University Press, 2003.

KITHINJI, Michael Mwenda. "An Imperial Enterprise: The Making and Breaking of the University of East Africa, 1949-1969." *Canadian Journal of African Studies* 46, no. 2 (2012): 195-214.

LEMA, Elieshi, Marjorie MBILINYI and Rakesh RAJANI. *Nyerere on Education. Selected Essays and speeches 1954-1998*. Dar es Salaam: Haki Elimu, 2004.

LEVI, Margaret, "A Model, A Method, and a Map: Rational Choice in Comparative and Historical Analysis." In *Comparative Politics: Rationality, Culture, and Structure*, ed. Mark I. Lichbach and Alan S. Zuckerman, 19-41. Cambridge: Cambridge University Press, 1997.

LUHANGA, Matthew L. *The Courage for Change. Re-Engineering the University of Dar es Salaam*. Dar es Salaam: Dar es Salaam University Press, 2009.

LUHANGA, Matthew L., Daniel J. MKUDE, Tolly S. A. MBWETTE, Marcellina M. CHIJORIGA and Cleophace A. NGIRWA, *Higher Education Reforms in Africa: The University of Dar es Salaam Experience*. Dar es Salaam: Dar es Salaam University Press, 2003.

Makerere University. *Fact Book 2009-2010*. Kampala: Makerere University, 2010.

MAMDANI, Mahmood. *Scholars in the Marketplace: The Dilemmas of Neo-Liberal Reform at Makerere University (1989-2005)*. Dakar: CODESRIA, 2007.

MBWETTE, Tolly S. A. *Managing University Crises*. Dar es Salaam: DUP, 1996.

MNGOMEZULU, Bhekithemba Richard. *A Political History of Higher Education in East Africa: The Rise and Fall of the University of East Africa, 1937-1970*. Houston: UMI, 2004.

MSEKWA, Pius and Thadeo L. MALIYAMKONO, *The Experiments. Education Policy Formation Before and After the Arusha Declaration*. Dar es Salaam: Black Star Agencies, 1979.

NYERERE, Julius K. *"Ujamaa". The Basis of African Socialism*. Dar es Salaam: Tanganyika Standard, 1962.

NYERERE, Julius K. *Freedom and Unity/Uhuru na Umoja: A Selection from Writings and Speeches 1952-1965*. Dar es Salaam: Oxford University Press, 1966.

NYERERE, Julius K. *Freedom and Socialism/Uhuru na Ujamaa: A Selection from Writings and Speeches 1965-1967*. Nairobi: Oxford University Press, 1969.

NYERERE, Julius K. *Ujamaa. Essays on Socialism*. London: Oxford University Press, 1973 (1968).

PIERSON, Paul, "Increasing Returns, Path Dependence, and the Study of Politics." *The American Political Science Review* 94, no. 2 (2000): 251-267.

PITCHER, Anne M. and ASKEW, Kelly M. "African Socialisms and Postsocialisms." *Africa: Journal of the International Africa Institute* 76, no. 1 (2006): 1-14.

PROVINI, Olivier. "Reforms in the University of Dar es Salaam: Facts and Figures." *Les cahiers d'Afrique de l'Est* 45, no. 45 (2012a): 77-86.

PROVINI, Olivier. "Les réformes à l'Université de Dar es Salaam: l'établissement d'un nouveau marché de l'enseignement supérieur." In *Universités, universitaires en Afrique de l'Est*, ed. Nicodème Bugwabari, Alain Cazenave-Piarrot, Olivier Provini and Christian Thibon, 275-298. Paris: Karthala, 2012b.

RANGER, Terence. "The "New Historiography" in Dar es Salaam: An Answer." *African Affairs* 70, no. 278 (1971): 50-61.

ROBERTSON, John H. "The Role of Science and Technology in Development Education." In *Nation-Building in Tanzania*, ed. Anthony Rweyemamu, 34-45. Nairobi: East African Publishing House, 1970.

SCHUTTE, Donald G. W. "The University of Dar es Salaam: A Socialist Enterprise." In *World Yearbook of Education 1972/3. Universities Facing the Future*, ed. W. R. Niblett, R. Freeman Butts and Brian Holmes, 75-96. Oxon: Routledge, 1972.

SLATER, Henry. "Dar es Salaam and the Postnationalist Historiography of Africa." In *African Historiographies. What History for which Africa?*, ed. Bogumil Jewsiewicki and David Newbury, 249-260. Beverly Hills: Sage Publications, 1986.

SHIVJI, Issa G. *Intellectuals at the Hill. Essays and Talks 1969-1993*. Dar es Salaam: Dar es Salaam University Press, 1993.

University of Dar es Salaam (UDSM). *UDSM Five-Year Rolling Strategic Plan 2005/2006-2009/2010*, Vol. 1: Main Document. Dar es Salaam: Dar es Salaam University Press, 2005.

UDSM. *Self-Evaluation of the Sida/SAREC Bilateral Research Cooperation Programme 1998-2008*. Working paper: Sida/SAREC, 2007.

University of Nairobi (UoN). *Annual Report and Accounts*. Nairobi: University of Nairobi, 2000-2011.

Chapter 12

Ward Secondary Schools, Elite Narratives and Nyerere's Legacy

Sonia Languille

In 2006, the Government of Tanzania led by Prime Minister Edward Lowassa decided to enact an electoral promise inscribed in the CCM Manifesto for the 2005 presidential elections: to build a lower secondary school in each ward (the administrative level between district and villages, named kata in Swahili). This decision unleashed a movement of rapid expansion of lower secondary schooling of an extraordinary magnitude. Between 2004 and 2011, the number of secondary schools was multiplied by four, from about 1,290 to about 4,370 schools, and the number of students enrolled at O'Level grew by 325%. The gross enrolment ratio for lower secondary education drastically improved from 12.4% in 2004 to 50.2% in 2011. However, from a learning perspective, this movement brought adverse outcomes. Between 2007 and 2012, the failure rate in the Certificate of Secondary Education Examination skyrocketed from 9.7% to 56.2%, fuelling intense debates in the media and in Parliament.

This policy, which has profoundly modified the Tanzanian educational landscape over recent years, represents a rupture with the educational trajectory followed by the country for more than four decades. During Ujamaa, Education for Self-Reliance posited primary education and literacy as the overarching objective of the country's educational policy; secondary education was construed as an education for few but free and of quality, a model of elitist but meritocratic education. Julius K. Nyerere's imprint on this educational organisation was decisive; year after year, he consistently reiterated his conviction about Tanzania's secondary education problem. This educational option was directly derived from Tanzania's low economic base. According to him, Tanzania, as a poor country, could not afford to expand secondary education: "[Secondary education] is not the right of all Tanzanians as Primary Education is" (Nyerere, 1984: 153). This statement, pronounced in 1984, clearly echoed an earlier declaration in 1967: "We cannot solve the problem of primary school leavers by increasing the number of secondary school places" (URT, 1967a: 78). In 1988, in the face of the expansion of government's programme for secondary education, Nyerere's tone became imbued with anger:

> "these [opening new public and private secondary schools] are not plans for teaching but for cheating (...) What will it benefit a child if he or she goes from a poor primary school to an even poorer secondary school, without facilities or even an adequate number of teachers? What we are doing is upgrading primary education for a few, and then pretending that it is Secondary Education.(...) Something which is secondary education only in name is a deception of an innocent child as well as being useless as a preparation for future service to the community. We are training for frustration and alienation" (Nyerere, 1988 in Lema et al, 2006: 184).

A couple of decades later, ward secondary schools came to materialise, on a large scale, Nyerere's ominous words. These are some of the labels used by my informants to describe the ward secondary schools: 'resort camps', 'advanced nursery schools', 'day care centres for grown-up children', 'garbage in, garbage out', 'in ward secondary schools, the product is nearly zero'. In a context where Nyerere remains a worshiped figure and a mandatory reference in political and policy-making spheres, how could a policy be enacted that so profoundly contradicts Nyerere's teaching? This chapter provides elements of response through an exploration of elites' narratives. It largely draws upon the notion of "public rhetorical common places" as defined by Patrick T. Jackson, that is, discursive resources "that can be utilized so as to render a given policy acceptable". Their availability is "an indispensable part of the process of public policy-making" (Jackson, 2006: ix). The analysis is based upon about 150 qualitative interviews conducted with members of the elite during a fieldwork conducted in 2011-2012 in Dar es Salaam and in Lushoto district.[1] The systematic analysis of elites' narratives[2] allows

---

[1] The author is grateful to the research centre REPOA for hosting her during fieldwork.

[2] The term 'elite' is here defined following Reis and Moore (2005: 2) as "the very small number of people who control the key material, symbolic and political resources within a country". This generic definition can be supplemented by Hossain and Moore's delineation of national elites as "the people who make or shape the main political and economic decisions: ministers and legislators; owners and controllers of TV and radio stations and major business enterprises and activities; large property owners; upper-level public servants; senior members of the armed forced, police and intelligence services; editors of major newspapers; publicly prominent intellectuals, lawyers and doctors; and – more variably – influential socialites and heads of large trade unions, religious establishments and movements, universities and development NGOs..." (2002: 1).

bringing into light these public rhetorical commonplaces mobilised to legitimise the ward secondary schools policy. Edward Lowassa, Prime Minister between 2006 and 2010, and President Kikwete's long-time close political ally, played a critical role in the decision-making process. The label 'Lowassa schools', coined by the press and used by few respondents, attests to a hardly uncontested paternity. However, the ward schools policy would not have occurred without a process of legitimation profoundly rooted into the country's specific historical process and ideology. Without the mobilization of these public rhetorical commonplaces, it is our contention, the reconfiguration of the post-independence educational settlement provoked by the ward secondary schools would not have been possible. Among these discursive resources, Nyerere's legacy, his educational ideas and practice of power have occupied a prominent position. The legitimation of the ward secondary schools policy, as an example of hybrid ideological construct, involved a re-articulation of the historical educational philosophy developed by Nyerere intertwined with the global neoliberal education discourse. This chapter argues that this recourse to Nyerere's legacy to legitimate a policy which is in blatant contradiction with his actual thinking was also made possible by contradictions in Nyerere's own discourse.[3]

The first section explores the significance of secondary education within the post-independence educational settlement and points out the contestation that Nyerere's vision for secondary education underwent. The second section deconstructs the egalitarian motivation that supposedly inspired the promoters of the 2006 policy. The third section argues that, behind imagined requirements of the global knowledge economy, conflated with the ambiguities of Nyerere's modernisation philosophy, the ward secondary schools, more than places of learning, constitute devices for the domestication of the poor youth.

---

3 The author is very much indebted to the editors of two volumes of collections of Nyerere's essays and speeches on education: Elieshi Lema, Marjorie Mbilinyi, Rakesh Rajani and Issa Omari. Their books were key to develop the author's understanding of Nyerere's educational philosophy.

Julius Nyerere and Secondary Education, an Enduring but Contested Educational Settlement

Secondary education and the post-independence educational settlement: an elitist education in a socialist nation

A specific educational settlement was forged during the Ujamaa period, within which secondary education occupied a specific position. The notion of 'education settlement' is forged from the concept of 'political settlement' commonly used in historical political economy. This concept refers to "the balance or distribution of power between contending social groups and social classes on which any state is based" (Di John and Putzel, 2009: 4). More precisely, Khan (2010: 20) defines a political settlement as a description of how a society solves the problem of violence and achieves a minimum level of political stability and economic performance for it to operate as a society. Following Melling who stressed that "social policies of the state formed part of a wider political settlement at key moments of development" (1991, quoted in Di John and Putzel, 2009: 4), the conditions of distribution of educational rights and entitlements across social groups can be considered as part and parcel of this political settlement. An educational settlement corresponds to a specific organisation of the access/quality/equity nexus, traditionally central to educational policy-making. The ward secondary schools policy has led to a profound reconfiguration of this nexus at secondary level: it has entailed a shift from elitist, merit-based, quality secondary education towards mass and poor quality secondary education. The patterns of educational enrolments at secondary level displayed in graphs 1 and 2 vividly illustrate the historical rupture provoked by the ward secondary schools policy. Its significance cannot be understood without a description of the post-independence educational settlement and of its meaning within Ujamaa broader political project.

Graph 1: Enrolment in secondary education (Government - Non Government) 1961-2010 Enrolment

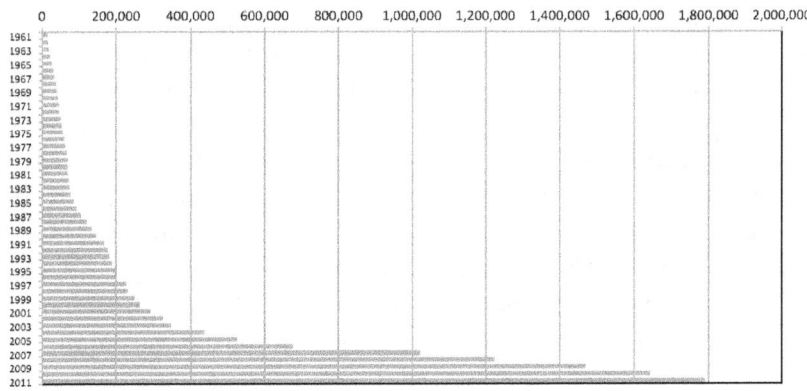

Source: URT-MoEVT (2011)

Graph 2: Transition Rate From Primary to Secondary Education (Government and Non- Government)

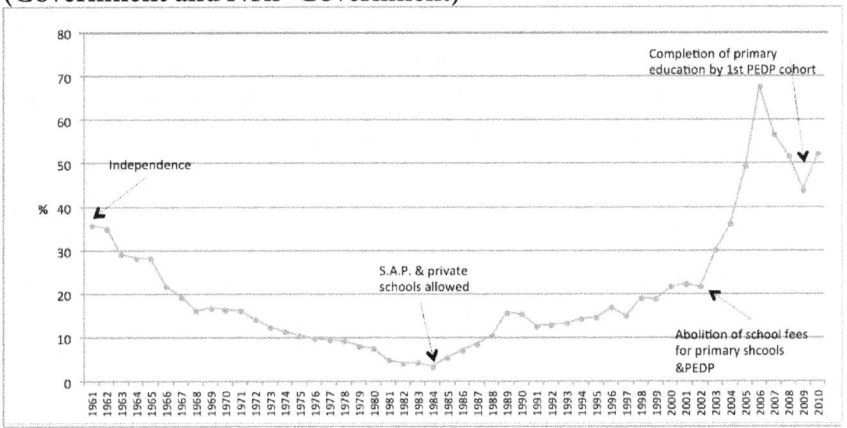

Source: URT-MoEVT (2011)

In 1967, with the Arusha Declaration, Education for Self Reliance was put at the heart of the Ujamaa development philosophy: education was understood as the fundamental instrument for a radical social transformation (Samoff and Sumra, 1994). The 1977 Constitution of the United Republic of Tanzania guaranteed the right to education for all citizens "up to the highest level according to his merits and ability"; it asserted that the "Government was made liable for creating the conditions for realisation of this right". But during Ujamaa, primary education and literacy programmes were regarded as the chief instruments for social equalisation through education. According to Nyerere, "Primary education is to the education of our nation what Agriculture is to the economy – the pivot on which everything else turns. It is not called Primary education for nothing; it is the education everyone has" (Nyerere, 1984: 150). Primary education was conceived as an end in itself: it was to prepare children to their role within the community rather than to give them an automatic entry ticket to upper levels of education. Secondary education was deliberately conceived as an education reserved for few students but delivered on a free basis. For decades, access to secondary education was restricted to a small minority. Between 1966 and 1981, primary education enrolment multiplied by six and the literacy rate grew from 20% to 90%; in 1977 the primary gross enrolment ratio reached 97%. In the same period, the transition rate from primary to lower secondary education fell from 35% in 1962 to 2.6% in 1981: "Tanzanian children (had) among the lowest probability of attending secondary school of all children in the developing world" (Lassibille et al, 2000: 4).

As pointed out in the introduction, the main rationale for a distorted educational pyramid – broad base and tiny summit – lay in Tanzania's narrow economic base. "The poverty of Tanzania does not allow for the kind of expenditure which would be necessary for such universal services [post primary education], however we would like them. Priorities have to be worked out and strictly adhered to" (Nyerere, 1971: 110). The intrinsic contradiction between a right-based, egalitarian discourse on education and this restriction of the right to upper levels of education to few privileged youth was pointed out by Nyerere himself: "Publicly provided 'education for education's sake' must be general education for the masses. Further education for a selected few must be education for service to the many. There can be no other justification for taxing the many to give education to only few" (URT, 1967a: 79). Secondary education expansion was only legitimate in relation to its service to primary education and the rest of the economy, "in providing a reservoir from which we can recruit teachers, agriculturalists, health workers, engineers, and so on. We have no other justification for providing secondary school education". During Ujamaa, the prevailing manpower policy derived the number of seats available in government secondary schools and university from the projected needs of the economy.

Within a self-identified socialist regime aimed at reversing the colonial legacy, such blatant built-in elitism in the education system needed to be legitimised. The educational settlement called indeed for an ideological apparatus and organisational measures to make it acceptable to the vast majority barred from a resource critical to access white collar jobs, power and wealth. First of all, a quota system attributed a specific number of seats in public secondary schools to each region and to girls. In parallel, legal restrictions put on the expansion of private schools was meant to contain the distorted educational patterns inherited at independence (Samoff, 1979a; Buchert, 1994).[4] Secondary schools also played a critical role in the process of the "reciprocal assimilation of elites" (Bayart, 1993): secondary education contributed to forming an 'esprit de corps' among the elite conducive to the integration of different, emerging and already established, segments of the elite. The fact that Tanzanian students attended secondary schools outside their region of origin forged within the elite a sense of national belonging that transcended tribal identities. This social blending process was a critical function that Nyerere attached to secondary schools. The implementation of Education for Self Reliance also implied critical changes in the curriculum aimed at inculcating students with a sense of serving the public and at preparing them to their role as drivers of rural development. Work had to become integral part of education and the secondary education curriculum to be 'vocationalised' so as to make it relevant to students' future life in the community. The continuity between the colonial education system and Education for Self Reliance – the philosophy and its practice – has already been pinpointed (Coulson, 1982; Mbilinyi, 1979). What has less been emphasized, however, is how much these mechanisms, working against the idea of wealth or tribal belonging as the origin of individual advancement, inscribed meritocracy at the heart of secondary education and therefore social promotion.

A contested educational settlement

In contemporary Tanzania, Nyerere has increasingly become the object of unanimous praise. Most informants, when questioned about the evident contradiction between Nyerere's educational options and the

---

[4] The colonial power promoted an economic specialisation of Tanganyika's territory between cash crops areas, food crops zones and labour force basins in a context of a rising racial segmentation, Indians and Europeans consolidating their control over the formal modern sector. The development of the education system was closely tied up to this economic strategy and organised to fulfil the needs of the emerging capitalist group. Historically, schools – governmental and missionary – were implanted in cash-crop areas, zones of European settlement, trade hubs or industrialising areas. The education system was also racially differentiated with a segment delivering an academic and elitist education to Indians and Europeans, mainly in government schools. The second segment dedicated to Africans would deliver a mass education, mainly in missionary and 'bush' schools led by indigenous local authorities.

ward secondary schools policy, dismissed this inconsistency as spurious. This refutation took various rhetorical forms.[5] These performative claims of full adherence to Nyerere's legacy seemed essential to guarantee the legitimacy of the ward secondary schools policy, as if mere hints of decision-makers' possible betrayal of Nyerere could dangerously shake the foundation of the current socio-political order. Nyerere's spectre haunts Tanzania's political and policy-making arenas; references to the Father of the Nation constitute an imperative for any public leaders' speech. However, in a same movement, within policy-making circles, Nyerere's material voice on the significance of secondary education for Tanzania is being silenced, confined to the unspoken.

Besides, these façade of unanimity and claims of absolute fidelity obscure the intense contestation that Nyerere's educational options were subject to, both during his time in power and after his resignation as President. Indeed, despite its enduring nature, the historical education settlement did not remain unchallenged. Samoff (1979b) showed, in particular, how the petty bourgeoisie in the Kilimanjaro region developed strategies to reinforce their social and political position inherited from the colonial period through a locally driven and funded secondary school expansion in contradiction with the national education agenda. The government itself implemented with flexibility its own policy on private education to accommodate the 'social demand'. The vocationalisation of the curriculum, at least as it was implemented through manual activities or cultivation of the *shamba* (school field), was resented by parents and conceived as a continuity of the colonial education system that refuted academic education for Africans (Buchert, 1994; Okoko, 1987).

The post-independence educational settlement was also subject to stern international critics. A 1990 famous World Bank comparative study of educational achievements in Kenya and Tanzania (Knight and Sabot, 1990) incriminated Nyerere's Education for Self-Reliance policy and especially the restrictions put on private secondary schools. Despite its methodological flaws and its denial of the actual financial constraints experienced by Tanzania's education system (Samoff, 1992), the 1990 document still influences aid agencies' economists today in Dar es Salaam. One of them referred to this "amazing study by Knight and Sabot" and implicitly characterised the Education for Self Reliance as an anti-egalitarian and obscurantist policy: he used the motto "don't

---

5 For instance a forceful denial of the characterisation of Nyerere's secondary education policy as restrictive or its reframing in positive terms.

educate anybody" to qualify the former 'Tanzanian way' in education.[6] The 1995 Education and Training Policy offers another illustration of the international disapproval of the secondary education configuration inherited from Ujamaa[7]. This policy document, largely drafted under donors' influence, constituted a clear formalisation of the neoliberal turn of the mid-1980s on cost-sharing measures and promotion of private sector. It incorporated a fundamental attack against one core element of the historical settlement over secondary education: it planned the end of the quota system on geographical origin and gender (URT-MoEC, 1995: 21). Since the private sector was now allowed to thrive, the quota system, portrayed as intrinsically unfair and inefficient, lost its relevance. The notion of 'merit', understood in relation to collective and historically constructed inequalities, was replaced by 'merit' viewed through an individualistic lens, in relation to 'natural' aptitudes, independent from the social origin and that the society needed to nurture: the government's role was to support the 'deserving ones'.

The 1995 Education and Training Policy also identified the construction of one secondary school in each ward as a key educational strategy for the country. The CCM Election Manifesto of 2000 and 2005 reaffirmed the strategy; Edward Lowassa did not invent the policy. However, in his inaugural speech to the Parliament on 30th December 2005, newly elected President Kikwete did not mention at all the ward secondary schools. Instead he prescribed the creation of 'Pan-Territorial Secondary Schools that will deliberately mix talented students from all corners of the country'[8] with the view of strengthening national unity: this programmatic vision had more resonance with the Ujamaa meritocratic model of government secondary schools than with a model of community-driven mass secondary education. The coexistence of these two options provides an evident sign of frictions within the state: the question of the type of secondary education that the country required or could afford was a contested site for the elite. Electoral objectives were undoubtedly not foreign to E. Lowassa's decision to

---

6 Interview with a Dar es Salaam-based foreign economist, major aid agency.

7 This policy was openly at odds with the Education for Self Reliance socialist ethos but in 2012 it was still considered by most Tanzanian actors in the education sector – Ministry officials but also members of the civil society – as a truly home-grown policy. This paradoxical sense of 'ownership' can be explained by a process, among the domestic elite, of internalization of donors' increasingly influential agenda after the mid-1980s and by the fact that the drafting process was very inclusive and participatory.

8 Speech by the President of the United Republic of Tanzania, Jakaya Mrisho Kikwete, on inaugurating the fourth phase Parliament of Tanzania, Parliament buildings, Dodoma, 30 December 2005.

launch the ward secondary school policy. This process cannot be analysed in disconnect with his well-known presidential ambitions and his personal efforts, on his route to the political summit, to assert his credentials as a statesman responsive to people's needs[9]. Nevertheless, if Lowassa's individual agency in leading the ward schools policy and his electoral strategy cannot be denied, they were also rooted in a broader, long-lasting intra-ruling class struggle.

Nyerere himself was very much aware of the pressure exerted by some segments of the ruling class to expand secondary education. "I know that virtually all the pressure for educational expansion comes in the form of demand for more secondary schools (…). I'm saying that it is the job of the Party and the Government, and in particular the Ministry of Education to resist this pressure' (Nyerere, 1984 in Lema and al, 2004: 153). In 1988, he vocally denounced public officials' support to the expansion of public and private secondary schooling as subverting the Party's programme: 'many of these new Private Schools are the results of public collections supported by – or even initiated by – Party leaders and prominent figures! (…) No one has suggested that it is part of our Party's Programme! (…) It would be a greater service to the people of Tanzania, to the children of Tanzania, and to education in Tanzania, if public collections were made and used for the upgrading of our primary schools. Our leaders should look again at their responsibilities to the mass of our people" (Nyerere, 1988: 184). In light of this vigorous admonition, addressed to 'deviant' leaders, one can grasp the magnitude of the actual rupture with Nyerere's legacy that ward secondary schools embody.

Next section pursues the investigation of elites' mobilisation of Nyerere's legacy in their legitimation of the ward secondary schools policy.

---

9 Despite catastrophic form 4 examination results from 2010 to 2012, Lowassa has continuously boasted his secondary education achievements to boost his political profile. His supporters also proclaim their champion's political superiority by drawing on the ward secondary school story. See for instance, 'Lowassa who is remembered for his influence in Ward Schools program' *In2EastAfrica*, 17 August 2012; 'Records have it that it was Lowassa's zeal and commitment to construct secondary schools in every ward' *Vox Media*, 4 July 2011.

Ward Secondary Schools: An Egalitarian Policy?

The 'social demand' narrative

One of elites' dominant narratives to explain the secondary education expansion relates to Tanzanian leaders' responsiveness to people's 'demand' in a context of mass primary education. Tanzania indeed embarked into its Primary Education Development Plan (PEDP) in 2000. Largely supported by donors, it entailed the abolition of primary school fees and consequently propelled a surge in primary enrolment. In 2005-2006, the first cohort of PEDP students was about to complete their primary schooling. The two words 'social demand' came again and again in all interviews, across all categories of elite members. The discursive mobilisation of the 'social demand' argument points to a specific understanding of the role of the state as 'servant of the people'. The state is seen as an entity committed to ensure the conditions of an equalization of social conditions.[10] This 'social demand' narrative certainly reflects the interdependent nature of the relations between the ruling class and the rest of the society. As argued in Gray (2012), "part of the political legitimacy of the Party constructed under socialism was its commitment to equality" and even after the economic liberalisation elite's political survival has continued to depend on their egalitarian credentials.

The pre-eminence, among the Tanzanian elite, of this idea of a 'social demand' for education, and specifically secondary education in the aftermath of PEDP enrolment success, should be analysed in conjunction with the existence of a profound disjunction between a powerful national imaginary invested in education that transcends social boundaries and the post-independence educational settlement that constructed secondary education as an education for the elite. Nyerere's educational philosophy and policies lie at the heart of this disjuncture. Despite calls for a classless state, secondary education was constructed, under Ujamaa, as a key site of class formation. A direct link was set up between secondary education and access to white-collar jobs: entry qualification for specific training schemes (like those for agricultural extension workers, teachers and many types of technicians) was upgraded to Form IV (Coulson, 1982: 203). English, commonly conceived as an indispensable resource to access influence, power

---

10 This perception is not specific to Tanzania nor developing countries. In the case of the United States, republican 'egalitarian virtues' propelled the 'high school movement' at the beginning of the 20th century (Goldin, 2001, 1997).

and wealth, was maintained as language of instruction for post-basic education levels, building up the distinctive social function of secondary education.[11] Against Nyerere's intent, secondary schools continued to be referred to as 'Bwana Kubwa' or 'big man' schools and primary school leavers who could not join secondary education continued to be labelled as 'failed'.

Despite its undisputable elitist nature, Ujamaa secondary education model was still perceived in 2012 by those who benefited from it as a tool to serve an egalitarian development strategy. Many respondents of this research expressed their gratitude towards a system that made their own social advancement possible. "[Nyerere] thought of rural people, he thought of poor people. Some people like us couldn't pay school fees. My father was very poor. But we were educated to university education".[12] One official of the Ministry of Education even refuted the word 'elite' to qualify government secondary education: "I don't believe that secondary education was for the elite. I don't. Not during Nyerere's time… Even at that time, education was for all".[13] Here the word 'elite' is implicitly associated with wealth-based schooling in contradiction with the meritocratic feature of government secondary education that officially allowed every child to attend secondary school, irrespectively of his/her social extraction, and to climb the social ladder. This egalitarian ethos is embraced, at least rhetorically, at the highest levels of the Executive. For President Kikwete, "most of us here, of my generation, would never have gone to school and reached this far in life had it not been for the far-sightedness and good social policies of our Founding Father".[14]

Despite the pervasiveness of an egalitarian ethos within both the administrative apparatus and the state power, the modalities of funding and implementation of the ward secondary schools policy profoundly vitiated decision-makers' egalitarian claims.

---

11 Swahili, the national language, is the language of instruction at primary level.
12 Curriculum developer, Tanzania Institute of Education.
13 Official, Direction of Secondary Education, Ministry of Education and Vocational Training.
14 Inaugural speech to the Parliament, Dodoma, 30 December 2005.

An enrolment expansion without budgetary expansion[15]

The high political priority given to secondary education in 2006 was not translated into budgetary terms and was not accompanied by a substantial expansion of the teaching force. Between 2003/04 and 2009/10, the secondary education budget remained quasi flat and its share within an expanding education budget went through a sturdy decline, from a pick of 18.2% of the education budget in 2004/05 to its lowest level of 6.2% in 2009/10 (graph 3). While enrolment in secondary schools (O and A levels) grew by 253% between 2003 and 2008, the number of teachers only increased by 42%.

Graph 3: Share of Sub - Sector Allocations in The Education Budget (in% 2002 / 03 - 2011/12)

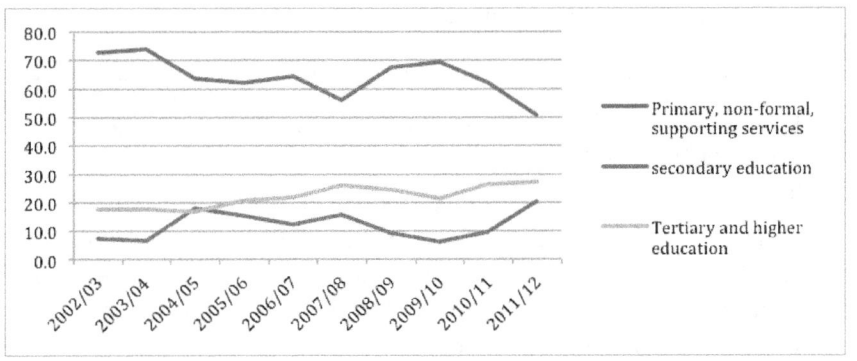

Source: the author based on URT-MoEVT (2011: 165)

The evolution of 'unit costs' illustrates, even more forcefully, the low budgetary priority granted to secondary education. Between 2002 and 2009, enrolment in public secondary schools (O and A levels) increased by 590% but the secondary education spending unit decreased by about 70% (graph 4). Over the 2002/03-2011/12 period, tertiary and higher education chiefly profited from changes in the pattern of sector resource allocation. During the pick years of the ward secondary schools policy, elites' budgetary choices reflected an actual material commitment to higher education and a disregard for the financial requirements of quality secondary education for the mass.[16]

---

15 The financial analysis in this part is by the author based on data from URT-MoEVT (2011).

16 These budgetary patterns were also largely influenced by aid agencies' allocative choices in education: between FY 2004/05 and FY 2009/10, donors' main sector of investment remained primary education. Over the period, this level absorbed between 77% and 50% of total education external assistance (author's own calculations based on budget books and donors'

Graph 4: Spending Per Student in Primary and Secondary Education 2002/03 - 2011/12

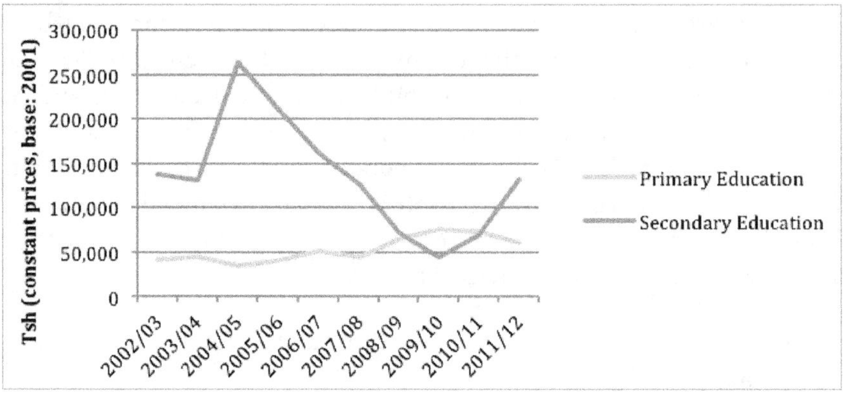

Source: the author, based on enrolment and budget data from URT-MoEVT (2011)

NB. Budget in constant prices computed via the GDP deflator, base year 2001. Due to data availability, by convention, the 'primary education spending unit' was computed using the enrolment in public primary public schools and the budget for 'primary, non-formal, other education institutions and supporting services'.

These elites' budgetary preferences stand in sharp contrast with patterns of education expenditures during Ujamaa. Indeed, the post-independence educational settlement had a financial dimension. The Education for Self-Reliance priority to primary and adult education was translated in budgetary terms: between 1966/67 and 1980/81, the share of primary and adult education in recurrent expenditures increased by 13% and by 37% in development expenditures. Over the same period, the share of secondary education in recurrent expenditures fell by 20% and by 19% in development expenditures (Buchert, 1994). This historical budgetary trade-off had a second facet: a high unit cost for secondary education. The state did not charge any school fee and covered lodging, transportation and food costs for all students attended public secondary schools. This exceptionally high unit cost[17] was, according to Nyerere, the price of a quality secondary education. Achieving quality education was indeed intrinsic to Ujamaa secondary education model, as acknowledged by many respondents. Zitto Kabwe, a young opposition leader, stressed both the egalitarian virtues and the quality

---

disbursements reports). The World Bank was the unique important international organisation that resolutely invested in secondary education.

17 In 1990, according to calculations by Lewin (1996: 370), Tanzania had the second highest ratio (after Uganda) of secondary to primary unit costs, among 62 countries with GNP per capita below US$5,000: the country spent 17.5 more on secondary students than on primary pupils.

of the former public secondary education system: "I come from a very poor family. I went to public school and I got my first shoes in Form 1 and 2, when a neighbour gave them to me because he was pleased of my results. At that time, public schools were centres of excellence. All good teachers were teaching there. Both parents of rich and poor families had the opportunity to send their kids to school and get quality education". This appreciation was shared by the international community: "Back to the 1980s and 1970s, Tanzania used to have a high quality secondary education. The paradigm then, under Nyerere, was to produce very good graduates but there was no concern about numbers".[18] Besides, Nyerere's commitment to the developmental role of higher education (Nyerere, 1970 (2004)) did not entail a budgetary preference for this sub-sector. In 1995, in an address at the 25th anniversary of the University of Dar es Salaam, severely hit by the budgetary implications of the financial crisis, Nyerere implicitly enunciated his order of precedence for the education budget: "Within the education sector, a government cannot decide to close down primary and secondary schools so as to make money available for the University, because the latter needs qualified entrants as well as money (…) within the educational sector, it is not a forgone conclusion that the balance between primary, secondary, technical and tertiary expenditures should be immediately tilted towards Universities" (Nyerere, 1995: 200).

In 2006-2007, the elite solved the fiscal conundrum posed by the ward secondary schools policy by transferring the burden to the poor.

Forced community contributions and ward secondary schools: a regressive tax on the poor

Right from the inception, which can be traced back to the 1995 Education and Training Policy, Tanzanian policy-makers envisioned the ward secondary schools policy within a locally-driven developmental perspective: "Urban, district, town, municipal, city councils and authorities, communities, NGO, individuals and public institutions shall be encouraged and given incentives to establish, own, manage and administer at least one secondary school in each ward (Kata) in their areas of jurisdiction" (URT-MoEC, 1995: 102). A specific 'social contract' underpinned the ward secondary schools policy enunciated by Prime Minister Lowassa: communities had to start the construction of schools then the state (government and districts) would cater for the roofing, cover for the biggest share of running costs through a Tsh 25,000

---

18 Interview with education aid manager, major aid agency.

capitation grant and allocate an adequate number of teachers. However, the state did not honour its part of the contract: peasants and parents bore a large share of the costs of the reform. Not only communities built schools but they have also been paying a wide range of fees to cover schools' running costs, including the salary of non-professional teachers.[19] In exchange, their 'return to investment' took the form of a massive examination failure and the vanished hope for a brighter future for their children. Wards schools turned into fools' game.

'Self-help' ideology has tainted development policies in Tanzania since colonial times; it constituted a prominent feature of Ujamaa development strategy (Samoff, 1989: 6). Specifically in the education sector, Kilimanjaro region has provided the rest of the country with a successful model of educational advancement driven by local initiatives and funding schemes but underpinned by a specific economic base (Samoff, 1979b). The enduring presence of 'self-help' ingredients within Tanzanian development policies does not imply that self-help projects have been time and space invariant. Over the decades, the very meaning of the notion has been subject to inflexions, reflecting evolving relations between state power, society and local state brokers. Jennings (2007) underlined for instance the shift from an initial framing of the 'self-help' concept in terms of participation to the nation-building project in the early years of independence to the post-Arusha Declaration period when compulsory participation was to serve state's control and management priorities. Nyerere's discourse on community-driven secondary education reflected these contradictory and evolving meanings. He fully endorsed the idea of communities contributing to education expansion through their labour but rejected the idea of their monetisation: "Constantly asking parents to buy for this or pay for that is self-defeating; sooner or later they will stop sending their children to school because they cannot provide what it is asked for. Silver and gold they have none: what they do have is their labour. That they can often provide: labour to build a new classroom, or a teacher's house, or to paint walls or repair a roof" (Nyerere, 1988: 183). He simultaneously stressed the fallacy of communities' labour contribution when the state cannot provide for quality education basic inputs. "When talking about secondary school expansion, we are quick to say that the people will put up the buildings by their own efforts. But the buildings are less important.

---

19 Personal empirical investigation conducted in Lushoto district in March-April 2012, that included the visit of 25 secondary schools, confirmed that parents' contributions constitute the main resource of schools to take charge of running expenses, including the hiring of contractual form 6 leavers to make up for the shortage of teachers.

(...) The important things in education are the teachers, the books, and for science the laboratories" (Nyerere, 1984: 154). In that sense Nyerere did not embrace the process of reformulation of the 'self-help' ideology prompted by the economic liberalisation of the 1980s. In the context of Structural Adjustment Programmes, authorities' call for communities' contributions strongly reverberated International Financial Institutions' promotion of cost-sharing measures to support the expansion of the education sector. Since the end of the 1990s, this convergent rhetoric has been reworked in a post-Washington consensus idiom largely appropriated by the Tanzanian elite: communities' contributions are key to build up local 'ownership', promote people's 'participation and empowerment' and strengthen public 'accountability', all ingredients of efficient 'social services delivery'. But the empirical reality, in Lushoto, has been one of communities pressurised to financially support a central state's policy as well as local politicians' ambition and struggles. However, the plasticity of the 'self-help' notion allowed decisions-makers to pride themselves on their direct lineage with Nyerere's developmental practice.

Another feature of the ward schools policy implementation modality – the recourse to coercion – is equally difficult to reconcile with the irrepressible social demand narrative. Mbilinyi (1979: 225) argued that "both coercive/repressive and ideological apparatuses are relied upon to increase social control over the peasant labour force". This applies to the ward secondary schools story. The two traditional ingredients of popular consent have indeed prompted communities' adherence to the policy and to its financial 'cost-sharing' premise. Undeniably, the belief in the power of education as an engine for individual, family, community progress does not constitute elites' specific attribute. Data from the 2006 Integrated Labour Force Survey confirms a broadly-shared social desire for education. To the question 'If given a choice, what would you like to do?', an overwhelming proportion of respondents replied: 'going to school full time'.[20]

---

[20] Focus groups conducted with parents in Lushoto confirmed that the valuation of education cuts across social classes.

Graph 5: People' preferred activities

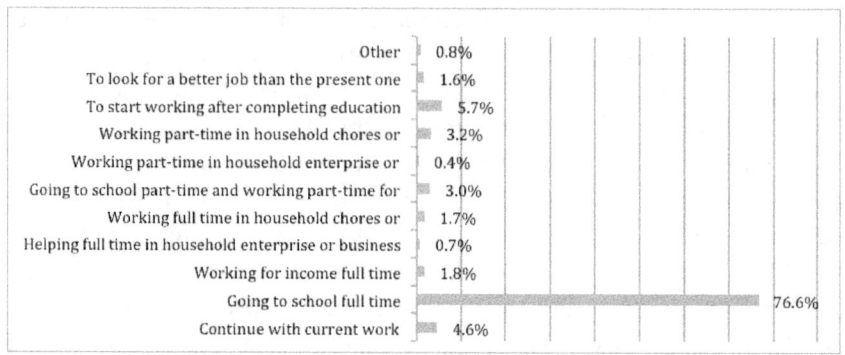

Source: URT-NBS (2006)

However, state's representatives at local level also resorted to coercion to gain the population's adherence through fine or even imprisonment. Villagers who were unwilling to pay were forced to contribute through the *uambozi* practice – the forced requisition of households' assets (cattle, furniture...). In that instance too, decision-makers could largely build their legitimacy from Nyerere's own contradictions. This policy bears indeed great resemblance with historical centrally-driven policies, implemented in a heavy-handed fashion by the state. For instance, Nyerere, who started the villagisation process as a voluntary scheme, finally resorted to coercive measures and forced groupings in the face of thin actual outcomes (Hyden, 1980).

The ward secondary schools policy has provided the elite with an answer to the financial conundrum posed by a narrow national fiscal space. But the state-society relation that made possible the implementation of the policy largely departs from an imagined benevolent state responding to a pressing 'social demand'. And with these under-resourced, poor-performing secondary schools, a three-tier secondary education system has taken shape – private schools,[21] old government schools still enjoying a selective entry system and community schools. Many informants explicitly interpreted this differentiated education system as the consolidation of a 'class-system' in Tanzania.

---

21 This label covers a diversified situation (high-fee, highly selective private schools and low-cost private schools not very dissimilar from ward secondary schools).

Ward Secondary Schools: Domestication of the Youth in the Time of the Knowledge Economy

A second dominant narrative mobilised to justify the ward secondary schools policy has been centred on the youth. It has intertwined two antagonist constructions of the category: the youth as a threat to the social order, and the youth as agents of modernisation whose skills will unlock the door of the global knowledge economy to Tanzania. Framing the 'youth issue' in such dialectical terms is not new. According to Burgess (Burgess, 2005: xviii), "the politics of generation after independence were at the same time inclusive and exclusive: the state recruited, celebrated and foregrounded the vitality of youth on the public stage. And yet the state excluded from its notions of citizenship images of youth that appeared to conflict with the nationalist imperative of building the nation".[22] With the ward secondary schools, this opposition between the 'idlers' to be 'purged'[23] and 'the servants of the nation', constant feature of Tanzanian 'politics of generation', is being rearticulated. This educational policy responded to social anxieties caused by the successful expansion of primary education between 2001 and 2006. A bulge of idle and disenfranchised primary leavers was about to threaten the society's peace and harmony; their capture within a state institution would ensure their domestication, the discipline of their mind and body and the taming of their violent or deviant behaviours.

'The youth roaming in the street' or 'the ticking bomb': secondary education expansion to ascertain elders' social order

In 2012, the two phrases: 'the youth roaming in the streets' and the 'youth ticking bomb' were permanent references in newspapers, official speeches and Parliamentary debates. The idea of a 'raw youth',[24] 'half-cooked' and half educated, came prominently in discourses. The growing pre-eminence of the 'youth' in public discourses in Tanzania predated 2011 uproars in the Middle East. In 2005-2006 indeed, Tanzanian authorities started to shift their concern from 'children' towards 'the youth', in an evident relation to secondary education expansion. Several policy options could have been envisaged to cater for the expected rise in

---

22 See also Brennan (2010) and Burgess (2010) for historical accounts of attempts by the socialist ruling power to incorporate 'idle and dangerous' youth into the state apparatus (TANU youth league in Dar es Salaam or youth labour camps in Zanzibar) to domesticate their perceived violence.

23 Word borrowed from Burton (2007).

24 The expression is borrowed from Burton (2006).

primary education leavers – and are indeed present in the public debate: the gradual construction of new schools, an expansion focused on existing schools with additional boarding facilities or the prior-training of teachers. In most cases interviewed officials – even bureaucrats who acknowledged their scepticism about or disagreement with Prime Minister Lowassa's choice – resorted to two related lexical fields to legitimise the policy and, implicitly, disqualify alternative policies: the ward secondary schools policy was a matter of emergency and the government had no choice. The 'no alternative' and 'emergency' rhetoric constitutes a classical feature of policy-making legitimation processes (Ball, 2012) and 'youth in the streets' was actually the only alternative envisioned by most officials. The word 'street' came again and again in interviews; a sort of catchphrase that seemed to embody elites' deepest fear. The government had to build a dyke to contain the youth tidal wave that threatened to unfurl on the Tanzanian peaceful order, like a bomb.

The 'social order' discourse has had a specific gender coordinate. Family planning considerations are indeed systematically mobilised to justify the ward secondary schools policy. As pointed out by a senior official within the Prime Minister Office-Regional Authorities and Local Government, "We've got a high birth rate in Tanzania due largely to early pregnancies. With secondary education, you diminish the number of young mothers and fathers. When they've finished secondary school (Form 4), they're young adults, they can marry". The last National Strategy for Growth and Poverty Reduction (Mkukuta II) is also rather explicit on the ultimate goal of girls' education: "Increased access to secondary education, especially for girls is expected to be one of the most effective measures to address issues of population dynamics, including reduction in fertility rate." (URT-MoFEA, 2010: 64). The ward secondary schools policy is being framed as a birth control device.

The very formulation of the ward schools policy – to build one secondary school in each ward –, very much different from a call for 'secondary education for all', implicitly posits an intrinsic relationship between education and population management. A formulation that puts the emphasis on the location of schools, within communities, tangles up welfarist considerations – the state bringing basic social services to the people – together with concerns over youth mobility. In a context of widespread social anxiety over the youth invading cities' streets, the design of an education policy in spatial – rather than learning – terms cannot be interpreted as a coincidence: ward secondary schools should contribute to fix the 'raw youth' in rural areas and prevent their migration to cities. As put by a former Member of Parliament in an interview: "It allows to concentrate kids in one area rather than letting them smoking marijuana". This policy formulation should be contrasted with old government secondary schools, mainly located in urban centres: their attendance would oblige students to quit the village and the farm to enter the urban world; 'migration' was, at that time, part and parcel of the secondary schooling experience.

This general anxiety over the exuberant and threatening 'youth body' – the violent male body and the sexualised female body – strongly resonates with the current international discourse unleashed by the Arab spring. Aid agencies have flooded the world with reports on the 'youth issue'. The 2013 World Development Report, entitled 'Jobs', drew the attention to the "621 million youth neither working nor studying" (p. 4), pointing that "in extreme cases a lack of job opportunities can contribute to violence or social unrest" (p. 6). The discursive concurrence has been underpinned by a lexical convergence: while the World Bank measures "rates of idleness among 15-24 years old" (World Bank, 2012: 6), the Tanzanian elite worry over the 'idle youth'. Aid agencies' strategic focus on girls' education and women empowerment also display a desire of domesticating girls' sexuality and remains firmly embedded within a patriarchal, essentialist perspective on girls.[25]

Girls' actual educational challenges and more generally women's subaltern social status correspond to a material reality. The uncertain prospects for Tanzanian girls are evidenced by current statistics: 'overall, 23% of women age 15-19 are pregnant or already have children' and 'young women with no education are more than 8 times as likely to have begun childbearing than women with secondary or higher education (52% versus 6%) (URT-NBS, 2010: 8). And if gender parity in access to primary education has been achieved, gender disparities grow at secondary and higher education levels and are also substantial in performances (URT-MoEVT, 2011). Current data on demographic and urbanisation trends have also provided a fertile soil for growing social anxieties over the 'idle youth'. Tanzania has one of the highest birth rates in the world, 65% of the Tanzanian population is under age 24 and Tanzanians aged between 15 and 24 represent 17% of the country's population (URT NBS 2010). The demographic growth is being

---

25 For instance, 2005 DFID's *Girls' Education Strategy* report, while recognising girls' education as a right, contains an evident assignment of girls to their traditional reproductive function within the community: 'educating girls helps to make communities and societies healthier, wealthier and safer, and can also help to reduce child deaths, improve maternal health and tackle the spread of HIV and AIDS' (DFID, 2005: 1).

accompanied by a rapid urbanisation process.²⁶ These demographic trends go along with a growing feeling of insecurity among the urban elite: press articles and official statements reflect the centrality of the crime issue within today's public debates.²⁷

The apparent novelty of the nexus 'idle youth / urbanisation / crime', contemporary to a 'primary school leavers crisis' driven by specific demographics and by the success of a specific educational programme (PEDP), conceals its long genealogy that can be traced into colonial and post-independence administrative discourses and practices. While in the mid-1950s, the colonial administration was already distressed by the 'primary school leavers' crisis' (Burton 2006), in 1967, Nyerere evoked the 'so-called problem of primary school leavers' that Education for Self Reliance was meant to address. Burton (2005) showed how the colonial administration lived in a constant fear of being submerged by 'raw' youth escaping rural areas. But, 'independence from colonial rule did not resolve debates and questions about the status of young people' (Burgess, 2005: xviii). Nyerere's discourse and politics revealed a distinctive ambivalence towards the youth (Ivaska, 2005) that fuelled an official rhetoric by which 'youth were supposed to serve as the indebted servants of a new order, but stood accused of some of its most flagrant transgressions' (Burgess, 2005: xviii). He constantly insisted on the pivotal role of the youth in the development process but this spearheading role was reserved to a particular category of youth, hard-working and committed to rural development (Ivaska, 2005). In contrast, young underemployed in the cities, the urban 'idlers', were castigated as internal enemies (Brennan, 2006). Their idleness was equated to mere betrayal of the socialist nation work ethics. In the Arusha Declaration, 'laziness, drunkenness and idleness' were cast as serious sins 'to be ashamed of' and 'to loiter in towns or villages without doing work' were depicted as unacceptable exploitive behaviour (URT, 1967b).

Nyerere's discourse on women exhibited similar ambiguities. His unabated commitment to universal primary education recovered an equal commitment towards girls' education: "In Africa if every child does

---

26 According to United Nations' population projections, the percentage of people living in urban areas in Tanzania is likely to grow from 24% in 2005 to 38% in 2030, a progression more than twice the rate of the population as a whole. By 2030, more than 25 million Tanzanians will be living in urban areas with Dar es Salaam among the ten fastest growing African cities between 2010-2020 (UN Habitat, 2010: 54).

27 Even if impressionistic evidence seem to corroborate the perception of rising crime rates in Dar es Salam and other Tanzanian cities, we will not question here the extent to which this social feeling corresponds to an actual social phenomenon.

not go to school those to be left out will be mostly the girls" (Nyerere, 1997: 211). The quota system to enter government secondary schools was used to address gender educational disparities. However, the Arusha Declaration drew a distinction between the frivolous and lazy urban (educated) woman and the industrious woman in the village: "Women who live in the villages work harder than anybody else in Tanzania. But the men who live in villages (and some of the women in towns) are on leave for half of their life... The energies of the millions of men in the villages and thousands of women in the towns (…) are at present wasted in gossip, dancing and drinking". Under Ujamaa, Brennan (2006: 404) argues, 'young unmarried women living in towns – alongside their male counterparts – formed major focal points of postcolonial nationalist anxiety'. Schoolgirls were similarly constructed as licentious beings, 'portrayed as unapologetically pleasure-seeking group that refused to observe public decorum and gendered or generational hierarchies of authority' (Ivaska, 2007: 227). This construction found a perfect echo in 2012 parliamentary debates when the Committee for Social Affairs rebuffed the Ministry of Education's proposal to end pregnant girls' expulsion from schools on the ground that this proposed change to the 1995 Education and Training Policy would encourage girls' promiscuous behaviour[28]. Schoolgirls' sexualised body has remained both a site of fixation of social anxieties and a contested domain within the ruling class.[29]

Finally, the dimension of space management embedded in the ward school policy also strongly resonates with ambiguities of colonial and post-colonial administrative practices. In attempts to control Africans' mobility, the colonial administration devised coercive measures (pass laws, resident permit, heavy taxation of 'informal' economy and repatriation schemes) but also considered compulsory education and the extension of the school system (Burton, 2005: 97). Similarly, under Ujamaa, the main argument to justify the villagisation process was centred on the provision of social services (Coulson, 1982: 256-57). But controlling patterns of space occupation through the construction of (primary) schools (and health dispensaries etc.) or the localisation of new settlements around existing social services like schools were certainly at the heart of this major social engineering project.

---

28 Interview with Member of Parliament, member of the Social Affairs Committee.

29 This obsession with family planning and sexuality echoes colonial states' 'domesticating impulse' riveted to the body of the colonised (Stoler, 1995).

Ward secondary schools, providing the youth with skills for the knowledge economy?

Tanzania has not been spared by 'planetspeak discourses':[30] the modernisation philosophy that underpinned developmental strategies and education policies, both under colonial power and socialist regime, is today being reworked in the 'globalisation' and 'knowledge economy' idiom. The justification of secondary education expansion has been directly fuelled by elites' anxiety of being left outside this contemporary modernisation movement.[31] Education is seen as one major instrument to avoid Tanzania a position on the fringes of the global world. The education system has to mould a population able to cope with this highly unstable, ever-changing, technology-driven globalisation. The 'globalisation-education' narrative is being framed along three inescapable imperatives: marketable skills, science and English. The lack of scientific knowledge jeopardises Tanzania's chance to insert into the global economy and benefit from it. Information and communication being consubstantial to the knowledge economy model, Tanzanian elites' desire of globalisation has crystallised into a quest for 'English' mastery. Finally, economic development would be blocked by a fundamental skills mismatch, rooted in an irrelevant and inefficient education system. Secondary education and vocational training need to impart youth with the entrepreneurial skills required by the labour market.

The saliency of skills, vocational training, sciences and English in elite discourses over secondary education has certainly mirrored donors' education agenda. For instance, World Bank Secondary Education Development Programme II (2010-2014) displays a strong 'science' emphasis, with a focus on laboratories, science textbooks and teaching practices in maths, sciences and language. In his opening statement to the 2011 Education Sector Review, the Canadian High Commissioner to Tanzania underlined the challenge of 'providing these young people with marketable skills' and the 'increased recognition of the importance of expanding post-secondary education, particularly Technical and Vocational Education and Training'. While donors shape their policies over the language of instruction in terms of scarcity of

---

30 The term is borrowed from Ball (2012) and refers to a "way of reasoning that seems to have no structural roots, no social locations and no origin".

31 The association between secondary schooling and modernity is not reserved to the elite. Stambach (2000) points to a similar perception, among northern Tanzania's population (Kilimanjaro), of secondary schooling as a site of emergence of modern identities.

competent English teachers and lack of teaching and learning materials, they also invoked the globalisation imperative to dismiss the possibility of a radical policy shift as regards the language of instruction, in a telling echo with Tanzanian proponents of English as the language of instruction. Tanzanian elites' romanticised view of the informal sector resonates with donors' entrepreneurship programmes and renewed emphasis on skills and vocational training.

This converging comprehension of quality education as science/English/skills cannot be interpreted as the mere outcome of an externally driven, imposed global agenda. In that instance too, Nyerere's educational legacy forms a constitutive ingredient of the ideological construct. Contemporary discourses on vocational training and skills are systematically underpinned by explicit or implicit references to Ujamaa education philosophy and practices. In 2012, the Planning Commission explained its current initiative to draft a national skill development strategy as an attempt to revive the logics underlying manpower surveys during Ujamaa.[32] Similarly, the introduction of a competence-based curriculum was interpreted as Nyerere's direct progeny.[33] The 'self-reliance' rhetoric is also systematically summoned in support to elites' glorification of self-employment in the informal sector as the venue for youth success and national economic development.

The argument here is not to deny the challenges faced by Tanzanian students in maths, sciences and English or to refute Tanzanian elites' desire to see their country occupy a position at the core of the global economy. But authorities' and donors' policy focus on maths, sciences and English, discursively tied to knowledge-economy inevitabilities, is problematic in many instances. Democratic deliberations, which would challenge this bounded and utilitarian definition of 'quality education', are potentially discredited on the ground of globalisation requirements. A high-rank official wondered: 'What about the poets, the art, the cinema? We need diversity. We need all competences besides maths and physics and science, social sciences, art. We need to bring diversity in our society. A focus on math and science is of course easier to justify'. Besides, claims over the irresistible demands of globalisation reinforce unequal dynamics within the education system. For instance, most

---

32 Interview with official, Planning Commission.

33 A curriculum developer in the Tanzanian Institute for Education wondered: 'What is the origin of competence-based education in Tanzania? Was it imported from other countries or did it have deep indigenous roots here? When I went to visit back the Arusha Declaration and Education for Self Reliance, I found the whole thing there: developing critical thinking among the people, developing Science and Technology, combining work and the education'.

students transit from primary schools, where Swahili is the language of instruction, to ward secondary schools with a very poor proficiency in English; there they hardly encounter proficient English teachers. At the same time, through the mushrooming of English-medium private primary schools, wealthy parents build their children's education premium from the (pre)primary level; they then cumulatively benefit from upper education levels. At university level, in line with the national priority given to sciences, students in sciences are eligible for a 100% loan, without mean-testing; but given that ward secondary schools have experienced a severe lack of science teachers and laboratories, most of the students who can continue sciences at higher level logically come from privileged schools, well-resourced in science teachers and equipment. In brief, "you make rich kids learn sciences" (Member of Parliament).

While the 'education-knowledge economy' narrative has been based on fuzzy empirical evidence,[34] claims over its direct lineage with the Father of the Nation contribute to its entrenchment and to the legitimation of the mechanisms of social reproduction it conceals. Indeed, Nyerere posited the transmission of skills and attitudes as the primary purpose of the Education for Self Reliance[35]. He also expressed a constant concern over the need to enhance scientific and technical knowledge in Tanzania, as a critical instrument for the country's economic development and international independence: "The realistic prospects for every country's development, even its chances of defending (or raining) its independent sovereignty within an increasingly interdependent world will depend heavily upon its wealth in knowledge– particularly science-based knowledge" (Nyerere, 1995 in Lema and al, 2006: 199). Yet contemporary invocations of the self-reliance ideology operate a displacement of its meaning by which it becomes construed through an individualistic lens. Self-reliance is no longer a collective endeavour, it is no longer the responsibility of the entire society, and the role of the government is just to create an enabling environment for the respectable and industrious youth in order to equip

---

34 Rigorous statistics on the labour market are scant. In enterprise surveys, businessmen do not identify the lack of skills as their main obstacle. The share of telecommunication and financial services in the national GDP has grown but like mining or construction, they remain capital intensive industries. Most jobs, mainly unskilled, are created in the informal sector. Bemused by a systematic conflation between language of instruction and language of communication, very few in the elite question the percentage of the labour force that competes on a globalised labour market where English could indeed make a difference.

35 "Our education has to provide skills to our children, young people, and adults. It also has to help to build attitudes appropriate to the development of our society" (Nyerere, 1984: 155).

them with the entrepreneurial skills that would enable them to be self-employed. At the same time, this rosy 'self-employment' tale conceals precarious working conditions stemming from unregulated relations of employment and earnings of bare subsistence level: people engaged in this segment of the labour market tend to remain trapped within its realm (Rizzo, 2011).

Nyerere's own contradictions offered a fertile ground for this displacement of meaning and for the naturalisation of the knowledge economy predicaments in the Tanzanian soil. Nyerere's own ambiguities over English – he was a fierce advocate of Swahili as the key ingredient of nation building but also translator of Shakespeare into Swahili – contributed to shape the elites' enduring belief in English as a construction site of the modern African self. Nyerere's educational philosophy also weaved together two discordant conceptions of education. On one hand, he forcefully promoted an emancipatory education geared towards individual and collective transformation - an education that would liberate human beings from their enslavement to the productive world.[36] On the other hand, both his philosophy and development practices firmly tied education to economic production[37]. The vocationalisation of the secondary education curriculum testified of his firm belief in the necessity to reconfigure the education-labour nexus in relation to the actual conditions of production in Tanzania. His manpower policy also set up a strict relationship between secondary education certificate and entry in the formal labour market. Blurring the boundaries between education and work was a core tenet of his educational thinking, as clearly stated in the following assertion: "What we are aiming at is converting our schools into economics communities as well as educational communities" (URT, 1967a: 91).

Nyerere's attempt to curb people's expectations for formal secondary and higher education was defeated by a widespread social disinclination for vocational education constructed as a vehicle of racial and social differentiation during the colonisation (Okoko, 1987: 63-68). For Nyerere, this unresolved tension between technical and academic education constituted a major setback for the country's development: "Our failure to emphasize science teaching, of all kinds and at all levels, and especially our indifference to technical and vocational training is the greatest failure of our educational system" (Nyerere, 1988: 179). At

---

36 'I want to be quite sure that our educational institutions are not going to end up as factories turning out marketable commodities' (1974: 126).

37 This contradiction was already pointed out in Mbilinyi (2006).

the end of his life, Nyerere endorsed the full correspondence between Education for Self-Reliance and the 'employability' rhetoric: "Their education must prepare them [the young people] to be Self-Reliant and self-employed if they cannot secure (...) paid employment. Perhaps in the language of today, we should say that education should help the young to develop a spirit of private enterprise' (Nyerere, 1998: 164). Contemporary discourses around the ward secondary schools testify that the general/vocational education nexus remains a highly contested domain in society at large, among educationists and within the ruling class.[38]

The discursive weaving of the employability, self-reliance and criminalisation of the youth rhetoric overshadows what is really at stake behind the valuation of vocational training by a segment of the domestic elite and by international aid agencies: the legitimation, in a context reconfigured by mass general secondary education, of the 'reproduction of the division between manual and intellectual labour' which is 'at the very heart of the production process and in society as a whole' (Poulantzas, 1978: 60). The recourse to a generic 'youth' category, if it allows to draw the attention on existing generational tensions, also eclipses the social differentiation that characterised the young population: despite an increased access to general education, the horizon of the poor youth remains manual work.

Conclusion

Because education policy choices are deeply rooted in national ideology, in the country's political economy trajectory and its economic basis, a systematic exploration of elites' narratives, their genealogy and their entanglement with global discourses, provides a fecund method to understand educational policy-making. The low-cost and poor performing ward secondary schools are the last offshoot of a process of remodelling of the nation's educational settlement initiated by the economic liberalisation of the 1980s. The ward secondary schools policy illustrates what Block called the "continuing tensions in a government programme between its integrative intent and its role in the accumulation process" (1977: 23): in a new context of quasi-universal primary education coupled with quality private education available for the wealthy, under-resourced ward secondary schools can be interpreted as a renewed educational settlement intended to resolve

---

38 For instance a high rank government official underlined the political sensitivity of the subject among policy-makers: "On the debate between skills and academic knowledge, the government is reluctant to take a strong position".

the structural tension inherent to education systems over the world. This might help explain Tanzanian elites' high level of tolerance towards massive exam failures at form four examination: one might argue that, from the elite point of view, the ward secondary schools policy, far from being a failure, was adapted to the actual conditions of production in Tanzania today – agrarian economy, capital intensive industrialisation, low-skilled service activities in the informal sector – and was pursuing an appropriate goal: a domesticated youth.

The profound resonance between elite narratives on the ward secondary schools, colonial power's policy and rhetoric and contemporary international discourses reveals the structural problem faced by the modern capitalist state over the social integration of the youth. In a context of essential scarcity of jobs, "a school system that kept students locked in an extended state of youth" (Stambach, 2000: 143) provides a temporary solution to the youth containment problem. The globalisation imperative disguises the inaptitude of the (domestic and international) ruling class to conjure up the contradiction between school expansion and the paucity of skilled jobs and to chart out a labour-intensive developmental path for Tanzania, and sub-Saharan Africa in general (Amsden, 2012: 114). In that context, constant invocations of Nyerere's mythic figure of infallible and uncontested leader committed to an equal society and the simultaneous muting of his actual voice and contradictions provide a thick smoke-screen to powerful mechanisms of social reproduction within the Tanzanian society.

References

AMSDEN, Alice. "Grass Root War on Poverty." *World Economic Review* 1 (2012): 114–131.

BALL, Stephen. *The Education Debate*. Bristol: The Policy Press, 2012.

BAYART, Jean-François. *The State in Africa: The Politics of the Belly*. Heinemann: London, 1993. Originally published in Jean-François Bayard, trans. *L'Etat en Afrique. La politique du ventre* (Paris: Fayard, 1989).

BLOCK, Fred. "The Ruling Class Does Not Rule: Notes on the Marxist Theory of the State." *Socialist Revolution* 33 (May-Jun., 1977): 6–28.

BRENNAN, James R. "Youth, the TANU Youth League and Managed Vigilantism in Dar es Salaam 1925-1973." In *Generations Pasts. Youth in East African History*, ed. Andrew Burton and Hélène Charton-Bigot, 196–220. Ohio University Press: Athens Ohio, 2010.

BRENNAN, James R. "Blood Enemies: Exploitation and Urban Citizenship in the Nationalist Political Thought of Tanzania, 1958–75." *The Journal of African History* 47, no. 3 (Nov., 2006): 389–413.

BUCHERT, Lene. *Education in the Development of Tanzania, 1919–1990*. London: James Currey Publishers, 1994.

BURGESS, Thomas G. "To Differentiate Rice from Grass Youth Labor Camps in Revolutionary Zanzibar." In *Generations Pasts. Youth in East African History*, ed. Andrew Burton and Hélène Charton-Bigot, 221–236. Ohio University Press: Athens Ohio, 2010.

BURGESS, Thomas G. "Introduction to Youth and Citizenship in East Africa." *Africa Today* 51, no. 3 (Spring 2005), 'Youth and Citizenship in East Africa': vii–xxiv.

BURTON, Andrew. "The Haven of Peace Purged: Tackling the Undesirable and Unproductive Poor in Dar es Salaam, ca.1950s-1980s." *The International Journal of African Historical Studies* 40, no. 1 (2007): 119–151.

BURTON, Andrew. "Raw Youth, School-leavers and the Emergence of Structural Unemployment in Late-colonial Urban Tanganyika." *Journal of African History* 47 (2006): 363–387.

BURTON, Andrew. *African Underclass. Urbanisation, Crime and Colonial Order in Dar es Salaam*. Nairobi: The British Institute in Eastern Africa, 2005.

COULSON, Andrew. *Tanzania. A Political Economy*. Oxford: Clarendon Press, 1982.

DFID. "Girls' Education Strategy." 2005.

DI JOHN, Jonathan and James PUTZEL. "Political Settlements, GSDRC Emerging Issues Research Service." Issues Paper, 2009.
FOUCAULT, Michel. *Histoire de la sexualité. La Volonté de savoir*. Paris: Gallimard, 1976.
FOUCAULT, Michel. *Surveiller et punir. Naissance de la prison*. Paris: Gallimard, 1975.
GOLDIN, Claudia. "The Human-Capital Century and American Leadership: Virtues of the Past." *The Journal of Economic History* 61, no. 2 (2001): 263-292.
GOLDIN, Claudia. "Why the United States Led in Education: Lessons from Secondary School Expansion, 1910 to 1940." *NBER Working Paper* 6144, 1997.
GRAY, Hazel. "Tanzania and Vietnam: A Comparative Political Economy of Economic Transition." PhD Diss., School of Oriental and African Studies, 2012.
HOSSAIN, Naomi and Mick MOORE. "Arguing for the Poor: Elites and Poverty in Developing Countries." IDS working paper, Brighton, Institute of Development Studies, 2002.
HYDEN, Goran. *Beyond Ujamaa in Tanzania. Underdevelopment and an Uncaptured Peasantry*. Berkeley and Los Angeles: University of California Press, 1980.
IVASKA, Andrew M. "In the 'Age of Minis': Women, Work and Masculinity." In *Dar es Salaam.Histories from an Emerging African Metropolis*, ed. James R. Brennan, Andrew Burton and Yussuf Lawi, 213-231. Dar es Salaam: Mkuki na Nyota, 2007.
IVASKA, Andrew M. "Of Students, 'Nizers' and a Struggle over Youth: Tanzania's 1966 National Service Crisis." *Africa Today* 51, no. 3 (Spring 2005): 83-107.
JACKSON, Patrick T. *Civilizing the Enemy, German Reconstruction and the Invention of the West*. Ann Arbor: The University of Michigan Press, 2006.
JENNINGS, Michael. "'A Very Real War': Popular Participation in Development in Tanzania during the 1950s & 1960s." *International Journal of African Historical Studies* 40, no. 1 (2007): 71-95.
KHAN, Mushtaq H. *Political Settlements and the Governance of Growth Enhancing Institutions* (unpublished), 2010.
KNIGHT, John B. and Richard H. SABOT. *Education, Skills and Inequality: The East African Natural Experiment*. New York: Oxford University Press, 1990.

LASSIBILLE, Gérard, Tan JEE-PENG and Sumra SULEIMAN "Expansion of Private Secondary Education: Lessons from Recent Experience in Tanzania." *Comparative Education Review* 44, no. 1 (2000): 1–28.

LEMA, Elieshi, Omari ISSA and Rakesh RAJANI. *Nyerere on Education. Nyerere kuhusu Elimu.* Volume II. 'Selected Essays and Speeches 1961-1997'. Dar es Salaam: HakiElimu and E&D Limited, 2006.

LEMA, Elieshi, Marjorie MBILINYI and Rakesh RAJANI. *Nyerere on Education. Nyerere kuhusu Elimu.* Volume I. 'Selected Essays and Speeches 1954-1998'. Dar es Salaam: HakiElimu and E&D Limited, 2004.

LEWIN, Keith M. "The Costs of Secondary Schooling in Developing Countries; Patterns and Prospects." *International Journal of Education* 16, no. 4 (1996): 367–378.

MBILINYI, Marjorie. "Introduction: Quality Education, Democracy and Social Transformation." In *Nyerere on Education. Nyerere kuhusu Elimu.* Volume II. 'Selected Essays and Speeches 1961-1997', ed. Elieshi LEMA, Marjorie MBILINYI and Rakesh RAJANI, vi–xvi. Dar es Salaam: HakiElimu and E&D Limited, 2006.

MBILINYI, Marjorie. "*Secondary Education*." In *Education for Liberation and Development: The Tanzanian Experience*, ed. *Hinzen* Heribert and *Volkhard H.* Hundsdorfer, 97–113. Paris: UNESCO, 1979.

MELLING, Joseph "Industrial Capitalism and the Welfare of the State: the Role of Employers in the Comparative Development of Welfare States. A Review of Recent Research." *Sociology* 25, no. 2 (May, 1991): 219–239.

NYERERE, Julius K. "Education for Service and Not for Selfishness", English Award of Honorary Doctorate of Letters Degree from the Open University, 5th March 1998. In *Nyerere on Education. Nyerere kuhusu Elimu.* Volume I. 'Selected Essays and Speeches 1954-1998', ed. Elieshi LEMA, Marjorie MBILINYI and Rakesh RAJANI, 160–164. Dar es Salaam: HakiElimu and E&D Limited, 2004.

NYERERE, Julius K. "Education and Development in Africa," Second Michael Scott Memorial Lecture, African Education Trust, London, 4th June 1997, as Chairman of the South Centre. In *Nyerere on Education. Nyerere kuhusu Elimu*, Volume I. 'Selected Essays and Speeches 1954-1998', ed. Elieshi LEMA, Marjorie MBILINYI and Rakesh RAJANI, 206–212. Dar es Salaam: HakiElimu and E&D Limited, 2004.

NYERERE, Julius K. "Address at the Twenty Fifth Anniversary of the University of Dar es Salaam", 1st July 1995. In *Nyerere on Education.*

Nyerere kuhusu Elimu, Volume I. 'Selected Essays and Speeches 1954-1998', ed. Elieshi LEMA, Marjorie MBILINYI and Rakesh RAJANI, 192–203. Dar es Salaam: HakiElimu and E&D Limited, 2004.

NYERERE, Julius K. (1988) "Twenty Years of Education for Self Reliance", Address at the Chakiwata Symposium, Marangu Teachers' College, 12th September 1988. In *Nyerere on Education. Nyerere kuhusu Elimu*. Volume II. 'Selected Essays and Speeches 1961-1997', ed. Elieshi LEMA, Omari ISSA and Rakesh RAJANI, 178–190. Dar es Salaam: HakiElimu and E&D Limited, 2006.

NYERERE, Julius K. (1984), "The Situation and Challenges of Education in Tanzania", Education seminar, Arusha, 22 October 1984. In *Nyerere on Education. Nyerere kuhusu Elimu*, Volume I. 'Selected Essays and Speeches 1954-1998', ed. Elieshi LEMA, Marjorie MBILINYI and Rakesh RAJANI, 146–158. Dar es Salaam: HakiElimu and E&D Limited, 2004.

NYERERE, Julius K. (1974), "Education for Liberation", Dag Hammarskjold Seminar, Dar es Salaam, 20th May 1974. In *Nyerere on Education. Nyerere kuhusu Elimu*, Volume I. 'Selected Essays and Speeches 1954-1998', ed. Elieshi LEMA, Marjorie MBILINYI and Rakesh RAJANI, 122–132. Dar es Salaam: HakiElimu and E&D Limited, 2004.

NYERERE, Julius K. (1971), "Living, Learning and Working Cannot Be separated", Excerpts from 'Ten Years After Independence' presented at TANU National Conference, September 1971. In *Nyerere on Education. Nyerere kuhusu Elimu*, Volume I. 'Selected Essays and Speeches 1954-1998', ed. Elieshi LEMA, Marjorie MBILINYI and Rakesh RAJANI, 108–114. Dar es Salaam: HakiElimu and E&D Limited, 2004.

NYERERE, Julius K (1970), "Relevance and Dar es Salaam University", Inauguration of Dar es Salaam University, 29th August 1970. In *Nyerere on Education. Nyerere kuhusu Elimu*, Volume I. 'Selected Essays and Speeches 1954-1998', ed. Elieshi LEMA, Marjorie MBILINYI and Rakesh RAJANI, 96–106. Dar es Salaam: HakiElimu and E&D Limited, 2004.

OKOKO, Kimse A. B. *Socialism and Self-Reliance in Tanzania*. London and New York: KPI, 1987.

POULANTZAS Nicolas. *State, Power, Socialism*. London: NLB and Verso Editions, 1978.

REIS, Elisa P. and Mick MOORE. *Elite Perceptions of Poverty and Inequality*, Cape Town: David Philip; London, New York: Zed Books, 2005.

RIZZO, Matteo. "'Life is War': Informal Transport Workers and Neoliberalism in Tanzania 1998-2009." *Development and Change* 42, no. 5 (2011): 1179–2005.

SAMOFF, Joel. Review of *Education, Work, and Pay in East Africa*, by Arthur Hazlewood; and *Education, Productivity, and Inequality: The East African Natural Experiment*, by John B. KNIGHT and Richard H. SABOT. *The Journal of Developing Areas* 27, no. 1 (Oct., 1992): 85–91.

SAMOFF, Joel. "Popular Initiatives and Local Government in Tanzania." *The Journal of Developing Areas* 24, no. 1 (Oct., 1989): 1–18.

SAMOFF, Joel. "Bureaucracy and the Bourgeoisie. Decentralization and Class-Structure in Tanzania." *Comparative Studies in Society and History* 21, no. 1 (1979a): 30–62.

SAMOFF, Joel. "Education in Tanzania. Class Formation and Reproduction." *Journal of Modern African Studies* 17, no. 1 (1979b): 47–69.

SAMOFF, Joel and Suleiman SUMRA. "Financial Crisis, Structural Adjustment and Education Policy in Tanzania." Paper presented at the Annual Meeting of the American Educational Research Association, New Orleans, LA, April 4-8, 1994.

STAMBACH, Amy. *Lessons from Mount Kilimanjaro: Schooling, Community, and Gender in East Africa*. New York: Routledge, 2000.

STOLER, Ann Laura. *Race and the Education of Desire: Foucault's History of Sexuality and the Colonial Order of Things*. Durham, N.C.: Duke University Press, 1995.

UN-Habitat. *The State of African Cities 2010: Governance, Inequality and Urban Land Markets*, Nairobi: UN-Habitat, 2010.

United Republic of Tanzanian (URT). *The Constitution of the United Republic of Tanzania*. Dar es Salaam, 1977.

URT. *Education for Self Reliance* in *Nyerere on Education. Nyerere kuhusu Elimu*, Volume I. 'Selected Essays and Speeches 1954-1998', ed. Elieshi LEMA, Marjorie MBILINYI and Rakesh RAJANI, 67–88. Dar es Salaam: HakiElimu and E&D Limited, 2004 (1967a).

URT. *The Arusha Declaration*. Dar es Salaam, 1967b.

URT-MoEC. *Education and Training Policy*. Dar es Salaam, 1995.

URT-Ministry of Finance and Economic Affairs. *National Strategy for Growth and Poverty Reduction II (Mkukuta II)*. Dar es Salaam, 2010.

URT-Ministry of Education and Vocational Training (MoEVT). *Basic Education Statistics of Tanzania (BEST). National Data 2007-2011.* Dar es Salaam, 2011.

URT-National Bureau of Statistics (NBS). *Tanzania Demographic and Health Survey.* Dar es Salaam, 2010.

URT-NBS. *Integrated Labour Force Survey.* Dar es Salaam, 2006.

World Bank. *World Development Report 2013: Jobs.* Washington DC, 2012.

www.ingramcontent.com/pod-product-compliance
Lightning Source LLC
Chambersburg PA
CBHW070808300426
44111CB00014B/2453